T0314007

CAPITAL AS WILL AND IMAGINATION

A volume in the series
Cornell Studies in Money
edited by Eric Helleiner and Jonathan Kirshner

A list of titles in this series is available at www.cornellpress.cornell.edu.

CAPITAL AS WILL AND IMAGINATION

Schumpeter's Guide to the
Postwar Japanese Miracle

Mark Metzler

CORNELL UNIVERSITY PRESS   **ITHACA AND LONDON**

First published 2013 by Cornell University Press
Printed in the United States of America

Library of Congress Cataloging-in-Publication Data

Metzler, Mark, 1957–
    Capital as will and imagination : Schumpeter's guide to the postwar Japanese miracle / Mark Metzler.
        p.   cm. — (Cornell studies in money)
    Includes bibliographical references and index.
    ISBN 978-0-8014-5179-9 (cloth : alk. paper)
    1. Capital—Japan—History—20th century. 2. Capitalism—Japan—History—20th century. 3. Saving and investment—Japan—History—20th century. 4. Credit—Japan—History—20th century.   5. Japan—Economic conditions—1945–1989.   6. Schumpeter, Joseph Alois, 1883–1950.   I. Title.   II. Series: Cornell studies in money.

    HC465.C3M48   2013
    330.952'04—dc23   2012028550

Cornell University Press strives to use environmentally responsible suppliers and materials to the fullest extent possible in the publishing of its books. Such materials include vegetable-based, low-VOC inks and acid-free papers that are recycled, totally chlorine-free, or partly composed of nonwood fibers. For further information, visit our website at www.cornellpress.cornell.edu.

Cloth printing   10 9 8 7 6 5 4 3 2 1

To Robert Eldredge Metzler, engineer and entrepreneur,
and to John Luke Metzler, again:
Der spiegelt ab das menschliche Bestreben;
Am farbigen Abglanz haben wir das Leben.

Contents

Tables

Acknowledgments

The collective enterprises of language and thought are life movements of which we all partake, and we perceive only glimmers of the sources of all we are given. Here I can acknowledge only the most visible help, starting with an appreciation of the field I've been working in. Economic historians lament that economic history in the United States has fallen between the two stools of academic history and academic economics, two disciplines that seem to have turned their backs on the subject (a subject whose lessons may deflate some current conceits of both). I can begin by acknowledging that I don't encounter this problem when it comes to Japan. Economic history inside Japan sets a world standard in its detail, sophistication, and sheer volume, though only bits of this work find their way into English translation. Outside Japan, dozens of expert foreign historians of Japan incorporate economic subjects integrally into their work, and the combination of economic with social, political, cultural, and intellectual history flourishes with new insights and approaches. I have too much to draw on, and my citations acknowledge only a fraction of it. More directly, parts or all of this manuscript have benefited from the critical reading and comments of Andrew Barshay, David Bruce, Simon Bytheway, Katalin Ferber, W. Miles Fletcher, Dane Hampton, Thomas R. H. Havens, Laura Hein, Tony Hopkins, Temple Jorden, Robert Metzler, Scott North, Scott O'Bryan, Mario Ōshima, Irwin Scheiner, Richard Smethurst, and Kohei Wakimura. A stimulus toward synthesis was provided by conversations with Katalin Ferber and Jean-Pascal Bassino. The series editors, Eric Helleiner and Jonathan Kirshner, and Roger Haydon at Cornell University Press, contributed greatly to its realization as a book. The work of writing it was done at the Departments of History and Asian Studies at the University of Texas at Austin, where special thanks are due to Alan Tully, and at the Institute for Research in Humanities at Kyoto University, where I finished the project thanks to the tremendous hospitality and encouragement of Naoto Kagotani. Earlier phases of research were done at the Faculty of Economics at Osaka City University, with the kind support of Mario Ōshima, and at the University of Tokyo's Institute of Social Science, where thanks are due to Nobuhiro Hiwatari. This project was assisted by research funding from the Japan Foundation, the University of Texas at Austin, the University of Texas Institute of Historical Research, the Institute for Research in Humanities at Kyoto University, the Northeast Asia Council of the Association for Asian Studies, and a Fulbright-Hays Faculty Research Abroad fellowship. Most important of all have been my family: my parents, Violet Metzler and Robert Metzler; my parents-in-law, Keiko Matsumoto and Shigeo Matsumoto; my spouse, Taeko, for her constant inspiration; and Miranda, Kairi, Tommy, Luke, and Elisey.

Abbreviations

For abbreviations used in the citations, please see the list at the beginning of the Notes.

BoJ	Bank of Japan (Nihon Ginkō)
EPA	Economic Planning Agency (Keizai Kikakuchō)
ESB	Economic Stabilization Board (Keizai Antei Honbu)
ESS	Economic and Scientific Section (of SCAP/GHQ)
IBJ	Industrial Bank of Japan (Nihon Kōgyō Ginkō)
MCI	Ministry of Commerce and Industry
MITI	Ministry of International Trade and Industry
MoF	Ministry of Finance (Ōkurashō)
RFB	Reconstruction Finance Bank
SCAP, SCAP/GHQ, or GHQ	Supreme Commander for the Allied Powers/General Headquarters; SCAP referred to General Douglas MacArthur but was applied by extension to the entire occupation administration. The two abbreviations, GHQ and SCAP, are used interchangeably.

Note on Terms and Conventions

References to other parts of the book are by section number, in the format (see x.x).

Japanese Names and Words

Names of Japanese people are given in the Japanese order (family name first), except in bibliographic citations for English-language works in which they were originally listed in the Western order.

When rendered into the Latin alphabet, Japanese words are pronounced more or less as they would be in Spanish or Italian.

Money

"¥" in the text means Japanese yen. "$" means U.S. dollars. Billion means 1,000 million.

The value of the yen diminished more than three-hundred-fold during the first four years after Japan's defeat, there was no unified market for foreign exchange, and it is therefore difficult to render yen during this period into dollar equivalents. In 1949, U.S. minister Joseph M. Dodge fixed the yen's exchange rate at ¥360 per dollar, and this rate was maintained until 1971.

Era Names

Names of Japanese eras since 1868 have been imperial reign names, as follows:

Meiji   1868–1912
Taishō   1912–1926
Shōwa   1926–1989
Heisei   1989–

CAPITAL AS WILL AND IMAGINATION

INFLATION AND ITS PRODUCTIONS

The stuff lies there: the problem is to win it;
That calls for art, and who can now begin it?

Es liegt schon da, doch um es zu erlangen,
Das ist die Kunst, wer weiß es anzufangen?

—From the capital-creation scene in Goethe's *Faust:*
The Second Part of the Tragedy (1832)

This book investigates the financial fountainhead of modern capitalist development: inflationary credit creation. For empirical material, it uses the experience
of Japan in the fifteen years after World War II, from the period of postwar recovery to the onset of "High-Speed Growth" in the second half of the 1950s.
Japan's High-Speed Growth itself was a hypercapitalist type of industrial development of tremendous intensity. This epoch-making innovation opened the
current, Asian age of world industrialization.[1] The inflationary creation of credit
by banks funded this industrial expansion, set its directions, and forced its pace.
Credit-leveraged growth also has built-in insustainabilities, as reflected recently
in the building up of debt bubbles on an unprecedented scale.

This investigation concerns the nature of modern capitalism itself, for which
Japan serves as an especially clear case study. When it comes to the nature of
capitalism, England has been taken as exemplary since the days of Karl Marx.
America has since inherited this normative role. It is not yet considered usual to
treat Japan, or any Asian country, as more than a special case. I ask the reader
here to set aside the presumed norms and reconsider Japanese experience as an
exemplar of general principles. Japan and East Asia offer more than a "comparative case." Rather, the system of capital provision in East Asia has been
stripped down to a purer form than it had in the countries where capitalism
originated, losing elements associated with its historical origins that turn out to
be more incidental than necessary. The insight to be gained from this new point
of view reflects back on those countries and practices that have been considered
normative.

1

To put it philosophically, this book is an essay on the two flows of the economy and their interworking. On one side are the material flows of energy and matter that physically constitute wealth. On the other are monetary flows: the representational or "ideal" flows that indicate social wealth. Part of the significance of Japan's postwar experience is that the physical economic flows were enlarged, year after year for two decades, at a rate that had never before been achieved in industrial history. This acceleration of the capitalist developmental process has since become normal in East Asian countries. At the time, the reality raced ahead of theoretical understandings and was not always credited as real. Even now, the subject is understudied and underappreciated outside the East Asian region.

In trying to grasp this process, I found that the name of the Austrian economist Joseph Schumpeter entered the story in a way that probably would have surprised Schumpeter, and in a way I did not imagine when I began the investigation. Also unanticipated has been the intrusion of a still more heterodox stream of energy-based conceptions of economic life. I did see at the outset that this was a story about inflation. And Schumpeter's realization was that inflation, caused by private credit creation, was intrinsic to the process of capitalist development.

High inflation, by definition, robs the purchasing power of stores of monetary wealth. The inflationary creation of new credit-capital—new purchasing power—, mainly by banks, is also the basic mechanism of capital creation under modern capitalism. In appropriate developmental circumstances, when properly modulated, inflationary credit creation has proven its functionality for rapid industrial growth. No past economic system has approached what industrial capitalism has achieved in this respect. In Japan's case, a rationalized system of "pure" credit-capital provision funded a kind of rapid growth that seemed almost miraculous. Or perhaps *Faustian* is a better description, for the allegory of paper money and capitalist development presented in Goethe's play, itself a document of the dawning of the modern age, has its own insights to offer. "The stuff lies there: the problem is to win it"—the one speaking here is the devil Mephistopheles, who sees no reason to wait for treasure to be dug out of the ground before spending it, and who understands that a credible, negotiable claim to money *is* money.

Postwar Japan illustrates these questions with great clarity. Japan as it was on the day of surrender, August 15, 1945, had suffered an enormous destruction of physical capital. Physical capital had to be rebuilt by physical labor and by sacrifices of current consumption, but this work was funded through an enormous inflation of paper claims to wealth. Although this system arose out of the circumstances of a wartime planned economy, it was essentially entrepreneurial. Japan desperately needed economic development, and this system of pure capital creation successfully financed it. Whether growth in the form it actually took was the best form of growth is another question.

Will and Imagination

I use the term *Schumpeterian finance* as a synonym for what Schumpeter called "credit inflation." The Japanese government's top economic planner, Ōkita Saburō, in a 1962 book on development planning, called it "inflationary accumulation." Schumpeter himself originally described it as "forced savings." By this he meant a specifically developmental type of credit creation, the financial counterpart to entrepreneurial innovation. These ideas are part of a simple and powerful synthesis first presented in Schumpeter's *Theory of Economic Development* in 1912. The term *forced savings* itself serves as an intellectual genetic marker by which one can trace the further progress of this idea.[2] Neither the idea of forced savings nor Schumpeter's larger synthesis will be found in "mainstream" neoclassical economic textbooks in the United States. On the other hand, this idea appeared in Japan's first and most influential textbook of neoclassical economics.

American economics textbooks do describe how banks create money (meaning credit and debt), and they explain that almost the entirety of the "money supply" consists of credit balances (i.e., debt balances) held in bank accounts. But textbooks then typically revert to describing banks as financial "intermediaries," leaving the reader with the impression that investment is only possible because of prior saving on the part of someone, somewhere. Compare this to the explanation given by Ōkita Saburō in 1957: "if the amount of new investment [were] to be confined strictly to the amount of savings collected by the financial institutions or by the government, not much could be done."[3] This is the point emphasized by Schumpeter, who explained that new credit created for new investment is essentially inflationary, as is the creation of any kind of new purchasing power. Temporarily, at least, it reduces the purchasing power of already existing money—it is a privately imposed "inflation tax" and in effect a fractional expropriation of purchasing power from others. Cycles of price inflation and deflation are not incidental to the capitalist developmental process but rather are *the very mechanism through which it operates*. Chapter 3 will walk through the steps of this operation.

In considering all of this, we confront basic questions about the nature of money. We see particularly the verbal or "communicative" aspect of money-capital. We see also its protean aspect. The business news regularly reports on the ways financial markets can "create" wealth and "destroy" it, often with arbitrary suddenness. Many of us stop to consider the paradoxicality of such constructions of wealth when translated into the world of actually existing buildings, machines, and physical goods, which do not suddenly materialize or vanish according to these financial gyrations. Such journalistic statements are of course statements about "paper" wealth or "virtual" wealth, about *claims* to wealth. These claims to wealth can plainly behave according to social and psychic laws quite different from the physical laws that govern physical things. At the same time, these claims to wealth serve as commands that direct the supply of human services and the production of physical things. The complex, shifting relations between these two worlds of real and virtual wealth are at the center of this book. Accordingly, I ask the reader to tolerate a degree of philosophical questioning not usually found in histories of financial practice and policy.

In ways explained below, virtual, financial capital is a kind of communicative *indication* or *direction*. Mechanistic, materialist analysis can capture only part of the process; the weight of words themselves becomes important in thinking about it. Poetic and philosophical methodologies have not been completely absent from economic analysis, but one has to dig to find them. I've cited Goethe as a source of inspiration; he seems also to have been a source of inspiration for Schumpeter. I casually appropriated this book's title from a younger contemporary of Goethe, Arthur Schopenhauer, who is otherwise unconnected with it.[4] What's provocative is Schopenhauer's title itself. In German, his book is named *Die Welt als Wille und Vorstellung*, but the title is unstable in English, translated variously as *The World as Will and Representation*, or *The World as Will and Imagination*, or *Will and Idea*, or *Will and Presentation*. The variable word, *Vorstellung*, in its most literal sense means "putting before." That literal sense is precisely apt. Together with the question of will—of the willing of worlds into existence—we thus have the question of "putting before," or presentation. The word *presentation* has multiple senses in English also, including the sense of making the potential present, and the senses of representing, indicating, and staging as a showman or impresario. The point of all of this is that financial capital is a performative act of social imagination, indication, and presentation and is not at all a thing or a substance. We are into the immaterial depths as soon as we begin really to consider it. I am not trying to be mysterious in saying this. It is rather the subject itself that is mysterious, in ways that can't be captured in the prosaic language in which it is commonly presented.

The Flow of the Argument

Schumpeter's theory focuses on creative, investment-driven inflation. However, the historical price profile of the twentieth century was even more conspicuously shaped by war inflation, or the "investment" of credit capital into death and destruction. Japan's High-Speed Growth system itself developed out of the practical experiences of a crudely planned wartime economy, and out of the more successful experiences of postwar "reconstruction inflation." As a backdrop to the analysis, chapter 1, "The Revolution in Prices," surveys the great wartime inflations of the twentieth century. Chapter 2 introduces some of the people who will appear in the story to follow.

Chapter 3, "What Is Capital?," presents the core of the argument. Defined simply, *capital* is money used to make money. This definition immediately shifts the question to the nature of capitalist money itself. Schumpeter's century-old insights into this question came to be broadly understood in 1950s Japan but even today are not grasped in most English-language writing on the subject. Chapter 4, "Flows and Stores," approaches the question of capital from another direction, by way of some basic ecological-economic conceptions. On the physical side, economic activity ultimately consists of flows of energy and materials. Money capital, on the other hand, although we name it with a thing-like noun, is not a substance that can flow but is instead a communicative relationship, the creating and assigning of claims to resources. These claims operate as orders that direct the use of social resources and shape the social order more generally.

The historical body of this book is chapters 5–11, which describe Japanese experience in the fifteen years from the beginning of the Allied occupation in 1945 to the Income Doubling Plan of 1960. Japan's national transformation was part of a wider international transition: from the deepest crisis in the history of modern capitalism, circa 1929–45, to the "golden age" of postwar industrial capitalism, circa 1950–73. The economic policy shifts of these pivotal years are thus of extraordinary interest. It is here that individual personalities become conspicuous: the inflationist promoter and publicist Ishibashi Tanzan; the deflationary restrictor Joseph Dodge; the arbiter of credit Ichimada Hisato; the mediating Schumpeterians Nakayama Ichirō, Tōbata Seiichi, and Tsuru Shigeto; the technocratic planners Arisawa Hiromi and Ōkita Saburō; the political entrepreneur Ikeda Hayato. Of course, the main work of recovery and growth was conducted by an army of working people, striving on both the workplace and the domestic fronts, directed by an officer corps of entrepreneurs. As explained here, the sacrifices of the purchasing power of those who were further from the sources of the money-creation process provided the capital for the entrepreneurs who were located at those sources. This inflationary funding process is a financial and monetary one that happens on a level distinct from that of value creation and exploitation operating within the process of production itself.

Chapter 5 describes the destabilization of Japanese capitalism in 1945–46. This was a consequence of the war but was also an outcome, partly deliberate, of

American policy, which aimed to destroy Japan's military-industrial potential and to decentralize and democratize the country. Japan's heavy-industrial complex survived this attack. Many companies were kept in business by means of the inflationary reconstruction policy championed by Ishibashi Tanzan, described in chapter 6. After U.S. authorities purged Ishibashi from office, his ameliorative liberal approach gave way to a more radical kind of statist, probusiness reformism under the slogan "modified capitalism," which had a brief ascendancy in 1947–48. Officials and favored businessmen utilized inflationary forced savings as a tool of industrial revival, but inflation was also socially and culturally destabilizing, generating severe social tensions and a wide sense of the chaotic transmutation and destruction of values.

Chapter 7 focuses on the credit restriction program that was imposed under U.S. orders and directed by American Bankers Association president Joseph M. Dodge in 1949. This "reverse course" reflected a great international political shift associated with the intensification of the Cold War; the new policy was implemented first in the western zones of Germany. This policy, dubbed the Dodge Line, induced a "stabilization panic" and depression.

Within the macro-level framework of Dodge's deflation policy, a new microlevel Japanese synthesis emerged, as described in chapter 8. Japanese countermeasures to work around Dodge's credit-restriction policy involved the privatization of the government's expansionary credit-creation policy: in effect, the private banking sector was remobilized to serve national ends. The result was a system of "superdirect," Schumpeterian finance.

Chapter 9 pauses to offer some interim conclusions about the successes of inflationary reconstruction, the end of the great inflation, and the beginnings of the "Schumpeterian boom" that followed. Chapters 10 and 11 discuss the High-Speed Growth system, focusing on the onset of the growth boom after 1955 and the questions of credit creation and planning. The Era of High-Speed Growth (Kōdo seichō jidai) has become a proper name in Japan, indicating the period 1955–73, and I use the term that way here. But *high-speed growth* is also a generic term, describing a process that has since occurred or is now occurring across eastern Asia. This fact gives to Japan's experience a much wider significance. Japan's financial system at the time pumped capital into Japanese industry in a way that supercharged growth and funded it with relatively low inflation. This dynamic balance was made possible by the great increase in production itself. The consultative national planning process that then developed would seem to be the last place one would expect to find the influence of Joseph Schumpeter, with his lifelong predilection toward laissez-faire. In fact, Schumpeter's ideas, represented by his leading Japanese students, were at the center of it.

Chapter 12 concludes the book by returning to the question of capital itself. After the heroic phase of industrial growth came the great bubble. These were two sides of a single process. If not checked, the system of creating credit capital not only can but must produce great debt crises. This is a point Schumpeter did not properly grasp in his theory. Japan's "asset bubble"—or debt bubble—when it reached its peak in 1989 was the biggest financial bubble in history up to that point. Foreign commentators imagined then that it was a uniquely Japanese problem. It now has the appearance of a precursor to the global credit bubble centered on the United States and Britain, which continued to build to its own peak in 2007–8. This brings us to some limits and blind spots in Schumpeter's analysis. It brings us also to the question we collectively face today: What comes after the age of Schumpeterian finance?

History is integral to the larger argument here, and the methodology of this book is essentially historical. The history presented is illustrative, however: more of an extended essay than an attempt at a comprehensive account of this very dense and complex period. Here too the value of this book will be in the questions it raises.

THE REVOLUTION IN PRICES

The war was financed as an enterprise through the purchase of goods and credit operations.

—Joseph Schumpeter, "Crisis of the Tax State" (1918)

It's been called Japan's inflation, but from my standpoint the inflation of whichever country is much the same, as war finance is largely impossible without depending on inflation.

—Ōuchi Hyōe, in conversation with Ichimada Hisato (1949)

Finance was never a limiting factor in the expansion of the war economy.

—Jerome Cohen, "Budget Analysis" (1949)

The twentieth century was the most inflationary century in history. This distinctive aspect becomes clearer as we leave the century further behind. Partly this had to do with the financing of great wars. Partly it had to do with the nature of modern capital creation. This book is mainly about the second question, but it is important to consider the first one as well. Major wars, in whichever country, are typically funded by major inflations. More precisely, newly created credit supplies the financial capital for war, as it supplies the capital for other forms of enterprise. This was true of Schumpeter's homeland, Austria-Hungary, in World War I, as it was true of imperial Japan in World War II. Japan's postwar reconstruction also proved to be impossible without inflationary finance. War inflation differs radically in its results from the capitalist-developmental inflation delineated by Schumpeter, but it reveals in a stark way some of the basic workings of inflation. Reconstruction inflation is also a special case, but it is a case that exemplifies the developmental process at an extreme. Inflationary reconstruction was also the matrix of the Japanese High-Speed Growth system.

1.1 Faustian Capital

The essential capitalist form described in this book has a classic literary representation in Goethe's *Faust*. Goethe himself served for years as the state minister of economy at Weimar, and he was actively interested in economic investigations, as he was in botanical, mineral, and alchemical ones. Goethe also lived through an age of revolution, world war, wartime inflation, and postwar deflation. Part 1 of *Faust*, written in advance of much of that, is the "tragedy of love." Part 2, finished in 1831, is the "tragedy of money."[1] It begins at the court of the emperor at a time when the empire is overburdened with debt. Mephistopheles and Faust appear, and Mephistopheles creates paper money for the emperor, explaining that the paper notes will represent the vast unknown treasure buried in the earth. As the legend on the notes declares,

> To all who want it, be it known:
> This Note is worth one thousand Crowns.
> As sure Deposit, to it secured:
> The Emperor's Land's buried Goods.[2]

The emperor's debts are erased at a stroke, and Mephistopheles and Faust earn a place at the emperor's side. This paper money represents nothing yet existing in humanly usable form. It is latent or possible wealth. Nevertheless, the creation of believable claims written on slips of paper is enough to enroll legions of followers and set them to work creating new productive resources. At the climax of the drama, Faust himself becomes an entrepreneur and developer of new productive resources for masses of people—it is now that he would stay the passage of the moment to savor his achievement. And now, of course, the devil comes to collect his debt.

Dr. Faust's venture into capital creation recalls an episode in history that Goethe certainly had in mind: the story of the Scottish financier John Law. In the aftermath of the "world war" of 1701–14, Law proposed to the French regent that the kingdom's land itself could be the basis for creating paper money. On that premise, he set up a state bank that issued paper banknotes and paid off the kingdom's immense war debts. The French regent, after hiring the British banker, is said to have fired his now redundant alchemists.[3] Joseph Schumpeter considered John Law's scheme an epoch-making capitalist innovation, notwithstanding that it gave rise to the great Mississippi bubble of 1719–20 (see 3.2.1). The problem with Law's plan, Schumpeter thought, was that it did not sufficiently separate the banking and entrepreneurial functions, meaning that new credit creation was not being properly directed to a commercial or industrial enterprise that would have repaid the social investment. As it happened, Law's new money lost its purchasing power, Law's bank collapsed, and Law fled the scene. "Hard" metallic money was restored, and France went through an extended period of deflation, depression, and anticapitalist reaction. Law's business associate Richard Cantillon, a Franco-Irish banker and bubble speculator, also had to flee Paris. It was Cantillon who later became the first social theorist to discuss the role of capitalist entrepreneurship. Cantillon further analyzed how the inflationary effects of newly created money differed according to where and how it entered circulation (see 6.3). On both points, Cantillon prefigured aspects of Schumpeter's theory.[4]

1.2 World War I and the Political Economy of Twentieth-Century Inflation

Major credit-funded wars are typically followed by a two-stage sequence of inflationary boom and deflationary depression. A classic example can be seen in the French revolutionary and Napoleonic wars, which were the world wars of Goethe's age. These wars, funded by paper money, set off an inflationary price wave across the European and Atlantic worlds in the first fifteen years of the nineteenth century. This great inflation was succeeded by a long deflation that ran from 1815 into the 1840s. In the 1860s the U.S. Civil War generated another great inflationary price wave, also internationally. The midcentury inflation was succeeded by another long deflation, running from the 1870s into the 1890s. In Japan's modern national history as well, a sequence of war succeeded by inflationary boom, succeeded in turn by deflationary bust, has occurred several times.

World War I set off a wave of credit-inflationary action and debt-deflationary reaction that was unprecedented in its magnitude and scope. After the war came the inflationary boom of 1919–20, which affected most of the world. Japanese military participation in the war was limited, but the inflationary boom was especially great in Japan. It culminated in the biggest speculative bubble in the country's historical experience up to that point. At the height of the bubble, in late 1919, Japanese monetary authorities, like those in Britain and the United States, deliberately checked the provision of credit in order to bring on "deflation"— which was then a new word in the international economic vocabulary.[5]

The post–World War I deflation was also an international phenomenon. Japan was the country where deflation happened to appear first, when speculation in the commodities and financial markets collapsed in the spring of 1920. The deflationary trend culminated in the early 1930s, in the Great Depression. In the long historical view, we thus see a sequence of *great war → great depression*. Thus the Great War, via the working of the credit/debt process, led directly to the Great Depression. To the extent that the volume of credits was great, and to the extent that they were preserved as debts, so too was there a great pressure of deflation and depression.[6]

The credit operations that funded World War I dwarfed all previous undertakings, but the basic mechanism was essentially capitalistic. As Schumpeter explained to fellow Austrians in an essay published a few months before the armistice, the war was financed *as an enterprise*—that is, by means of credit creation and the purchase of resources. (The great exception was in the conscription of military-labor services by direct state command.)[7] Unlike the financing of an industrial enterprise, however, this massive creation of new credit-money did not induce a corresponding flow of useful production. World War I did produce a conspicuous industrial boom in the United States, Japan, and many neutral countries. For the European combatant countries, however, despite some boom-like investment phenomena, the war on the whole consumed and destroyed resources, eating deeply into the stock of existing physical capital. This newly created purchasing power thus reduced the purchasing power of existing money all around. It produced as a counterpart a great stock of debt certificates, said to represent future public obligations to pay millions on millions of units of national currency.

It was also during World War I that characteristic institutions of the twentieth-century type of political economy first came together as a system. The new policy package included foreign-exchange controls, deficit spending, managed currencies, and industrial subsidies. This was an essentially inflationary system. Together with these were devices to modulate and enable inflationary financing, including price controls, semicompulsory war bond drives, rationing of goods, and wage indexing. With mass conscription and mass austerity in the offing, state elites also incorporated labor parties into national governing coalitions, for the first time in most of the combatant countries. The worldwide inflations that developed later in the century were a continuation of World War I–style inflation. Wartime materials-mobilization planning, in Germany especially, became a prototype for future economic planning in both the capitalist and socialist countries. This twentieth-century policy package first appeared in Europe. It also took shape to a greater degree than is usually recognized in the United States.

Postwar inflation in Germany, before it entered its final phase of exponential increase, also functioned as a kind of "forced savings." This aspect is clearly described in Constantino Bresciani-Turroni's classic study of the German inflation. Bresciani-Turroni himself worked in Berlin as a member of the Allied financial control apparatus through the period of post–World War I inflation and deflation, and he explained how industrial subsidies drove the inflation, which had the character of an inflationary boom up until 1922. After this, hyperinflation went out of control. Quoting an anonymous German banker, Bresciani-Turroni noted also that inflationary capital creation "gave industry and commerce the opportunity to do without foreign loans."[8] In 1946, Ōuchi Hyōe published a partial translation of Bresciani-Turroni's book in Japanese as part of his own anti-inflation campaign, and it was also widely read in post–World War II Japan.

Notably, this institutional package did not come together in Japan during World War I—that happened twenty years later, during and especially after World War II. Wage indexing and the partial accommodation of labor leadership mainly happened after August 1945, as part of a great social battle. Although the immediate institutional effects of World War I were less profound in Japan than in Europe, the inflationary boom itself had a great impact. From 1915 to a peak in March 1920, Japanese retail prices doubled. Wholesale prices increased by about two and a half times. The Japanese government in 1917 suspended the gold standard, which was already a highly managed system, and began to operate an even more purely managed monetary system. Rice prices soared in 1917 and 1918, and nationwide rice riots broke out in August and September 1918.[9] An unprecedented wave of strikes broke out simultaneously, and massive universal suffrage demonstrations followed. These public manifestations, together with the surge of interest in Marxism and feminism, were the Japanese aspects of a worldwide revolutionary wave.

This great and sudden widening of demands for political and social inclusion helped to force a series of liberal political changes on the Japanese government. Inflation itself automatically widened the national electorate, for the right to vote still carried a property qualification. In the view of conservative political and financial authorities, the rise in prices also appeared to be a cause of new social divisions, labor militancy, and the spread of "dangerous thought." Women as managers of household consumption were blamed for the perceived overspending of the inflation era. The "restorative" deflation policy of the 1920s thus involved a whole set of restoration-minded political, social, and cultural attitudes and concerns, in addition to the more obvious fiscal, monetary, and industrial ones.[10]

1.3 Postwar Stabilization

World War II was also followed by a worldwide inflation. *The fact that no great depression resulted from World War II*, the greatest of great wars, is one starting point of this book. By historical standards, we thus see a "partial" sequence of a great war followed by a great inflation, but with no great deflation following.

This difference hinges on the question of debt. Each of the world wars was funded by immense amounts of new credit-capital. Credit means debt, and most of these debts were ultimately unrepayable. It was the financially driven effort to preserve the inflated international debt structure after World War I that led to the great collapse. Here is one place where the results of World War I and those of World War II ended up being nearly opposite. Economic stabilization after World War II was in this way the second part of a two-part process. Powerful learning effects were at work.

Postwar deflation, as Schumpeter emphasized, was not just an automatic response to inflation but was rather an act of political will.[11] After World War I, national governments could partially or entirely inflate away debts denominated in their own national currencies. This is what happened in the defeated countries of central and eastern Europe, where hyperinflation followed the war. It also happened to a significant extent in badly damaged "victor" countries like Italy and France. The governments of the victorious creditor countries, led by the United States and Britain, in 1919 and 1920 adopted deflation policies to preserve the value of existing monetary claims denominated in their own currencies. British and American bankers then took the lead in directing monetary "stabilization" policies internationally, also with an eye to preserving or enhancing the purchasing power of existing debts. The result was a series of austerity programs and policy-induced depressions, much in the style of the "structural adjustment" and "shock therapy" programs imposed by creditor countries through the International Monetary Fund (IMF) and other agencies in the 1980s and 1990s. International debt claims—in the 1920s meaning, above all, U.S. dollar debts—thus remained an immense and increasingly heavy load on the present, until they were finally more or less repudiated in the crisis of the world depression.[12]

The economic journalist Ishibashi Tanzan (1884–1973), who appears as a protagonist in this story, first became famous as an economic commentator for his criticism of the Japanese deflation policy in the 1920s and early 1930s. Ishibashi also began to disseminate in Japan the critique of Britain's deflation policy made by John Maynard Keynes. In the context of that place and time, Ishibashi's analysis seems to me to have been essentially correct. Deflation went out of control in the early 1930s, and there followed in Japan a great turn in policy, in a reflationary Keynesian direction, directed by the veteran finance minister Takahashi Korekiyo. This new phase of worldwide inflation thus began first in East Asia. It was again connected to war, as Japanese military agencies initiated what was often called in Japan a "quasi war" in northeastern China in September 1931.

Reflation was thus yoked to a militaristic and imperialistic policy that both Ishibashi and Takahashi opposed.[13] Ishibashi's opposition to militarism and imperialism was, in regard to its political possibility, a generation ahead of its time. Instead, the Japanese state's bellicose policy led to a total war in China in July 1937, twenty-six months before the German state launched a total war in Europe.

The people who directed economic stabilization and reconstruction programs after World War II bore in mind the lessons of World War I. There was no real attempt at deflation. Ishibashi Tanzan himself served as finance minister in 1946–47, when he directed an inflationary capital-creation program that earned him the backing of Japanese industrialists and got him fired by the U.S. occupation authorities. In this and in his later political activity, Ishibashi helped create the policy framework of the High-Speed Growth system. In contrast to the failure of deflationary stabilization after World War I, postwar economic management after World War II was thus a case of successful "inflationary stabilization." Debts were erased by means of inflation, and prices were stabilized after 1949 at levels many times higher than prewar levels.

1.4 The Great Inflation of the 1940s

In the first months of 1920, prices in Britain and the United States briefly surpassed the highest price levels of the nineteenth century, but not by very much. Prices then fell sharply later in the year. The international deflation that began then continued into the 1930s. Thus, if one looked back over the historical record of British or American price statistics from the temporal vantage point of the deflationary 1920s, one would conclude that the nineteenth-century price regime still *held* rather than that it had been broken. In later twentieth-century retrospect, however, in view of the institutional innovations associated with the war's financing and provisioning, World War I itself appears as the decisive break, and the "restoration" of the 1920s looks like an impossible effort to return to a world that was already gone. In any case, the price plateau of the long nineteenth century was manifestly left behind during World War II.

In Japan, the great inflation that followed World War II was the single most intense episode in the series of price inflations that have defined Japan's modern history. It was a boom time for some but a time of desperate want for most. In 1949, the deflation policy imposed by the U.S. adviser Joseph Dodge greatly moderated the inflation, but it continued until the final year of the Allied occupation, 1951. On the face of things, Japan's postwar inflation was very different from the type of developmental inflation analyzed by Schumpeter and explained in chapter 3. But in fact, what we see here reveals those developmental processes taking place in a forced and extreme way.

The first step in the great inflation can be dated to the last weeks of 1931. It was then that finance minister Takahashi Korekiyo ended the former deflation policy and resuspended the gold standard, making the yen purely a managed currency. The yen's "fiat money" character was heightened over the course of the "quasi-wartime" and wartime periods (1931–37, 1937–45). The new situation was legally recognized in the new Bank of Japan Law of February 1942. In the meantime, the volume of cash currency (mainly Bank of Japan notes) had increased from ¥1.8 billion in 1931 to ¥7.9 billion in 1941. It reached ¥56.7 billion at the end of 1945. The volume of account balances in Japanese banks simultaneously grew from ¥11.1 billion in 1931, to ¥41.5 billion in 1941, to ¥119.8 billion in 1945. By the time the great inflationary wave ended in 1951, cash currency in circulation came to ¥510 billion. Bank balances amounted to ¥1.5 trillion.[14]

Metallic money became a thing of the past. Gold had long since disappeared from ordinary monetary circulation—in Japan, this had happened already in the great inflation that accompanied the opening of the country to international trade in the 1860s. In actual circulation, silver, too, was largely replaced by paper notes in the 1870s. The "silver standard" during the years 1885–97 and the "gold standard" of 1897–1931 made these metals the theoretical bases of a paper-money system administered by the Bank of Japan. In actual use, these metals were reserved for making foreign payments.[15] Japan has thus had a domestic paper-money system since the beginning of the modern yen system in the 1870s. During the Pacific War, copper also became too valuable to be used for subsidiary coins. That was when the present type of ultralightweight aluminum 1-yen coins came into use. These aluminum coins were themselves about to be pulled from circulation and replaced with ceramic tokens when the war ended.

What is often overlooked is that the wartime inflation was also an investment phenomenon. The dimensions of this movement are outlined in table 1-1. To put these numbers in context: total government spending, including war spending, increased from ¥10 billion in 1936, to ¥85 billion in 1944, to ¥100 billion in 1945.

1.5 Exporting Inflation

Japan's domestic monetary expansion was modest compared to what Japanese authorities did overseas. There, localized military control of the creation of "war capital" turned into a method of self-financing imperial expansion. Ōuchi Hyōe in 1947 described his country's recent history as a megalomaniac psychosis.

TABLE 1-1. The industrial-investment war, 1936–1945 (year-end totals, in billions of yen)

YEAR	NEW INDUSTRIAL INVESTMENT	NEW LENDING TO INDUSTRY	INCREASE (DECREASE) IN BoJ LENDING*	INCREASE IN TOTAL BANK LENDING†
1936	1.6	0.6	(–1.0)	0.5
1937	3.7	1.8	(–1.2)	1.4
1938	4.6	2.0	(–1.2)	1.3
1939	6.9	3.8	0.6	3.1
1940	7.6	4.1	(–0.2)	3.6
1941	8.0	3.3	(–0.1)	3.0
1942	10.5	5.2	0.9	4.7
1943	12.2	6.9	1.8	5.6
1944	19.2	14.8	5.3	18.8
1945	50.4	47.0	28.9	46.5

Sources: Nakamura 1989a: 34–35; Nihon Ginkō Tōkeikyoku 1962: 69–70, 77–78; Nihon Ginkō Tōkeikyoku 1966: 192–93. Industrial lending was almost entirely from banks.

*Bank of Japan lending to banks (excluding BoJ lending to government).
†Total bank lending exclusive of BoJ lending.

"This patient," he wrote, "nourished a megalomaniac fallacy also with respect to currency." Japanese military forces were ordered to supply their needs locally in the territories they occupied. They appropriated goods and labor services by formally monetary means, purchasing them with local yen notes produced by new Japanese-run central banks or with paper scrip that the military produced for itself. On the face of it, they were financing the war "as an enterprise," but the enterprise was a violent conquest. This newly created money was thus the vehicle for a massive looting of wealth from the people of the occupied territories, who were paid for their goods and labor in paper claims whose purchasing power rapidly diminished into nothingness. From the standpoint of Japanese imperialist designs, this devolution of money-creation power to military authorities also had the perverse effect of creating independent monetary spheres unable to trade with each other. As Ōuchi anatomized it:

> Within each sphere of control, bank-notes or military scrip were inflated in an independent manner and economic relations of one area with another were completely cut off. Thus each of the Oriental nations was divided into several sections and the economic system in each of these [un]coordinated, small independent economic zones was destroyed by the inflationary process.[16]

The farther from Japan, the worse the inflation. By August 1945, price levels in Shanghai were 7,000 times higher than those of December 1941. In Singapore, prices increased by 35,000 times. In Burma, prices increased by nearly 200,000 times.[17] This inflation in the occupied territories threatened to spill back into Japan. At the end of the war in August 1945, ¥30.2 billion in Bank of Japan notes was outstanding in the Japanese home islands (*naichi*). In Taiwan and Korea, the Japanese-occupied territories longest assimilated to the Japanese system, there was ¥9.5 billion in colonial central bank notes. In Manchuria and Mongolia, there was another ¥10.7 billion. In the recently conquered Southeast Asian territories, there was ¥18.0 billion in Southern Development Bank notes. In the occupied areas of China, the Japanese-controlled central banks issued more than ¥3.1 trillion in notes. There were also vast unknown amounts of military scrip in the recently conquered territories.[18]

This note issue amounted to forced "loans" levied on the occupied populations. This point was quite forgotten by most Japanese who criticized the expenses of the Allied occupation and the reparations Japan was now going to have to pay. "Logically," Ōuchi pointed out, "the Japanese government ultimately should assume responsibility for cash payment against these notes." But to do so would create hyperinflation in Japan. "How can these huge monetary obligations of Japan be settled? This is the problem laid before the Allied Powers, and it is linked with their respective reparation claims against Japan."[19]

The upshot of this balance of claims was predictable: the Japanese government was required to repay the prewar bonds owed to British and American creditors. They did this with alacrity, so that the channels of foreign credit could once again be opened. The billions and trillions in forced loans on the public of invaded countries went unredeemed (though over the years, reparations payments to their governments did come to a significant amount).[20]

1.6 The Inflation Comes Home

During the war, Japan's domestic inflation was restrained by official price controls. Prices were frozen by government order at the time of the outbreak of the war in Europe in September 1939. Ongoing market adjustment by means of the basic price mechanism thus became illegal. Black marketeering became general by 1943, and despite official controls, consumer inflation averaged more than 20 percent per year from 1939 to 1945.[21]

The domain of freely market-determined price formation became a kind of demimonde during the wartime and occupation periods. During the war, the growth of black market transactions charted out an "entropic process" that expanded "in inverse proportion to Japan's deteriorating war condition," in the description of Owen Griffiths. Price controls were inaugurated in March 1938.

They developed into a comprehensive system of materials rationing, price controls over goods and services, and economic policing. "The black market expanded with each new layer of control."[22] Authorities made two million arrests for market infractions in the first fifteen months after the October 1939 price freeze ordinance. People's daily caloric intake simultaneously began to fall. The share of it provided by official rations dropped even more, meaning that most people depended on black market purchases. Producer goods and labor also came increasingly to be allocated by illegal markets. This illegalization of market activity went further with the great looting of stockpiles after the surrender. The economic roles of violent gangs also expanded greatly during the war. After U.S. forces took Saipan in July 1944 and began heavy bombing of the Japanese mainland, black market prices rose greatly, and the gap between black market and official prices widened. Barter became common. Urban residents who had not been evacuated to the countryside began to make regular trips to the countryside to buy food.[23]

Within the macro-level context of inflationary war finance, the government's wartime savings drives served to absorb money circulating among the people: savings were needed in order to maintain the value of the monetary unit. Great increases in credit creation for industry were thus supported by efforts to encourage popular savings and austerity. These were combined with effectively compulsory savings programs.[24] Increased savings thus followed rather than preceded money creation and investment (see 11.1). In this case, however, wartime "saving" also ended up as simple expropriation, when high postwar inflation reduced the value of people's stored monetary claims to almost nothing. When personal saving was again made voluntary after the war, the inflation made it illogical to save money. In any case it was impossible for many families. Savings as a means of monetary control was thus temporarily unavailable.

The most intense phase of inflation came after the war's end, when there was an enormous jump in prices. Statistics involving monetary values during this revolution in prices become arbitrary and chaotic, with such great volatility and such gaps between officially determined prices and black market prices that price surveys undertaken using different methods yielded very different numbers. In any case, the overall magnitude of the price rise is clear, as is its abrupt, stepwise character. Even many officially controlled prices increased by annual rates in the triple digits during the first half of the occupation. Black market prices for food and other necessities rose at similar rates. Roughly speaking, wholesale prices rose by three or four hundred times over prewar levels. The rise in retail prices was substantially higher than that. This was more than enough to wipe out the monetary value of savings and debts that existed at the war's end. At the same time, however, the rise in prices happened slowly enough that people did continue to use national money rather than dispensing with it altogether. They just used it as quickly as they could.

Postwar inflation was a worldwide phenomenon. In the defeated countries—Japan, Germany, Italy, Hungary, and Rumania—and in combatant countries experiencing civil war, such as China and Greece, there was near or outright hyperinflation at the end of the war. There was a worldwide scarcity of goods, and the imbalance between increased money creation and the limited production of goods created inflationary pressures everywhere. Even in the United States, whose industrial and farm production now supplied so many other countries, inflation appeared immediately in November 1946, when most wartime price controls (except for those on rents) were lifted. Japan's inflation was two or three orders of magnitude less than the inflation in China and other formerly Japanese-occupied territories. Nor did it approach the unimaginable billions reached at the furthest point of the German inflation in 1923. All the same, many commentators did call it a hyperinflation, and economic decisions of every kind were conditioned by inflationary considerations.

Both monetary and supply-side factors drove the inflation. The war itself consumed vast material resources. Stores of physical wealth of all kinds were used up or destroyed. More than two million houses and their contents were burned up in the U.S. bombing attacks. The production of new flows of wealth was severely restricted. On the monetary side it was different. A stock of monetary claims is a "stock" of representations. The bulk of these representations were not touched by the fires, and banking authorities continued to create new claims right through the crisis. The "supply" of claims multiplied, while the fund of resources they could command was radically diminished.

Inflation slowed somewhat in 1948, to about 60 percent per year in wholesale prices.[25] In 1949, when U.S. fiscal czar Joseph Dodge imposed a deflation policy, black markets began to close—free markets were relegalized—and prices were relatively stabilized. This policy was dubbed the "Dodge Line" by Ōuchi Hyōe, who tended to approve of it, despite the depression it caused. But it is also clear from the price statistics that price stabilization only "began to begin" with the Dodge Line. Full price stabilization happened only with the return of national independence in 1952. And this is still to speak of wholesale prices—people as consumers continued to pay an "inflation tax."

The postwar inflation was much more than an automatic response to war. It was also the result of a distinctive proinflationary and "Keynesian" policy of massive industrial subsidies. This policy was conceived and promoted by finance minister Ishibashi Tanzan, who was an economic liberal and opponent of state controls. Before considering that process, the next chapters introduce some of the people who figure in this story, and then the question of financial capital itself.

DRAMATIS PERSONAE

As military action must be taken in a given strategic position even
if all the data potentially procurable are not available, so also in
economic life action must be taken without working out all the
details of what is to be done. Here the success of everything
depends upon intuition, the capacity of seeing things in a way
which afterwards proves to be true.

—Joseph Schumpeter, *The Theory of Economic Development* (1912)

After World War II, the thought leaders of the generation who directed economic reconstruction and stabilization looked back reflexively to the problems
that had followed World War I, which they had witnessed in their youth. In Japan, several influential members of this generation had absorbed these lessons in
postwar Germany itself. The experience of the defeated countries of central Europe thus has multiple levels of relevance to Japan's postwar circumstances a
quarter-century later.

Joseph Schumpeter's Japanese students and translators were Nakayama Ichirō (1898–1981) and Tōbata Seiichi (1899–1983). They were part of a larger wave
of young Japanese intellectuals who went to Germany to study during the 1920s.
Ōuchi Hyōe (1888–1980) was a senior member of this cohort, and he spoke for
most of them when he recalled his "good old days" in Germany (or as he phrased
it, in a Japanese-language book, "meine gute alte Tage"). Ōuchi's student and
younger colleague Arisawa Hiromi, then an enthusiastic Marxist, studied in Berlin from 1926 to 1928. Nakayama and Tōbata studied in Bonn between 1927
and 1929 and became enthusiastic Schumpeterians.[1] Arisawa, Nakayama, and
Tōbata became enormously influential economic policy advisers after the war.
The three together were sometimes called the *gosanke,* or "three great houses." The
allusion is to the lords of the three Tokugawa branch houses who were privileged
to advise the Tokugawa shogun. The three appeared together in pivotal national
planning committees again and again during the fifteen years after World War II,
together with the d'Artagnan of the team, the young power-grid planner turned

economist Ōkita Saburō (1914–1993). Ōkita's own overseas learning experience happened in the 1940s, in wartime occupied China. The "Weimar" cohort also included the postwar Bank of Japan governor Ichimada Hisato. Joseph Schumpeter's own experience of the aftermath of war and defeat also deserves an introduction. It will be interesting to start with a comment on his intellectual reception in wartime Japan.

2.1 "The Schumpeter Vogue"

Schumpeter's theory of development became easily accessible to Japanese readers with the publication of Nakayama Ichirō's *Pure Economics* in 1933, followed by Nakayama and Tōbata's translation of Schumpeter's *Theory of Economic Development* in 1937. Schumpeter presented his complete system with the publication in 1939 of his two-volume work *Business Cycles: A Theoretical, Historical, and Statistical Analysis of the Capitalist Process. Business Cycles* was published first in English, in the United States, but met with little response there, where Schumpeter's work was now quite overshadowed by that of Keynes. It had a much greater appeal to Japanese economists, many of whom read English. Part of the appeal was Schumpeter's dynamic, historical, and developmental approach. *Business Cycles* meshed also with a surge of interest in theories of technology. It also appeared at a time of authoritarian reaction against the former Marxist vogue. Exponents of Marx's system, including Ōuchi Hyōe, were silenced. Schumpeter's translators Nakayama and Tōbata were conspicuously active, editing and writing volume after volume. In his memoir *Fifty Years of Economics* (*Keizaigaku gojūnen*, 1959), Ōuchi wrote the following concerning this "Schumpeter vogue":

> In this period of [wartime] reaction, one type of economics that had the external aspect of neutrality had a vogue especially in Japan. That was Schumpeter. Schumpeter's translation and dissemination was mainly carried out by Mr. Nakayama Ichirō and Mr. Tōbata Seiichi, but there were also people besides these two gentlemen who disseminated Schumpeter. For example, Mr. Yasui Takuma.[2] As for the fact that those big two volumes of Schumpeter [*Business Cycles*] were so widely read, while it may have been unconscious, after all it met the demands of an age that wanted to take refuge somewhere from the storm of Marxism. This is to say that the man Schumpeter was in his scholarship actually gifted in cunning. He slashed right through both the warp and woof of the economy, considering one part as dynamics and one as statics.

Then, on each of those stages, he made a highly delimited place for the various factors within each, while in fact giving them an extremely idiosyncratic character; and then he presented these [factors] moving on the stage. Then people who were watching this dual stage from a distance thought, yes, indeed, this is economics! This, so to speak, is a peculiar economic set. It is not classical economics. Of course it is not Marxist economics. The thought-materials used on this set are clearly in large part from the stream of the Austrian school, but as for the set's inner mechanism itself, it is a converted use of the results of Marxism. But that is hidden. So, this economics, as against the classical school and as against Marxism, has the external shape of a third empire. For this reason, in appearance this was not reaction.

As to the origins and social base of Schumpeterian economics, Ōuchi offered: "in the first place, Schumpeter's genealogy was that of a child of mixed blood," born of "German, particularly Viennese" economics and socialism. "In that period of strange coexistence of socialism and capitalism before and after World War I," Schumpeter was also "a stage director of prodigious acrobatic stunts."

This Schumpeter, already in this era [after World War I] had a mysterious influence in Japan. Then, after the Second World War, at the time of the vogue for the "new economics," he was once again revived in this relation. Through these two periods he had a similar social base. Denying classical economics, putting on a display of social concern, more than anything pedantry.[3]

Schumpeter's own display of social concern was not conspicuous. On the contrary, he disbelieved in human equality, detested Franklin Roosevelt's New Deal, and expressed a nostalgia for aristocratic values. Some of his American students understood his open admiration for Japanese culture as another expression of this longing. On his visit to Kyoto in 1931, as he admired some exquisite artistic productions of the Edo period, he remarked that if exploitation were necessary to produce such achievements, then he was not against exploitation.[4] On the other hand, his students Nakayama Ichirō and Tōbata Seiichi clearly expressed and energetically acted on their own respective "labor" and "farmer" social concerns in the 1950s. Ōuchi's statement evidently referred to them, and to the wider set of positions they represented. As to the maintenance of an "aspect of neutrality," it is also the case that Nakayama and Tōbata prospered in their careers during the war years, when things were not easy for Ōuchi.

2.2 At the Monetary Bonfire

As described in the next chapter, Schumpeter located the creation of credit by banks at the core of the capitalist developmental process. He understood inflation to be an intrinsic part of that process. From his own historical vantage point, as he completed his *Theory of Economic Development* in 1911, he looked back over the first century of industrial capitalism and saw nearly a century of deflation. Prices in the Western countries had in fact reached their historic lows around 1896 and had risen since, but price levels in 1911 still remained well below those of the early nineteenth century. Schumpeter thus came to the conclusion that the type of developmental inflation he described was intrinsically self-liquidating. Schumpeter was already famous as an academic economist when he got a chance to test his theories in practice after World War I, first as Austria's minister of finance and then as a banker and capitalist. But now Austria was in the midst of its postwar hyperinflation.

In the revolutionary tumult of early 1919, the Austrian Schumpeter began his short career in public service in German Berlin, as a member of the Commission for the Preparation of the Socialization of Industry. Politically, the moment that followed World War I in Germany and Austria would foreshadow aspects of the situation in Japan after World War II. One commonality is the experience of a brief interval of Socialist–Conservative cooperation. The Socialization Commission itself brought together a remarkable spectrum of leading figures from both the proto-communist left wing (the Independent Socialist Party of Germany) and the proto-socialist right wing (the Majority Socialist Party of Germany) of the Socialist movement, together with non-Marxist members such as Schumpeter.[5] As a cooperative bourgeois conservative, Schumpeter worked closely on the Socialization Commission with socialist intellectuals, including Karl Kautsky, himself one of the earliest members of the Socialist Party of Austria, and the Austrian Marxists Rudolf Hilferding and Emil Lederer. (Lederer a year after this became Ōuchi Hyōe's teacher and friend at Heidelberg.)[6] Other commonalities were the fact of a postwar energy crisis and the Socialization Commission's special focus on coal and steel. In this context, Schumpeter actually advocated the nationalization of coal production. After this experience, Schumpeter returned to Vienna to serve as finance minister of the new Austrian republic in March 1919. Again he played the role of politically unaffiliated conservative in a Socialist-led cabinet.

Unlike Japan after World War II, Austria was neither bombed nor occupied as a result of World War I, and its housing stock and infrastructure remained intact. In certain economic respects, however, its postwar situation was nearly as extreme. As Japan would be, Austria was separated from its former economic

hinterland (its empire). In this case, however, the economic weight of that empire was relatively much greater, and the end of empire meant the division of an
economically integrated continental state into separate national entities. The
greater part of the former empire's factories and mines were now in the Czecho-
Slovak republic, while the major sources of grain and coal supply were in the
Hungarian republic. The Austrian republic did retain for itself the capital city
and some Alpine scenery, as people liked to say. It also retained an empire-sized
administrative apparatus and an astronomical war debt. Other circumstances
were preminiscent of the aftermath of World War II in Japan. Viennese survived
on rations of 1,270 calories per day. Coal was in critically short supply. So, too,
was foreign-exchange money. At the same time, reparations obligations of a
great but still undetermined amount hung over the heads of state financial officials. Inflation mounted by stages into hyperinflation. Revolution was in the air.
In neighboring regional capitals—Budapest in March 1919, Munich in April—
there were Communist-led political takeovers, followed shortly by violent conservative reactions.

In these circumstances, Schumpeter put together a stabilization plan that was
mainly orthodox and conservative. It called for new taxes, a capital levy (a one-
off tax on wealth, in order to restore "the parallelism between the world of goods
and paper values"), exchange-rate stabilization at a reduced gold parity, the
separation of the central bank from state control, and the inducement of foreign
investment. Schumpeter also maneuvered to foreclose Otto Bauer's plan to so-
cialize key national industries. Schumpeter's plans for an enterprise-oriented
recovery came to nothing. The proposed capital levy, suggested in his famous
1918 essay on the "crisis of the tax state," had recommended him to the Socialists but alienated his own conservative backers. Schumpeter's temperament also
did not fit the job, and as a politician he was not successful. Currency circulation
doubled under his eight-month watch from 4.7 billion crowns in March 1919 to
10.8 billion in October, so one could not say that he restrained inflation either.[7]

Next came a boom-and-bust career as a banker, capitalist, and man about
town. On leaving ministerial office in October 1919, Schumpeter was awarded a
license to operate a bank. He parlayed this restricted privilege into the chair-
manship of the Biedermann Bank, a long-established partnership that through
his participation could now be formally incorporated as a bank. Schumpeter
stayed out of the bank's day-to-day operations and made a fortune by investing
borrowed capital amid the frenetic financial churning of the hyperinflation period. Ōuchi Hyōe, then visiting Vienna from Germany, has left us his own description of the city in 1922. The formerly brilliant Habsburg capital was "literally pitch black" at night, for even in the city center the electric streetlamps were

turned off, and it was dangerous to walk. "On those dark streets, many women of the night came and bumped into me. Yet if you went to the restaurants where foreigners gathered, the lights were bright there and there were many people dancing." The theatres were full of people.[8] Schumpeter, standing at the sources of the money-creation process, was among those who lived high during the inflation period, fancying a life as the greatest lover in Vienna and the greatest horseman in Austria. But this venture into credit creation also failed in 1924, and Schumpeter was left with a damaged reputation and a portfolio of personal debts.

Schumpeter's personal failure came at the point when postwar inflation turned to postwar deflation. This was Austria's national "stabilization crisis," which happened when the Austrian government agreed to an Allied-backed deflation program and restored the gold convertibility of the national money. Schumpeter's own ideas concerning monetary stabilization were also on the orthodox side. He fully recognized the artificial and managed character of the prewar gold standard, but he also thought that on balance it was preferable to return to it, even though the operation cost him personally.[9] For Austria as for Germany, this kind of "stabilization" ended up being socially and politically destabilizing in the extreme. In exchange for foreign-currency loans, the new republic traded away a substantial degree of national financial sovereignty and created a framework for years of austerity, as required by a newly erected structure of foreign creditor claims on future Austrian production.

The stabilization program in Austria was evidently successful in the short run. It inaugurated a series of such programs, forerunners of modern IMF-brokered programs that involve a similar set of arrangements. As happened in country after country during these years, Austria's "stabilization" began with a stock market crash and depression.[10] The post–World War II analogy, as we will see, is to Japan's "stabilization crisis" in 1949, when U.S. banker Joseph Dodge directed a policy of credit restriction and austerity. What was different after World War II was that U.S. banks were not authorized to engage in "controlled loans" to the defeated countries, and short-term monetary stabilization did not depend on the erection of a massive structure of ultimately destabilizing debts. It truly was a stabilization.

The 1924 stabilization crisis wiped out Schumpeter's paper profits, and he found himself caught up in lawsuits over business deals gone bad.[11] In the ensuing age of deflation, it took him a decade to repay his debts. Schumpeter now rebuilt his academic career. He was rejected for a university post in Berlin on reputational grounds. The Economics Faculty of the University of Tokyo offered him a post at this difficult time, something Schumpeter always remembered with gratitude. Professor Kawai Eijirō visited him in Vienna to discuss terms, which

Schumpeter seemed ready to accept. But Schumpeter was also negotiating his second marriage at the same time, and his fiancée told him that Japan could not be part of the deal. He instead took a professorship at Bonn University.

In the summer of 1925, in the space of six weeks, Schumpeter suffered the sudden death of his mother, to whom he was exceptionally close, followed by the death of his beloved wife, who died in childbirth together with their newborn son. Schumpeter addressed prayers for inspiration to his mother and his wife ever after, and lived mainly in his work. Bonn "robbed joy" from his life, as he later said.[12] In this soul-searching and depressed frame of mind, Schumpeter revised and condensed his *Theory of Economic Development* for republication in 1926. Not long after that, he got to know the young Japanese economists Nakayama Ichirō and Tōbata Seiichi, of whom he formed a high opinion.

2.3 The Marxists

Tokyo University professor Ōuchi Hyōe was postwar Japan's most famous expert in fiscal policy. He was also the most consistently committed critic of both capitalism and inflation among the economists introduced here. Before World War II ended, Ōuchi anticipated the great inflation that would follow. After the war, he emerged as a prominent critic of the government's inflation policy. Notwithstanding his Marxist politics, he was personally close to top government officials. Later, he even had the opportunity of lecturing to the emperor (on the *Communist Manifesto*, no less).[13] These connections to power reflect the unquestioned status of Tokyo Imperial University as Japan's top university. They reflect especially the university's primary function as a state institution for recruiting, training, and socializing the elite corps of imperial officials who themselves constituted the state executive.

Ōuchi himself graduated from Tokyo Imperial University, worked for a few years in the Ministry of Finance, and was then hired into the university's Faculty of Economics, at the time when it was established as a separate department. Ōuchi was a leader among the first generation of Tokyo University Marxists, and the Economics Department later became a center of Marxist studies in Japan, as it would continue to be into the 1970s. In 1920, Ōuchi's political radicalism resulted in his temporary suspension from his post. He took the opportunity to study in Germany, first going to Berlin in 1921 and then to the University of Heidelberg, which was a center of Marxist thought. The existentialist and sometime Marxist philosopher Miki Kiyoshi and the Marxist historian Hani Gorō were also studying in Heidelberg. Ōuchi spent the years 1921 and 1922 in further study of Marxism, and he closely followed contemporary events during the period of postwar turbulence. Working with a language tutor, he also studied Goethe's *Faust*.[14] For Ōuchi it was a self-funded trip, but the Japanese yen at this time went very far against the depreciating German mark. In 1921, the inflationary postwar boom still continued in Germany. By 1922, four years after the war's end, as Ōuchi reported, prices were beginning to stabilize. Then, however, came the reparations question and the Franco-Belgian occupation of the Ruhr industrial zone, and hyperinflation began.[15] Ōuchi left Germany in January 1923, just before the final and most extreme phase of the hyperinflation, and resumed his position at Tokyo Imperial University.

When it came to intellectually shaping the direction of postwar Japanese economic development, Arisawa Hiromi (1896–1988) was probably the single most influential person.[16] He was closely affiliated with Ōuchi, who was his senior by eight years and his economics professor at Tokyo Imperial University, where Arisawa also was hired. Both were associated with the non-Leninist "Labor and Farmer" (Rōnō) wing of the Japanese Marxist movement, which was connected politically with the Socialist Party after World War II. Arisawa studied for two years in Germany, 1926–28, and also became a Germanophile. At the end of his life, Arisawa returned to work on one of his favorite subjects, the history of the Weimar Republic. At the time he went to Germany, the country had already been through its postwar hyperinflation and two-year "stabilization panic." German capitalism's life pulse seemed to have run out, Arisawa said, "but then like a phoenix it revived." During this interval of momentary economic stabilization, Arisawa, who had a brilliant grasp of economic magnitudes and statistics, intensively studied Germany's economic experience during and after World War I, drawing lessons that later shaped his own theory of managed economy. Arisawa would retain a Marxist-derived structural understanding and general socialist sympathies, but by 1934, together with many Marxists of his generation, he was embracing the idea of the "controlled economy" (*tōsei keizai*). For Arisawa, this was one step in a kind of conversion to serving the Japanese state.[17] His research work also appeared useful to military authorities. In 1934, he wrote a book on the economics of "total war," *Industrial Mobilization Planning* (*Sangyō dōin keikaku*), which surveyed economic mobilization during World War I. Germany's example was influential here, but Arisawa also surveyed U.S. wartime economic planning, which has a significance that is still quite underregarded (especially in the United States itself).[18] By 1937, Arisawa thought that state capitalism was the wave of the future and was the only way out of the deadlock of the existing form of semiregulated capitalism.

Politically, these Marxist professors walked a fine line in 1930s Japan. In February 1938, Arisawa, Ōuchi, and several other Marxists employed at elite universities were arrested in connection with the so-called Popular Front incident.[19]

They were prosecuted under the Peace Preservation Law, which made it a crime to associate with any organization that denied the "system of private property" or sought to change the "national essence" (as much a catchall phrase in Japanese as in English). Arisawa was released fifteen months later. Still defending himself from prosecution, he quietly entered government circles and took a leading part in designing the economic plan for the totalitarian "New Order" planned by the Konoe Fumimaro cabinet. Ōuchi retreated to a politically safer kind of study—of Adam Smith.

The ideas Arisawa developed during the war concerning coal, iron, and steel would reappear in the Priority Production System, which he designed in 1946. At the time, Arisawa was also employed as an adviser at Toshiba and conducted research for the Imperial Army's Akimaru Institute. In the course of this work, he studied the input-output analysis that Wassily Leontieff had developed in his analysis of the U.S. economy. This too Arisawa would later apply to the design of the Priority Production System. Arisawa's relations with the Japanese state were thus complex and ambiguous. At the same time, his integration of Marxist and capitalist-developmental ideas had a consistency of its own, typifying the *jissen* (actual practice) style of Japanese applied social economics. In fact, an outstanding feature of postwar Japanese development is the role played by Marxism in people's understanding of the process. This is true not only of outsiders to the system: the unexpected point is that many theorists and planners approached the business of *capitalist* development from the standpoint of Marxist economics.[20]

2.4 The Capital Creator

Germany's experience after World War I also served as a personal reference point for an up-and-coming Bank of Japan official, Ichimada Hisato (1893–1984), who witnessed the end of the hyperinflation.[21] Between 1946 and 1954, Ichimada was governor of the Bank of Japan. The power of financial indication he exercised over Japanese industry was such that he was dubbed "the pope of Rome." The postwar central bank governor thus shared a common frame of experience with the Marxist fiscal expert. Unlike Ōuchi Hyōe, Ichimada had also witnessed the effects of the postinflationary "stabilization" crisis in Germany. This experience would become significant in Ichimada's later resistance to imposing a similar deflationary regimen on Japanese industry.

Ichimada learned other lessons from his connection with Bank of Japan governor Inoue Junnosuke. Ichimada was a native of Ōita prefecture in Kyushu, and he was attracted to a career in banking by the example of his seniors from Ōita,

Yamamoto Tatsuo and Inoue Junnosuke, both of whom were governors of the Bank of Japan who later became cabinet ministers. Inoue Junnosuke himself had entered the Bank of Japan as a protégé of Yamamoto Tatsuo. In 1918, Ichimada graduated from the Law Department of Tokyo Imperial University and joined the Bank of Japan under the patronage of Inoue, who became the central bank's governor in 1919. Ichimada was thus a Bank of Japan man "in the strictest sense."[22] As Inoue had been, he was groomed for the top from the time he entered the bank, rising step-by-step to become bank governor twenty-eight years later.

From February 1924 until 1925, Ichimada was posted to Germany for overseas training. There he viewed postwar monetary stabilization from a front-row seat inside the German Reichsbank. In the process, he came greatly to admire Reichsbank governor Hjalmar Schacht, whom he took as an anti-inflationary role model. "Even now," Ichimada recalled in 1950, "strongly carved in my imagination is the image of Schacht, deciding according to what he thought was the highest good of the nation, being faithful to his beliefs without retreating one step." Schacht, he thought, exemplified the proper "independence from politics" of the central banker:

> As for Reichsbank governor Schacht, if I can say so, if you took Inoue [Junnosuke] of Japan and made him a bit more international and a bit purer, that is the kind of person he was: he was a pure person without the degree of political attitude of Inoue.

Ichimada also called Schacht a "centralist democrat" and praised his "patriotic enthusiasm" and "enthusiasm for the liberalism of that time." This image of Schacht the progressive democrat is a far cry from Schacht's autocratic persona as Nazi economic czar in the 1930s.[23] This gap in Ichimada's evaluation of Schacht runs parallel to a gap between Ichimada's own self-perception and the pontifical authority that others would later see vested in him.

As in the Austrian stabilization plan, Schacht's stabilization of the currency was packaged with a program of Allied financial controls, combined with private "controlled loans" by U.S. and British banks. This program likewise brought on a stabilization depression. Germany's first round of stabilization depression was followed by a strong recovery, but that recovery was succeeded shortly by further waves of deflation and depression. At the depth of the depression in 1933, Schacht took on the role of "Hitler's banker" and exercised extraordinary powers of control over the funding of German industry. He also designed a comprehensive system of foreign-exchange control that would, after World War II, be adapted and carried over in the Soviet trading sphere.[24] Nazi-era central banking also strongly influenced the 1942 reorganization of the Bank of Japan, just at the point when Ichimada moved to a position at the center of things there (see 8.1.2). It was thus not the model of the liberal 1920s but rather that of the Nazi-era Reichsbank that Ichimada and his fellows would actually take as their standard.

Ichimada returned to Japan in 1926 and worked for two years at the BoJ's pivotal management office (*eigyō kyoku*). He served also as Inoue Junnosuke's secretary when Inoue returned for a second tenure as central bank governor to clean things up after the great bank panic of 1927. In this central posting, Ichimada was following the pattern of Inoue's own career. This was the time when the Ministry of Finance and Bank of Japan began to authoritatively direct the consolidation of the Japanese banking system. Another lesson came with the deflation policy of 1929–31, which was directed by Inoue Junnosuke, now as minister of finance. In a grim parallel to the policies of Germany's "Hunger Chancellor," Heinrich Brüning, the Inoue deflation intensified depression at home just at a time of internationally synchronized depression around the world. Inoue's campaign ended with his assassination in 1932, and with the discrediting of the entire liberal system.

In 1941, Ichimada was involved in the reorganization of the central bank along Reichsbank lines. He subsequently became responsible for running the Nationwide Financial Control Association. This placed him at the executive epicenter of the national credit allocation system, in its authoritative wartime form. Thus, from a post a few organizational rungs below the BoJ's highest executive level, Ichimada guided the organization and management of the wartime industrial financing system. In this role, he was in effect both a banker and an executive manager of a state economic planning board. This identity of banking and central planning roles becomes extremely interesting in light of Schumpeter's ideas concerning the commonalities of modern capitalism and socialism (see 3.4).

2.5 The Schumpeterians

Nakayama Ichirō and Tōbata (or Tōhata) Seiichi were fast friends and devoted Schumpeterians. They first met at Bonn University, where they both studied with Schumpeter. They went on to become the most prominent non-Marxist economists of their generation in Japan. With Arisawa Hiromi, they also had the greatest influence on policy, serving between them on dozens of major government commissions from the 1940s into the 1960s.

Nakayama Ichirō studied economics at Tokyo Commercial University. He graduated in 1926 and spent his career there as a professor of economics. In 1949, he became the university's president, and the university was renamed Hitotsubashi University. (The university motto is the Schumpeterian-sounding "captains of industry," although the use of the catchphrase is traced back to the university's founder, Mori Arinori.) In fact, Hitotsubashi University, to which Schumpeter donated much of his personal library, has had a lineage of "Schumpeterian" presidents, including Nakayama Ichirō, Tsuru Shigeto, and Shionoya Yuichi, one of the world's leading Schumpeter scholars.

Nakayama's teacher was the pioneering economist Fukuda Tokuzō (1874–1930). Fukuda himself studied in Germany with the famed Lujo Brentano, and he developed and brought back to Japan an in-depth understanding of the ideas of the German historical school and of labor and welfare economics. His ideals were close to what Germans came to call the "social market economy" after World War II. Fukuda also had a big part in introducing both Marxist and neoclassical economic ideas to Japan, in another indication of the eclectic sources of Japanese economics. The young Joseph Schumpeter was one of many contemporary Western economists whose writings Fukuda introduced to a Japanese intellectual public.[25] When Nakayama went to Germany to study with the great Schumpeter, he thus followed a path similar to that of his teacher.

After World War II, Marxism became predominant at many Japanese academic institutions. These included the Economics Faculty of Tokyo University, where Ōuchi, after his wartime purge, became a revered senior figure. Hitotsubashi stood out as a bastion of pro-capitalist economics, though of a strongly empirical, historical, and institutional sort. Hitotsubashi economists accordingly had a prominent place as advisers in official policy circles. In this, Nakayama's personal influence was itself an important factor.

Tōbata Seiichi, a professor of agricultural economics at Tokyo University, grew up in a middle-class farm family. As a student, he was personally impressed by the significance of food-supply economics when he witnessed the 1918 Rice Riots, which was Japan's own most intense experience with World War I–era inflation. It was the Rice Riots, he said, that taught him that "people in the mass have great energy." After studying at Tokyo Imperial University and getting a teaching appointment there, Tōbata in 1926 won a fellowship from the International Education Foundation (Rockefeller Foundation) to study agricultural economics at the University of Wisconsin. There, he studied the U.S. agricultural system intensively. He was inspired especially by the achievements of the U.S. agricultural extension system, which was itself a kind of entrepreneurial support system. Tōbata made extensive study trips around the United States and ended up staying until the beginning of 1928. Immediately on his return to Japan, the Ministry of Education sent him for two years of further study to the University of Bonn in Germany. It was there that he became friends with Nakayama Ichirō and studied with Joseph Schumpeter.

As preparation for that, Tōbata spent the summer of 1928 reading Schumpeter's works. The chief of these was the newly revised *Theory of Economic*

Development. In partnership with Nakayama, Tōbata studied with Schumpeter through 1929, and then departed for home in October of that year. As Tōbata recalled, it was a gift of an extra year for him, which he spent "studying like crazy, as if in a dream." He said he felt that day by day, Schumpeter was clearing the mist from his mind.[26] Tōbata returned via the United States, at the moment just after the Wall Street crash. He reached Japan in March 1930, at a point when crop prices were collapsing, intensifying the already existing agrarian debt crisis. Tōbata resolved to use what he had learned to help develop a progressive Japanese agricultural economics. He undertook this task with extraordinary energy.

In January and February 1931, in the midst of the world economic crisis, Nakayama and Tōbata helped host Schumpeter during an extended lecture tour of Japan. Schumpeter met many Japanese economists and gave public lectures on business cycles and economic theory in Tokyo, Osaka, Kyoto, and Kobe. One of his lectures was broadcast on Radio Osaka. After this point Schumpeter's ideas became part of current economic discussion in Japan and began to diffuse to a wider public. Schumpeter loved Japan. Reading the *Tale of Genji* left a strong impression; he later confided to Tsuru Shigeto that he would like to meet a woman like Lady Murasaki Shikibu "and slowly talk through the night with her."[27]

In 1933, Nakayama published his book *Pure Economics* (*Junsui keizaigaku*), borrowing the title from Schumpeter's idol Léon Walras. This book would be for many years the standard text for teaching neoclassical "equilibrium" economics. In fact, it presented a rather dynamic and Schumpeterian approach to the subject. Nakayama prefaced his book by mentioning the resolution he had formed together with Tōbata in Bonn "to somehow take a step beyond Schumpeter." He later prefaced his twenty-nine-volume collected works with a tribute to Schumpeter's influence, and he wondered whether he had actually accomplished this goal. Nakayama's account of economic development in *Pure Economics* was a neat digest of Schumpeter's *Theory of Economic Development*. It included a clear explanation of the inflationary creation of credit capital and the process of "forced saving," as discussed in the next chapter.[28] One won't find such an account in U.S. neoclassical economics textbooks; in Japan it was there at the beginning.

Nakayama's approach was also eclectic, and he led in disseminating Keynesian economics in Japan and in translating Keynes's works into Japanese. Indeed, he said, Keynes's *General Theory* of 1936 "completed" Schumpeter when it came to the theory of money.[29]

Tōbata Seiichi's 1936 book *Process of Development of Japanese Agriculture* (*Nihon nōgyō no tenkai katei*) was also influenced by Schumpeter's conception of capitalist development. Tōbata put entrepreneurship at the center of his analysis. However, he argued that the prime entrepreneurial movers in the development of Japanese agriculture were not the small-scale farmers and landlords, who were little involved in the marketing side of the process. Rather, the true entrepreneurs were, first, the commercial processors of agricultural products, and second, the government itself, acting through experimental stations and agricultural associations.[30] This conception of state agencies as entrepreneurs was in fact already a step beyond Schumpeter.

Together, Nakayama and Tōbata carefully translated Schumpeter's *Theory of Economic Development*. It was published by Iwanami in 1937 as *Keizai hatten no riron*. Schumpeter wrote a new preface for the occasion. In it, he indicated his high regard for Japan and for Nakayama and Tōbata personally. He also highlighted his twin intellectual debts—to the static equilibrium economics of Walras and to the dynamic developmental analysis of Marx.[31] The latter comment was striking to readers in 1937 Japan, when Marx's name had become a dangerous one with which to associate.

It was for this reason that Ōuchi Hyōe called Schumpeter's work "a child of mixed blood" (*ai no ko*). He used the same phrase to describe Japanese economics as a whole.[32] Ōuchi, with his own great stake in Marx's system, was not being complimentary in saying this. His comment was also sharply perceptive: Schumpeter's work indeed appeared to be a "third empire" between Marxist and neoclassical economics; Schumpeter had adapted the Marxist "mechanism" but had turned it to other purposes.

Tōbata Seiichi and Nakayama Ichirō were drawn into government work during the war. Tōbata, like so many other policy experts of his generation, also ventured into colonial policy. With Ohkawa Kazushi of Tokyo Commercial University, he conducted a study of Korean agriculture, published in 1937. He added the subject of colonial development policy to his teaching responsibilities from 1939 through the end of the war. In 1943, Tōbata went to the Philippines as a member of the Philippines Investigation Committee and helped produce a massive report on social and economic conditions. With other members of the committee, he would return to the Philippines in 1953, as a member of the Reparations Committee. This is one of many examples of how Japan's war reparations to Asian countries carried over directly into its later program of overseas developmental funding, under the rubric of Official Development Assistance (ODA). Those initiatives continued to be structured around ideas of "wide-region development." In Tōbata's case, the positive character of his wartime relations with Philippine scholars and their evaluation of the quality of his work is attested by his being given the Ramon Magsaysay Award in 1968.[33]

After the war, with near-famine conditions at home, Tōbata worked on problems of national rice supply and distribution. In May 1946, when Yoshida Shigeru formed his first cabinet, he invited Tōbata to serve as minister of agriculture and forestry. Tōbata declined, but in December 1946 he did accept a post as the first director of the Agriculture Ministry's new Research Institute of Agricultural Economics and Rural Sociology. There he worked successfully to develop a cadre of members trained in both technology and economics, an ideal we will see embodied also in the work of Ōkita Saburō and Gotō Yonosuke.

Nakayama Ichirō during the war period headed the Domestic Section of the army's Economic Research Institute (the Akimaru Institute), established in 1940 to investigate Japan's capacity to fight a war double the scale of the ongoing war in China. Arisawa Hiromi headed the Britain-America Section of the institute. Both Nakayama and Arisawa knew that war with the United States was far beyond Japan's means, and their reports demonstrated this in statistical detail. Army leadership ordered the burning of the institute's research results and dissolved the institute.[34] Toward the end of World War II, Nakayama began to participate in a research group on "postwar management" led by Bank of Japan adviser Miura Shinchichi. It was here that he began to focus on labor issues, which would become the most important focus of his postwar policy activity. Nakayama began with the questions posed by the demobilization of military forces, by investigating Germany's experience of demobilization after World War I. In the summer of 1945, Nakayama and Tōbata joined the Greater East Asia Ministry's Special Survey Committee, which would serve as a seedbed for developing ideas of postwar economic planning.

The youngest of Schumpeter's three famous Japanese students was Tsuru Shigeto (1912–2006), another eclectic, institutionally minded economist. In 1947 Tsuru became a leading figure at the Economic Stabilization Board during the period of its greatest influence. Tsuru himself had an elite family background. His father was the president of Tōhō Gas, and Tsuru later married a niece of Kido Kōichi, who as lord keeper of the privy seal was in the inner circle around the emperor. In Tsuru's student days in higher school (an elite institution somewhat like the old German *Gymnasium* system) he became involved in the leftwing anti-imperialist student movement, and in 1930 he was arrested and expelled from school. He wanted to go to Germany to study, but his parents feared he would become more radicalized there and sent him instead to a small college in Wisconsin. At Lawrence College, Tsuru was taught by Harry Dexter White, later the main American framer of the Bretton Woods agreement (and still later himself targeted as a communist). On White's recommendation, Tsuru finished his undergraduate education at Harvard, where he then completed a Ph.D. in economics, working after 1935 with Joseph Schumpeter and joining a cohort of graduate students who would become some of the most famous names in postwar U.S. economics. Tsuru's doctoral dissertation was a historical study of business cycles in Japan. He took great inspiration from Schumpeter, who was at the time completing his own massive study of business cycles. After nearly a decade in America, Tsuru found himself caught there at the time of the Japanese attack on Pearl Harbor. He subsequently had the unusual experience of spending time in wartime America in a comfortable internship together with German and Italian diplomats and their families. He was then sent to Japan in a repatriation exchange, by way of Mozambique. Back in Japan, Tsuru under Kido Kōichi's sponsorship entered the Ministry of Foreign Affairs. In June 1944, he became a pawn in the conflict between the militarist group around Prime Minister Tōjō Hideki and the group around Kido, who favored an attempt at a negotiated peace. Tōjō had Tsuru drafted into the infantry. Kido managed to get him released, and he was then sent in the spring of 1945 to the Soviet Union as a diplomat, escaping in this way the bombing of Tokyo.[35] For Tsuru, as for others, this period of violent political division and war was also a time of extraordinary intellectual fusion and effervescence. Tsuru's own mix of Marxist, American institutionalist, and Schumpeterian thought was another intellectual "child of mixed blood."

WHAT IS CAPITAL?

Capital is nothing but the lever by which the entrepreneur subjects to his own control the concrete goods which he needs, nothing but a means of diverting the factors of production to new uses, or of dictating a new direction to production.

—J. A. Schumpeter, *The Theory of Economic Development* (1912)

The typically Schumpeter-type development, that is, credit creation → carrying out of *new combinations*, represents the financial aspect of Japanese economic development since the latter part of the 1800's more definitely than in the case of the other advanced nations.

—Shinohara Miyohei, "Factors in Japan's Economic Growth" (1964)

The ideas advanced by Joseph Schumpeter are now enjoying boom times. His conceptions of entrepreneurship and innovation have had more influence in thinking about those subjects than those of any other scholar. Schumpeter pioneered the study of economic development and of technological "paradigm shifts," and he is widely credited as a forerunner of the emerging field of evolutionary economics. But he is not thought of as a theorist of credit-supercharged high-speed growth. This is what he became in postwar Japan, for reasons described in the following chapters. At the heart of this understanding is Schumpeter's conception of capital.

Capital in its economic sense can be thought of in two ways, as money-capital and as physical capital.[1] Despite the confusion of naming, the two are quite distinct and behave according to distinct sets of principles. This chapter considers capital mainly in the first, financial sense. This is the sense in which Schumpeter used it. Capital, as Schumpeter explained it, is the means of *diverting the factors of production to new uses*. "What is this lever, this means of control?" he asked. Simply, "it is a fund of purchasing power." It has a "protean" quality.[2] Schumpeter did not quite say it, but the word *Faustian* comes also to mind.

As a theoretical description of the capitalist process, Schumpeter's explanation is useful and provocative. In a way that he would not have anticipated, it also became significant as *pre*scription in postwar Japan. The channel of influence here was by way of Japanese economists who studied with Schumpeter and took his ideas to heart.[3] More than a matter of Schumpeter's ideas influencing Japanese development, however, it was a matter of these economists finding that Schumpeter's ideas confirmed their own intuitions, and finding in those ideas a description of what they saw happening around them. As Shinohara Miyohei suggested, postwar Japan's credit-funded development may have been more purely "Schumpeterian," in the financial-capital sense described here, than that of any other country. This is thus a matter of parallel insights into a common capitalist process, but there was some direct influence also. Shinohara Miyohei was himself a student of Nakayama Ichirō, making him a "grand-student" of Schumpeter, in a country were such filiations are especially important. In a memorial on Schumpeter's death in 1950, Arthur Smithies said that Japan had probably extended "more esteem and admiration" to Schumpeter than had any other country. From the other side, as Jean-Pascal Bassino pointed out, Schumpeter was one of the first European or American economists to take Japanese development seriously.[4]

I myself am not writing here as a "Schumpeterian," and my goal is not to explain or apply Schumpeter's entire system. My point is to explore how Schumpeter's ideas of credit-capital creation elucidate basic features of the modern capitalist process that are usually glossed over or misunderstood. They offer insights that Karl Marx's critical analysis of capitalism did not encompass and that most procapitalist analyses shut off from discussion (including many analyses that otherwise draw on Schumpeter's account).[5] This is not to say that Schumpeter's view is complete; but he asks questions that can bring us to a next level of understanding. The fact that Japanese participants in the creation of the High-Speed Growth system took hold of these ideas makes them doubly interesting.

Schumpeter first presented his description of the capitalist process in his *Theory of Economic Development*, published in German in 1912. The second (1926) edition of the *Theory of Economic Development* was published in English in 1934 and, as described already, published in Japanese in 1937.

3.1 When New Capital Comes onto the Stage

"*All new capital*, in the first instance, comes onto the stage, that is, onto the market—commodities market, labor market, or money market—still as *money*, money that through definite processes would transform itself into capital."[6] This was Karl Marx's starting point on the subject of capital, in volume 1 of his massive life's work on the subject. Marx's main concern was what happened next in the process, after money-capital was invested into production. A starting point of this book is with a prior question, which Marx left out of consideration: What is this money-capital itself? And how does it come to be? For Schumpeter, the creation of new money-capital and, more specifically, credit-capital, was the financial counterpart of innovation under capitalism.

Schumpeter's own exploration of the dynamic, developmental nature of capitalism began with the idea of economic *flow*—"a continuous flow of goods and a continuously moving economic process"; "a stream of goods being continually renewed." This idea of the flowing or "revenual" character of the economic process will recur repeatedly in the following pages. Ultimately, as Schumpeter clearly perceived, "one can actually speak of 'stocks' [of goods] only in an abstract sense"—stocks of goods really resolve into regulated flows.[7]

Analytically, Schumpeter distinguished two circuits of credit circulation. The first is a circuit of circulating credit for the reproduction of existing operations. These funds can be thought of as flowing out of established revenue streams. His attention was directed to the second circuit, that of new investment for new undertakings. This was capital presented for the creation of "new combinations."[8] The calling of the entrepreneur, the archetypal hero of Schumpeter's story, was to divert portions of the economic flow into new channels. "It is the carrying out of new combinations that constitutes the entrepreneur"; most businesspeople were not entrepreneurs in this sense. Schumpeter's definition of "new combinations"—*neue Kombinationen*, which he later called simply *innovations*—is well known but should be repeated. New combinations could consist of:

1. The introduction of a new good . . . or of a new quality of a good.
2. The introduction of a new method of production . . . [or] new way of handling a commodity commercially.
3. The opening of a new market. . . .
4. The conquest of a new source of supply of raw materials or half-manufactured goods. . . .
5. The carrying out of the new organization of any industry, like the creation of a monopoly position . . . or the breaking up of a monopoly position.

The *discontinuous* creation of new combinations is thus the really significant developmental process.

Those who carry out the entrepreneurial function include not only "'independent' businessmen," "but all who actually fulfil the function . . . even if they are, as is becoming the rule, 'dependent' employees of a company."[9] Schumpeter thus recognized that within the modern corporate order—which was still very new when he first began writing—entrepreneurship itself was becoming a managerial function. Schumpeter did not say it here, but one could read by implication that entrepreneurial innovation was becoming or could in the future become a delegated and even routinized group function. Japanese business groups, and in particular their general trading companies (*sōgō shōsha*), would later make it precisely this. And Japanese planning officials who built on Schumpeter's idea would later understand entrepreneurship further as a *national* function.

This is not what Schumpeter emphasized at the time. His explanation of the role of the entrepreneur is individualistic, idealized, and celebratory. His explanation of the role of the banker is only slightly less so. His schema also brings into focus, and into relationship with one another, key points concerning the way banks create new monetary claims, the nature of inflation, and the process of new development. It is worth working through this often overlooked part of Schumpeter's analysis step by step, for it goes to the heart of the capital-creation circuit.

3.2 The Distribution of Promises

Schumpeter began his chapter "Credit and Capital" by returning to the idea of "new combination." Fundamentally, he said, "the essence of economic development consists in a *different* employment of *existing* services [*Leistungen*] of labor and land." (To this we should add the "services" of *natural resources* such as coal; the point will return in chapter 4.) So, innovation consists in *a different employment of existing productive capacities*—the statement seems trivially obvious. But it makes clear the next point, "that the carrying out of new combinations takes place through the *withdrawal* of services of labor and land from their previous employments." In other words, nothing in the material economic realm comes from nowhere. The entrepreneurial organization of "new combinations" is necessarily a matter of diverting existing resources. Or, we might say, of diverting existing energetic and material flows.

Money, on the other hand, is a socially imagined construction that can—Schumpeter says must—be created de novo. To put it philosophically, money belongs to the ideal, or communicative, realm. Money is also an *irreducible* part of the process. "Processes in terms of means of payment are not merely reflexes of processes in terms of goods." That is, money is not merely a reflection of material economic flows, nor merely a veil over them. But to say so was a "heresy," Schumpeter pointed out, according to the standards of the nineteenth-century economists who held that economics was essentially exchange, and that exchange was essentially barter, with money serving only as a convenience. Schumpeter's point that money—specifically, newly created, *additional* money—was essential to the capitalist process leads to the fundamental point. This is that innovation and development—"a different employment of the system's productive powers"—"cannot be achieved otherwise than by a disturbance in the relative purchasing power of individuals. . . . It is always a question of drawing goods out of the circular flow."[10]

3.2.1 Money Created by Banks

The *redistribution of purchasing power* is thus a starting point of the developmental process. How is this new purchasing power created? Here we come to the special role of banks in the capitalist system:

> This creation of means of payment centers in the banks and constitutes their fundamental function. . . . *The creation of money by the banks establishing claims against themselves*, which is described by Adam Smith, and indeed by still earlier authors in a way quite free from popular errors, has become a commonplace today.

Here it should be inserted that by the time Schumpeter was writing, the greater part of money in the countries of capitalist development, even by narrow definitions of money, no longer consisted of physically existing currency (banknotes and coins). Rather, most money, by accepted functional definitions of money, was "book money," or bank balances, existing physically only as accounting entries. And bank balances mean *credits*:

> These circulating media come into being in the process of granting credit and are created especially . . . for the *purpose* of granting credit. A bank is, according to Fetter, "*a business whose income is derived chiefly from lending its promises to pay.*"

There was nothing controversial in this statement, Schumpeter said, anticipating resistance. "No one can reproach me with offending against, say, [David] Ricardo's statement that 'banking operations' cannot increase a country's wealth, or with making myself guilty of, say, a 'vapory speculation' in [John] Law's sense." But in fact, Schumpeter said, Ricardo's statement "is not quite correct." That is, it seems that banking operations *could* increase a country's wealth.[11]

As for "vapory speculation," we have some forthright statements in Schumpeter's notes on John Law, published after Schumpeter's death by his third wife, the economist Elizabeth Boody Schumpeter. Here he wrote: "Manufacture of money! Credit as a creator of money! Manifestly, this opens up other than theoretical vistas." Here Schumpeter credited John Law with "the discovery that money—and hence capital in the monetary sense of the term—can be manufactured or created" by banking operations. Law's national bank project of 1718 meant the birth of "the idea of Managed Currency," an idea "which was subsequently lost to the large majority of economists until it forced itself upon them after 1919." That is, it forced itself on them during the great inflation and bonfire of debts that followed World War I. And, Schumpeter continued, this was to speak of managed currency "not only in the obvious sense of the term but in the deeper and wider sense." This deeper sense was a macroeconomic and indicative one, in which management of currency and credit was "a means of managing the economic process" as a whole.[12]

At this point it becomes necessary to address a common confusion, perpetuated by banks' self-representation concerning their own business and perpetuated by the very words that economists persist in using to describe the process. Bank balances continue to be routinely described, including in the banking statistics, as "deposits." In fact, banks' creation of credit means that actual paid-in deposits form only a fraction in the total of bank balances. "In some countries"—Schumpeter indicates England—"perhaps three-quarters of bank deposits are simply credits." That is, the only thing "deposited" in a bank in these operations is the bank's promise to pay; this amount is credited to a borrower's account, in exchange for the borrower's promise to later repay the bank. But this basic fact is kept obscure, as

> only a few banks show in their periodical statements what part of their deposits consists of real [primary] deposits. . . . Strictly speaking, moreover, *all* bank deposits are based upon mere credits. . . . [*only*] *credits which arise out of "sums paid in" are* covered *in a special manner and do not increase the purchasing power of the depositors.*

Monetary sums paid in by depositors, which merely "relocate" their purchasing power, are the kind of deposits that most people usually think of, but they occupy only a fraction of what gets accounted as bank deposits. And in fact, from the standpoint of the banking system as a whole, much of those "sums paid in" themselves originated as credits credited to the accounts of employers and then paid out as wages to their employees. What most entrepreneurial holders of bank balances hold on "deposit" are actually credits extended to them by the bank, which do increase their purchasing power. In this way,

> the businessman as a rule first becomes the bank's debtor [by taking out a loan] in order to become its creditor [as the holder of a deposit credited against the bank], . . . he first "borrows" what he *uno actu* "deposits."[13]

These newly created funds do not leave the banking system as long as they "circulate" (as bookkeeping entries) from one bank account to another. In practice, this means that as long as they circulate among company accounts, these newly created promises-to-pay remain within the banking system and do not have to be paid out as actual physical currency. In practice, they are mainly paid out in cash when paid as salaries and wages (or when used for business purposes in black market transactions).

It is thus confusing if not actively misleading to call these newly created credits *deposits*, which in its primary sense implies the deposit with a bank of already existing cash currency. For this reason, Schumpeter later clarified his terminology: this creation of new purchasing power was "the creation of *balances*, misleadingly and insincerely called *deposits*." In the twenty-first century, it is still routine to describe all bank balances as "deposits" and to describe banks' role as that of "intermediaries"—that is, between savers and borrowers. At the level of the banking system as a whole, this language itself is essentially false. In the typical case described by Schumpeter, only a tiny fraction of the bank's loan corresponds to already existing savings. The "loan" itself is a new creation of new purchasing power by means of a new bookkeeping entry in the borrower's account. When the borrower needs to draw on this account for making payments, the sums paid out will typically be rerecorded as an entry to someone else's account in another bank. (Ideally for the bank itself, they would be paid to another account within the same bank.) Hence, Schumpeter explained, "only a negligible fraction of all transactions are and can be effected by money [cash currency] in the strict sense." Seen from the standpoint of cash money, the circulating media created as bank credits "exist in such quantities that they could not possibly all be redeemed at once." This point is well known. The most important point here is the further observation that these circulating media "not only replace, for the sake of convenience, sums of [cash] money which previously circulated, *but also appear newly created side by side with the existing sums.*"[14]

3.2.2 Promises as Capital

With this we come to the essence of the capitalist developmental process:

> The entrepreneur—in principle and as a rule—does need credit, in the sense of a temporary transfer to him of purchasing power, in order to produce at all, to be able to carry out his new combinations, to *become* an entrepreneur. . . . He can only become an entrepreneur by previously becoming a debtor. He becomes a debtor in consequence of the logic of the process of development, or, to put it in still another way, his becoming a debtor arises from the necessity of the case.

In fact, the entrepreneur "is the typical debtor in capitalist society." More than that, "the entrepreneur is also a debtor in a deeper sense . . . *he receives goods from the social stream*—again in principle—*before he has contributed anything to it*. In this sense he is so to speak a debtor of society."

To sum up, "the essential function of credit," meaning new purchasing power,

> consists in *enabling the entrepreneur to withdraw the producers' goods which he needs from their previous employments*, by exercising a demand for them, and thereby to force the economic system into new channels. . . . The nature of the process . . . consists in creating a new demand for, without simultaneously creating, a new supply of goods. . . . By credit, entrepreneurs are given access to the social stream of goods before they have acquired the normal claim to it. . . . Granting credit in this sense operates as an *order* on the economic system to accommodate itself to the purposes of the entrepreneur, as an order on the goods which he needs: it means entrusting him with productive forces.[15]

Of course the entrepreneur, as debtor, must deliver on these promises. The entrepreneur does this by organizing production, earning revenues, and transferring part of those revenues back to the bank that created the credit in the first place. From the side of the banking system, the individual bank must in time honor its promise to pay. But most of those payments take place within the banking system, and the banking system as a whole has created something from nothing. The expected end result of these "new combinations" will be more, better, and cheaper production, enlarging the social flow of resources.

This new production takes time to realize. For this reason, credit is needed to bind present and future. There is "a *gap* to bridge in the carrying out of new combinations." This is the time-gap between the entrepreneur's purchase of means of production and the flow of new products that will eventually result. "To bridge [this gap] is the function of the lender." The lender "fulfills it by placing purchasing power created *ad hoc* at the disposal of the entrepreneur. . . . Thus the gap is closed which would otherwise make development extraordinarily difficult, if not impossible in an exchange economy where private property prevails."

And to repeat, considered from the standpoint of the material flow of the economy: "the purchasing power [so created] really represents nothing but *existing* goods."[16]

Or more precisely, it represents *new* claims to existing goods.

3.3 Credit Inflation the Mechanism of Capitalist Development

The creation, ad hoc, out of nothing, of new monetary claims to already existing goods and services: by this point, the question of price inflation may have come up in the reader's mind. Inflation is in fact an essential part of the capitalist developmental process. It also begins to explain its business-cyclic nature. That is, the new demand for the purchase of already existing means of production comes first, before any addition to supply:

> If now credit means of payment, *new purchasing power* in our sense, are created and placed at the entrepreneur's disposal, then he takes his place beside the previous producers and his purchasing power its place beside the total previously existing. Obviously this does not increase the quantity of productive services existing in the economic system. Yet "new demand" becomes possible in a very obvious sense. *It causes a rise in the prices of productive services.* From this ensues the "withdrawal of goods" from their previous use, to which we have referred. The process amounts to *compressing the existing purchasing power.* . . . No goods and certainly no new goods correspond to the newly created purchasing power. But room for it is squeezed out at the cost of previously existing purchasing power.

Previously existing means of payment lose a part of their purchasing power proportional to the amount of the newly created means of payment. As Schumpeter assured the reader, paradoxical as it might seem at first glace, there is really "nothing illogical or mystical" in any of this. What Schumpeter is describing here is the *preemption*—literally the "buying before"—of resources. Or more precisely, it is the "buying for more" of resources.

Schumpeter noted that the price increases induced by the creation of these new means of payment ought logically to proceed in a certain order:

> In the first place, the purchasing power of previous producers in the market for producers' goods will be compressed, then the purchasing power in the market for consumption goods of those people who receive no share or no adequate share in the increased money incomes resulting from the entrepreneur's demand. This explains rising prices in periods of boom.[17]

There is more to say about this question of *where* new money enters the economic process and about the order in which price increases proceed. This is the question of which social groups benefit and which pay. We should not suppose the answer to be the same in every inflation.

As for naming this process, Schumpeter noted, "if I am not mistaken it was von Mises who coined the extremely happy expression "*forced savings*" [erzwungenes Sparen] for this process." The term is an analytical touchstone. Machlup attributed to Schumpeter himself the most important place in the development of this idea.[18] Schumpeter did not use the term "forced savings" himself, but in 1926 he did not yet disapprove of it. Nakayama and Tōbata translated this term as "forced economizing" (*kyōsei sareta setsuyaku*), which is a still better expression, as opposed to other Japanese words for *saving* that would instead highlight accumulation on the part of a saver. In this kind of "forced economizing" by means of price inflation, the masses of people subject to the process do not *personally* save at all. Rather, they are fractionally expropriated; these forced austerities can be considered "savings" only in a special social sense. We could also call it forced investment. The point, as Schumpeter's friend and critic Fritz Machlup put it, is that

> investments can now exceed [personally] intended saving; that is to say, capital formation can be in excess of what people saved out of their previous income; the extra capital formation is "forced," so to speak, upon the community through monetary witchcraft.[19]

Schumpeter thus brings the reader—he presumes a resistant reader—to this point: that the involuntary withdrawal of resources from the rest of society is what enables the entrepreneur to gather and mobilize the resources to undertake something new. He now names the capitalist developmental process:

> When the price changes [i.e., increases] which thus become necessary are completed, . . . the units of purchasing power now existing are all smaller than those existing before and their distribution among individuals has been shifted. This may be called *credit inflation*.[20]

Schumpeter contrasted this type of productive credit inflation with a *consumption inflation*, wherein "the goods withdrawn are consumed, the means of payment remain in circulation, the credit must be continually renewed, and prices have risen permanently." In historical actuality, the two are not so easily separated. "Consumption inflation," Schumpeter argued, requires a separate deflationary operation to liquidate the new means of payment and restore prices to their former level. One thinks here of the deflationary financial policies that followed World War I, though Schumpeter first wrote in 1911 in advance of all that.

Unlike a consumption inflation, the process of credit inflation in support of new, *productive* entrepreneurial combinations ought to be automatically self-correcting, Schumpeter thought. This in itself would generate cycles of inflation and deflation. For this self-correcting, developmental process to operate, the entrepreneur must not only repay the loan itself: "he must also economically repay commodities to the [social] reservoir of goods." If all goes according to plan, at the end of the process the entrepreneur will have "enriched the social stream with goods whose total price is greater than the credit received. . . . Hence the equivalence between the money and commodity streams is more than re-stored, the credit inflation more than eliminated, the effect on prices *more* than compensated for." What has happened is therefore "only a non-synchronous appearance of [newly created] purchasing power and of the [newly produced] commodities corresponding to it, which temporarily produces the semblance of inflation."

Ultimately, as Schumpeter imagined it in 1911, there remains "no credit in-flation at all in this case—rather deflation," owing to the ultimate increase in social production. This is the idea of "automatic deflation" (see 12.3). "This alone," he claimed "would explain falling prices in periods of depression."

This result seemed to be confirmed empirically by the price history of Europe since 1815: there had been business-cyclic ups and downs of prices, but these happened around a long-run declining price trend. This developmental process of enlarging the production stream "actually explains the secular fall in the price level in times when no other causes, for example gold discoveries, prevent it."[21] Significantly, Schumpeter would later describe these periods of falling prices as *periods of harvest.* World War I had generated a great inflation, it is true, but this Schumpeter set aside as something caused by war, which he took to be external to the capitalist process. The return of deflation in the 1920s gave him no reason to change his mind.

All of this raises many further questions, which come up repeatedly in the pages that follow.

3.4 Capital as Indication

Concerning the creation of credit capital, Schumpeter introduced a final consid-eration that will be fundamental for the discussion that follows. This may be described as the *indicative* aspect of capital, the way credit capital acts as an "or-der" on the economic system.

Schumpeter began his analysis of the command and control of productive labor and resources with the observation that financial capital has its own mar-ket. This is true in a much more concrete, much less metaphorical way than is the case for many other "markets" that have no concentrated, easily observable form. This is the "money market," where

> on the demand side appear entrepreneurs and on the supply side pro-ducers of and dealers in purchasing power, viz. bankers, both with their staffs of agents and middlemen. What takes place is simply the ex-change of present against future purchasing power. In the daily price

struggle between the two parties the fate of new combinations is decided.

In this market for purchasing power, "all kinds of economic projects are first brought into relation with each other, and contend for their realization in it." It is this mandatory or indicative aspect that Schumpeter emphasized:

> The money market is always, as it were, the headquarters of the capital-ist system, from which orders go out to its individual divisions, and that which is debated and decided there is always in essence the settle-ment of plans for future development.[22]

For Schumpeter, this idea of capital-as-indication (my term, not his) was sharpened by its resemblance—more resemblance than contradiction—to the idea of state planning under socialism. When Schumpeter first wrote, socialism existed only as an imagined social system. Twenty-seven years after he published his original account of the capitalist development process, he returned to the subject in his 1939 magnum opus *Business Cycles*, in the chapter "How the Eco-nomic System Generates Evolution." With the intervening emergence of a cen-trally planned socialist system as an actual system of government, it seemed all the clearer to Schumpeter that banks under capitalism functionally resembled a state planning board under socialism:

> Since the central authority of the socialist state controls all existing means of production, all it has to do in case it decides to set up new production functions is simply to issue orders to those in charge of the productive resources to withdraw part of them from the employments in which they are engaged, and to apply the quantities so withdrawn to the new purposes envisaged. We may think of a kind of Gosplan as an illustration. In capitalist society the means of production required must also be withdrawn from their employments . . . and directed into the new ones.[23]

Thus, "credit creation by the banks"—their "issue to the entrepreneurs of new means of payment created *ad hoc*"—"corresponds in capitalist society to the order issued by the central bureau in the socialist state."

Whether under socialism or under capitalism, innovation involves the shift-ing of existing factors from old to new uses. But there is a difference between the two methods of shifting factors that bears directly on the question of inflation. "In the case of the socialist community the new order to those in charge of the factors *cancels* the old one." "But if innovation is financed by [capitalist] credit creation, the shifting of factors is effected not by the withdrawal of funds—

'canceling the old order'—from the old firms, but by the reduction of the purchasing power of existing funds. . . . The new 'order to the factors' comes, as it were, on top of the old one, which is not thereby canceled."[24] The inflationary price effects generate a series of consequences that are responsible for many of the characteristic features of the capitalist process, including business cycles on both longer and shorter timescales (see 9.1). In case the reader might have missed the point, Schumpeter repeated it: banks function as a kind of capitalist authorizing agency corresponding to a state planning board.[25]

3.5 The Capitalist Process as an Ideal–Material Circuit

The procapitalist Schumpeter took the anticapitalist analysis of Karl Marx as one of his starting points. The thrust of his entire project was, opposite Marx, to establish a procapitalist picture of capitalism as a dynamic developmental system. But Schumpeter wrote not only against "Papa Marx" but also with him, sometimes expressing a kind of filial affection for the old man (who died in the year Schumpeter was born).[26] Marx's analysis of capitalist development, with its sense of historical dynamics and structural change, was also part of the intellectual heritage that informed Japan's postwar *capitalist* development. Marx's ostensibly materialist view of the basic capital circuit also clarifies some questions at the heart of this book.

As described by Marx, it is with money that the capitalist process begins. The basic capitalist circuit consists of *money* (M), invested into *commodities* (C), to be sold for *more money*. To abbreviate, this is the circuit *money-capital → commodity → money-capital + profit*, or $M \rightarrow C \rightarrow M + \Delta M$. For Marx, "capital" was thus manifested in a succession of phenomenal forms, as money or as commodities, as it passed through the stages of this circuit.

On the whole, however, Marx's view of money was, more or less like those of the classical economists he wrote against, undeveloped and still partially substantive. In fact, he often seemed to be thinking mainly of precapitalist forms of metallic money rather than of modern credit-money. But as we have seen, even by the time Marx published the first volume of *Capital* in 1867, most money in Britain, the leading capitalist country, already consisted of bank balances rather than cash currency. If we adopt instead a view of money that recognizes the actualities of modern capitalist practice, the fundamental *money → commodity → money* circuit appears as a circuit of ideal (or *indicative*) and material forms. Marx, at points when he approaches the edges of his materialist philosophical system, comes close to taking this view himself.

Neither of these forms can play its part in the process without the other. In the precapitalist production-for-use circuit, a producing household makes commodities for sale, in order to purchase and consume other commodities. But in the capitalist production-for-profit circuit, it is not the commodity but the indicative "idea," money capital, that comes first. It is then with more money that the circuit can be completed. "It is under the form of money that value begins and ends, and begins again, every act of its own spontaneous generation," wrote Marx. But "unless it takes the form of some commodity, it does not become capital."

We see here a recursive, self-creating process in which capital, as Marx understood it, is "value in process, money in process," continually augmenting itself within its circuit, undergoing embodiment as a commodity and disembodiment back into the money form. Marx's description provided a departure point for Schumpeter. However, under Schumpeter's relatively restrictive (hence useful) definition, capital *only* exists as money—as purchasing power. As Schumpeter would say, money becomes capital only *in the act* of being invested. With that done—being spent—the capital is *gone*, from the standpoint of the entrepreneur. It has been converted into technical means of production.

As for the modern type of capital, Schumpeter agreed with Marx: the transformative modern type of capital was not the "antediluvian forms" of merchants' capital and moneylenders' capital. The transformative modern type (or application) of capital was rather industrial capital. The added value rose out of the production process.[27]

Marx, in common with classical "bourgeois" economists, also tended to imagine "value" as a kind of substance that was somehow conserved through these various transformations, something like the conservation of energy. Here, too, Marx approached the limits of a strictly materialist logic: "While productive labour is changing the means of production into constituent elements of a new product, their value undergoes a metempsychosis. It deserts the consumed body, to occupy the newly created one."[28] The classical economists' long quest for a unitary conception of economic "value" does not seem worth pursuing. On the other hand, Marx's description of the basic money–commodity circuit sharpens some fundamental questions, which were taken up productively by Schumpeter.

This description of the money–commodity–money circuit also makes clear another fundamental point that has already come up: to complete this process calls for *more money* than was there at the beginning. The process of capitalist production generates—and requires—not only a continual augmentation of commodities but also a continual augmentation of money itself. Commodities must be sold for *more* money than is invested into them (or into their production), or the whole process will seize up. This is so for the individual capitalist, and it is so collectively, for the entire system. This is the so-called capitalist "realization problem." It leads to the question where this additional money will come from.

All new capital first comes onto the stage as money. And more money is needed at the end of the process. But where does money capital itself come from? When it came to this question, Marx adopted one of the worst intellectual habits of "bourgeois" economists and assumed away the troublesome question. Marx's simplifying assumption was to take *gold* as the universal money commodity; and an essential characteristic that qualifies gold for monetary use is that it *cannot* be produced at will. Marx's justification for making this assumption was that it was after all only a question of detail, for money was ultimately reducible in its essence to a measure of labor power: "Money as a measure of value, is the phenomenal form that must of necessity be assumed by that measure of value which is immanent in commodities, labour-time."[29] (Here is the value-substance that Marx thought was conserved through the entire transformative process.) Money *must*, somehow, represent condensed labor. However, when it came to explaining exactly *how* labor-time might be so embodied in money—*incarnated*, Marx says repeatedly—his discussion became tangled and obscure. (And in fact, Marx came close to confessing that he could not really see how this actually happened.) As with more modern economists, this was a case of assuming away a problem that, if clearly understood, would nullify entire sections of the analysis subsequently put forward.

In fact, the capitalist essence of the nineteenth-century gold standard was certainly not the millennia-old practice of digging gold from the ground and using this scarce and durable metal as a token for trade. The capitalist essence of the system was rather that gold served as the commodity basis for an increasingly grand and elaborate superstructure of paper money and bank credit. This structure of credit was nothing less than a *governing* (or cybernetic) system of representation and indication. This complex development, which was racing ahead at the time Marx published the first volume of *Capital* in 1867, was of the essence of the system of capitalism that he undertook to describe. Marx did later discuss "means of payment" and "credit-money," but he considered them mainly as Adam Smith had, as a "substitute" for money (implicitly assumed to be metallic money). Again, Marx offered the conventional account given by the bourgeois economists whom he otherwise criticized so sharply.

When it came to the subject of money, Marx thus ended by reproducing the dominant ideological constructions rather than cutting through them. And altogether, he treated the question as a secondary rather than as a foundational one. As Schumpeter pointed out, it was common to nineteenth-century academic economics in general to leave money outside real theoretical consideration. And this was so even as money surreptitiously constituted the entire theoretical system. In the system of classical economics, money quietly stood in for that ineffable substance of "value." Economists could never finally agree on what this core construct of *value* was, but in practice everyone knew that it must be a lot like money. And subsequently in the neoclassical system, money stood in, "as a convenience," for the ineffable psychic calculus of "utility." No one could really say what the core neoclassical construct of *utility* actually was, or how the mind of *Homo oeconomicus* might compute it, much less how one might directly measure it as a scalar value. But again, in practice, everyone knew that the utility of something must be measured by money.

Marx's own materialist analysis, up to a point so concrete and clear, thus ran into difficulties in dealing with this system of ideal "flows," which at times seems to map directly onto the world of material flows but at other times, most evidently at moments of crisis, operates in ways that are not possible in the material world, in which nothing can come from nowhere and in which objects cannot be in two places at once (unless, perhaps, when one enters the self-reflexive quantum physical worlds discovered in the twentieth century). Here, particularly when trying to rescue a one-factor labor theory of value, Marx typically retreated into Hegelian-style mystifications (though it also sometimes happens that out of these difficult passages come some of his philosophically most suggestive ideas).

To repeat the question: the presentation of money capital initiates the capitalist circuit, but how is this money-capital itself brought into existence? Marx, in agreement with conventional economic opinion, insisted that the money-capital that an entrepreneur brings to the markets for commodities and labor is value *saved* or appropriated from *past* production—in effect, that it represents past, embodied labor. But does it really? Schumpeter tells us that, more than that, newly created money-capital in the hands of the entrepreneur is a claim on present resources based on a draft on *future* production. Or, we could say, it *presents* (in German, *stellt vor*) rather than *represents* (*stellt dar,* which is the term Marx used in trying to understand money-capital as representing embodied labor). That is, this newly created credit-capital "represents" nothing yet existing, but its "presentation" nevertheless *claims* existing resources.

Under Schumpeter's relatively restrictive definition, only the initial presentation of money really constitutes capital. Contra Marx, capital in Schumpeter's view is no more "embodied in goods" than coal is "embodied" in a steel rail. That is, it is "embodied," wrote Schumpeter, only "in the sense that the use of coal has led to the creation of the steel rail." But the coal has been burnt, and the capital has been spent. Only "elliptically" can the productive services purchased be considered as capital.[30]

There is no reason to be dogmatic about this definition of capital—the important point is to distinguish indicative credit-capital from material capital goods and services. This book takes the former, "ideal" aspect of capital as its main thread. For this purpose, Schumpeter's account raises many profound problems for consideration. It is above all invaluable for directing attention to a set of processes governing fundamental social choices that "mainstream" economic ideologists work consistently *not* to elucidate.

So far, the focus has been on credit. All credit, of course, is identically debt. Schumpeter, thinking from the side of the entrepreneur, used the word *credit* again and again in his explanation. The word *debt* tends to appear in his account only in more specialized usage. Schumpeter likewise thought that the inflation inherent in the capitalist process was a necessary but passing, self-liquidating process. Closer examination reveals problems with both conceptions. The energy-economic conceptions developed by Frederick Soddy and others since him throw the problem into sharp focus.

FLOWS AND STORES

> **Capitalism . . . is still, to coin a word, *revenual*. . . . The wealth of the community is its revenue, which, in the last analysis, is a revenue of energy available for the purposes of life. . . . It is impossible to save or store this flow to any appreciable extent.**
>
> —Frederick Soddy, "Cartesian Economics" (1921)

> **Why is it that such high savings could be produced from such a low standard of living? Such a high savings rate doesn't arise out of that kind of poverty. After all, it was funding that came first, and growth that came first. And so savings was the *result*.**
>
> —Nakayama Ichirō, "Japanese Capitalism Seen from the Standpoint of Economic Selfhood" (1960)

Schumpeter's theory of capital focuses attention on the "two flows" of the economy: on the one hand flows of materials and energy and on the other flows of financial claims. Economic activity is "a combination of two unavoidable circulations," Schumpeter wrote, "which express two irreducible forms of activity," industry and finance.[1] Frederick Soddy also commenced from the starting point of *flow*, seeking to ground economic understanding in a physical conception of energetic flow. This view of human economy as energetic process leads in a still more heterodox direction, connecting to a stream of ecological-economic thought that is only recently coming together in the pages of journals such as *Ecological Economics*. This perspective also highlights constitutive contradictions built into the capital-provision process, drawing attention from the "credit" side to the "debt" side of the credit/debt process. Here we see that monetary savings, from which investment is conventionally said to "flow," is socially speaking a kind of debt.

4.1 Energy, Capital, and Debt

Energy, as defined by Vaclav Smil, after an extensive survey of existing definitions, is the ability to transform a system. This idea of energy has parallels to

Schumpeter's protean conception of capital. Other writers have taken up the comparison directly and see in energy and capital a kind of identity. "*Coal is the real capital,*" Frederick Soddy wrote in 1921, "out of the consumption of which the capitalist civilisation has been built up." As opposed to this, money-capital was not real but rather "virtual" capital, a form of debt to be paid out of future real economic flows.[2] Where Schumpeter saw credit, Soddy saw debt, and the shift of emphasis reveals other sides of the capitalist process.

As chapter 1 discussed, one result of World War I was the invention of a new political economy of managed inflation, in which industrial subsidies played a central role. This experiment got wildly out of control in Germany particularly. Another result of World War I was the new salience of energetic and materials-flow conceptions of economy and of national power. These concerns reflected the experience of wartime shortages, the demands of wartime materials-mobilization planning, and the greatly increased strategic salience of petroleum. In the early 1920s, these concerns were confirmed and even intensified by perceptions of looming global energy shortages, which were also reflected in Japan.[3] Energetic-strategic thinking was also framed in positive developmental terms. Most of the new "energetic" thinking, however, happened outside of or at the margins of the world of academic economics.[4] The sterile abstraction of neoclassical economics was not relieved by this new thinking, and the new thinking remained fragmented and undisciplined when it came to its engagement with economics. Physical scientists and engineers were prominent in developing these new, critical conceptions. Their critiques often verged into new technocratic social visions. They also frequently reflected an older stream of populist and socialist critiques of financial capitalism, which were reinvigorated amid the global deflation and depressions that followed World War I.

Frederick Soddy (1877–1956) has a significant place in the annals of twentieth-century science as a pioneer researcher in radiochemistry and developer of the theory of isotopes, for which he received the Nobel Prize in chemistry in 1921. Soddy was one of the first scientists to realize and publicize the possibilities of atomic energy, which he thought probably powered the stars. As a potential energy source for powering human civilization, he thought atomic energy would be little short of miraculous in its implications. He was also one of the first to think that, under the prevailing system of social and economic organization, people were not ready for such power and would turn it to the creation of horrific tools of destruction. Soddy's book *The Interpretation of Radium* was a source from which the writer H. G. Wells drew long passages verbatim in writing his science-fiction novel *The World Set Free*, published early in 1914. In it, Wells presented the history of a future world war, fought in the 1950s, in which cities would be destroyed by the fire of atomic bombs. Wells's novel in turn sparked the imagination of the Hungarian-born physicist Leo Szilard, who helped lead the Manhattan Project and later worked on the development of nuclear power. (Szilard at the end of the war also opposed using the atomic bombs on Japan; after the war he was a prominent antiwar activist.) In the context of this book, it is also interesting to note that Soddy, in his deep research into the "transmutation of elements," drew inspiration from a source that Goethe had studied in depth but that was very unusual for a modern physical chemist: alchemy.[5]

As Soddy explained it, his own inquiry into economics "commenced with the attempt to obtain a physical conception of wealth that would obey the physical laws of conservation"—recall Marx's attempt—rather than imitating, as money did, "the capricious behaviour of the subject-matter of psychical research."[6] It was in this context that Soddy explained the basic incommensurability between the physical flows of the economy and "virtual" monetary flows. The contradictions between the two flows gave rise to inflation and deflation, speculative excess and depression. Soddy's inquiry also arose out of the conjunctural context of the deflation and debt crises that followed World War I. Soddy's books were not translated into Japanese, but energy-based conceptions of the economy came in via other routes. In the 1920s and 1930s, the U.S. "Technocracy, Inc." movement helped popularize Soddy's and similar ideas. The energy-economic vision developed by the Technocrats and others was picked up by electrical engineering professor Baba Keiji (1897–1961), who was making it a lively concern just at the point when young Ōkita Saburō began to study with him at Tokyo Imperial University in 1934. Baba, who earned a second degree in economics and later moved into the Economics Department, is remarkable for exemplifying the new confluence of engineering and economic thought that inspired Ōkita and other thought leaders of his generation. Baba also wrote books about technology and management, developed a systems-theoretical approach, and later founded the Japan Systems Analysis Society. Ōkita in his autobiography singled out for mention Baba's books *Technology and Economy* (*Gijitsu to keizai*, 1933) and *Technology and Society* (*Gijitsu to shakai*, 1936). These books made extensive reference to current European and American technological and energy perspectives and to the U.S. Technocracy movement. In fact, they were mainly a digest of such materials. In his account of the ideas of the Technocracy movement, Baba described them as deriving from Frederick Soddy.[7]

Baba's books, in the timing of their publication, were at the leading edge of a great burst of Japanese scholarly writing on technology. This work also drew heavily on German and North American sources and coincided with the onset of wartime mobilization and the comprehensive "planification" of the economy after 1937.[8] Schumpeter's *Business Cycles* itself, with its account of the historical succession of technological paradigms, could be considered part of this movement, which included the work of Lewis Mumford, R. Buckminster Fuller, and many others. The American "Technocracy, Inc." movement was thus the self-conscious, eccentric fringe of a much broader and deeper movement. This Technocracy with a capital *T* made a flashy media debut in the 1920s, but the antics of the movement's flamboyant leader, Howard Scott, caused the organization to be marginalized. In Canada, Technocracy, Inc. was even banned in 1940 because of the fascist overtones it had taken on.[9] However, technocracy with a small *t*—technocracy as actual practice—had a heyday in the 1940s, in the context of war production and postwar reconstruction. This happened in the heart of the great administrative apparatuses of state. It was virtually a worldwide movement that passed right through ideological boundaries.

The U.S. Technocracy movement conspicuously advocated an energy theory of money. This seemingly simple idea, also taking inspiration from Soddy, was that a unit of money should be defined in energy units. This was another attempt to grapple with the worldwide problems of postwar inflation, deflation, and debt that dominated the economic landscape of the 1920s. Reading these monetary proposals, one immediately perceives their various difficulties. Soddy himself pinpointed the debt-money problem and isolated a core contradiction in capitalist economics, as discussed further below. The problem's solution is another question. It is easy to end up agreeing with Smil's considered judgment that single-factor "embodied energy" theories of value do not work. What these energy-economic theories do clarify is the need to theorize energy as a factor of production.[10]

4.2 Flows of Production

The ideas mentioned here have an affinity with the new systems thinking that was coming together in the mid–twentieth century, as represented in Japan by people like Baba Keiji and Ōkita Saburō.[11] In line with this thinking, it is instructive to consider the basic systems-theoretic concepts of flows and stores in terms of energy and in terms of financial claims. Soddy, like Schumpeter, offered an essentially flow-based world picture. But compared to Schumpeter, he began at a much more fundamental level: "life depends from instant to instant on a continuous flow of energy, and hence wealth, the enabling requisites of life, partakes of the character of a flow rather than a store." This flow of energy was real, living wealth. In the final analysis, "the means of subsistence are derived from the daily revenue of solar energy, through the operations of agriculture." The most critical production cycles remain dependent on the diurnal cycle and on the annual cycle of the seasons: "the wealth of the community is its *revenue*, which, in the last analysis, is a revenue of energy available for the purposes of life."

As for the storing up of wealth, "it is impossible to save or store this flow to any appreciable extent."

> True, you can dam a river, at great expense, and make a reservoir. But, even if not used, the accumulated waters evaporate and leak away. You can under . . . even more unfavourable terms, store electric energy. But to contemplate storing wealth on a national scale for even a day is something like contemplating a storage battery large enough to satisfy the demand of the world for electric power for one day. True, nature has stored [energy] in coal by processes requiring geological epochs, but what we do is *unstore* it, an easier matter, and convert it into a flow before it is of the least possible use to us. Again, for short periods, the flow may be embodied in some concrete commodity. . . . Such accumulated assets, at best, are classified not as accumulated wealth, but as aids and accessories in the maintenance and increase of wealth out of the available revenue of energy. The wealth is the revenue, *and it cannot be saved.*[12]

There is some rhetorical exaggeration here. Soddy was so focused on flows that he seemed to discount the question of the accumulation of stocks of physical capital—railways, factories, power stations, and so on—that most economists understand to be fundamental to economic growth. On a geological timescale, the scale on which Soddy often thought, stocks are just slower flows. Or as Schumpeter said, stocks are actually regulated flows. That is, the distinction between flows and stores is a function of the timescale being applied. But on the timescale of human lifetimes, this question of faster and slower makes every difference. Indeed, the course of human history could be told as a story of capital-stock accumulation, especially if we consider that process in the broadest sense as encompassing human knowledge and capabilities. The building up of national physical-capital stocks is certainly foundational to the high-speed growth process considered in this book. For present purposes, however, it is enough to refer the reader to the classic studies of physical-capital accumulation by Ohkawa Kazushi, Henry Rosovsky, and other members of the Hitotsubashi-centered team involved in the Long Term Economic Statistics project.[13] The point remains that stocks of physical capital equipment will stand idle and deteriorate quickly without a continual input of energy, a reality dramatically illustrated in the conjoint coal and food crises that followed World War II. Life itself, and living human civilization, is a real-time energetic flow, which depends on real-time caloric flows, and modern industrialization can also be described in the increase and articulation of energy flows. "This is the great paradox of Capitalism," Soddy concluded: notwithstanding this name we have given it, "as regards its necessities" capitalism is still essentially "revenual."

4.3 Stores of Promises

We return now to the financial-capital side of the question. *Wealth*, as Soddy defined it, consisted of "humanly useful forms of matter and energy." This is what Schumpeter's entrepreneur organized the production of, in ever new and improved forms, ever more efficiently, in ever greater quantities: this is the process of economic development. Operating parallel to this "revenual" world of faster and slower material-energetic flows is the world of "virtual wealth," to apply another term coined by Soddy. This kind of wealth—socially recognized claims to wealth—is rather easily recorded and secured in social memory. When we attempt to save wealth, it is largely in the form of such social claims. Under stable monetary-institutional circumstances, this virtual, monetary wealth can be preserved for multiple human lifetimes, coming in the course of things to govern human relationships of all kinds. Accordingly, the socially acknowledged wealth of an individual is something quite different from the flows of "revenual" wealth of the community considered as a whole:

> The ordinary modern individual member of the community in the vast majority of cases does not possess enough [real] wealth to keep him alive for a week. By means of a token, legalised as a form of currency, whether a cowrie, stone or a metal counter, but now, more and more exclusively, a simple paper note, the community acknowledges its indebtedness to the holder of the token, and empowers the individual to indent upon the revenue of real wealth flowing through the markets at any time.[14]

Again, Soddy seemed not to know of Schumpeter's ideas (not translated into English until 1934), but their respective "flow" visions of the economy are notably similar. Similar also is a shared emphasis on distinguishing actual goods and services from claims to goods and services.

Soddy's initial insight was that *at the level of the whole society*, it was untenable to identify the possession of debts with the possession of actual wealth. This was not only a theoretical recognition; on a timescale of multiple decades, owing to the rapid "natural increase" of debt claims, it was true practically as well:

debts are subject to the laws of mathematics rather than physics. Unlike wealth, which is subject to the laws of thermodynamics, debts do not rot with old age and are not consumed in the process of living. On the contrary, they grow at so much per cent per annum, by the well-known mathematical laws of simple and compound interest.[15]

Again we see the "virtual," representational character of financial claims. However, "the process of compound interest is physically impossible," for it would lead over time "ever more and more rapidly to infinity." Here was a basic contradiction between imagined social-mathematical constructions and physical realities. Naturally, the social constructions will have to yield in the end, but this does not happen without a painful, wasteful process of social turmoil and suffering.

Plainly, money-capital and physical capital are fundamentally different. As Schumpeter emphasized, money-capital constitutes socially sanctioned "orders," not things. As Soddy emphasized, monetary claims are debts. By a mathematical logic, endless monetary accumulation is possible according to the "miracle of compound interest." In social actuality, the increase of monetary claims recurrently finds its own definite limits. These take the form of debt defaults and bankruptcies, or debt alleviation by means of monetary inflation or debt-relief measures. Historically, debt defaults have tended to happen collectively, in great waves. This point is integral to the cyclical capitalist developmental process as analyzed by Schumpeter, but it is a point that he largely left out of consideration. The compounding of debt claims and the eventual impossibility of their realization in the material world thus means that debt crises—or more precisely, *debt-destruction crises*—are systemic and inescapable. It may be possible, for a time, to build up physical wealth at rates corresponding to the compounding of interest—but, as Herman Daly interpreted Soddy's ideas, "having a physical dimension, its growth sooner or later encounters limits." Consequently, "at some point the growing liens of debt holders on the limited revenue will become greater than the future producers of that revenue will be willing or able to support, and conflict will result. The conflict takes the form of debt repudiation," whether by means of inflation, bankruptcy, or confiscatory taxation. "Conventional wisdom considers the latter processes pathological, but accepts compound interest as normal. Logic demands, however, that either we constrain compound interest in some way, or accept as normal and necessary one or more of the counteracting mechanisms of debt repudiation."[16] And this question brings us to the bubble economics of the late twentieth and early twenty-first centuries (see 12.4).

It brings us also to Schumpeter's own vision of development through cycles. For Schumpeter, the recessionary-deflationary phase of the cycle had two contrasting aspects. On one hand, it was a time of "harvest": repayment by the entrepreneur to the social stream in the form of increased production, and repayment by the entrepreneur of debts to banks and other creditors. With this repayment, at least part of the new purchasing power created by the original credit would be extinguished, Schumpeter thought. On the other hand, the recessionary-deflationary phase was one of "creative destruction," as the flood of new production and falling prices forced insufficiently profitable enterprises to disband and drove entrepreneurs to develop new methods and forms. Schumpeter emphasized the creative aspect of "creative destruction," explaining it as a process driven by innovation. He downplayed the importance of the type of debt-deflation dynamics described by Irving Fisher.[17] A theoretically fuller and historically more realistic picture would incorporate the two.

And to pursue the question of savings-as-debt to a conclusion: people as savers, Soddy said, seek "to convert wealth that perishes into debt that endures." That is, we seek to become social creditors "in order to derive a permanent future income" from stored monetary claims. This is not a question of a rentier stratum only: even to maintain oneself in old age, a person "must convert his non-storable surplus into a lien on future revenue, by letting others consume and invest his surplus now in exchange for the right to share in the increased future revenue."[18] We can think of those entrusted others as Schumpeter's entrepreneurs. In conceptualizing monetary savings, Soddy's idea also agrees with Schumpeter's. Again, Soddy: "Although it may comfort the lender to think that his wealth still exists somewhere in the form of 'capital,' *it has been or is being used up* by the borrower either in consumption or investment, and no more than food or fuel can it be used again later."[19] Like the fuel burned to make the steel rail, money invested as "capital" is money spent. This was Schumpeter's definition also: one cannot have one's capital and use it too. Wealth in the material economic world resolves into present streams of usable wealth, which are in the last analysis energetic flows. Saving, for the individual person or individual enterprise, means the storing up of claims against future production by others. Countries may even store up claims on other countries. But at the level of the whole economic world, *where there are no outside others*, what *is* saving? This connects to another fundamental question: What is taxation? This question is also addressed later (see 6.4).

There is much more of interest in these energetic-flow conceptions, and this discussion only touches on a few relevant insights. Some of these insights are surprisingly close to certain Buddhist conceptions of life. It has also been pointed out that Schumpeter's statement on capitalist development, with its sharp consciousness of presentation, duration, and creative flux, shares something with the views of Henri Bergson, whose *Creative Evolution* was published while Schumpeter was formulating his own ideas and who may have been an unacknowledged source of inspiration.[20]

4.4 Saving Follows from Investment

In a fundamental economic-philosophical sense, monetary saving thus consists of the storing up of claims, or of promises to pay. These are claims on the future production of other people. But the investment of capital, as we have seen, involves the diversion of *existing* productive services to new uses. Entrepreneurs do not go through a process of storing up coal, or land, or workers, before putting them to use. In empirical fact, monetary savings under modern capitalism may be more the result of investment than the source of it (see 11.1).

How can investment happen in advance of saving and even be a cause of it? Considering this in connection to Japan's own developmental history, both Nakayama Ichirō and Ōkita Saburō described a process that was essentially inflationary and Schumpeterian. High savings "was born as a result" of high investment and growth, Nakayama wrote; "or to consider it the other way around, it's completely impossible to think that such high investment happened because of [prior] savings." This point was "the key to explaining various questions that come out of Japan's economic growth." Ōkita likewise explained that "in the early state of Japan's modernization, government and banks first created money and credit, which stimulated the establishment of various enterprises, and then later collected private savings in money form."[21] Ōkita thought that this process "was almost the reverse of that of the development of banking institutions in Western countries." Or at least it is the reverse of the conventional and continually propagated image of banking in Western countries. The Western reality (again following Schumpeter) is not necessarily so different.

The remainder of this book considers capital mainly in Schumpeter's monetary sense, not Soddy's energy-flow sense. That is, it concerns what Soddy would call *virtual* capital. But the worlds of virtual capital and of physical-energetic economic flow mutually form one another. The generating and managing of energy flows is also where the power-systems engineer Ōkita Saburō got his start in wide-region growth planning, and his ideas impinge here as well.

4.5 Power and Planning

Ōkita Saburō, notwithstanding his often blandly bureaucratic public presentation, is one the most interesting postwar Japanese economists of all.[22] Ōkita worked at the center of Japan's postwar economic planning system—no one was more centrally located—and his career as a national and international economic planner reveals new aspects of most of the subjects touched on in this book. In his dynamic systems approach, one sees an energy-based vision of economic flows. One can see also the tight connections between the historical development of electrical-power networks, the emergence of systems thinking, and national-level economic planning.

Ōkita was born on November 3, 1914, in Japanese-occupied Dairen (Dalian), in the Kwantung Leased Territory. The place itself precociously exemplified the new twentieth-century style of state-capitalist development. Here, Japanese administrators conducted their own "experiment on a living body," as they explored a new style of intentional development that could be tried out most freely in the environment of a colonized territory. Dairen was the regional headquarters of the parastatal South Manchurian Railway Company, a giant transportation, energy, and industrial corporation that acted as the de facto administrative government of the railway zone, which was seven hundred kilometers long. The city itself was an early model of high-modernist urban planning.[23] Ōkita's father, a politically minded newspaper publisher, returned to Japan in 1927 and later started a company to manufacture carburetors, at a time when the Japanese state was beginning active efforts to build up a national automobile industry. Ōkita passed the examination for admission to the elite First Higher School, a gateway to Tokyo Imperial University, and studied there in the company of schoolmates who went on to become top government officials, corporate executives, and intellectuals. He graduated in 1934. Like Tsuru Shigeto, he was thus a member of the generation of higher-school students who experienced the Marxist boom of the early 1930s and its dramatic suppression.[24]

At Tokyo Imperial University, Ōkita studied electrical engineering from 1934 to 1937, where he was especially inspired by Professor Baba Keiji. At a time when light-electrical engineering (electronics and communication engineering) had already emerged as the glamour field, Ōkita chose instead to specialize in electric-power engineering. He was attracted by the economic dimensions of the field. He graduated in April 1937 and entered the Ministry of Communications. Three months later, Japanese forces launched their all-out invasion of China, and national economic mobilization began at home. In addition to telecommunications, broadcasting, and postal services, the Ministry of Communications was then responsible for regulating electric power (a domain later shifted to the Ministry of International Trade and Industry) as well as marine transportation and aviation (later shifted to the Ministry of Transport). The ministry was also a center of technocratic advocacy.[25] Ōkita's appointment was a joint one between the ministry's Electricity Bureau and its Engineering Bureau, which was responsible for telecommunications. The latter bureau was headed by Kajii Takeshi, who would later become Ōkita's father-in-law. This turned out to be a highly strategic family connection, as Kajii later became the ministry's administrative vice-minister and was then appointed founding president of the new parastatal telecommunications monopoly, Nippon Telegraph and Telephone (NTT). Ōkita also joined the Communications Ministry as a member of the technical engineering staff rather than as a higher civil servant. Here he found that he was in a subordinate position compared to fellow Tokyo Imperial University graduates from the elite Law Faculty, and he took part in the organization of a "technicians' movement," led by Matsumae Shigeyoshi, that worked across multiple ministries.[26]

In 1939 Ōkita was posted to wartime Beiping (Beijing). His job was to plan the electrical power grid for North China. It was in Beijing that he began to work closely with Gotō Yonosuke. Gotō, Ōkita's junior by four years, had followed a very similar career path, studying electrical engineering at Tokyo Imperial University, entering the Communications Ministry, and moving on to a career as an economist and planner. This team, who became known as Ōkita "the hatchet" and Gotō "the razor," was sharp indeed. They worked in tandem until Gotō's troubled death in 1960.[27] Gotō, later Ōkita's junior colleague at the Economic Planning Agency, became nationally famous as the author of the economic white papers of the late 1950s. He is known above all for the consciously Schumpeterian vision of the 1956 "postwar is over" White Paper (see 10.2).

Ōkita was recalled to Tokyo in 1941 and transferred to the Greater East Asia Ministry, where he was a member of the research staff, specializing in planning the energy and industrial development of occupied China. He joined the Shōwa Academy (Shōwa Juku), a junior organ of the Showa Research Association (Shōwa Kenkyūkai) for a critical period of several months. This brought him into close contact with members of prime minister Prince Konoe's "New Order" brain trust, an intellectually high-powered milieu in which Marxist, fascist, and technocratic ideas mixed.[28] Ōkita's task was to calculate Japan's iron and steel capacity. It became clear to him, he said later, that Japan must lose the war, by an inescapable physical logic of materials, energy, and production flows. Brain-trusters Arisawa Hiromi and Nakayama Ichirō reached the same conclusion. Carefully quantified economic research and planning, and the economic integration of Japan and Asia, would occupy most of the rest of Ōkita's career.

Ōkita and Gotō were involved in secret postwar planning from June 1945, supported by Ōkita's superior, Arata Sugihara. Their team was first called the Research Group for the Self-Sufficiency of the Japanese Mainland.[29] In this connection, Ōkita and Gotō traveled through northeastern Japan and had two remarkable meetings. One was with the militarist Ishiwara Kanji, the former army planning chief and advocate of a totalitarian controlled economy, who had masterminded the Japanese takeover of Manchuria in 1931. Ishiwara himself had studied "total war" theory in Germany as a military attaché in the years 1922–25. He had begun then to develop a vision of a future "World War II" with America and of the consequent necessity of an Asian bloc economy, a vision that had provided his fellow young officers with the imaginative roadmap to disaster.[30] Ōkita's and Gotō's second meeting was with the liberal anti-imperialist Ishibashi Tanzan, a visionary of another kind of peaceful capitalist Asian co-prosperity, who a year later would become postwar Japan's minister of inflationary reconstruction finance.

JAPANESE CAPITALISM UNDER OCCUPATION

Let us assume that an insular nation, which has an active trade with other nations and whose economic system may be conceived as in full development in our sense, is cut off from the outside world by an enemy fleet. Imports and exports alike are obstructed, the price and value system is shattered, obligations cannot be kept, the anchor chain of credit snaps . . .

—Joseph Schumpeter, *The Theory of Economic Development* (1926)

It was like a kind of experiment on a living body, the various processes of one economy returned to an extremely primitive point by the destruction of war; then developed into a modern economy; and all happening, both from the side of policy and from the side of the phenomena themselves, in a concentrated way.

—Ōkita Saburō, in conversation with Arisawa Hiromi (1966)

As a consequence of the war, energetic and material flows were constricted to famine levels. Sources of basic materials were cut off, and transportation and supply infrastructure was in a shambles. Essential foodstuffs and other materials that did continue to flow increasingly did so through illegal channels. At the same time, the circulation of money was amplified and speeded up, as if a great commercial boom needed to be financed. The contradictory movements of these two flows meant an immediate inflation of prices and set off a series of systemic transformations.

Japanese industry was already in crisis by the time of Japan's surrender on August 15, 1945. Production and distribution were choked off by competitive hoarding of scarce strategic materials, the near cutoff of inward shipments by the U.S. naval blockade, and air raid destruction. A panoply of state controls also made production look less and less capitalistic. Financial capital flowed mainly through a complicated administrative circuitry that combined de facto state funding for private industry with de facto forced loans from private industry to the state. After the surrender, business owners who had expected the procapitalist United States to deliver them from bureaucratic control were disappointed.[1]

Instead, prolabor U.S. officials liberated their employees. By the end of September, Japanese business elites thus found themselves between a hammer and an anvil. From the base of the production hierarchy, workers collectively rejected the conditions under which they had been existing. The workers' uprising began within days of the surrender, in the coal mines, the energetic fountainhead of the industrial economy. By November, hungry and now militant workers in various industries were subjecting business executives to public struggle meetings and setting up their own committees to take over control of production.[2] Workers rushed to form unions, and newly reorganized Communist and Socialist groups took a lead in the organizing. Meanwhile, from "above the clouds," in their stations in the new supergovernment that they placed atop the existing state hierarchy, U.S. occupation authorities rapidly dismantled police-state controls. They also identified big business as part of a military-industrial complex that had conducted and profited by Japan's wars of aggression. Accordingly, they mandated the breakup of the *zaibatsu* big-business groups and began to purge from office the upper ranks of conservative business leadership and their politician allies. Shipyards and other industrial facilities were shut down and slated for removal as war reparations. Thus, the first U.S. policy initiative vis-à-vis Japanese industry undertook to dissolve Japanese capitalism as hitherto constituted.

These circumstances added up to the most uncertain conditions in Japan's modern industrial history. A program of new and capitalistically successful responses came out of this crisis. As for the "anchor chain of credit," it did have to be let out considerably.[3] But it did not snap.

The economic policies of the U.S. occupation authorities during the first two and a half years of the occupation were an amalgam of activism and laissez-faire, of intense focus on some areas and tolerance of surprising Japanese government latitude in others. Japanese authorities compensated for their loss of control in areas targeted for reform by new initiatives elsewhere. Here, the ability to foresee new developmental possibilities under radically new environmental conditions was critical. In this respect, those who were most identified with the old order of things tended to be most at a loss.

5.1 Imagining Postwar Development

Ōuchi Hyōe later recalled the setting. "For about a year after the war," he wrote,

> I often went to this burnt-out South Manchurian Railway Building [in
> Tokyo] and in that cold, unheated place we discussed Japan's future. . . .
> Those meetings mobilized nearly all Japan's economic experts, who

engaged in discussion with all the *élan* of patriots of the Meiji Restoration.[4]

The methodological vision that came out of those meetings continued to guide Japanese development thinking and international advising into the twenty-first century. These meetings, organized by Ōkita Saburō of the Greater East Asia Ministry, began with a group of ten people on August 16, the day after the surrender. Many people experienced a kind of mental numbness at the war's end. Others were powerfully focused during this moment in between; both death and liberation were in the air. The hard-driving Ōkita remembered the intensity of the effort: "I don't think I ever worked harder in my life." Through this effort, he said, "I completed my metamorphosis from electrical engineer to economist."[5] Ōuchi Hyōe served as committee chair. Joining them were the Schumpeterian economists Nakayama Ichirō and Tōbata Seiichi, who would, with Ōkita, be at the organizing center of so many policy and planning councils over the coming years.

This planning response was more powerful for the fact that it happened in a kind of planning vacuum. Toward the end of the war, while U.S. forces prepared to invade the Japanese mainland, the Imperial Army did develop postwar contingency plans—to mount a guerrilla resistance, to cache arms around the country, and even to hide a member of the royal family to serve as a potential hidden emperor.[6] But civil officials could not talk openly of defeat and occupation, and they developed no systematic plans for these increasingly certain eventualities. A few economists working in government offices and private research institutions secretly began to analyze the probable economic consequences of defeat, and they later recalled their fear of being found out by the military police. Many of these economists emerged as influential decision makers and public intellectuals in the early postwar years.

Ōuchi Hyōe, after his arrest and expulsion from Tokyo Imperial University, was forced to withdraw from public life. He was given an office in the research department of the Bank of Japan, and in the months before the surrender he quietly began to study how his country could cope with the economic consequences of defeat. He was assisted by Yoshino Toshihiko (1915–2005) of the BoJ's research staff. Around the same time, finance minister Kaya Okinori asked Takahashi Kamekichi, who ran his own private economic institute, to begin planning for postwar economic eventualities. (That effort was "practically useless," Takahashi later said, because, while it assumed the loss of Japan's overseas empire, it did not reckon on unconditional surrender and occupation.)[7] Ōkita's efforts, however, were actualized, through the Coal Subcommittee established by prime minister Yoshida Shigeru and later through the Economic Stabilization Board.

Also taking part in those first meetings were several economists who had been associated with the former Shōwa Research Association, with which Ōkita had been affiliated as a junior member.[8] In this way, Ōkita's committee brought together a group of planners who had been active in the days of the Konoe cabinet's "New Order" movement in 1940–41. The Ministry of Greater East Asia, under whose auspices these first meetings were held, was itself a wartime formation that combined sections of the Ministry of Foreign Affairs with "an intelligence organization" (in Ōkita's words). Ten days after the August 16 meeting, the Greater East Asia ministry was dissolved in preparation for the occupation, and most of it was recombined with the Ministry of Foreign Affairs. Ōkita and Gotō Yonosuke were transferred to the Research Bureau of the Ministry of Foreign Affairs, under whose auspices the "Special Survey Committee" meetings were continued. Hence the Committee is also called the Ministry of Foreign Affairs Committee. Yoshida Shigeru, who became foreign minister in September, supported the group's efforts. Yoshida, a conservative, had himself been arrested by the military police in April 1945, suspected of plotting a negotiated settlement to the army's "sacred war."[9] Although Yoshida became known as a great enemy of the left, he was also personally close to several of the leftist committee members. The group was enlarged to include Arisawa Hiromi (who participated from the fourth meeting, in October) and others as central members.[10] Arisawa later headed the Coal Subcommittee, which grew directly out of the Special Survey Committee and which designed the Priority Production System.

The Special Survey Committee's final report, mainly written by Ōkita, did not appear until November 1946. In many ways, it was a brief for heavy industrial, high-technology development, an implicit rebuttal to U.S. reparations plans that would have removed much of Japanese heavy industry. The report's deeper significance lay in its vision of the existing world situation, its sense of future developmental possibilities, and its understanding that Japan would develop in the context of the industrialization of the wider East Asian region. In this way, Ōkita and the luminaries he gathered together were themselves intellectual entrepreneurs, in a dimension Schumpeter thought was essential: "the capacity of seeing things in a way which afterwards proves to be true."[11]

Within this group, Nakayama Ichirō was closest to being a representative of the neoclassical economic tradition. Four decades later, Ōkita and Arisawa recalled those days:

> Ōkita: If you look at it now, there were all kinds of people [in the Special Survey Committee]—neoclassical [*kinkei*] economists, Marxist economists from both the Kōza [Leninist] and Rōnō [Social Democrat] wings. . . .

Arisawa: (laughing) "There weren't any neoclassical economists."

Ōkita: "Nakayama Ichirō was there, and you can say Nakayama was neoclassical. . . ."

Arisawa: (laughing) "He's not a real neoclassical economist."[12]

This is an interesting judgment concerning the economist who wrote the standard textbook on neoclassical economics.

Nakayama Ichirō and Tōbata Seiichi, who were at the center of what Ōuchi Hyōe derided as a "Schumpeter vogue" during the war years, were thus also at the center of postwar planning councils within which Marxist economists were initially prominent. Immediately at the end of the war Nakayama began to participate in many other policy councils, including the Postwar Currency Policy Committee, which was set up by finance minister Shibusawa Keizō. It was this committee that determined the "new yen" reform of February 1946 (see 5.5). Nakayama subsequently participated in the economists' lunchtime meetings hosted by Yoshida when Yoshida became prime minister. Out of this emerged the Priority Production System. Nakayama later chaired numerous other government policy councils—the activity level of all of the economists highlighted here is astounding. He also had a leading role at the Japan Productivity Center.[13]

Nakayama's explanation of the role of these councils is also interesting. Many of them, he said, "had the characteristics of administrative agencies, even when they were termed councils." That is, "their policy decisions were called advice, but in reality some of the committees held strong administrative powers."[14] Nakayama's most significant political role was to chair the Central Labor Relations Commission from its establishment in 1946 until 1960. Under Nakayama's leadership, this commission was the center of collective wage determination in Japanese industry, at the time when the framework of postwar labor relations was established.

5.2 First Responses: Burning, Looting, and Printing

The work of these "systems entrepreneurs" conveys a sense of broad oversight, coherence, and order. Such a state of awareness was highly exceptional at the time. The Japanese government surrendered on August 15, and the Allied occupation began at the beginning of September. The nation's governors thus had two weeks to prepare for being governed by an enemy army. During these few days, several key decisions were made and several feats accomplished. These included actions that set off Japan's new price revolution.

The Japanese central government offices, like the adjoining financial district, were relatively spared by the American firebombing that had leveled so much of the rest of the city. They now stood out against the burned-out, abandoned back-drop of what had formerly been Tokyo's densely populated downtown districts. With coal, charcoal, and firewood in severely short supply, and with gasoline nowhere to be found, the clear skies in postdefeat Tokyo were striking. Smoke did rise for these few days across the government district of Nagatachō from bonfires of government documents. Ōkita Saburō recalled:

> at the end of the war, before the Allied forces arrived, each ministry was ordered to destroy evidence of wartime activities by burning all docu-ments relating to the war. This was a very stupid thing to do. . . . The documents being burnt in courtyards and other places included mobi-lization documents, production capacity surveys and many basic eco-nomic materials, many of which would help our work in planning the postwar economy. Consequently I went along to those places where documents were being burnt and secretly brought some home.[15]

Ōkita ran into his fellow economic planner Inaba Hidezō (1907–1996) doing the same thing. Inaba used the documents he systematically collected to start the Research Institute of the National Economy. There, Inaba worked in parallel with Ōkita's foreign ministry group and produced his own detailed report also in November 1946.[16]

While state officials were destroying archives of stored communications (in-cluding those pertaining to the sources and disposition of stored goods), they also ordered the undocumented release of great stores of goods. The opportunis-tic "privatization" of military stockpiles was partly spontaneous, partly orga-nized. The black market in consumer goods, which Ōuchi Hyōe described as a "night of a hundred demons," was highly visible.[17] A black market for produc-ers' goods also developed. It took on a massive scale with the emptying of gov-ernment warehouses. One participant, a criminal gang member, recalled the scene at one government depot after August 15: "it was the biggest supply depot in the country. You name it, they had it. And within two weeks of the end of the war the whole lot had disappeared. . . . There were plenty of [railroad] sidings inside the base, and every morning dozens of freight cars came in for us to load. Most of it was steel plates, brass, sheets of copper, duralumin, and other al-loys."[18] Goods stockpiled under the system of wartime materials provision were thereby released into black-market channels. A system of collusive underground market operations in this way succeeded to the former place of the military in governing key materials bottlenecks of industrial provisioning. Military and civil officials and corporate officers entered into business dealings that were now formally defined as organized crime. Thus, money-capital was diverted into hoarding of and speculation in materials. Much of this trading was illegal, and it involved the illegalization of large swathes of the formerly legitimate economy.

With this came a privatization of coercive violence. As open-air markets sprung up, so too did a structure of "protection" and informal governance, expanding the preexisting structure of semitolerated, semicriminal gangs. When U.S. occupation authorities disbanded the military and secret police and disarmed the regular police, some political authorities also turned to violent gangs, which had a prior history of political usefulness as an underground reservoir of coercive power. One can therefore speak of a hidden and informal state-gang complex.[19] Another aspect of this illegal or semilegal economy is relevant here. Violent gangs have historically functioned in Japan as debt collectors, and the Japanese financial system in its entire and true shape also encompasses a financial system–gang nexus. The connections appear indirect, in that "bad debt" claims held by "honorable" tiers of the financial system may pass through the hands of intermediaries before being turned over to criminals. But these connections are also constitutive and systemic.

The National Diet's Hoarded Goods Investigation Committee later estimated that military and other government goods held at the time of the surrender were worth at least ¥50 billion in current yen. No one really knew, and as so often, those who knew the most did not talk about it. Other estimates range up to ¥500 billion. Moving and storing this volume of goods would have been impossible without the cooperation of government officials and large companies. Many companies thus shifted their focus from production to speculation in black-market commodities.[20] And, to return to Schumpeter's analysis, the investment of newly created money not for new production but for speculative buying of already existing goods was bound to cause inflation without any redeeming developmental features.

The high end of the looting business belonged to the world of finance. Here, authorities distributed an enormous amount of new monetary claims to resources. The Bank of Japan, also fearing runs on the banks, began to make massive cash payouts immediately after the surrender. Even private printing companies were mobilized to print new banknotes. On August 15, the BoJ note issue stood at ¥30.2 billion. Two weeks later, it was ¥42.3 billion, an increase in the national monetary base of some 40 percent.[21] "All four gates to the Bank of Japan were opened and trucks just kept pulling up one after another," wrote Ōuchi Hyōe, who witnessed it from his temporary office there. "They left stuffed full of new wooden boxes filled with 100 yen bills that the bank had hoarded during

1944 and 1945." Ōuchi already had the image of Germany after World War I fixed in his mind. His first thought at this sight: "*Inflation! Inflation!*"[22]

5.3 The Amplification of Monetary Flows

A precondition for the story that follows was *the preservation and maintenance in the hands of Japanese political and banking authorities of the power to create money.* Japan during the occupation underwent a kind of political and cultural colonization in many domains. Its external relations were tightly controlled. However, this was not the case in regard to the creation of money and credit. The Japanese state preserved its fundamental monetary independence even under military occupation.

American forces came to Japan having already printed their own yen-denominated military scrip for use in acquiring goods and services in Japan. This was what Allied occupation forces had done in Germany, which unlike Japan was placed under direct military government. It was also what Japanese forces had done in the territories they occupied in Asia. It was thus of decisive importance that the Japanese government succeeded in heading off U.S. plans to use military scrip. The key role was played by finance minister Tsushima Juichi, an expert English speaker and international financial negotiator who spent most of two decades before the war in London and New York as the Japanese government's international financial commissioner. Meeting with U.S. military officials early in September, Tsushima persuaded them not to use military scrip by assuring them that their needs could be supplied with Bank of Japan notes. (In fact, U.S. planning had anticipated this.)[23]

The government's wartime debts to industry, much of it to compensate companies' wartime losses, added up to ¥95 billion. At the end of the war, anticipating that occupation authorities would intervene to stop it, the Japanese government rushed to pay these off. In the three months after the surrender, they succeeded in paying out ¥26.6 billion. These lump-sum payments were equivalent to one-third of the total budgetary expenses of the entire eight-year war from 1937 to 1945. These "indemnities" to munitions firms were also conceived as a way to bail out the banking system, by allowing these companies to pay off their bank loans. Some 20 percent of the 1946 general account budget was set aside for these payments, before the Americans did put a stop to them. When they were cut off, it meant massive company liquidation and reorganization.[24]

This flood of paper yen, funneled through the industrial companies, was highly inflationary. By the beginning of 1946, the BoJ note issue had reached

¥60 billion, double the level of August 15. At the same time, the volume of bank balances actually declined in the last months of 1945, when about ¥5 billion was withdrawn from bank accounts and converted into cash, because of fears of a capital levy or freeze on bank deposits. This was a temporary reversal of the long-run historic trend, which was for bank balances to form an ever larger share of the national money supply (see appendix table A-1). The cash went into black-market purchases, contributing still further to the run on scarce commodities. This great shift into cash continued a movement that had begun during the war years. By 1947, currency in circulation had increased to nearly equal the total of bank balances.[25] This "drain" into cash would begin to reverse itself with the 1949 deflation policy implemented by the U.S. banker Joseph Dodge (see 7.4.1).

5.4 The Constriction of Material-Energetic Flows

Analyses of Japan's postwar history often begin with an accounting of the destruction. There is a lot to account for. Some 2.7 to 3 million Japanese people died in the war. Most of them were young men entering the prime years of their working lives. A comparable number were in prisoner-of-war camps. More than 4 million people were seriously ill or disabled. Nine million people were homeless, after the partial or near-total destruction of sixty-six cities. Added to this was the sinking of most of the merchant fleet; the loss of one-third of national industrial production facilities; and the drastic fall-off of both industrial and agricultural production.[26] Some of these catastrophic effects are shown in table 5-1. To understand the economic development that followed, however, it may be more revealing to start with an accounting of what remained.

Despite the post-apocalyptic appearance of the country's urban landscapes, Japan on August 15, 1945, remained the world's fifth- or sixth-largest industrial power, although dwarfed by the United States and now by the USSR also. Japanese industry remained capable of producing more than 5 million tons of steel per year, more than it had produced in 1935. Production capacity for other metals had also increased. In the production of machine tools, there remained the capacity to make more than 50,000 units annually—more than double the capacity of 1937, when the war began.[27] For many militarily oriented industries such as steel, the greatest contraction of production actually came after the war. Japanese industrialists, experiencing the reality behind these statistics, could easily conclude that it was less the war itself than U.S. policies during the first two

TABLE 5-1. The expansion and collapse of industrial production, 1936–1947

YEAR	IRON AND STEEL	MACHINERY	TEXTILES	CONSUMER DURABLE GOODS	TOTAL MFG.
1936	21.9	11.4	74.9	9.6	31.5
1937	25.3	15.3	**85.3**	9.6	37.2
1938	29.0	16.8	70.4	9.6	38.2
1939	31.1	20.6	70.4	9.7	42.1
1940	32.4	25.0	63.7	**10.8**	44.3
1941	33.4	28.8	51.5	7.9	45.8
1942	35.3	29.9	40.7	6.5	44.5
1943	**39.5**	32.8	26.7	4.8	45.0
1944	36.9	**38.6**	14.2	2.1	**46.2**
1945	13.1	16.4	5.5	0.7	19.6
1946	4.3	5.0	9.1	2.3	7.4
1947	5.7	6.0	12.2	3.7	9.2

Sources: MITI data, given in Nihon Ginkō Tōkeikyoku 1966: 92–93.

Note: Index: 1960 = 100. Year of peak production is indicated in boldface type. Weighted index of value-added for each product category. See also table A-4.

years of occupation that actually brought the national economy to its lowest point. This would be to ignore the fact that many of the goods produced during the war were actually "negative" capital goods: at best, it was production-for-destruction that was simply lost and wasted; at worst, it was used to destroy other people's lives and wealth. But Japanese industrialists did tend to draw the conclusion that U.S. policies were opposed to industrial recovery.

Economically speaking, Japan after the war also experienced a kind of systemic closure, due to the restriction of inward resource flows and the restriction of Japanese travel and business abroad. Thus, during the first phase of Western occupation, Japan was economically more isolated from the rest of the world—more closed in terms of material trade flows relative to the scale of total domestic flows—than it had been since the end of the Tokugawa shogunate's "closed country" regime in 1859. The naval blockade and particularly the effects of U.S. submarine warfare had already stopped the inflow of raw materials. And "in effect," Kōsai Yutaka pointed out, "this blockade was continued by postwar restrictions that the American occupying forces imposed on foreign trade."[28] A phase of relative closure continued even after 1949, with the closure of trade with Communist-governed mainland Asia, also at U.S. direction. Economic recovery and growth in the 1950s thus had a strongly domestic, investment-led aspect. Japan would not regain prewar levels of overseas trade until well into the period of High-Speed Growth.

5.4.1 The Postwar Energy Crisis and the Workers' Revolt

Viewed in energy terms, there was a general caloric crisis in the autumn and winter of 1945. Coal production fell to one-third to one-fourth of the normal level. The autumn rice crop was only two-thirds of normal. The harvest shortfall was caused in part by drought and in part by severe shortages of chemical fertilizer. Energy itself was a primary input in the manufacture of chemical fertilizer, so the energy shortfall meant that fertilizer was in short supply. Low river flows meant that hydroelectric power was also diminished.

Food consumption fell below the Japanese government's per capita norm of 2,150 calories per day as early as 1941. It began to fall drastically in 1945. The end of food imports from Korea, Taiwan, and Manchuria cut off about 20 percent of Japan's former inflow of food supplies, mainly grain, sugar, and soybeans. Total fisheries production fell off by 40 percent, due especially to the decline of the sardine catch, owing to the loss of fishing vessels and lack of diesel fuel. Vegetable production fell 20 percent. Korean rice, however, continued to be shipped to Japan, now as a smuggling trade, alleviating the food shortage in Japan and worsening it in Korea.[29]

The cutoff of imports also meant that the country was temporarily closed in on itself in terms of fuels. In 1936, the last year before full-scale war mobilization, coal supplied 51 percent of total national energy consumption. Manufacturing industry depended especially heavily on coal. Electric power, mainly produced by run-of-river-type hydropower, provided 21 percent of total energy consumption.[30] Charcoal and firewood remained primary household energy sources, constituting 19 percent of national energy consumption. Petroleum accounted for 8 percent of total energy usage but was critically important for transportation (diesel fuel for shipping and fishing fleets, gasoline for trucks and cars). The buildup of military-oriented heavy industry in the 1930s greatly increased the demand for energy, supplied mainly by increased production of coal, whose share of total energy inputs rose to 66 percent in 1940.

Imports of oil were practically shut off in 1944 and 1945 by the U.S. blockade. In October 1945, occupation officials shut down the Japanese oil refineries. No crude oil was imported into Japan again until 1949. United States forces brought in fuel for their own use, and only very small amounts of petroleum products were imported for Japanese use. Coal imports were also cut off. *Zaibatsu* mining companies had invested heavily in their richer and more capital-intensive overseas mines in Korea, Taiwan, South Sakhalin, and above all Manchuria, where highly mechanized strip mines produced coal for Japan. The giant Fushun mine in South Manchuria produced 10 million tons in 1936, at a time when total coal production in Japan itself came to less than 50 million tons.[31]

Immediately after Japan's surrender, an energy crisis emerged with explosive social force. Japan's coal mining industry had operated historically on the basis of superexploited, often semifree or unfree labor. In this way, until August 1945, the modern industrial energy order depended to a large degree on extraeconomic coercion. "The feudal quality of the labor system is most severe in the coal mines," as a Socialist Party statement put it. This was not empty rhetoric but a fair description of a system that historically employed large numbers of penal convicts and held entire families in practical debt bondage. This exploitative aspect was greatly intensified under wartime fascism, when non-Japanese were forced to work in the mines in concentration camp conditions.[32] By the last year of the war, 128,000 Korean miners, many forcibly conscripted, made up some 32 percent of mineworkers. About 40,000 Chinese, mostly prisoners of war, worked in the mines, together with other Allied POWs. Many thousands died there.

It was also here that the postwar struggle for freedom and democracy first broke out into an open fight. Democratization from below and the energy crisis were thus two faces of a revolutionary systemic transformation. About 4 million metric tons of coal was mined per month during the war. Historically, this was the highest level that Japanese coal production ever attained. Coal production fell off sharply immediately after the surrender in August, when POW and conscript workers began refusing to work. A severe energy crisis thus began immediately after the surrender. The September production level fell to 890,000 tons. Allied authorities rapidly repatriated foreign workers, and Japanese workers took up their own fight.[33] In November, coal production fell to 554,000 tons, barely one-eighth of wartime levels. The railroads were given priority in receiving coal, and even they did not have enough.

Electric power generation also fell off sharply. Thermal (coal-fired) generation did not regain its 1940 level until 1951. Hydropower temporarily provided more than 90 percent of national electric power, but even hydropower generation fell, temporarily limited by the same drought conditions that limited the 1945 harvest. But hydropower generation quickly recovered its former level in 1946 and continued to increase during the occupation period. Fuel for home use, still mainly charcoal and wood, was in critically short supply. Many mountainsides had been stripped bare during the war. Wood and charcoal production was down to two-thirds the level of the 1930s, and charcoal briquette production fell to only 40 percent of prewar levels. Hydroelectric power being the most available energy source, people in urban areas now turned to the use of crudely made electric hotplates for cooking and heating.[34]

5.4.2 The Crisis of Capitalist Reproduction

"The economy of a country essentially organic in structure must be grasped and diagnosed as an organic whole." This was the dynamic and holistic approach taken in the first of the annual white papers on the state of the Japanese economy produced by the Economic Stabilization Board in July 1947. It was written mainly by the Marxist-Institutionalist-Schumpeterian economist Tsuru Shigeto, working closely with Ōkita Saburō. The situation depicted by Tsuru, Ōkita, and their colleagues on the ESB research staff was of a country that was quickly running through accumulated stocks and had already entered a dire cycle wherein the scale of production was diminishing day by day. All material factors of production were involved. National land was severely deforested during the war, and investment in afforestation in 1946 was proceeding at only one-seventh of the prewar norm.[35] Deforestation combined with insufficient maintenance of river banks contributed to severe flooding and destruction of fields. Capital equipment of all kinds was badly deteriorating. Breakdowns of train equipment of the national railways had gone from a rate of 3.9 cases per million miles before the war to a rate of 102 in 1946. Owing to the deterioration of equipment, the actual generating capacity of coal-fired power plants had fallen to less than half of their authorized maximum capacity of 2.9 million kilowatts. In manufacturing, productivity per worker was only one-third to one-half of prewar levels, owing to damaged equipment and shortages of energy and materials. At the level of individual households, people in the cities faced a "bamboo shoot livelihood," so called because of the way families survived by "peeling off" layers of clothing and household goods for sale to pay for daily necessities. Most dangerously, the people's health was deteriorating. After the poor rice harvest in 1945, there was a good harvest in 1946, but basic food shortages continued. Grimly illustrating this diminishing scale of reproduction, elementary school children in 1946 were "retarded nearly one year in both height and weight" compared to children in 1937.[36]

Arisawa Hiromi particularly emphasized the threat of a cycle of diminishing reproduction. This was specifically a crisis of *capitalist* reproduction. During the war, state authorities had ordered the conversion of ever more of civilian production to military production. The war also brought assured profits to companies engaged in military production. War's end brought a severe crisis. Corporate profits turned negative, falling in 1946 and 1947 below the depression-era low of 1931. (The chaotic year 1945 itself was a statistical hiatus.) Within this overall contraction of production, the corporate share of national income also collapsed relative to that of other social sectors.[37] Outside of the statistics, many companies engaged in black-market trading on a massive scale and collected unreported cash profits. Minimally, this sudden drop indicates a severe crisis of legitimate capitalism and "life-threatening" circumstances for many enterprises. Depression levels in corporate income persisted through the first part of 1950 and were transcended only with the onset of the Korean War in June 1950. In the context of the movement for workers' production control and unionization in 1946 and the great strike wave that began in 1947, there was an acute perception of a capitalist system in crisis. This sense was present on both sides of a suddenly sharp capitalist-versus-anticapitalist divide.

5.5 Liquidating Japanese Capitalism

The occupation of the Japanese mainland began with the arrival of General Douglas MacArthur and the signing of the surrender agreement on September 2, 1945. Japan's remaking got under way in earnest in October, when MacArthur's General Headquarters, Supreme Commander for the Allied Powers (GHQ/ SCAP) was set up to conduct the nonmilitary aspects of the occupation. United States authorities initially disavowed economic responsibility for Japan but did begin to deliver food aid to avert famine. At the same time, they directed a sweeping political, social, and economic reformation.

The American plan to remake Japan constituted a direct attack on the existing system of Japanese capitalism. General MacArthur's charter orders for conducting the occupation were contained in the top secret document "United States Initial Post-Defeat Policy Relating to Japan" dated August 22, 1945, which was clear in its statement of goals: "The existing economic basis of Japanese military strength must be destroyed and not be permitted to revive." It further directed the Supreme Commander "to favor a program for the dissolution of the large industrial and banking combinations which have exercised control of a great part of Japan's trade and industry."[38] This dissolution of large combinations did happen on the commercial and industrial side. However, except for the splitting of the giant Imperial Bank, it did not happen on the banking side.

On October 31, 1945, GHQ ordered the freezing of *zaibatsu* assets. The idea was to break up the combines and sell shares in the subsidiary companies to the general public. It was said that this would democratize ownership in the American style. "Democratic" is not a good description of this type of ownership structure; in actuality, this reform would create *managerial* capitalism—also in the American style. In theory, this breaking up of private concentrations of economic power could be seen as the taking down of some of the big trees that had shaded out the smaller ones, opening a field for new entrepreneurial initiative. *Zaibatsu* dissolution and economic deconcentration thus had an aspect of "creative destruction."[39] The extent to which this "deconstruction" was actually creative is controversial. The firms broken up, far from being moribund or ossified, constituted the most advanced and technologically efficient parts of the economy. The company-groups targeted were Mitsui, Mitsubishi, Sumitomo, Yasuda, Asano, Furukawa, Fuyo, Kawasaki, Nisso, Nichitsu, Nomura, Okura, Riken, and Shibusawa. Finance minister Shibusawa Keizō was in charge of the process. Ishibashi Tanzan strongly criticized it.[40]

Many historical analyses that look at the longer run minimize the final significance of the dissolution of the *zaibatsu*. Despite ambitious American plans that grew to target hundreds of companies, in the end only eleven business groups were dissolved. The movement was then stopped during the probusiness course reversal that began in 1948. Further, the new Anti-Monopoly Law, which the Americans had intended to maintain this dissolution, was not enforced. The major *zaibatsu* groups thus reconstituted themselves as *keiretsu* ("series" or "linkages") in the 1950s. In this light, it might seem hyperbolic for Ishibashi Tanzan to write, as he did in 1951, that "the dissolution [of the *zaibatsu*] destroyed Japan's economic order and proved to be a major cause of obstructing her economy."[41] But while U.S. efforts did fall short of the goals of GHQ's "*zaibatsu* busters," the companies they broke up in fact constituted the industrial and commercial core of Japan's economic order. Notwithstanding their happy talk about the efficiency of small business and free competition, many American contributors to the anti-*zaibatsu* policy also made it clear that they saw economic deconcentration as a way to take Japan down a notch industrially. On the Japanese side, people across the political spectrum attributed such a motivation to the American policy. As an assessment by the Japan Communist Party later put it, the United States "carried out the 'democratization policy' to weaken Japan."[42] Probusiness conservatives agreed. The economic deconcentration policy also contributed to the so-called capital strike and the collapse of industrial production during the early years of the occupation. Beginning in January 1946, GHQ also began to purge business executives who had directed the war economy. A total of 453 businessmen were directly purged. A similar number resigned under threat of purge, while a few hundred others were barred from certain posts.[43]

Reparations were another way Allied authorities intended the Japanese people should pay for some of the damage they had caused to other countries. The threat of reparations also caused the directors of large companies to hold off on reinvesting in their own operations. Japanese concern over the prospect of reparations began immediately after the surrender. In early December 1945, the U.S. Reparation Mission issued a report (the "Pauley report") that recommended immediate substantial reparations in the form of industrial equipment. Ultimately this did not happen, but uncertainty on this point continued until 1949.

Beyond making the Japanese people pay the costs of their own occupation, however, GHQ authorities did not attempt to exploit Japan economically, owing in part to MacArthur's determination to keep American companies out. As early as the autumn of 1946, efforts were coming out of Washington to insert big-business representatives into the occupation's economic administration; MacArthur for several years kept them at a distance.[44]

The occupation ended in 1952 with the U.S. government contributing substantial subsidies to the Japanese government, which by that point had become a U.S. client state. But the occupation began with the defeated Japanese government paying financial subsidies to their foreign occupiers. For the Japanese government, this was easy enough. The Bank of Japan simply issued more money. But the real resources had to come from somewhere, and this, too, meant more inflation. Japanese government payments for occupation expenses, given the euphemistic label "termination of war expenses," became the largest single budget item, consuming some 30–40 percent of budgetary expenditure. The costs of the occupation itself were thus criticized as a source of inflation, for example by the right-wing Tokyo University economist Hijikata Seibi, and more discreetly by Ishibashi Tanzan.[45] The other side of this arrangement was that easy money creation continued.

In regard to economic stabilization policy, the six months from August 1945 to the implementation of emergency stabilization measures in February 1946 were a period of "indecision."[46] By war's end, Ministry of Finance officials understood wartime price, wage, and materials controls to be functioning poorly. Directly after the surrender, they began to rethink them and planned a general lifting of controls, except for necessities. General Headquarters rejected this. At GHQ urging, the Ministry of Finance conducted an elaborate currency reform in February 1946. This was the first systematic effort at economic stabilization. Existing bank accounts were frozen—that is, the payment of debt obligations by financial institutions was halted—and a "new yen" was created. There was also a special capital levy (as Schumpeter had proposed for Austria in 1918 and then failed to implement as finance minister).[47] The freezing of bank accounts was, in effect, a general debt moratorium for the banks. The banks were further shored up because people had to deposit "old yen" cash into bank accounts in order to convert them to new yen, which could be withdrawn only in limited quantities. The reform was also egalitarian, at least in the short run, as households got access to their accounts, while most other accounts were blocked. These emergency measures temporarily slowed the rise of prices in early 1946. However, price pressures picked up again later in the year. Altogether, wholesale prices in 1946 rose by almost three times, and consumer prices more than doubled. The bank-account freeze also made people leery of banks, while the wealth levy made people leery of leaving wealth where it might easily be found. There continued to be an extraordinary shift into cash. Many interbusiness dealings assumed a black-market aspect, and as tax-collection efforts became a greater source of social pressure, tax evasion became ubiquitous. It was in these circumstances that Ishibashi Tanzan became minister of finance in May 1946.

INFLATION AS CAPITAL

It is a curious paradox that a country whose people are so devoted to frugality and thrift should have such a strong propensity to inflation as does Japan.

—Jerome Cohen, *Japan's Postwar Economy* (1958)

Reconstruction of basic industries was made possible by the forced savings caused by hyperinflation.

—Noguchi Yukio, "The Development and Present State of Public Finance" (1986)

Was the postwar inflation caused by shortages or by overspending? This is the way the question was often posed; and even after the fact, the production-oriented Ministry of International Trade and Industry (MITI) and the funding-oriented Ministry of Finance tended to come down on opposite sides of it. In a retrospective survey of Japan's postwar economy written in 1956, the chief of MITI's Research Section thus explained that after the war, "the acute shortage of food-stuffs, raw materials, fuel, and electric power soon brought on a vicious inflation." His counterpart in the Ministry of Finance emphasized instead that it was the great increase in the money supply that drove the inflation.[1] Both were correct, but to emphasize one side or the other implied a choice between opposed policy positions.

The inflation was also understood as a case of "forced savings" by many analysts. As such, it had a capitalist-developmental aspect in line with Schumpeter's account. Schumpeter claimed (without investigating it empirically) that the social subsidy received by industrialists with superior access to credit came at the expense of other industrialists competing for the same productive services.[2] In practice, cost increases were not so neatly contained, and the "inflation tax" was much more widely paid. "We cannot deny," the Bank of Japan's Yoshino Toshihiko acknowledged in 1957, "that economic reconstruction has been enforced through the sacrifice of wage and salary earners." Yoshino himself was the main author of a substantial study of Germany's post–World War I inflation and stabilization produced by the BoJ in 1944–45. He then took part in reconstruction planning as the BoJ member of the committee that developed the Priority Production

System. Wage levels, as Yoshino explained, "caught up with price levels only after 1954, when postwar inflation was halted."[3] Thus wage earners subsidized industrial investment.

Industrial recovery by means of inflation contributed a core component of the reformed capitalist order that was consolidated in the early 1950s. This capital-provision aspect of the inflation has often been overlooked by Anglo-American analysts, although in fact Joseph Dodge came to perceive it clearly. Politically, the inflation policy was identified above all with Ishibashi Tanzan, who was among the visionaries of Japan's postwar growth. Many Americans then and since considered Ishibashi's policy a manifest and even foolish failure. Many Japanese have perceived instead a substantial degree of success under difficult conditions. From the standpoint of industrial recovery, there is much truth in this. In other circumstances such an outcome would not have been possible, but in the special local and international circumstances after World War II, it was. Some of the ideas and institutions confirmed and created out of these successes later became dysfunctional and damaging, but this is a story of more recent times.

6.1 The Ishibashi Line

On the face of it, a Keynesian liberal like Ishibashi Tanzan would seem to have been exactly the sort of person GHQ's "New Dealers" would have wanted in office in newly democratizing Japan. Since the 1910s, Ishibashi had been known as a critic of Japanese expansionism and as a proponent of social reform and representative government. As a writer for and later publisher of Japan's biggest business newsweekly, the *Tōyō keizai shinpō* (Oriental Economist), he also had a platform for making his views known. Economic journalist Kimura Kihachirō, in an English-language account written to introduce Ishibashi in 1946, explained that Ishibashi was "a liberalist of the classical type, who strictly adheres to the doctrine expounded by Adam Smith," who opposed state controls, and whose ideas "verg[ed] upon ultra-individualism." "Thus Ishibashi was consistently crying down the controlled economy during the war and now is in a most earnest manner urging for a comeback of the free economy of the pre-war period."[4] But Ishibashi conspicuously failed to play the part of a member of a defeated nation, and he persistently irritated the occupation authorities by criticizing their policies, in their own liberal terms, with the attitude of one who held the moral high ground. Moreover, Ishibashi's liberalism encompassed great liberality to the munitions companies and *zaibatsu* to whom the government owed giant wartime debts, at a time when these companies were on GHQ's hit list.

This probusiness version of liberalism put Ishibashi at odds with reform-minded occupation officials concerning the relative dangers of bureaucratic state power versus big business power, for the "free economy of the prewar period" was also an economy dominated by the big *zaibatsu*. Ishibashi had developed strong ties over the years with many business leaders. From the last months of the war to the time of his appointment as finance minister, he also sat on several government advisory committees concerned with economic issues. In late 1945, he publicly took up the cause of the *zaibatsu* in opposition to GHQ's dissolution plans.[5] For this, he gained great credit with the business world, which backed his appointment as minister of finance in the first Yoshida cabinet in May 1946. During his term as finance minister, much of the business world became deeply indebted to him for the funds he directed their way. For the same reasons, Ishibashi was purged by GHQ in May 1947 after only a year in office.

Ishibashi's liberal and pro-*zaibatsu* views were joined with a famously expansive vision of government-sponsored capital creation and spending. Ishibashi became known as an inflationist's inflationist—a "latter-day oriental John Law," in the words of GHQ economist Martin Bronfenbrenner. The comparison is instructive, for the Scottish financier had undertaken to dispose of the French government's immense war debts by setting up a state bank and replacing the debt with paper money. But as Schumpeter emphasized, Law's plan was not linked to an industrial investment policy that would have created an enlarged production flow to correspond to the new money, and the result was the infamous Mississippi bubble of 1719.[6] In any case, Law had discharged state debts with inconvertible paper money and caused them to vanish into oblivion.

Ishibashi's attention, unlike Law's, was focused on industry from the beginning, and his policy was far more than a ploy to eliminate debt. (Indeed, as explained in later chapters, the Japanese state did not need to worry about its domestic debt.) Ishibashi's policy began from the lessons of Japan's Great Depression. As he saw it, the depression that began in 1929 was immeasurably worsened by the mistaken deflation policy conducted by the government of the time, which had been fixated on restoring the gold standard. In Japan as in Germany, the depression, intensified by the deflation policy, fostered the rise of the right-wing and militarist movements, which nearly destroyed the country. Thus, Ishibashi said, "I was worried that postwar Japan might repeat the same mistake."[7] When Ishibashi became finance minister in 1946, he applied this lesson: the great danger was postwar deflation and depression. What was demanded was a "positive" deficit-spending policy of the sort that had rescued Japan from the Great Depression in 1932. Unlike Takahashi Korekiyo, the author of the 1932 policy, with whom Ishibashi now compared himself, Ishibashi was an avowed practitioner of Keynes's doctrine.[8]

In opposing deflation in the 1920s, Ishibashi had opposed the international policy tide of that time. The trend of the times had now caught up with him, and he moved swiftly with the new tide. All the same, Ishibashi continued to see himself as a lone voice against a tide of opinion that was mistakenly fixated on inflation. Already in September (as the inflation was taking off) he was warning publicly of the danger of deflation.[9] He reasoned that war spending had propped up the economy. With the withdrawal of that spending, contraction and acute deflation would follow. Despite the severe inflation that followed, he held to this view.

In 1946, Ishibashi decided to go into politics and joined the Liberal Party.[10] As a result of the April 1946 general elections, Liberal Party president Yoshida Shigeru was able to form his first cabinet. Yoshida showed a remarkable political eclecticism in putting together his cabinet. He first offered the job of finance minister to Ōuchi Hyōe, a Marxist with ties to the Socialist Party. Yoshida's predecessor, Hatoyama Ichirō, had already attempted to recruit Ōuchi for the post. Ōuchi was also, unlike Ishibashi, fiscally orthodox. In this sense, Ōuchi was a practitioner of "classical economics," according to his one-time research assistant Yoshino Toshihiko.[11] When it comes to Ōuchi's staunchly anti-inflationary position, there is no mistake in this judgment, and when it came to monetary questions, Marxists traditionally had taken a conservative "classical" approach. In any case, Ōuchi declined the offer, thinking that the anti-inflation policy he favored would not be politically palatable or achievable.[12] Yoshida then offered the post to the neoclassical-Schumpeterian-Keynesian economist Nakayama Ichirō. Nakayama also declined. Only then did Yoshida offer it to Ishibashi. Yoshida was reportedly not personally sympathetic to Ishibashi but made him finance minister in response to the demands of big business, who trusted him.[13] Yoshida was also willing to leave economic policy to his subordinates. He did have a strong aversion to the wartime military regime, to the wartime controlled economy, and to economic planning, which he viewed as communistic. In all this he and Ishibashi more or less agreed. Nevertheless, the politics of the Yoshida's first cabinet were unlike those of his more conservative second cabinet. Not only was what Bai Gao has called the "institutional inertia of the managed economy" very strong but Yoshida also remained personally close to the talented group of economists and economic bureaucrats introduced in the previous chapter, who advocated ideas of planning and economic control. These included Arisawa Hiromi, who designed the Priority Production System under Yoshida's auspices. They also included Wada Hiro, who as Yoshida's minister of agriculture directed the agricultural land reform and later, as a leader of the left wing of the Socialist Party, headed the Economic Stabilization Board.[14] This was Yoshida Shigeru's own moment of postwar socialist–conservative cooperation.

6.1.1 "Famine Prices" Demand More Investment, Not Less

The Yoshida cabinet was inaugurated on April 22, 1946. At the press conference that day, Finance Minister Ishibashi declared his policy plainly. First, he said, the inflation was caused by shortages. One could not remedy shortages by simply restricting the currency. Second, the task of financial policy was to concentrate funds on the increase of production. Third, the February 1946 emergency financial measures (the bank account freeze and other controls that had accompanied the "new yen" reform) were harmful and should be abolished as quickly as possible.[15]

Ishibashi's analysis reflected his Keynesian stance. Ishibashi's Keynesianism also clarifies why Shinohara Miyohei could say that the ideas of "Schumpeter and Keynes" described the way things worked in postwar Japan: the essential point was the creation of new funds for industry (see 11.1). The present inflation, Ishibashi said, was not a "true inflation," because many people were unemployed and industrial capacity was going unused. The shortage of production was caused especially by bottlenecks such as the shortfall of coal production. Japan had the manpower and resources to solve these problems. What was lacking was the financial capital to mobilize these resources, and that could by created by government and banks. In other words, expansionary measures were needed. This analysis was much like Takahashi Korekiyo's reading of Japan's situation during the depression of 1929–32. The great difference between these two moments was that when Takahashi Korekiyo took office as finance minister in December 1931, wholesale prices were falling by more than 15 percent per year. In April 1946, inflation was already surging, and wholesale prices for the year would increase by about 80 percent.[16]

Ishibashi's first great task was to protect the flow of government payments to industry. This is the point where reconstruction finance connects to the question of the wartime debts owed to industry (see 5.3). Ishibashi, representing on this issue the viewpoint of the entire government, was adamant that these debts be repaid. Without this funding, he feared that production would collapse. GHQ's Economic and Scientific Section (ESS) refused. They saw these payments (as did many Japanese observers) as more high-level looting:

> It was indeed strange at first to observe the efforts of the Japanese officials to maximize government outgo and redemption of wartime obligations. But the rationale behind these concerted efforts soon emerged. . . . It was another attempt to shift the burden of war losses from the industrial and financial owners to the Japanese people—by the simple expedient of maximizing government compensations [to business].[17]

Another GHQ official charged more pointedly that Ishibashi's policies "earned the [Liberal Party] the solid backing of the *shin-yen* [new yen] class of postwar profiteers—blackmarketeers, contractors, and miscellaneous racketeers."[18]

In halting the payments, the ESS offered a "compromise" formula: the government would be permitted to pay the munitions companies, but the companies had to return the funds straightaway to the government via a 100 percent tax on the payments. Through his first month in office, Ishibashi resisted the American plan. It was when he tried to appeal directly to General MacArthur over the heads of ESS that GHQ's Government Section, on ESS advice, resolved to purge him. However, GHQ's new policy was to refrain from giving direct orders, so as to support the newly elected Japanese government, and it took eleven months before Ishibashi was actually removed from office.[19] In this way, Ishibashi unknowingly conducted practically his entire tenure as finance minister on borrowed time.

With Yoshida's support, Ishibashi held out for a direct GHQ order concerning the wartime debts, thereby forcing GHQ to take the blame publicly for the extraordinary tax. In June 1946, GHQ finally got the payments stopped. The results were as Ishibashi had anticipated. By autumn industrial production dropped off, even while inflation, propelled further by shortages, continued to accelerate.[20] The capital-provision policy was not stopped, however, but rather was forced into new channels, as Ishibashi moved to organize a new governmental bank designed to invest money directly into basic industries. This was the Reconstruction Finance Bank (RFB), which was conceived by a committee Ishibashi established in late June 1946 and which began to operate in August 1946.

This was the context of Ishibashi's July 1946 financial policy address to the Diet, in which he explained to the nation the imminent danger of depression and laid out his goals. The "greatest goal," at a time when workers were involuntarily unemployed and production facilities were idle, was "full employment." A true inflation would call for deflationary remedies, Ishibashi said, but real inflation could occur only in conditions of full employment. Here he invoked Keynes, who had died three months before. During the wartime period, productive resources had been fully employed, and Japan had indeed had a truly inflationary situation. But one could not solve the present problem of idle people and resources by idling more people and resources via a deflationary policy. The current high prices were rather "famine prices," caused by great shortages, especially of food. Far from being a true inflation, the present situation was "like a famine or a depression."[21]

Indeed, it was like a famine—only U.S. food aid kept it from being a terrible one. Large shipments of U.S. food aid began in the spring of 1946. By mid-1946, the United States was supplying some 37 percent of staple foodstuffs.[22] And the great idling of facilities and falloff of production was indeed like a depression. It was certainly unlike the inflationary boom phase of a normal business cycle. In this respect, Ishibashi said, Japan's postwar inflation was not like Germany's inflation after World War I, because Germany had had a full-employment boom up to 1922.[23]

Famine prices, Ishibashi explained, could only be remedied by increased production. The need was therefore *to mobilize productive resources*, even if the government must run a deficit and issue more currency in order to do so. And though the present crisis was like a depression, Ishibashi argued, it was not at all a usual business-cyclic recession but was the consequence of war and defeat. Usual countercyclic measures were therefore not appropriate. Eight years of war had exhausted the nation, and it was necessary to face up to and write off the economic losses of the war. This process of postwar adjustment would inevitably be deflationary. Therefore, a "positive policy" was needed to prevent the imminent turn to deflation.[24]

The term "positive policy" (*sekkyoku seisaku*) was part of a policy binary that carried strong political resonances in Japan's recent history. In Ishibashi's usage, "positive policy" invoked above all the reflationary antidepression policies of Takahashi Korekiyo, who in the years 1932–36 had employed a "positive" deficit-spending policy as a countercyclical macroeconomic tool.[25] To forestall deflation, Ishibashi thus proposed his own positive policy, consisting of five points:

1. Special promotion of pivotal industries
2. Reconstruction finance
3. Industrial rationalization (not a "negative contraction of operations" but a "positive" promotion of increased productivity in order to increase incomes)
4. An unemployment policy
5. Economic democracy[26]

Ishibashi's first point, the special promotion of pivotal industries, would be concretized in the Priority Production System. The second point, reconstruction finance, was connected to the first and pointed toward Ishibashi's initiative to organize a special reconstruction finance bank. It was in this connection that Ishibashi's policies became most famous. The third point, enhancing productivity, carried forward another long-standing concern also held by Takahashi Korekiyo.[27] An unemployment policy would counteract the effects of adjustment and rationalization. The final point, "economic democracy," was little more than a slogan. Ishibashi made this clear by explaining that although Japan in the past may have had big landlords and very rich people, now they were all gone. Thus, Ishibashi said, whether it was desirable or not, there was now only small-scale agriculture in Japan.[28] There were now also many small shareholders, he pointed out. Therefore, he concluded, "our economic democratization is already halfway there." What was still needed was democratic morality and democratic culture.

GHQ's termination of the wartime compensation payments was written into law in October 1946. This measure would have bankrupted most major companies, who counted those government obligations as capital. Therefore, the government simultaneously enacted a package of ameliorative measures, including the Enterprise Reconstruction and Reorganization Law, the Financial Institutions Reconstruction and Reorganization Law, and the Reconstruction Finance Bank Law.[29] The Reconstruction Finance Bank would be Ishibashi's main legacy as finance minister.

6.1.2 Priority Production and Reconstruction Finance

To understand the specificity of an inflation, including its social character and effects, one needs to know how and where newly created money enters circulation. Inflationary reconstruction in postwar Japan was based on industrial subsidies, mainly to a few priority industries. These were provided as direct government subsidies and in the form of lending by the Reconstruction Finance Bank. The RFB began operations in August 1946 as the Reconstruction Financing Department of the Industrial Bank of Japan (IBJ), which itself was a specially chartered parastatal bank. It is easy to accept Schumpeter's judgment that a country's national budget reveals the skeleton of the state, "stripped of deceptive ideologies."[30] One can say further that the state budget combined with the account books of the parastatal banks constitutes such a document concerning what can be called the *extended state* (see 8.1.1). Under the Reconstruction Finance Bank Law of October 1946, the RFB was itself chartered as a special bank, wholly owned by the government. The new bank remained closely connected to the IBJ, from which many of its personnel were drawn.[31]

The direction of these state and bank subsidies was guided, from the spring of 1947, by the Priority Production System. This system, whose chief architect was Arisawa Hiromi, aimed to rebuild key energy and materials industries, beginning with coal, electric power, steel, and chemical fertilizer. The planning and management of the Priority Production System was conducted by another new organization, the Economic Stabilization Board (ESB), called in Japanese by the more military-sounding name Keizai Antei Honbu (Economic Stabilization Headquarters), or "Anpon" for short. The Economic Stabilization Board was itself established in May 1946 as a result of GHQ concerns to control inflation and ensure fair distribution. It, too, went into operation in August 1946. The new board was to coordinate policy between ministries and was given charge of price controls and rationing. It acquired an array of control powers over production, financing, distribution, and transportation, and over economic planning, broadly defined. These powers would not become really effective until 1947.

The Priority Production System developed out of the discussions among a group of economic experts who met weekly over lunch with Prime Minister Yoshida at his out-of-the-way second office. These meetings began around October 1946. This group was the successor group to the "Special Survey Committee" introduced in the previous chapter. Ōkita Saburō, now working in the Research Bureau of the Ministry of Foreign Affairs (where Yoshida also continued to serve as minister) again served as the group's secretary and organizer. The core members were Arisawa Hiromi, Inaba Hidezō, Yoshino Toshihiko of the Bank of Japan research staff, and Ōkita's junior colleague Gotō Yonosuke, joined by Satō Naoyoshi of the Ministry of Commerce and Industry and Ōshima Kan'ichi from the Ministry of Finance. All agreed that a solution to the vicious cycle of production decrease must begin with coal, whose production remained at critically low levels. To work out the details, the Coal Subcommittee was formed, chaired by Arisawa and including Ōkita, Inaba, and Tsuru Shigeto. It was there that Arisawa developed his idea for a system of "tilting" or "priority" production (*keisha seisan hōshiki*). The same group, with Arisawa serving as an outside adviser, became the top planners at the Economic Stabilization Board a year later.[32]

The principle of "priority production" agreed on in late 1946 was intended to govern all "supply and demand adjustment programs," over which the government had authority under the Temporary Supply and Demand Adjustment Law of September 30, 1946. In fact, the phrase "supply and demand adjustment" directly replaced the no longer palatable wartime term "mobilization." To boost coal production, allocations of materials to other sectors would have to be cut. But a bootstrapping problem entered in here: to mine more coal, more steel was needed, but to make more steel, more coal was needed. "Somehow or other we had to break this vicious circle," Ōkita said. Shipments of U.S. fuel oil turned out to be the way out. The U.S. authorities allowed the fuel-oil shipments following a direct request from Prime Minister Yoshida. It was Ōkita who drafted the request.[33]

Finance Minister Ishibashi initially criticized the broad range of controls given to the Economic Stabilization Board. The controversy over the ESB again aligned Ishibashi against GHQ's Economic and Scientific Section, which backed the ESB and thought that Ishibashi was again trying to sabotage their plans. Prime Minister Yoshida then appointed Ishibashi himself chairman of the ESB in January 1947. Other sections of the Japanese government had viewed the ESB negatively as a GHQ invention. With Finance Minister Ishibashi in charge, it finally became an effective organization, now dedicated to the project of priority production.[34] This access to power of the "Ishibashi ESB" happened just at the point that Arisawa, Ōkita, Tsuru, Nakayama, and Tōbata all abruptly distanced themselves from Yoshida over his antilabor stance (see 6.2). By May 1947, when Ishibashi was finally purged by GHQ, the Economic Stabilization Board had expanded to include ten bureaus employing 2,000 people. It would gain much more power under the subsequent Socialist-led cabinet.

Reconstruction financing also ballooned. The Reconstruction Finance Bank went into business under its own name in January 1947. Within three months, by the end of March 1947, RFB lending already came to almost 10 percent of all bank lending. One year later, it came to almost 30 percent of all lending. The RFB was funded by the government directly and by being allowed to issue its own bonds, which were purchased by the Bank of Japan. One could also say that it was funded by inflation. From February 1947 until Joseph Dodge shut down the RFB in March 1949, 32 percent of the huge increase of the Bank of Japan's note issue was accounted for by the BoJ's holding of RFB bonds. This happened at a time when the BoJ was also increasing its loans to private banks.[35] One might thus reckon, roughly, that the RFB alone accounted for a third of the monetary inflation of 1947–48. It also funded much of the recovery of production that took place in 1948, so its final net inflationary effect must be understood as the ratio between the two.

At the Bank of Japan, governor Ichimada Hisato agreed that "to extinguish inflation, there is ultimately no way but to increase production." The central bank's Loan Mediation Bureau (Yūshi Assen Bu) also had a critical role.[36] This system was initiated in March 1946 and fully established over the course of the next year. In 1948, this BoJ bureau "mediated" (meaning originated) 18 percent of all bank lending. When the RFB was shut down under the Dodge Line in 1949, the bureau's share increased to 24 percent. Most of this credit was directed to members of the IBJ and Fuji Bank (former Yasuda) groups. Its operation was also linked to the Priority Production System. It is also notable that the Loan Mediation Bureau was under the direct control of BoJ governor Ichimada Hisato (see 8.3.1). In effect, Ichimada thus continued to function in the position he had gained during the war. This bureau closed in 1954 when Ichimada resigned as BoJ governor.

The RFB's lending decisions were made by a committee chaired by the minister of finance. The director-general of the Economic Stabilization Board was vice-chair. Ishibashi Tanzan simultaneously held both positions from the time of the bank's establishment in January until March 1947. Lending decisions were made according to the quarterly plans drawn up by the Economic Stabilization Board, in line with the Priority Production System. Most RFB loans were disbursed in Tokyo, and most of the money went to a few hundred large enterprises.

The "RFB inflation" thus originated with the spending "orders" of these enterprises. These were not just capital loans but huge operating subsidies.

Reconstruction Finance Bank lending to priority businesses was a main source of industrial funding. Government price subsidies were a second source. Under the Priority Production System, scarce rationed inputs into other production processes (e.g. coal) were designated as priority goods. The Economic Stabilization Board fixed sale prices for these at artificially low levels. The government then provided direct subsidies to companies to make up the difference between these low sale prices and the actual costs of production. Such subsidies equaled 30 percent or 40 percent of total cost. This, too, was a kind of capital creation. These subsidies amounted to nearly one-fourth of the FY 1947 budget.[37]

The Priority Production System was also a response to the challenge from labor, especially in the energy sector. Reconstruction Finance Bank lending thus went also to support wage increases, the construction of workers' housing, and new hiring in the coal mines especially. In November 1945, the number of coal miners had fallen to 210,000. By 1949, it was back up to 460,000.[38] Coal mining was still mainly pick-and-shovel work, and this manpower made a critical difference in coal production, which also recovered to prewar levels in early 1949.

The inflation continued. The food crisis also continued. In early 1947, urban households were paying out about 70 percent of their living expenses for food alone. Diets improved, according to the Cabinet Statistics Bureau's Consumer Price Survey, from a level of less than 1,300 calories per person per day in January 1947 to more than 1,600 calories in April. This was still well below the Japanese government's norm of 2,150 calories per day. Families were still buying 20 to 40 percent of their total dietary intake from so-called black-market sources. Because of the much higher prices there, black-market purchases absorbed about three-fourths of total spending on food.[39] In 1947, black-market food prices continued to surge upward month by month, roughly tripling over the course of the year.

Finance Minister Ishibashi admitted that inflation was a problem in his second budget speech on March 3, 1947. However, he continued blithely to dismiss monetary and fiscal factors as causes of the inflation. He also claimed to have balanced the budget. (This was done by moving budget deficits "off budget" to the government's special accounts.) He further claimed to have restricted lending by the Bank of Japan and other financial institutions. Thus, Ishibashi assured the Japanese public, "as far as measures to prevent inflation from the side of fiscal and monetary policy, we can say that we have completely achieved the perfect state. The remaining questions are the production and circulation of goods."[40]

6.1.3 Ishibashi's Purge

GHQ finally purged Ishibashi in May 1947. It was perhaps the most controversial and politicized purge of the occupation. To justify it, GHQ conducted a public relations hatchet job on Ishibashi, accusing him of having promoted Japanese imperialism in the 1930s. The charge lacked convincing power because Ishibashi had been known so long as an anti-imperialist.[41] He seems to have been genuinely surprised and shocked by the accusations against him, and he was at pains to defend his record against GHQ's public charges—all of which were beside the real point.

GHQ's true, economic-policy motivations are apparent in a secret Economic and Scientific Section memorandum on Ishibashi's purge dated May 1, 1947. Here, ESS officials charged that "the record of Mr. Ishibashi as Minister of Finance is one of continuous obstructionism toward occupation economic objectives." This was supported by the following items:

1. Ishibashi had stonewalled SCAP on the issue of the extraordinary tax [on government indemnity payments to industry], forcing General MacArthur's intervention.
2. "Mr. Ishibashi has publicly advocated and practices pro-inflationary financial policies in contravention to expressed SCAP deflationary policies." Ishibashi wanted to lift financial controls as soon as possible. Moreover, "the pro-inflationary tendencies of Mr. Ishibashi have been explained by his associates as a reflection of his prime sympathy for the interests of large industrial groups who stand to profit by the inflation."
3. Ishibashi failed to implement effective price controls.
4. Ishibashi had "become in effect the economic spokesman for the Government." He also controlled the Economic Stabilization Board. He helped to extend bank loans indiscriminately.

Further, ESS had been pushing for a single consolidated government budget for the year, but Ishibashi had resisted this.[42] (That is, he maintained the existing system of multiple "off budget" special accounts.)

Ishibashi himself suspected another American motivation, as his magazine the *Oriental Economist* later reported in 1957, when Ishibashi himself had just become prime minister: "The real reason" that drove SCAP to remove Ishibashi from office, the magazine reported (in English) was "his stern attitude, as Minister of Finance, toward cutting huge expenditures which the Japanese Government had to make out of the meager budget for extravagant building plans for occupation personnel such as numerous swimming pools, spacious golf links, and large hydroponic farms."[43]

At any rate, Ishibashi was purged from office and banned from public life for the remainder of the occupation. His vice-minister, Ikeda Hayato, protested GHQ's decision. So did Bank of Japan governor Ichimada Hisato, together with prominent journalists and political leaders.[44] Prime Minister Yoshida conspicuously failed to come to Ishibashi's defense.

In light of the high inflation that accompanied Ishibashi's policy, his views would also seem manifestly to have been mistaken. Officials within the Ministry of Finance itself had deep misgivings. These doubts apparently extended to Ikeda Hayato, who in 1952, shortly after the end of the occupation, criticized Ishibashi's policy without naming him directly: "The economic policy of that time had an increase of 'production' as the most important point. Thus it didn't touch the sickness itself, and in the meantime the inflation rapidly marched ahead." On the other hand, Shimomura Osamu, who later became Ikeda's economic policy adviser and was then a Ministry of Finance official working in the Price Office, thought that Ishibashi's policy, notwithstanding its drastic side effects, revived the entrepreneurial will to increase production.[45] Bank of Japan president Ichimada Hisato later averred that he, too, had favored a more contractionary policy but at the time had been forced to issue more money to cover the government's deficits. This is not what he said at the time, and Ishibashi had hardly been alone in thinking that the essential thing was to increase production. Economists opposed to inflation had also understood this need, and GHQ itself had implicitly agreed.

The Yoshida cabinet itself resigned soon after Ishibashi's purge, on May 24, as a result of the April 1947 elections. Under the subsequent Socialist-led cabinet, the recovery process was openly guided by a theory of comprehensive economic planning that did in fact make Ishibashi appear "a liberalist of the classical type." The inflation rolled on.

6.2 The ESB Line: "Modified Capitalism"

Between Ishibashi's Keynesian "new liberalism" and the "classically liberal" deflation imposed by Joseph Dodge in 1949 came a phase of experimentation with corporatist-style capitalist stabilization. This policy is well described by the contemporary term "modified capitalism" (*shūsei shihonshugi*). This policy too was inflationary, although it also appears that by 1948, the combination of increased production, price controls, and taxation was beginning to moderate the rate of price increases.

The period when Japan lost its sovereignty and fell under U.S. occupation was, paradoxically, the historic high point of the Japanese civilian bureaucracy's control over the economy, as Chalmers Johnson emphasized in his classic account. Although occupation authorities abolished various wartime mobilization measures, they also inadvertently delivered new influence into the hands of the Japanese economic bureaucracy by eliminating the military and the *zaibatsu* as competing power centers. Severe shortages, the tasks of reconstruction, and the inflation itself constituted an ongoing national emergency; the continuation of government-administered rationing and price controls seemed unavoidable. Nor did GHQ's New Dealers necessarily see governmental controls over the private economy as an evil. Their outlook, like that of their Japanese counterparts, had been shaped by their own experiences of the Great Depression and the wartime controlled economy in the United States. Looking at it from a Marxist standpoint, Ōuchi Hyōe directly equated the ideas of the U.S. New Deal with Japanese "modified capitalism" theory.[46]

This was also a period of ascending bank control: the extension of state administrative control and the extension of bank control over "orders to the factors of production" went hand in hand. The system that later funded high-speed growth is already clearly visible here. The BoJ exercised actual monetary control by extending short-term credits to the banks, managed on a monthly basis; their infrequent use of announcements concerning the discount rate was mainly demonstrative.[47] This system enabled differentiated quantitative and qualitative micro-level regulation of the provision of credit-capital. Under "orthodox" central-bank regulation of private-bank lending by price (interest rate) and volume, capital will go by default to the places that offer the highest returns. In circumstances of severe material shortages, this would mean the flow of capital into commodity hoarding and speculation. In the free ("black") markets, this is where cash-capital did in fact flow. Micro-level qualitative direction of capital flows, by industry and by individual company, was thus quite different from "orthodox" macro-level regulation.[48] There thus emerged during the early postwar years a dual economy in which a free-market sector, much of it now consisting of illegal trading, existed next to a sector of administratively guided capital and resources, centered around the Priority Production System. Companies and people participated to varying extents in both, yielding a complex picture that requires its own specific analysis and theorization.

The new democratically minded corporatism also reinvigorated a stream of overt economic planning—that is, centralized direction of capital—that had first developed in a militarist context around 1940. Technocratic direction appears here as a free-floating element, a "neutral" developmental tool that was at home in both fascist-militarist and New Deal–social democratic contexts. It would have been at home also in an authoritarian-socialist context. This aptness to authoritarian use contrasts with the ethical, "progressive" self-understandings shared by leading planners like Arisawa Hiromi and Ōkita Saburō concerning their own life-missions.[49] "Renovationist militarism" and "technocratic democracy" were thus alternate, overlapping universes very close to one another. Their overt system goals were at odds, but their critical economic functions were imagined and guided by the same economic planners. In the quick historic sequence from the one to the other, we see from the side of policy a very temporally concentrated "experiment," as Ōkita and his fellows understood.

Ōkita Saburō and the members of the Coal Subcommittee had served as a technocratic brain trust for Prime Minister Yoshida. As a group, they fell out with him following his denunciation of labor leaders as "a lawless bunch" (*futei no yakara*) in his national radio address on New Year's morning of 1947. Yoshida broadcast this insult at a moment when government officials were engaged in critical negotiations with the coal miners' unions in an effort to get them to accept longer working hours to help resolve the national energy crisis. The early postwar moment of progressive–conservative national unity dissolved. Yoshida's attitude spurred forward the movement for a national general strike, to be staged February 1, which was intended to force the Yoshida cabinet to resign. The Coal Subcommittee's collaboration with Yoshida also fell into abeyance. Thus, just at the point when the Priority Production System was set to start, the lunchtime meetings ended, as Arisawa, Tōbata, Nakayama, Kaya, Hori Yoshiaki, Wada Hirō, and Ōkita all absented themselves. Ōkita, because of his disagreement with Yoshida, also resigned from his research position at the Foreign Ministry.[50]

The high tide of the postwar leftist surge, from the standpoint of the Japanese labor movement, is usually perceived to have come at this point, when General MacArthur banned the general strike and set a limit to direct political action. But the management of economic recovery continued to move in a more "leftward" direction. In this domain, limits of another sort were established by the Socialists' participation in the coalition governments of 1947–48, the last time the Socialists would be part of a Japanese cabinet until the even more ill-starred effort of the mid-1990s. Simultaneously and for the moment still externally to the Japanese system, policy shifts in Washington, D.C., set another sort of limit to the "leftward" movement, as discussed in the next chapter.

GHQ pushed Yoshida to do more about the economy. Far from counseling economic decontrol, U.S. authorities at this point continued to call for more effective control, of prices especially. MacArthur underlined this in a March 22, 1947, letter to Yoshida that urged strengthening the Economic Stabilization Board, saying that coordination, planning, and control were needed for industrial revival. The ESB was accordingly reorganized as of May 1. The secretariat was enlarged, and new bureaus were set up: Finance, Foreign Trade, Construction, and Supervision—the latter equipped with a staff of economic investigators.[51]

In the national elections of April 25, 1947, the Socialist Party gained 26 percent of the vote. This was more than either of the main conservative parties. Accordingly, the Socialists were able to put together a "middle way" coalition cabinet with the Democratic Party, led by Ashida Hitoshi, and the National Cooperative Party, led by Miki Takeo.[52] The new prime minister was the moderate socialist Katayama Tetsu (1887–1978), who was also Japan's first openly Christian prime minister. The new cabinet took office on June 1.

Socialist Party leaders took the British Labour Party as a model. Main planks of their program were coal nationalization (which was implemented by Britain's Labour government in January 1947) and a comprehensive welfare state, which the British socialists were also putting in place. The Democratic Party (formerly named the Progressive Party) sought to take a mediating position between the Liberal Party on the right and the Socialist Party on the left. They adopted the slogan "modified capitalism," reflecting the ideas of the Japan Committee for Economic Development (Keizai Dōyūkai), as described below. The Democratic Party's March 1947 platform thus called for a middle way between old-fashioned capitalism and socialism, "breaking away from the deep rooted evils of capitalism and modifying the unrealistic character of socialism."[53] The party saw the path to recovery as "democratizing industry on the basis of a comprehensive economic plan." It declared that it would work to "separate capital and management in large firms, seek partnership between management and workers, and in particular respect the important role of labor by making use of managerial councils and establishing a system of profit sharing." The National Cooperative Party espoused similar ideas. "Modified capitalism" thus had a basis in party politics.

It had an even stronger base in the bureaucracy, above all in the Economic Stabilization Board and in the Ministry of Commerce and Industry. As a government agency, the ESB did not openly espouse a political program, but the idea of "modified captitalism" describes what it did in practice. Arisawa Hiromi himself exemplifies the new "middle" position. Arisawa turned down repeated invitations to head the ESB, whose basic program he had designed, and remained at Tokyo University as chair of the Economics Faculty. He did serve as an influential adviser to the ESB. The new director-general of the ESB was Wada Hirō (1903–67), a former official in the Ministry of Agriculture and member of the Cabinet Planning Board (Kikakuin). With Inaba Hidezō, Wada had been arrested in the "Cabinet Planning Board incident" in 1941 for having socialist ideas and affiliations. As agriculture minister in Yoshida's first cabinet, Wada was responsible for the highly successful implementation of GHQ's land reform. Wada joined the Socialist Party and became a top leader of its left wing. He also headed the Price Office. Those who had participated in Yoshida's lunchtime meetings reunited in June 1947 in the "Wada ESB." Tsuru Shigeto was appointed an

ESB director. Ōkita Saburō resumed his career as a government official as chief of the ESB's Research Division, which was greatly enlarged. This was the heyday of the ESB, which was for a time a kind of economic control headquarters.

Equally critically and less expectedly, "modified capitalism" had a powerful platform in the business world itself, where the idea was championed by leaders among the younger generation of business managers. These leaders organized themselves in April 1946 as the Keizai Dōyūkai (literally: "Society of Economic Friends" but originally named in English the Japan Committee for Economic Development). These young managers were in many ways the business-world counterparts of the young "renovation bureaucrats" who had risen to influence in the 1930s. They promoted the idea of a dawning "age of management" that transcended old-fashioned "feudalistic" capitalism. To translate these terms into an alternate vocabulary, they reflected the transformation of the prewar "class society" into a postwar "system society."[54] The Keizai Dōyūkai thus rejected both the *zaibatsu* order of the 1920s and the state control of the 1940s and, in the context of the challenge from the working-class and leftwing movements, sought to define a new capitalist path. The Keizai Dōyūkai situated themselves politically as the progressive wing of the *zaikai*, the politically organized business world. Vaguely, they called for economic democratization via a "transformation of the labor issue."[55] Concretely, they called for broader participation in management by department and section managers. This vision of the bureaucratically organized firm as a kind of managerial republic is close to what came to be in many large Japanese companies. It is called "employee sovereignty" in many later analyses, though it was not company members as a whole who were sovereign but rather the managerial hierarchy as a body. The new managerial ideologists presented management as a technical function mediating various interests, with functions and prerogatives that were independent of the existing capitalist system.[56] One might also say that Keizai Dōyūkai members were maneuvering to protect their positions even in the event of socialization: whether capitalist or socialist in its ownership structure, modern industry would still require expert managers. This idea of the corporation as a public entity could also be a self-serving justification for receiving public investment funds. This too—the dispensing of direct government subsidies and RFB loans—was the specific context of the new tide in thought.

From the side of the business managers who adopted the idea, "modified capitalism" thus meant *managerial capitalism*. This idea is reflected also in the 1946 report of the Special Survey Committee, authored mainly by Ōkita Saburō: "able business managers, who are valuable national treasures, must be protected from the arbitrary nature of capital."[57] In fact, the idea of "separation of capital [ownership] and management," current also in the United States and Europe, was formulated and championed in the Japanese context in the late 1930s by Arisawa Hiromi, among others. It meshed with his advocacy then of a "controlled economy" and "state capitalism," reflecting Marxist planning ideals combined with the German theory of "total war."[58] Stripped of the latter burden, the postwar rhetoric of modified capitalism sounded shiny and democratic. It also reflected and described actually unfolding institutional realities.

On June 11, 1947, ten days after taking office, the new coalition cabinet proclaimed a program of emergency economic measures. Their goals were to increase production of capital goods, to create a "sound and planned" distribution system, and to end the inflationary spiral. The Emergency Economic Plan thus retightened the materials-allocation and rationing systems, as well as price and wage controls, with the goal of moving transactions out of the black market and into the official (controlled) economy. The Priority Production System was the core of the program. This was a return to more economic control after the movement to dismantle wartime controls led by Ishibashi Tanzan.

The Economic Stabilization Board now gained enormous latitude and autonomy. Its administrative powers were authorized by the Temporary Supply and Demand Adjustment Law of September 30, 1946, which "replaced the wartime General Mobilization Law" (in the words of an official EPA report) and provided the "legal basis for the centralized control upon production, distribution and consumption of essential materials and goods." Materials were rationed via a coupon system. "Public Corporations" (Kōdan) were set up to manage the distribution of coal, oil, fertilizer, and foodstuffs. They were also set up for foreign trade, industrial reconstruction, shipbuilding, and price adjustment. These Public Corporations were state agencies "adopted in lieu of the war-time control associations." Their capital was provided by government funds and RFB loans.[59]

In July 1947, the ESB released its first "Economic White Paper," which was inspired by the British Labour government's recent economic white paper. The lead author was the historian of business cycles Tsuru Shigeto, one of Schumpeter's favorite students. The main work on it was Ōkita Saburō's responsibility. The Economic White Paper inaugurated the authoritative and widely referenced series that was later carried on by the Economic Planning Agency, and it set an example that other government agencies followed. Simultaneously, Ōkita also directed the writing of an economic five-year plan, the Economic Rehabilitation Plan of 1948. If it had been adopted, this would have been postwar Japan's first five-year plan. Ōkita's view at the time indicates another connection between planning and "forced savings": the recovery of basic industries was being enabled by "forced savings based on the issue of credit by the government." This inflation-funded process was proceeding in postwar Japan as it already had in postwar France and elsewhere, "whether consciously or unconsciously." And in order to achieve the least inflation and greatest increase in production, *planning* was essential.[60]

The Katayama government, with GHQ backing, thus built up the Economic Stabilization Board into the main economic planning center of the national economy. The ESB also became a center of economic policing, and the work of economic policing instituted during the war continued. The Economic Investigation Board Law of August 1, 1948 authorized the establishment of a central office and forty-nine prefectural and regional offices, which were given broad powers of investigation and liaison with the police. Mass arrests of ordinary people for black-market transactions continued. Police made 1.22 million arrests for marketing infractions in 1946; 1.36 million in 1947; and 1.5 million in 1948.[61] This was the coercive and punitive face of the experiment in economic controls.

The benefits of reconstruction policies also began to be more widely distributed in 1948. Workers were now organized into unions and backed by a sympathetic government in which the Socialists were coalition partners. This was when wages for workers in more advantageous positions began to catch up with the inflation in living costs.[62] For business executives, this was an unwanted side of "modified capitalism," as were workers' claims for representation in management. An employers' counteroffensive followed in 1949, simultaneous with the "course reversal" in occupation policy directed by Joseph Dodge.

6.3 Inflation and Social Leveling

World war and postwar reconstruction had socially leveling effects internationally, whether along capitalist or communist lines.[63] This was true in the United States. It was even more the case in countries within the Eurasian war zones. Leveling effects were especially strong in Japan—among the strongest in the noncommunist world. Conscious leveling reforms, above all the land and labor reforms mandated by GHQ, had large and enduring effects. Land reform worked together with the unintended consequences of food shortages and inflation to redistribute wealth from the formerly privileged urban sector to the formerly exploited farm sector. In this and in some other dimensions, inflation itself was a powerful leveling force. In other ways, it produced new inequalities.

This question of the distribution of social production connects to a point made by Hayek: that to understand the effects of an increase of money in circulation, we need to consider *where* the additional money enters circulation. *Timing* is the second essential point in considering the redistributive effects of inflation. As Richard Cantillon pointed out in the aftermath of the Mississippi

Bubble, the people who benefit from an increase in the quantity of money are those whose incomes rise early in the course of the inflation. Those whose incomes rise later are the losers.[64] To expand on the point: analysts often imagine the national "money supply" as a homogenous quantitative aggregate, but this is a static abstraction that describes only one dimension of a dynamic and multidimensional reality. "Money supply" in this sense is also a conception of money as a stock, when in fact we are considering a set of processes, operating through a socially specific circuitry of monetary flows. Within this system of flows, there are "upstream" and "downstream" locations. That is, "money supply" processes have their own microhistorical and geographical structures. This is the question of the *social structure of money supply*, conceived as a set of processes.

The high-inflation period brought dramatic social shifts in the balance of wealth and purchasing power. The war itself constrained popular consumption, boosted corporate profits, squeezed medium and small businesses, and led state authorities to limit agricultural rents in the interest of effective food procurement. GHQ's directives in late 1945 to break up the biggest corporations, legalize labor unions, and redistribute farmland to tenants had more profound redistributive effects. The collapse of production and the inflation itself had effects that acted even faster on the distribution of income and wealth.

The most extraordinary transformation was in agriculture. About half of the national population was engaged in farming, but in 1944 the agricultural share of national income was only about 13 percent. Rural Japan was poor in both relative and absolute terms. After the war, the agricultural share ballooned to about one-third of national income in 1946. Food shortages and inflation both benefitted farmers, who enjoyed considerable price-setting power in illegal markets. As a sector of society that typically carried heavy debt loads, agricultural households benefited doubly by the way inflation erased the burden of monetary debts. Former tenant farmers benefited triply, because the interaction of inflation and land reform allowed them to purchase the land they had tilled for practically nothing.[65] In effect, this combination of land reform and inflation amounted to a comprehensive agrarian debt-relief program. In this respect it was comparable to simultaneous land reforms in the Communist-governed areas of North China and in North Korea, which stabilized and solidified Communist Party rule. Land reform in Japan ended up stabilizing conservative party hegemony.

In 1930, "rentier income" in the form of interest and rent receipts formed a total of 24 percent of national income. By 1944, this portion had fallen to about 15 percent. After the war, rental and interest income shrank to almost nothing. In 1960, the two together still formed only 6 percent of national income. Even though new (interest-bearing) credit was being created in great volume in 1960, interest income comprised only about 4 percent of national income, as opposed to nearly 13 percent in 1930.[66] Landlord and rentier income thus had little weight within the High-Speed Growth economy.

In many national instances of inflation during the twentieth century, the wages of organized industrial workers have been indexed to the cost of living, resulting in at least the acquiescence of organized labor to inflationary policies. In occupation-era Japan, organized labor was a new and still poorly incorporated political element. Systematic wage indexing in Japan began when electric-power workers organized in the Densan union succeeded in tying their wages to the cost of living. This set a new standard framework for the national wage system, putting a floor under the real-wage losses that better positioned employees would suffer from inflation. Densan workers were also at the forefront of pushing for comprehensive societal planning and for labor involvement in management.[67] As a group, however, industrial workers suffered greatly from the decline in real wages brought about by inflation. In fact, the inflation's most vehement critics were the working-class organizations and especially the Communists, who persistently criticized inflation-funded subsidies as a giveaway to big business and a theft from everyone else. Officials in GHQ's Economic and Scientific Section agreed that inflation reduced workers' standards of living while enriching the same industrialists who had profited by the war and who now profiteered from shortages.[68] Industrialists also gained from the fact that inflation caused the value of their own "necessary" debts (as Schumpeter described them) to dwindle to insignificance.

Industrial subsidies, working in a poorly modulated "Schumpeterian" process, were a primary source of postwar inflation. The realities of this process contrast with a common view of twentieth-century inflation in general, which sees inflation as a political result of the advent of mass-based politics. More specifically, one often reads in the postwar U.S. literature the claim that inflation is driven by the wage demands of industrial workers, distant though workers would seem to be from the actual processes of money creation. In an influential explanation developed by Charles Maier, for instance, inflation is a "major form of distributive conflict," a way of handling class conflict without directly dealing with it as such. Weakly based political coalitions seem to be especially prone to inflationary financing for this reason. This idea fits occupation-era Japan. But the political coalitions behind twentieth-century inflation, according to Maier, tended to be led by the working class, and inflation typically meant the "redistribution of resources toward the working class."[69] Japan's experience contradicts this explanation. As we will see, however, U.S. Federal Reserve economists in 1948 would interpret Japan's inflation as a consumption-led inflation. In fact, the sources of inflation lay elsewhere. In the twentieth-century United States as well, investigation would surely reveal that workers' paychecks were not the first stop that newly created money made upon springing out of the banking system and onto the stage of economic life. The heart of this story may lie in the balance of mass savings versus mass consumption, although here, too, not quite in the way usually presented (see 12.1.1).

Can this redistributional view of inflation be combined with Schumpeter's picture of self-liquidating developmental inflation? These are not "either–or" situations but rather a case of multiple complex balances of gains and losses. These gains and losses vary across sectors, and indeed from one firm or one household to the next, and they vary across time, even in the very short term. High inflation brings these distributional questions into sharper focus, but they are present always and everywhere that enterprise is funded by newly created means of credit or cash payment. That is, a monetary redistribution of resources—"inflationary appropriation"—happens whenever new monetary claims are created. It is intrinsic to bank-based capitalism even in macroscopic conditions of no inflation or deflation. Even in a deflationary macro-level environment, purchasing power is being created or extinguished in socially differential ways, and deflation, too, always has redistributional effects.

6.4 Taxation as Monetary Regulation

Postwar inflation reflected shortages of goods, and it reflected more money chasing these scarce goods. In this second, money-creation aspect, inflation functioned as a kind of taxation. Government funded its own operations and those of essential industries by creating new money and credit and was thus on the receiving end of this transfer of wealth. On the providing end, the general public, as recipients or holders of depreciating money, ended up paying. The people paid; the government and its clients received: this is the essential relationship that constitutes taxation. Yet this kind of fiscal inflation is not literally a tax in the normal usage of the word, for taxation also has the sense of being a *direct* contribution. This raises the question of why direct taxes are necessary at all, when governments can easily create means of payment. More simply: *What is taxation?*[70]

In accord with the "common sense" that money is an independently existing substance, it is commonly thought that governments must tax people in order to "get the money" to fund government operations. By the middle of the twentieth century, this was not the way things worked in most of the world, and certainly not in Japan. Governments and banks could create money readily enough, and finance, as such, was not a limiting factor in either war or reconstruction. On the other hand, the inflation caused by new money and credit became an important limiting factor. Here is where taxation was needed, to "absorb" the "excess" of new purchasing power that found its way into the hands of people other than those on whom the financial authorities were aiming to bestow it. In practice, this meant final consumers. Taxation thus served to preserve the value of monetary (or debt) claims—it was needed as a means of regulating the value of money.

In this, taxation functioned in a way parallel to personal monetary savings. In times of stabilized currency values, personal saving is an alternative mechanism for absorbing purchasing power. Personal saving also functioned this way under the mandatory saving schemes of the wartime period, which worked together with price controls and rationing to limit price increases. In the end, of course, these so-called savings programs were not really savings at all for those concerned, as these supposed stores of virtual wealth depreciated into insignificance after the war. After monetary values were restabilized in the 1950s, voluntary saving resumed this modulating function. During the first postwar years, however, high inflation made it a losing proposition to save money. Economic hardship made saving in any case impossible for most households. This put all of the pressure on taxation. In fact, the function of taxation in modulating a system of inflationary financing is so vital that taxation itself is a core part of the social constitution of money.[71]

By the 1940s, the function of taxation in absorbing purchasing power "after the fact" seemed obvious to economists. Carl Shoup, a U.S. tax expert who designed a comprehensive reform of the Japanese tax system in 1949, himself did a study in 1941 on how to decide "the amount of taxation needed to avert inflation."[72] In theory, a fair and well-designed tax system is also much more just and rational than inflation, where the apportionment of social costs and benefits is anything but open and transparent. Before the Shoup reforms, Japan's tax system was itself far from fair, and it is hard to say which method was the more unjust.

By 1948, taxation was also showing some success in achieving monetary control. As GHQ economist and Shoup commission adviser Martin Bronfenbrenner described it, the use of taxes to absorb purchasing power in the hands of the public "checked a rampant inflation," in advance of Joseph Dodge's arrival in February 1949. At least it had moderated inflation significantly. But this was accomplished "with a patchwork tax system" held together with "chewing gum and baling wire."[73] "To raise the aggregate amounts required to check inflation," Bronfenbrenner said, "a bewildering multitude of direct and indirect taxes were in force." Reliance on taxes to control inflation pushed this system to its limits.

As the pressure on the tax system increased, it seemed to tax authorities that the nation faced a potential tax revolt with a dangerously revolutionary edge. In a postoccupation memoir published in 1952, Ikeda Hayato, who spent the first half of his career as a tax official, frankly acknowledged the truth of the popular postwar understanding that "if you pay your taxes honestly, you'll be hung up to dry."[74] (The Japanese metaphor might suggest, more than putting out the laundry, a picture of hanging up gutted fish or squid.) Ikeda explained that taxation in the high-inflation period was caught in a "vicious circle." Tax collectors were pressed by their superiors to deliver more taxes, so they squeezed taxpayers harder. This provoked more evasion and resistance, leading to reassessments of millions of taxpayers and ever more resistance. The inflation made people's incomes appear to swell in monetary terms, which made more and more lower-income earners subject to the income tax, notwithstanding the catastrophic decline in actual living standards. Ikeda indicated that taxes took in a total 24 percent of national income in 1948 and 26 percent in 1949. But this statistic does not begin to tell the story. Leftist critics pointed out that in current impoverished circumstances, two-thirds of household spending went for food alone. Out of the one-third of household income that remained after eating—insufficiently—taxes thus took almost 60 percent. Relative to actual consumption levels, Japanese taxes were therefore outstandingly high in international comparison.[75] The combination of inflation and taxation drove workers to insist, as a matter of family survival, that they be paid in goods, which could not effectively be taxed. Tax resistance also took on a desperate edge.

Under pressure to deliver their quotas, tax collectors adopted more forceful methods. Tax collection also became more uneven, arbitrary, and corrupt. At the center of the national tax system was the income tax, which relied on self-assessment. This system functioned during the war, according to Ikeda, but broke down in the postwar environment. As Bronfenbrenner summarized it, in this environment of ubiquitous underreporting, "arbitrary mass reassessments were carried out periodically at wholesale, as each local tax office strove to meet or exceed its quota of collections"—

> Honest and dishonest suffered alike, and taxes were collected in the presence of armed Occupation troops, almost literally at gun-point. Widespread evasion was met with widespread extortion, and accompanied by widespread corruption of the underpaid tax personnel. The tax collector had replaced the policeman as the nation's bogey; "bad taxes" were a main economic talking point of the Japanese Communist Party. Capital accumulation, either individual or corporate, required tax evasion almost as a *sine qua non*.[76]

Taxation turned into "a fight with the people as a whole," as Ikeda recalled it. Groups of angry taxpayers subjected individual tax collectors to *tsurushi-agé*—ad hoc people's courts. There was an outbreak of attacks on tax offices. The antitax movement led by the Communist Party developed out of this situation.[77] Facing this side of things, Ikeda was much less sanguine about inflationary finance than was Ishibashi Tanzan. As Ikeda explained it, his own enduring desire to cut taxes developed out of this situation; and he understood halting inflation to be a prerequisite for cutting taxes.

6.5 The Limits of Modified Capitalism

In 1948, as production began to recover and taxation intensified, inflation did begin to slow. There has been, therefore, a strong feeling in Japan ever since that time that Joseph Dodge's 1949 deflation policy was excessive and mostly unneeded when it came to controlling inflation, even among those who have acknowledged the Dodge plan as a decisive and mainly beneficial turn away from economic controls. For producers, the great inflation also ended before it did for consumers. Black-market prices for producer goods increased by nearly four times in 1947 but then largely stabilized early in 1948.[78] Consumers, to their detriment, lived at this point in a more "free market" economy than did large producers. By late 1948, however, the extreme inflation of prices for consumer goods was also largely over.

At the same time, it was also clear that the administered price system was itself forcing ever more adjustments and intervention. Like drug therapy, each new measure induced bad side effects, which demanded further interventions, and so on—the government was trying to substitute direct controls for the market system's self-governing capacities. Controls also caused evasion, which required more policing and more controls. This compounding of complexity began to be reminiscent of the extreme irrationalities of the war economy. These measures were mostly understood to be temporary by their advocates, but once established they acquired their own institutional inertia. On the other hand, it seemed equally obvious to Japanese observers that simply to "leave things to nature" would be like turning everything over to the black-market system, and would mean a slide back into a vicious cycle of shrinking reproduction.

Under the Priority Production System, new capital funds, invested according to highly rational considerations, were created in an inflationary way. But high inflation itself guided business investment decisions in socially irrational directions, by encouraging investment into a socially counterproductive (and proinflationary) stockpiling of scarce goods. In fact, inflation tended to force the pace of investment, spurring further investment expansion as companies with access to credit raced to turn monetary claims into real goods. An ESS report in March 1948 expressed the concern that "industry is rehabilitating or expanding ahead of its current requirements on borrowed funds as a hedge against inflation."[79]

This was another side of the picture of low reported corporate profits indicated above: for multiple reasons, investment, especially in stocks of goods, seemed much more advantageous than the taking of money profits.

The subsidy system did help production to recover. It was also wasteful, poorly controlled, and increasingly corrupt. The system was widely criticized on all of these counts; its inequities were more sharply felt to the extent that one was outside of its core circuits. The excesses of the credit-subsidy system were also the immediate political cause of the collapse of the center–left coalition.

The Socialist Party had hoped to initiate the outright socialization of production by nationalizing the coal mines, but this project went nowhere. In a cabinet shuffle in March 1948, Democratic Party president Ashida Hitoshi became prime minister, and the three-party coalition continued for a few months longer. It was brought down by the bribery scandal involving the Shōwa Electric Company (Shōwa Denkō), a major recipient of funding from the Reconstruction Finance Bank. In October, Economic Stabilization Board director Kurusu Takeo was arrested, and the cabinet resigned. Former prime minister Ashida was arrested in December. The scandal also greatly exposed the workings of the Reconstruction Finance Bank itself.[80]

The "modified capitalism" coalition thus collapsed in October 1948. Pending national elections, scheduled for January 1949, Liberal Party president Yoshida Shigeru returned to office as prime minister at the head of a caretaker cabinet.[81] This was the beginning of Yoshida's long term as prime minister, which would last through 1954. Yoshida would later move to gut the Economic Stabilization Board. The business community also rejected the idea of "modified capitalism" in 1948. Thus, political authority swung back to the conservative Liberal Party, making "middle way" politics and "modified capitalism" the story of a road not traveled. At least not overtly. In less visible ways, however, and not under that name, the ideas of modified capitalism, with the critical omission of a managerial role for labor, were also the wave of Japan's near future. The "state control" tendency would be partially rolled back during the occupation's course reversal after 1949, but only partially. The "bank control" tendency would gain new force, while continuing to be guided by BoJ and MoF direction.

In considering the failure of the socialization program, Arisawa Hiromi looked back to Weimar Germany. In Berlin in 1926, Arisawa had begun a detailed study of Germany's postwar revolution and counterrevolution, inflation, and interim stabilization. "I never dreamt," he said, "that twenty years later my native country would fall into the same fate." But it had:

> I myself was placed in the midst of practically the same situations and
> problems that I had taken as my research subject twenty years ago in

Berlin. The international environment in which Japan was put had fundamentally different features from Germany's situation. The economic difficulties were more severe than Germany's. However for that reason, I thought all the more that Japan's postwar economic reconstruction and the solution to the inflation had to be based solidly on socialization, and that the thoroughgoing completion of democratization must not dissolve simply into a struggle for higher wages.

Instead:

Historically, I have to think that things have repeated. . . . The tracks of Japanese economic reconstruction are now being laid out according to one policy. It is already hard to change. Since the end of the war, one period has almost passed.[82]

INTERLUDE (DEFLATION)

"Total war" under modern conditions calls for a concentration of effort much more stringent than the mechanism of capitalist markets can achieve. Wartime planning by government in fact suspends the normal operation of capitalist processes. In doing so it develops, on the one hand, economic structures and situations and, on the other, new social organs and positions of power which do not automatically disappear with the emergency that brought them into existence. They have to be liquidated, if at all, by a series of distinct measures which naturally meet resistance. We have seen that the outcome of the ensuing struggle will not depend on any abstract desirability of a return to prewar ways but on the political forces marshaled for and against it.

—Joseph A. Schumpeter, "Capitalism in the Postwar World" (1943)

Deflation is surgery not therapy.

—Joseph M. Dodge, "Inflation Notes" (1949)

Wartime planning, succeeded by recovery planning, went far beyond the hitherto normal operations of capitalist markets. In Japan, the wartime control system came much closer—in detail—to the Soviet model of centralized planning than is generally realized. At the same time, it was also true that "the war was financed *as an enterprise* through the purchase of goods and credit operations," as Schumpeter had said of World War I.[1] But this "enterprise" did not repay the social investment by returning goods to the social stream. It only consumed resources, while creating immense financial debts. The great inflation followed, driven forward by the demands of reconstruction finance. Both inflation and the materials-mobilization type of planning would be liquidated together—partially—by political action in 1949. This chapter investigates the role played in this "restoration" movement by the United States–directed deflation policy of 1949–50. Japanese responses in the domain of financial capital provision are discussed in chapter 8.

During the first three years of the occupation, American reformers performed one sort of social surgery in Japan, by excising perceived militarist, fascist, and feudal institutions and attempting to transplant the institutions of political liberalism.[2] They broke up many large enterprises and radically destabilized the Japanese business world. In the face of a more or less disapproving occupation stance, Japanese authorities managed to keep big companies on life support via a massive flow of reconstruction financing, or capital creation in Schumpeter's sense. The deflationary surgery conducted by money doctor Joseph M. Dodge (1890–1964) was another kind of operation.[3] Dodge intended to get the government out of business and restore normal capital circulation. For Dodge, this meant radically restricting new credit creation. He launched this program immediately on his arrival to Tokyo in February 1949, enforcing a "one-stroke" stabilization plan that ended government price subsidies and ended lending by the Reconstruction Finance Bank. These were the main pillars of the Priority Production System. While Schumpeter's entrepreneurial impresario, empowered by drafts of newly created credit-money, played the expansive, Jovian part in the cyclical process of development, here, in a concentrated form, was the saturnine, destructive side of Schumpeter's "creative-destructive" process. This settling of accounts was quite unwelcome to the Japanese business world.

7.1 Joseph Dodge and the Theory of Capital Restriction

Schumpeter's explanation of how new capital comes onto the stage was explored in chapter 3. In this process, bankers have an "authorizing" role in advancing to entrepreneurs new monetary claims to social resources. Bankers also play a constraining and validating role. As Schumpeter explained, this role has a strongly "critical, checking, admonitory" aspect. The question of bankers' own moral character looms large in his explanation, as it does in the traditional self-presentation of many bankers themselves.[4] Joseph Dodge, head of the American Bankers Association (ABA) and president of the Detroit Bank, exemplified this face of the capitalist process, in both his theoretical understanding and in his own conservative and upright character. To control inflation, Dodge thought, one needed a complement of what can be described as "negative" virtues:

> The art of financial management calls for patience, restraint, and the steadfast pursuit of long-term objectives, rather than direct and dramatic action. What is wanted is a maximum effect with a minimum of direct action. This can usually be done with the remedy of a vigorous and ruthless dose of credit control.[5]

Officially, Dodge insisted that his program be called disinflation, not deflation, and his comments that deflation was surgery, to be conducted via ruthless doses of credit control, were not for public consumption. Privately, he did not observe this nicety.

Joseph Dodge, whom everyone called Joe, was a down-to-earth, no-nonsense man. The son of a Detroit sign painter, he was, as a banker, a self-made man. His formal education ended with high school, but that education was evidently a solid one. He learned his trade working as a bookkeeper and then worked as a bank examiner and accountant. By the 1920s he was managing the finances of Detroit's largest automobile dealership. The depression of the 1930s was especially hard in Detroit. After cutting his own salary and doing his best to rationalize the dealership's accounts, Dodge voluntarily resigned his position as vice president of the dealership because he thought it could no longer afford to pay him. After several months of unemployment, he returned to banking, and at the Detroit Bank he rose to the post of president, greatly expanding the bank's business on the basis of U.S. government credit programs.[6] During the war, Dodge worked in the U.S. military purchasing administration and was appointed chairman of the War Department Price Adjustment Board. He gained such a reputation there that he was elected president of the American Bankers Association in 1947. In 1945–46, he served as a financial official in the U.S. occupation of Germany. Germany's experiences of postwar stabilization thus provided an important reference point for Dodge, too, both personally and intellectually. After returning from Germany, Dodge as ABA president promoted an anti-inflation campaign in America. Later, he would also help negotiate the Austrian peace treaty. In February 1949, the U.S. government dispatched Dodge to Japan to take command of monetary stabilization. He was not eager to do this, and it took personal pressure from President Truman to get him to return to government service.[7]

Dodge's thinking on inflation is revealed in a forty-five-page treatise titled "Inflation Notes," which he wrote out, apparently for his own use, after his first return from Japan in the summer of 1949. He "selected, abstracted, and paraphrased" these notes mainly from Constantino Bresciani-Turroni's study of Germany's inflation after World War I, supplemented by books about post–World War II currency stabilization in Belgium, Italy, and France by Leon Dupriez, Bruno Foa, and Pierre Dieterlen and Charles Rist.[8] Bresciani-Turroni particularly seems to have opened Dodge's eyes to the role of industrial subsidies in Germany's post–World War I inflation, and in Japan's current inflation.

Dodge was also convinced that revival could happen only through a "stabilization crisis," the essence of which was *the lack of working capital for business.*[9]

This restraint of credit creation would manifest itself in high rates of interest, the closing of unproductive firms, suspension of new plant construction, and the rationalization (or downsizing) of production—in other words, an induced economic depression in the style of the 1920s. Indeed, Dodge seemed to believe that it was a moral necessity for Japan as a nation to fully manifest and understand its own true poverty; only then could the nation begin on the difficult road to recovery.

In this connection, the differences between the inflationary versus the deflationary redeployment of people and resources are worth considering further. In the inflationary process of "new combination" described by Schumpeter, banks' provision of newly created monetary claims gives entrepreneurs the ability to hire or purchase existing services of labor and productive resources. They are able to *preempt* these productive services by hiring or purchasing them at higher prices. This is the process of "buying before" and "buying for more" (see 3.3). The liquidation process promoted by Dodge reversed this order of operations. First, a lack of working capital for business forced the release of productive services by squeezing firms to consolidate and downsize, and by bankrupting some of them, idling people and resources. The restraint of capital creation thus "freed" workers and productive resources from their present employments and made them available for eventual redeployment elsewhere. The stabilization crisis, as Dodge saw it, thus ended "the excessive immobilization of capital which occurs during the inflation."[10] The surviving enterprises that end up rehiring these laid-off workers or purchasing and redeploying these liquidated resources will be able to hire or purchase them *for less*. One can describe waves of entrepreneurial inflation as "hot" phases of profuse, multiplicitous growth. Periods of deflation, typically promoted by bankers concerned to preserve the value of monetary claims (i.e., debts), are "cold" phases of consolidation and aggregation. In the case of the inflationary redeployment of resources, there are multiple claimants for limited resources: it is "a race for means of production," owing to the creation of new claims. Investment comes first and saving after. Contrariwise, the deflationary release of resources creates pools of unclaimed productive services—it raises the ratio of productive services to monetary claims, by restricting monetary claims. Bank of Japan governor Ichimada Hisato described this, also in the summer of 1949, as the shift from a "sellers' market" to a "buyers' market."[11] In an inflationary "hot" phase, the benefit accrues to those who have superior access to new claims (new money) and to those who hurry. In a deflationary "cold" phase, the benefit accrues to those already holding monetary claims ("old money") and to those who wait. Saving may seem to exceed investment, and to precede it. Significantly, the latter conjunctural situation more nearly corresponds to the scenario described by Marx, who understood capital as concretized *past* labor. This is not surprising, for Marx came of age in a long era of price deflation, which ran in Europe from 1815 to 1850. The fact has not been noticed and its implications not appreciated, but the capitalism Marx first anatomized, with its falling prices and reserve armies of the unemployed, was that of an age of systemic deflation.[12]

7.2 The Sphere of International Capital

This book focuses on the domestic creation of money-capital within a national economy. Around the world, most national economies became much more domestically oriented in the early postwar period, and international investment remained subject to state controls. This was very much true in Japan. Nonetheless, the outer world of international monetary circulation impinged on the sphere of domestic capital creation, often in determinative ways. Access to U.S. dollar capital served as a license granting access to a field of high-tech capital goods and imported materials otherwise beyond the reach of entrepreneurs, in Japan and in the rest of the world. The creation of U.S. dollar credit-capital was, like the creation of domestic yen capital, an act of social will and imagination, but it was one whose control then belonged exclusively to U.S. institutions.[13] The provision of long-term foreign capital loans was also political in the strictest sense, in that it was decided through negotiations at the highest circles of the government and banking worlds, rather than through a process of bidding by a large number of agents in a competitive market.

7.2.1 Headquarters of the International Capitalist System

"According to the Bretton Woods Agreement, international exchange transactions and loans and investment in the postwar period will be placed under the unified control and influence of the powerful international financial institutions headquartered in the United States"—this was the view of Ōkita Saburō and his coauthors in the 1946 "Special Survey" report.[14] As a result of World War II, the Wall Street money market became "the headquarters of the capitalist system," to borrow Schumpeter's phrase—of the whole capitalist world, a world within which even London and its empire occupied a contained and secondary position. The business of the money-center banks was to create credit capital: orders to the "individual divisions," constituting "plans for future development" (see 3.4). These capital orders now structured a global field of resource circulation. It was in this enlarged role that Wall Street bankers approached the remaking of Japan, in which they showed a new interest after 1947. They did this from peak positions within the U.S. central government administration itself.

In September 1947, as part of a great and mostly unheralded reconstitution of the U.S. government structure, the Department of Defense was created. A primary organizer of this enterprise was James Forrestal (1892–1949), who as the first secretary of defense personalized and helped to institutionalize the postwar Wall Street–Pentagon nexus. Forrestal was also a self-made man to a degree unusual in the "Eastern establishment" of the time, rising from a modest background to become president of the Wall Street investment bank Dillon, Read and Company. As part of the informal foreign-lending cartel of the 1920s, Dillon, Read had been active in lending to Germany especially. It also did business with Japan, arranging bond issues for Daidō Electric Power and Tokyo Electric Power.[15] During World War II, Franklin Roosevelt appointed Forrestal undersecretary of the navy, in charge of procurement and production. This position placed Forrestal at a critical administrative interface in the military-industrial complex at the moment when it was taking shape. In 1944, Forrestal was promoted to secretary of the navy. He was also close to the "Japan crowd" around former ambassador Joseph Grew, who favored a negotiated peace with Japan.[16]

Forrestal's deputy was another Wall Street investment banker, General William Draper, Jr. Draper had been Forrestal's number-two man at Dillon, Read, where he became vice president in 1937. During the Pacific War, Draper served as a regimental commander (far under MacArthur). He was then appointed chief of the Economic Section of the Allied Control Council in Germany and worked as economic adviser to General Lucius Clay. This made Draper the chief official in charge of economic policy in the American occupation zone of Germany. Joseph Dodge served at the time as finance executive there.[17] When Forrestal became secretary of defense in September 1947, he appointed Draper undersecretary of the army, giving him oversight of the occupations of both Japan and Germany. In effect, Draper now became the final authority for the economic decisions governing the latter part of the occupation.

The administrative ascent of bankers like Forrestal and Draper was part of a great restoration of Wall Street's political fortunes. The original consolidation of peak U.S. financial markets in Wall Street went back to the late nineteenth century. During World War I, Wall Street banks, chiefly J. P. Morgan and Company, rose to international primacy by financing the war enterprise of the British and French states. In the 1920s, U.S. banks began to provide long-term capital to foreign central and local governments and to foreign public utilities. This wave of international lending began with giant consortium loans to the Japanese and German governments in 1924, connected to the deflationary "stabilization" campaign of those years. The Wall Street banks also funded a wave of foreign investment by U.S. firms. Thus U.S. credit capital began to shape development in numerous countries. But this was also an unstable and in fact destabilizing kind of international primacy, as was shown in the serial collapses of foreign loans, U.S. capital markets, the international gold standard, and large swaths of the U.S. domestic banking system in the years 1929–33. The collapse of the financial bubble discredited the money-center banks, and the inauguration of Franklin D. Roosevelt and a populist-minded Democratic congress in 1933 opened them to political attack.[18] The age when top Wall Street bankers had enjoyed casual access to the highest levels of government ended, and the years from 1933 to 1939 were politically a brief "winter period" for Wall Street.

The war in Europe in 1939 and the U.S. entrance into the war and renewal of the United States–British alliance in December 1941 produced a turn back toward Wall Street by the Roosevelt administration.[19] But simultaneously, as in other countries, the war subordinated the interests of financial capital to those of production. War brought business recovery, but it also brought a system of formal and informal controls over materials, wages, prices, and capital. All of these had the effect of extending the New Deal controls to a new level.[20] In the United States as in Japan, the war thus institutionalized a kind of government-business interpenetration that may well be called "modified capitalism," as Ōuchi Hyōe suggested. This corporate-government partnership was animated by a new sense of world leadership.

In the U.S. congressional elections of November 1946, the Republican Party won majorities in both houses of Congress. This reaction was in part a broad-based public rejection of the wartime controlled economy. But—to return to Schumpeter's comment quoted at the opening of this chapter—the new economic structures developed in the United States by the war and the "new social organs and positions of power" were only partially liquidated. It was much more the case that new structures of power were consolidated—but as happened also in Japan, they were consolidated in a semiprivatized way. In the balance of power between Wall Street and Washington, D.C., there was now a partial shift back toward Wall Street. Big banking and financial interests began to weigh in on military and foreign-affairs questions, and a comprehensive shift in policy followed. Working within a Democratic Party presidential administration that still held to many New Deal tenets, a more conservative group of financiers thus moved into key executive positions. "Typically from big business, big finance, and big law circles in the Northeast," in the words of GHQ official Theodore Cohen, these top officials of the State and Defense departments shared a "remarkably uniform" viewpoint that was internationalist, economically orthodox, and antipopulist. They were also leading architects and advocates of the new

Cold War system. Forrestal was a senior spokesman among this new group of policymakers, who included army secretary Kenneth Royall and State Department planning chief George Kennan.[21]

Although it is not the focus of this book, the Cold War context was transformative, and it cannot help but enter the story. Joseph Dodge himself remained focused on fiscal questions, but in recruiting him for the job, President Truman had emphasized not only the importance of "the economic situation in Japan" but also "its relation to what has been happening in China."[22] Historians have also studied the Cold War context of the occupation's "reverse course" in detail.[23] Here, it is analytically useful to set that question mainly to one side, in order to focus on the question of capital. Had there been no Cold War, questions of postwar inflation, deflation, reconstruction, and stabilization would have remained. At an abstract level, of course, the struggle between U.S.-centered *capitalism* and state-socialist systems of economic governance has everything to do with the present subject. To frame the question of the Cold War in capital-system terms: what U.S. financial leaders feared was the prospect of a contracting sphere of private credit-capital circulation. They perceived this danger at the level of the whole international economy, and they perceived it at the domestic national level, within "mixed" national political economies that had expanding publicly owned sectors.

At the same time that Japanese officials were inventing the economic bureaucracy of the postwar developmentalist state, U.S. officials thus created the bureaucracy of their own postwar "national security state"—the Department of Defense, Central Intelligence Agency, and National Security Council, all three established September 18, 1947. These agencies gave institutional—and budgetary—structure to the Cold War system and sustained its momentum as a kind of permanent "emergency" system.[24] The point is significant for the American system of credit-capital creation also. In the postwar U.S. economy, the government's issuance, through the banking system, of a very large, regularized flow of government debts—promises to pay—became the prime channel for the entry of new "high-powered money" into the system (see 12.1.2).

7.2.2 The Financial Course Reversal in the Occupied Territories

As we have seen in the cases of both Japan and America, policy experimentation that would arouse intense opposition at home is much more freely carried out under the administrative despotism that can be practiced in an occupied territory. The democratic-reformist phase of the U.S. occupation of Japan was one kind of "experiment on a living body." William Draper and Joseph Dodge then conducted a politically opposite sort of experiment. In 1950, GHQ economist

Martin Bronfenbrenner called the Dodge plan "an orientalized picture of what [U.S.] domestic economic policy might now be" if the Republican Party had won the presidency in 1948—and "a test-tube version of what it may become in the future if financiers increase their influence in its framing."[25] This was prescient, for when the Republicans did win the presidency in 1952, President Eisenhower brought Joseph Dodge to Washington as his first budget director and raised the status of that position to cabinet rank. But what Dodge would be able to do in Washington was strictly limited compared to his domain of authority in Japan. Occupied Japan, now itself the captive social laboratory in someone else's empire, thus experienced the shifting political winds in Washington in an intensified fashion, whether more liberal or more conservative.

The policy shift was carried out first in Germany, which was then a much greater focus of U.S. concern. United States policy there followed a two-stage sequence of reform followed by consolidation, broadly parallel to that in Japan. Directly on being named to office in September 1947, army undersecretary Draper led a mission to Germany and recommended that policy be reoriented from its emphasis on reparations and de-Nazification and toward the rebuilding of German industry. De-Nazification essentially ended in Germany in 1949. MacArthur and Dodge echoed these thoughts in regard to Japan. The problem was no longer to keep Japan down, as Dodge explained to an American audience in the summer of 1949—"our problem is to keep Japan up."[26] Dodge was here quoting MacArthur, who had himself been quoting Winston Churchill's new view of Germany: the stories continued to run in parallel.

Differences remained over what it meant to "keep up" a country. Like Japanese officials, German officials tended to emphasize "production recovery first," as opposed to the "monetary stabilization first" approach favored by U.S. authorities. In Germany, the Colm-Dodge-Goldsmith monetary reform plan of 1946 had recommended against pursuing production recovery first, but full implementation of monetary reform was delayed. As Germany's recovery lagged and inflation continued, the feelings of the German public, recalling the post–World War I hyperinflation, swung toward the need for currency reform as a precondition of recovery. A German currency reform was carried through in 1948, and rapid industrial recovery followed. The German currency reform thus appeared to have better early results than the Dodge Line in Japan. Part of this was a question of timing, for the German economy faced renewed problems during the international recession of 1949. In Japan's case, the 1949 recession hit the country simultaneously with Dodge's deflation plan in a kind of double shock.

Looking at Japan, members of the new group of policymakers in Washington were dismayed at the influence of New Dealers within GHQ and at the extent of the democratic reforms they had implemented, which George Kennan and others derided as "socialization." Draper followed his September 1947 visit to Germany with a trip to Japan, where he pressed GHQ officials to end the purge of business leaders and to halt the breakup of the *zaibatsu* groups.[27] In March 1948, Draper went to Japan a second time as part of the Draper-Johnston mission, which was chaired by Percy Johnston, chairman of the board of Chemical Bank. They recommended a revision of policy similar to the changes Draper had directed in Germany. This was the first articulation of the policy that later became known as the Dodge Line. In the western zones of Germany, occupation authorities had broken up the big banks during the reform period. After the occupation ended, German financial authorities then painstakingly reconsolidated the national banking system. Trustbusters in GHQ's Economic and Scientific Section also wanted to break up the big banks in Japan, but already in 1948, officials in the ESS Financial Division viewed the bank deconcentration in Germany negatively and worked to block similar measures in Japan. The Draper-Johnston mission backed them up, recommending that the banks, including the Industrial Bank of Japan, be taken off of the deconcentration list. Thus, the Mitsui, Mitsubishi, and Sumitomo *zaibatsu* were broken up into hundreds of separate companies, but the *zaibatsu* banks remained uniquely concentrated and undisturbed.[28] After the occupation, these banks formed the nucleus of the reconstituted *keiretsu* corporate groups.

The Draper-Johnston mission was followed in June 1948 by an economists' mission led by Ralph Young of the Federal Reserve Board's Research Division. This mission was organized by the Treasury and the Federal Reserve, whom Draper in effect enlisted as allies against MacArthur. The Young mission spent eighteen days in Japan and concluded that it was necessary to restrict popular consumption and reduce the real wages of Japanese workers—which, as they reported, were still only 65 percent of their 1934–36 levels. Thus, the report came close to counseling a 1920s-style stabilization depression. This harsh and uninformed verdict was opposite to GHQ's policy up to that time, which had been to raise real wages. In addition, the inflation itself had functioned as a system of popular austerity, or "forced savings." Now, Draper and his allies argued that inflation reflected excess consumption and that deflationary austerity was the solution. As they saw it, anything that increased domestic consumer demand would only use up a country's resources that could otherwise be put into exports and industrial reconstruction.[29] MacArthur resisted the new, financially oriented line, but by the beginning of 1949, he had largely lost control of occupation policy, and Draper's group was in charge. This movement was backed by a hard-edged public attack on MacArthur's conduct of the occupation conducted by Henry Luce's mass-media group.[30] James Forrestal himself, suffering from acute mental depression, left the scene at this point. Dismissed from office by President

Truman, he entered Bethesda Naval Hospital, where he died in a fall from a window in May 1949, an apparent suicide. Draper remained in charge, and he carried out the financially oriented course change in both western Germany and Japan.

In 1948, President Truman, the Joint Chiefs of Staff, the National Advisory Council, and the National Security Council had all taken up the issue of the Japanese economy. The new policy was announced in December 1948 in the Nine Point Economic Stabilization Plan. The nine points were (1) balance in the consolidated budget; (2) strengthening tax collection; (3) limiting credit extension; (4) achieving wage stability; (5) strengthening price control; (6) improving foreign trade controls; (7) improving allocation and rationing; (8) increasing production; (9) improving food collection.[31] The first four of the nine points reflected monetary stabilization goals; the latter five reflected established GHQ economic-control policies. Joseph Dodge was to implement the new policy. In practice, he ignored the latter five control objectives and implemented only the fiscal and monetary stabilization side of the plan.

Dodge arrived in Japan on February 1, 1949, accompanied by a staff of U.S. Treasury officials, and assumed supreme authority over economic policy. He was appointed directly by President Truman with the title "Financial Advisor to the Supreme Commander for the Allied Powers, with the personal rank of Minister." Dodge's policies would be attacked from many sides, but he was not a man to be snowed, and few doubted his financial expertise or personal integrity. He was also politically shrewd and formidably capable and focused. Unlike many young GHQ officials, he was well prepared for his task.

Dodge immediately set to restricting the government's creation of new money and dismantling what he called Japan's "greenhouse" economy. His policy was simultaneously a matter of taking control and of letting go, of both restriction and deregulation. In more recent times, Dodge's policy mandates would be called free-market reforms, and Dodge might also be called Japan's "minister of liberalization." The Dodge Line meant the return to Japan of a universalist liberal economics resembling the deflationary "stabilization" policies of the 1920s. It also resembles the IMF-sponsored "structural adjustment" programs and free-market reforms of the 1980s and 1990s.[32] Like these other programs, it was part of a struggle over who would create money-capital and how.

7.3 Ministers of Restriction

Price stabilization in Japan thus came together with a conservative course reversal and the restabilization of established hierarchies of authority and ownership. This coincidence has moral, social, and political dimensions, about which Joseph

Dodge had definite ideas, and in this conforms to a repeated historical pattern.[33] The new U.S. policy in Japan was an expression of a political shift in the United States and in the larger international system. In Japan, too, there was a major domestic political shift, which happened just in advance of Dodge's arrival. In the January 1949 elections, voters gave a landslide win to the Liberal Party, confirming Arisawa Hiromi's judgment that the Socialists' postwar window of opportunity was closed. With an absolute majority in the National Diet, Yoshida's cabinet, formally inaugurated on February 28, was the first single-party cabinet since the war. Because of its position as the right wing of the conservative parties, the Liberal Party also benefited from the new bipolarization of Japanese and international politics. Tsuji Kiyoaki called it "the strongest cabinet in Japanese history since the Meiji era."[34] This may be, because Japan's political world was now itself contained within a U.S.-directed political environment, from which the Yoshida cabinet derived special backing. But by the same token, Joseph Dodge would greatly restrict the new cabinet's freedom of maneuver. Japanese officials who supported the conservative and probusiness thrust of Dodge's policy also worked simultaneously to circumvent many of his directives at the microeconomic level.

Not only did the "modified capitalism" coalition break up at this point, but so did its constituent parties. The Democratic Party split in early 1949, when many of the more conservative members left to join Yoshida's Liberal Party. The Socialist Party kept only 48 seats in the 1949 election, down from 143 seats after the 1947 election, and party infighting intensified. The Socialists also dropped their big nationalization plans and refocused on smaller and more immediately practical projects. In January 1950, the left and right wings of the Socialist party openly split, and they functioned as two separate parties for the next five years. Yoshida's Liberal Party prepared to return to more classically liberal economic principles as well. Under U.S. orders, they ended up taking part in a more radically liberal attack on the institutions of modified capitalism than they had intended.

The finance minister in the new cabinet was Ikeda Hayato, who had been vice-minister to Ishibashi Tanzan. Ikeda later succeeded to Yoshida's position of party leadership and became prime minister in 1960. He is best remembered for the Income Doubling Plan of 1960, which earned him a place in the "positive policy" pantheon with such luminaries as Takahashi Korekiyo and Ishibashi Tanzan. But Ikeda's budding career in national politics first unfolded under the stingy aegis of Minister Dodge, who also became, after Ishibashi, virtually one of Ikeda's teachers. It was Ikeda who relayed Dodge's orders while seeking, with little success, to modify them. Practically speaking, he thus remained something like vice minister to Minister Dodge. The Americans granted considerably more leeway to Bank of Japan governor Ichimada Hisato, who was a rival to Ikeda.

While Ikeda's fiscal policies were frustrated, Ichimada on the monetary side thus quietly reformulated policy in response to the Dodge Line. In doing so, he succeeded in establishing the semiprivatized financial circuit of the High-Speed Growth system, as described in the next chapter.

Finance Minister Ikeda's secretary and English-language interpreter was Miyazawa Kiichi, who was then a Ministry of Finance official on the elite track. Miyazawa later headed the Economic Planning Agency, inherited the leadership of the Ikeda–Ōhira faction of the Liberal Democratic Party, and was himself finance minister and prime minister in the 1980s and early 1990s, and then again senior finance minister and advocate of a Keynesian "positive policy" during the postbubble recession of the 1990s. Miyazawa was present at all of Ikeda's meetings with Dodge. He also ghostwrote Ikeda's 1952 memoir of the occupation. In his own 1956 memoir, Miyazawa described his and Ikeda's memorable first meeting with Dodge in February 1949.[35] Dodge, he reported, got straight to the point, telling the Japanese that things had now changed in their relationship with the United States. Dodge told them he had spoken extensively with President Truman and the heads of the U.S. government. From their perspective, Japan was making poor use of the aid received from America. It was necessary to stop inflation and balance the budget. This naturally would cause problems for the Japanese government and people. However, this was only to be expected after such a miserable defeat—

> Now, the most necessary thing for the Japanese people was, in a word, austerity. The most necessary thing for the Japanese Government and Occupation army was to have the courage to force the Japanese people to endure austerity.

People must stop dreaming and start from a "heartless," realistic position.[36] "We thought that a fearsome old man had come," said Miyazawa. "But still, we did not at all expect that for one or two years it would be just as he said." Dodge's first address to the Japanese public also created a sensation. The Japanese economy was like a person walking on stilts, Dodge said. One stilt was government subsidies, and the other was U.S. aid. This was rendered in Japanese as "economy on stilts" (*takeuma keizai*), a phrase that immediately became current. It was a "rigged economy," Dodge said, and he set to cutting it down to size.

The threat to the system of industrial finance was clear. But Japanese officials also perceived an opening. "Not only we were surprised," said Miyazawa. So were U.S. occupation staffers, for Dodge was at the same time announcing the new policy to GHQ itself, which Miyazawa and Ikeda saw as filled with "mostly relatively extreme New Dealers" with extreme beliefs in favor of economic planning. Miyazawa described his conversation with Ikeda after their first meeting with

Dodge: "At that time, the thing Japanese officials most exercised their brains about was over how they could use the absolute authority of the occupation army to their own ends." Many, he said, succeeded through the use of flattery. There were a few cases of open opposition. (We know how Ishibashi Tanzan fared.) And then, Miyazawa said, there was the classic method of creating divisions among the authorities and taking advantage of the gaps between them, reversing the idea of "divide and rule." In line with this strategy of dividing the rulers, Ikeda and Miyazawa excitedly talked of how to divide Dodge and the New Dealers. "Until that time," Miyazawa continued, "the Japanese financial authorities had been bullied continually by a figurehead named Marquat [chief of the Economic and Scientific Section] and the New Dealers under him." Finance Ministry officials, by long years of training, disliked giving out money. They preferred retrenchment, and they resented the New Dealers' interference. Hence,

> we were not without a feeling of trying to borrow and use the power of this unknown but apparently stubborn old man named Dodge. At the least, we felt that it would be easier to ride on Dodge's boat than on that of the New Dealers. However, when it came to actually riding on it, things were much stingier than we expected and we were forced to go on a rough voyage; but that was later.[37]

Thus, many Japanese leaders agreed with many of Dodge's principles, even while they resisted many of the specifics of his policy and pushed for changes in it. Inflation was a serious problem for almost everyone, but the demands of reconstruction and the balance of domestic political forces made it difficult to cut industrial subsidies or to force workers and taxpayers to bear even heavier austerities. Dodge's program promised to end inflation as a political deus ex machina. Dodge himself fully understood this point and was prepared to play the heavy, knowing that he would be the shield behind which Japanese politicians could hide. Whatever else conservative elites may have thought about Dodge's approach, they could also accept his new line as an attack on New Deal or socialistic policies.

7.3.1 The Dodge Line

Dodge enunciated the main principles of his policy in a four-hour meeting with Ikeda on March 1. It was Ōuchi Hyōe who dubbed this "the Dodge Line."[38] Dodge demanded:

1. A balanced, consolidated budget. All special accounts (described on the Japanese side as a capital-investment budget) were to be brought into the general account.

2. Elimination of hidden subsidies. All subsidies were to be brought into the general account with a view to abolishing them. (For this reason, if one looks at the general-account budget numbers, it appears that there was a great increase of subsidies in 1949.)

3. No further extension of the borrowing power of the Reconstruction Finance Bank.

4. A special import account to which aid "counterpart funds" would be credited. Government and Relief in Occupied Areas (GARIOA) funds were to offset present subsidies, and Economic Rehabilitation in Occupied Areas (EROA) funds were for debt reduction.[39] (Dodge's longer term goal was that U.S. aid capital would in the future be replaced by U.S. private investment.)

5. Tightening of the allocation of imported raw materials and linkage of import allocations to production for export.

Ikeda told Dodge he agreed with these principles—except, crucially, for the limitation of the Reconstruction Finance Bank. While he acknowledged the RFB's role in the inflation, he said the bank's lending had helped increase production. Dodge prohibited further RFB lending in April 1949. The bank was later wholly dismantled. It was reconstructed in a new form with the return of Japanese sovereignty in 1952.

The new policy was felt directly in the newly consolidated budget, which Dodge required to operate at a surplus. The Ministry of Finance called this a "superbalanced" budget. These spending cuts were a great embarrassment to the Liberal Party, which in its recent electoral campaign had promised a "positive" budgetary package that included substantial tax cuts and a big ¥100 billion public works budget. Dodge's budget immediately cut this package in half. Moreover, Finance Minister Ikeda could not say publicly that the austerity budget was a GHQ order and had to present Dodge's budget as his own.[40] Again and again, Ikeda asked Dodge to allow a tax cut and to release more funds for reconstruction expenses and regional public works. He told Dodge he agreed that "the patient" was ill and needed treatment but suggested the medicine could be "sugarcoated" to help it go down. Even a token tax reduction would serve as a "sedative" to relieve the shock. Dodge refused such public-relations gestures and insisted that present tax revenues be maintained "to create the maximum pressure on consumption"—that is, to absorb purchasing power (see 6.4). The need was to control inflation "and to reduce domestic consumption." "Siphoning off funds and materials and labor beyond absolute needs was inflationary."[41]

At times, however, Ikeda also seemed to present himself as the formulator rather than merely the administrator of the Dodge Line policies. Thus, despite a series of frustrating meetings with Dodge, Ikeda told Dodge in April 1949, toward the end of his first visit to Japan, that he had been "continuously borrowing the ideas of another person [meaning Dodge] in answering all of the problems in connection with the budget but had become so used to these ideas that they were now his own." Further, he said, he hoped to see the Dodge group return "because of their neutral position toward existing problems." Doubtless some flattery was intended, and Ikeda followed this compliment with his usual argument for a token tax cut, which Dodge, as always, rejected. At the same time, Dodge noted that "Mr. Ikeda's proposals are in some respects more drastic than my own."[42] Thus, Dodge wanted to stop any expansion of RFB lending but would have permitted the bank to make new loans out of the collection of existing loans, in order to encourage its collection activities. Ikeda now said that the RFB should not be permitted to make any new loans. This effectively put the bank into liquidation. It also removed a possible new source of pressure for companies to repay their RFB loans—which previously had been collected very little or not at all.

Not that Ikeda was happy to have to truckle to Dodge. In his 1952 memoir of the occupation, written after the return of national sovereignty left him free to speak his mind, Ikeda told Japanese readers that while he did not want to say anything bad about the other party after the relationship had ended, his purpose in writing was to let future generations know "how bitter and how ridiculous things were under the occupation." Ikeda, the veteran tax official, added that Dodge did not understand taxes and, more than that, that he refused to understand.[43] In fact, a wide range of economic thinking was at odds with Dodge's prescriptions. A secret U.S. State Department report of May 1950 said that "every major power element in the Japanese body politic considers itself injured and its interests jeopardized" by the Dodge plan.[44] The business world, as represented by the newly organized Federation of Economic Organizations (Keidanren), expressed its support for currency stabilization by means of a "balanced budget, wage stabilization, stimulation of export trade etc." But Keidanren opposed any restriction of credit: "our inflation is very acute. However in order to effectively stem inflation, credit expansion is necessary for bolstering production. In this sense, the present currency is far from excessive in its quantity but, we should say, rather short."[45] Because production levels remained far below normal, Keidanren representatives said, "any currency reform measure for absorbing excessive currency or purchasing power is not warranted at all." Ishibashi himself may have been sidelined politically, but the Ishibashi line retained its big-business support.

7.3.2 Consumption versus Investment; Government Inflation versus Private Inflation

Dodge's understanding of Japan's inflation also appears to have changed significantly over the first six months of his mission. He came to Japan holding views
similar to those presented by the seventy-page Federal Reserve Board (Young
mission) report that had served as his briefing book.[46] Thus, looking at Japan's
economy in March 1949, Dodge imagined that the problem was excess consumption. It was "a consumption inflation," he declared, unconsciously using a
term Schumpeter had also used to describe the nondevelopmental type of inflation. Dodge thus lectured Ikeda and Liberal Party leaders that "in an inflationary
situation the pressure should be on incomes and through taxation on the consumer." Dodge recommended a sales tax as a good means of limiting consumption. He also called for an increase in passenger rail rates; these, together with
postage rates, were raised by 60 percent. The tax burden should be heavy, he explained to Ikeda: "in principle the time had come for [the Japanese] to pay for
some of their past mistakes." Moreover, "public works of any kind were inflationary in a shortage and inflationary economy and were a device to meet depression not inflation." The Japanese had it easy compared to other occupied
areas he knew of, Dodge told Ikeda. "Japan had been travelling on soft rubber
tires supplied by the U.S." He did recognize that certain industries had been
"feeding at the trough" of government subsidies.[47]

In fact, the expenses that pushed Japanese government finances into the red
were not social subsidies but industrial subsidies (together with subsidies to pay
for the Allied occupation itself). By the summer of 1949, Dodge began to perceive that Japan's inflation was mainly driven by industrialists and happened at
the expense of working people. The phrase "forced savings" entered his vocabulary. Dodge came to appreciate this point in reading about Germany's phase of
"reconstruction inflation" after World War I; he noted, quoting Bresciani-
Turroni, that

> such obvious and conspicuous advantages for producers can be derived
> from inflationary phenomenon, that naturally they become the most
> convinced supporters of monetary inflation. Wages increase only at a
> great distance behind the rise in sale prices.

In inflation, Dodge concluded, the economically strongest reap the greatest advantages by the general ruin.[48]

Thus, unlike many later probusiness analyses of inflation, Dodge did not
blame labor. Rather, he saw working people as victims of inflation. Dodge and
the Japanese Communists actually agreed that inflation was a great public enemy

and that industrial subsidies were to blame. Ōuchi Hyōe understood the same thing. In fact, the leftist Ōuchi was in late 1949 quite positive about Dodge's policy, saying in conversation with BoJ governor Ichimada Hisato and Arisawa Hiromi that people must be prepared to endure the deflation policy, for as long as it took. (It was Ichimada who expressed reservations.)[49] None of this altered Dodge's sense of the necessity for a traumatic crisis. It just shifted his sense of who was to blame:

> The stabilization recession is not the result of an act of government, or by any other authority, it is the result of certain segments of the business, industrial and financial world, which have contributed to bring about the inflationary situation through their selfish and irresponsible behavior.[50]

On the question of "forced savings," Dodge wrote that stabilization meant the end of the process that provided entrepreneurs with capital at the expense of owners of "liquid capital" (i.e., monetary claims) and of salaried and wage workers: "Once stabilization has been achieved, it is impossible to continue the financing of business by forced savings. Voluntary savings become the sole source of capital."[51] This statement, however, was not really thought through, or not quite frank. In fact, when Dodge was finished with his reform, it was only the state, and the state reconstruction bank, that would cease to create credit-money in advance of monetary savings from out of the national income stream. Private banks would continue the preemptive financing of business as before. Here was a contradiction in Dodge's thinking, which he was evidently not inclined to dig into. He recognized a distinction between a "government inflation" and a "private inflation," and he did not fail to perceive the reality of the latter. (To judge by its absence from most American economic textbooks, the possibility does not exist.) What he called a "private inflation," although he did not name it this way, is more precisely a credit inflation, or a bank inflation:

> A government inflation is provoked by continual demands made on the Central Bank by the state. A private inflation is the creation of paper money for businessmen by bank credit. . . . The extension of bank credits, like the issue of notes on the account of the state, profits some classes and imposes losses on others.[52]

Dodge consistently regarded government budget deficits and the central bank's issue of money to cover them as the most fundamental cause of inflation, and he acted to halt the fiscal inflation. But except for closing the government's Reconstruction Finance Bank, he left the private credit–inflation process alone.

7.4 "The So-Called Stabilization Panic"

The new policy provoked a depression, which Dodge was fully prepared to sit through, but which brought tremendous pressure to bear on the Japanese government. In 1946, Ishibashi Tanzan had insisted that the postwar inflation was not a true inflation, because the country's productive resources were radically underutilized. Ikeda Hayato as finance minister now presented the mirror image of Ishibashi's idea. The "so-called stabilization panic," Ikeda insisted, was not a real depression. On this point, Ikeda sounded like Dodge: "in the transition period from an 'inflation economy' to a 'normal economy,' this kind of phenomenon inevitably follows, and is different from 'depression' [fukyō] in the real meaning of the word." Companies premised on inflation were bound to fail, Ikeda said. Their mistaken views were to blame; to try to support them would only restart the inflation. Only by passing through the stabilization crisis could Japanese businessmen regain a true entrepreneurial spirit. Ikeda thus derided the previous policy of what might be called socialism for capitalists, admonishing business managers against "the sweet preconception of a 'debt economy,'" where business losses would somehow be made good.[53] Authentic business management meant "fighting with real swords":

> I believe that to regain the spirit of the old-fashioned entrepreneurs, who felt the bitterness of a debt economy to the marrow of their bones, is to return to the roots of a normal economy. If there are people who have forgotten this kind of entrepreneurial spirit, can we not say, to speak without irony, that there is "danger" in the attitude of such people?[54]

Even after the return of national independence in 1952, Ikeda thus went out of his way in identifying himself with the stabilization depression. He expressed this most notoriously in his public unconcern over the news that several bankrupt small business owners had committed suicide. Questioned on this point in the National Diet, Ikeda said only "it is unavoidable that people will go bankrupt because of the depression during the process of economic adjustment. For the time being, we must walk a thorny road."[55] To develop a more appealing and democratic political persona would take him some time. Ikeda's views of capital and entrepreneurship were thus very far from those of Ishibashi, or of Schumpeter. A "debt economy" was for Schumpeter the essence of capitalist development, and the entrepreneur was "the typical debtor" in the capitalist order, a necessary rather than accidental debtor (see 3.3). In practice, however, Ikeda also recognized the centrality of credit and worked to keep it flowing (see 8.3).

The brunt of the Dodge Line depression was borne by small businesses and laid-off workers, who were now "let go" from their employment in large numbers. Ikeda, for his part, told Dodge that the Yoshida cabinet was committed to reducing government staff, and that the government would "set the example on employee dismissals."[56] The biggest layoffs happened in the public sector. The national railways were reorganized into Japan National Railways (JNR), and national telephone and telegraph was organized into Nippon Telegraph and Telephone Public Corporation (NTT), which were both to be run as self-supporting, profit-making operations. (The latter was directed by Kajii Takeshi, the father-in-law of Ōkita Saburō.)[57] Japan National Railways laid off almost 100,000 people. NTT laid off 220,000. In private industry, MITI reported 400,000 "persons adjusted" from the beginning of the Dodge Line in February 1949 to the beginning of the Korean War in June 1950. The greatest number of these layoffs were in the coal-mining and metals industries, which had previously received the greater part of RFB funding. The Dodge Line also brought a severe recession and a wave of reconsolidation in the emerging electrical goods industry. Matsushita Electric reduced its 15,000-person workforce to 3,500. Most small radio manufacturers, most of which had only recently formed, also failed at this point.[58]

The paternalistic Douglas MacArthur expressed some worry about this, but Dodge saw simply a return to economic normality. As he explained to MacArthur,

> comparison is always made with peaks of employment created by unusual circumstances and [with] figures which include many who under any normal circumstances would not be employed. It has been well said that an acceptance of nothing less than full employment (actually over-employment) is the road to disaster. We need a reasonable mobility of labor as well as a mobility of capital.[59]

What Dodge called "mobility" had until the Great Depression of the 1930s been called "liquidation"—the term had become discredited. "It is a tough job to halt a 'Santa Claus' economy," Dodge told Marquat in September 1949, in connection with the layoffs and restriction of public works. Or to cure a drug-addicted economy, he further suggested, because stopping inflation "is like stopping the dope habit, there is always an uncomfortable period."[60] Many Japanese people, and knowledgeable U.S. officials on the spot, doubted that a wave of liquidation and bankruptcies was really what the country needed at this point.

Various interests and agendas converged in the political struggle to liquidate new "structures and situations" and "return to prewar ways." Japanese industrialists seized on the chance to try to liquidate and reorient unions by purging their leadership, especially targeting Communists and union activists. The revision of the trade union law in June 1949 opened the way for a general attack on union contracts negotiated during the previous period of labor strength. Deflation thus came together with political and social counterrevolution. This movement intensified in 1950. In the first half of 1950, as semicovert skirmishing intensified in Korea, the "red purge" in Japan also got into full swing.[61] MacArthur stopped just short of outlawing the Japan Communist Party, on advice that to do so would look too much like a return to the former imperial police state.

For Dodge, however, the simple and essential point was to end inflation. This happened as he had intended. His promarket antagonist Ishibashi Tanzan described black-market prices as the most indicative of the true economic situation. By that index, prices actually fell. Black-market producer prices headed downward as early as March 1949, when the Dodge Line began to be enforced. Black-market consumer prices peaked a month later and began to fall in May. The price decline continued until June 1950, when the Korean War began. By that point, black-market prices were down more than 40 percent from their early 1949 peaks.[62] By the middle of 1950, black markets were disappearing, owing to the combined effects of deflation and deregulation. One could describe this abstractly as a liberation of "markets." It was also a liberation of ordinary people, in their daily activities, from police harassment and threat of arrest.

7.4.1 From Cash to Credit

For the banking system, the Dodge Line was a boon in that it reduced the "drain" into cash-currency and resulted in a large increase in the amount of monetary balances inside the banking system. Here, rather than imagining a national "money supply" as a single pool of "liquidity," we need to consider two spheres of domestic monetary circulation, each with distinct rules and dynamics. In between these two spheres is an interface in the banking system. In the sphere of cash-currency circulation, physically tangible forms of currency (mainly paper notes) circulate physically as counterflows to the provision of goods and services. This is the sphere to which most "common-sense" views of money refer. Historically, of course, it is the most continuous with older practices. In 1950s Japan, this daily-life sphere of cash-currency circulation was still quite large. In fact, the use of currency remains much greater in Japan than in many other industrialized countries.

The sphere of cash-currency is not the one that is mainly significant for the process of capital creation considered in this book. This capitalist process happens in the second sphere, that of bank balances. In this sphere, corporate accounts predominate. Here, all money consists of credits (debts), with interest charges attached. Quantitatively—with the significant exception of the immediate postwar period—this sphere became in the twentieth century much the larger of the two. As described already, the volume of cash-currency increased greatly after the war, and by 1948 it was nearly equal to the volume of bank balances (see 5.3). This happened at a time when the volume of bank balances was also increasing at record rates. This relative increase in cash-currency was reversed during the first year of the Dodge Line. By the end of 1949, the level of bank balances had rebounded to a level double that of currency in circulation. This shift from cash-currency into balances held in banks meant a de facto reprivatization of the larger share of the national money supply.

These two spheres, of cash-currency and bank balances, also corresponded in a very rough way, in 1950 much more than now, to the two standard measures of price levels. That is, the cash-currency sphere corresponded to the world of consumer prices, which refer to transactions between businesses and the public and to interpersonal transactions. Black-market transactions were made in cash. The sphere of corporate bank balances corresponded to the world of wholesale prices, which refer to interbusiness transactions. When we speak of consumer versus wholesale price indices in the 1950s, we are thus speaking not only of different markets, different kinds of goods, and different parties to transactions but also, as a rule, about different forms of money, albeit forms immediately convertible one into the other.[63]

The greatest channel from bank balances into cash—the greatest "leakage" out of the banking system—was the payment of wages and salaries (see 11.2). That is, the banking system as a whole—any banking system—is not called on to pay out cash-currency as long as the newly created purchasing power remains within the banking system and is transferred, for example, from one corporate account to another. The monetary interface between the bank-money and cash-money sectors thus becomes a critical point for the governing of the money system as a whole.

7.5 Inside Money and Outside Money

The Dodge Line also established a new regime in the relation of domestic (Japanese) money to (American) foreign-exchange money. The significance of this shift is clearer when seen in a longer historical context.

Through the entire modern period, beginning with Japan's forced monetary opening in 1859, Japanese authorities were concerned to concentrate scarce foreign-exchange money and control its use, until the need for this was obviated by the great trade surpluses and foreign-exchange balances that accumulated in the 1980s. The parastatal Yokohama Specie Bank, founded in 1880, and the Bank of Japan, after 1882, were intended to fulfill this role. They did this by lending yen funds (domestic credit-money of their own creation) to exporters on the security of their export bills and then taking payment in British pounds or in silver and gold specie. A large part of these foreign-exchange payments were handled in London, in the form of drafts on London banks. Centralized management of foreign-exchange funds continued through Japan's gold-standard era (1897–1931). Far from being a system of monetary laissez-faire, the gold standard was a highly managed system under which gold coins did not circulate domestically but instead were held by the Ministry of Finance and the Bank of Japan and reserved for external payments.[64] During World War I, the MoF imposed formal foreign-exchange controls, as a supposed temporary measure. Following the disastrous experience with decontrol in 1930–31, the MoF reimposed and extended exchange controls after 1932.

This was not only Japan's experience. Depression and war made national foreign-exchange controls ubiquitous in the 1930s and 1940s. This situation continued after World War II, when there was an acute worldwide shortage of dollars. What was distinctive about Japan's postwar foreign-exchange controls, among industrialized capitalist nations, was their exceptionally long retention after the war, and the systematic way they were articulated with a centralized system of foreign-exchange budgeting. The 1949 Foreign Exchange and Foreign Trade Control Law restricted foreign-exchange transactions in principle, requiring Ministry of Finance permission for all foreign-exchange transactions. Sakakibara and Noguchi called the 1949 law (still in force when they wrote in 1977) "the bulwark of Japan's closed monetary system."[65]

This emphasis on concentrating foreign exchange and on concentrating capital in general is closely connected to the question of industrial finance. As Ōkita Saburō emphasized, imports of foreign capital had a limited place in Japan's industrialization. It was, however, a highly strategic place, as Simon Bytheway has demonstrated.[66] Japan desperately needed dollar funds to pay for necessary imports of all kinds, and in 1949 the country was critically dependent on U.S. aid funds. Joseph Dodge's view in setting up the "counterpart fund" system was that economic normalization would in the future lead to the replacement of U.S. aid funds by U.S. private capital lending, to be repaid out of the earnings from Japanese exports, mainly to less industrialized Asian countries. In fact, foreign capital in the 1950s first came into Japan in the form of loans managed by governmental or semigovernmental agencies. Substantial lending came through the World Bank, which actually insisted on effective government planning as a condition for constructive use of funds.[67]

Ōuchi Hyōe had begun his secret presurrender research in the spring and summer of 1945 by looking into the implications for Japan of the new international monetary order announced at Bretton Woods in July 1944.[68] As it worked out, the new international monetary system had a delayed significance for Japan, for the country was practically cut off from international monetary exchanges for several years after the war. A fundamental purpose of the Bretton Woods system was to reestablish a system of fixed exchange rates among the world's major currencies, to replace the nonsystem that had followed the breakdown of the international gold standard in 1931–33. The Bretton Woods system is often described as a U.S. dollar standard and is sometimes even called a gold-exchange standard. For Japan, this is not what it was. Most of Japan's imports had to be paid for in dollars. But the country's dollar reserves did not form the basis of the domestic monetary system in the way that British pounds and U.S. dollars indeed had done under Japan's gold-standard system between 1897 and 1931.[69]

These questions are ones of private credit creation also. Before 1914, the British pound was the world's pivotal currency. This status gave a privileged place to British banks, able to create the world's most universally potent means of payment. The British pound under the gold standard thus formed the basis for the first truly global system of credit-money creation. The United States became Britain's great creditor during World War I. The pound sterling entered into a long cycle of depreciation, punctuated by repeated attempts at restoration, and the U.S. dollar became the world's "hardest" major currency, although it was still far from dominant in international financial arrangements in general. The Bretton Woods agreement established a pivotal position for the dollar, but the British pound continued at the end of World War II to be the invoice currency for about one-half of international trade. This was due partly to the relative "softness" (i.e., availability) of sterling and relative "hardness" (i.e., scarcity) of dollars. (One can compare the international situation of the "softer," more abundant U.S. dollar and the "harder," scarcer Japanese yen and European euro in the early twenty-first century.)[70] The dollar had a remarkably small place as an international reserve currency as late as 1947—only 12 percent of the world's official foreign-exchange reserves were in dollars, with sterling accounting for the remaining 88 percent.[71] This changed very rapidly after 1947, which was also the year that the British government tried and failed to return the pound to convertibility (meaning dollar convertibility). Other countries now took steps to replace inconvertible sterling with dollars.

During the first phase of the occupation, GHQ tightly controlled Japan's foreign trade, which was conducted under a complex system of multiple exchange rates. To ease the import of goods needed as industrial inputs, the yen was valued at rates as high as ¥80 per dollar for the purchase of cotton for domestic use and ¥67 per dollar for pig iron. (The latter rate would signify an even stronger yen than the historically high yen-dollar rate reached in 2011.) In order to promote exports, exchange rates for export sales valued the yen much lower, from ¥200 down to ¥600 per dollar.[72] This system of extraordinary case-by-case administrative decision-making began to resemble a semibarter trade system. Here, the Dodge Line meant a grand resimplification. In April 1949, U.S. authorities fixed a single exchange rate between the yen and the dollar, at ¥360 to $1. This fixed rate lasted until August 1971. It may be regarded as the definition of the Bretton Woods system as far as Japan was concerned.[73]

There was no formal or direct link between foreign-exchange reserves, controlled by the Ministry of Finance, and the creation of money by the Bank of Japan and the private banks. There were indirect links, visible in the "fast-slow" growth cycles of the 1950s, which were modulated by the cycle in Japan's international balance of payments (see 10.1). But the connection was buffered. Japan's domestic money and credit system formed an autonomous system, and foreign-exchange signals were mediated through nationally managed controls that partially insulated the domestic system from the fluctuations of the trade balance. The really remarkable thing, emphasized already (see 5.3), is that Japan's money and credit system remained autonomous and semiclosed even under conditions of foreign military government. There was an essential continuity of Japan's core capital-creation circuits in a time of extraordinary tumult and transformation.

It was here that Dodge attempted to intervene, by acting to restrict domestic capital creation and replace it, in part, with U.S. aid capital. Dodge anticipated that sufficient retrenchment and liquidation would create the conditions for a future influx of foreign loans: "The objective must be to achieve self-support so as to warrant continuation of U.S. aid and ultimately create the conditions favorable for foreign credits."[74] In the context of the time, "foreign" credits could practically only have meant U.S. credits. This was also a goal Ichimada Hisato supported at the Bank of Japan, where he formed his own committee to publish a series of English-language promotional reports. Such a restoration of U.S. capital lending to Japan would also have been a partial return to the world of the 1920s, for the inducement of U.S. capital had also been the goal of the deflation policy of Inoue Junnosuke, and of the U.S. bankers who had advised him to tie the yen to the dollar in 1929. Dodge was a man of considerable personal honor whose public service was not motivated by crude self-interest on his own part. Nonetheless, this goal, of incorporating Japanese development into the field of credit creation by U.S. banks, completes a circle that connects Dodge's policies to the collective interests of U.S. financiers. Those who put Dodge on the job in

Japan in the first place—William Draper and his firm Dillon, Read—were, for their part, quick to cash in on their new influence in Japan.[75]

Dodge also insisted that domestic demand be suppressed and that the Japanese must work harder to supply overseas demand: "internal rehabilitation and expansion necessarily falls into second place behind the need for a priority of exports." To redirect productive resources into production for foreign consumption "will require continued limitations on domestic consumption and an emphasis on the needs of the export consumer."[76] Dodge therefore promoted "mobility" (or liquidation) of resources in the expectation of remobilizing these resources for export industry, which would earn foreign-exchange money, which would repay foreign loans. For these reasons, the single exchange rate and export promotion were integral to the Dodge plan. From Dodge's standpoint, it also went without saying that credit creation by Japanese financial institutions could not fund overseas demand. Here, too, it would be a matter of international, chiefly U.S., credit creation, in a dollar-based trading world.

This export-oriented policy almost immediately received a heavy blow from events in the larger international economy. Dodge's vision was a return to the logic of the 1920s. The Keynesian critique of the deflation policies of that era emphasized that if all countries attempted to gain balance by constricting domestic demand, it would be a formula for universal poverty, with no sources of demand anywhere. That is, it would yield once again the world economic situation of the 1930s, with its competitive devaluations, export dumping, and trade wars. And in the fall of 1949, with global recession and a wave of currency devaluations taking place, exactly this situation seemed to be bidding to repeat itself.

7.6 The World Economic Crisis

In late 1948, a phase of postwar deflation and recession began in the United States. From a peak in August 1948, U.S. prices fell by 8 percent by the end of 1949.[77] As of this writing, the 1948–49 deflation remains the last "classic" deflationary recession on record in the United States (though the possibility has seemed suddenly more real since the collapse of recent financial bubbles). The onset of recession in what was then the single motor of world trade made many people think that with the war at an end, chronic depression would again be the way of things. Japan's outlook seemed especially poor. Not only critics of capitalism felt this way. As *Fortune* magazine's attack on GHQ put it in the spring of 1949, "the Japanese face a future uniquely bleak in a bleakish world." The Supreme Commander shared these fears. Writing to Dodge in Detroit in July 1949, MacArthur assured him that he was confident that Dodge's stabilization program would "come through in good style"—"unless there is a world wide depression, which might develop."[78] Again the United States seemed to be overproducing relative to effective demand, while much of the rest of the postwar world could not afford to consume sufficiently even for basic needs.

American planners' vision for future Japanese exports was for a recovery based on textiles and other light-industrial exports in branches of industry where the U.S. was no longer competitive. This idea was quite explicit. This, too, implied that Japan should return to the industrial structure of the 1920s. Affirmatively, this vision meant U.S. support for securing other Asian markets and sources of supply for Japan as an alternative to China, which meant tying Japan into an island and peninsular "great crescent" around communist Asia. It was Dodge who told Ikeda that "your natural markets are in countries whose standard of living is below that of Japan." He reassured Ikeda that U.S. dollar aid to Southeast Asia could contribute to the demand for Japanese goods there.[79] This idea did not accord with existing economic realities. It also failed to see the emerging reality of general East Asian industrialization. In this it contrasted with the perception of Ōkita Saburō and others, who realized that Japanese industrial development was taking place in a dynamic Asian context, meaning that Japan's labor-intensive light-industrial goods would before long have to compete with those of lower-wage neighboring countries, and that rapid technical upgrading was the only way forward.

The U.S. recession caused a drop in American imports of raw materials from countries in the sterling area, which included much of the projected Asian crescent. This led to a new sterling crisis. On September 18, 1949, British authorities devalued the pound from $4.03 to $2.80. This happened eighteen years to the day after the British government's decision to abandon the gold standard and let the pound depreciate in 1931.[80] In a wave of devaluations that was also reminiscent of 1931, thirty other countries devalued their currencies, including all the sterling-area countries except Pakistan. This left Japan's new exchange rate suddenly 30 percent higher relative to the sterling area and European countries. Like Japan, the European countries were also striving to bring their industrial production back on line, and they were likewise starved for dollars to pay for their own desperately needed imports of food, raw materials, and industrial machinery. Dodge had originally considered the exchange rate of ¥360 to the dollar as a de facto devaluation that would boost Japanese exports. However, the majority of Japanese exports still went to sterling-area countries, mainly in Asia, and they were now being priced out of these markets.[81]

Dodge's restriction of credit induced another systemic transformation that had not been anticipated. In fact, it did not end the Japanese government's policy of subsidized priority investment. Rather, it displaced it into private banking channels, which Dodge left unregulated. In this, the Dodge Line set in place the final piece of the integrated state-bank mechanism that would form the financial core of the High-Speed Growth system. The sources and control of capital thus assumed the distinctive forms of the classical age of Japanese capitalism.

THE STATE-BANK COMPLEX

Although in terms of ideology Japanese society underwent a drastic reorientation after the end of the war, the economic system—particularly the institutional system for financial control—was retained essentially intact. The result was . . . an acute gap between understanding and reality.

 . . . Extensive regulation applied through the money market controlled the flow of capital, strongly influencing the industrial structure and the pattern of economic growth. Financial control was implemented through the Bank of Japan and other financial institutions, particularly large banks, with support from the bureaucracy in the economic field. The banks and the economic bureaucracy functioned as a general staff behind the battlefield in this total war called high economic growth.

—Noguchi Yukio and Sakakibara Eisuke (1977)

[The banker] makes possible the carrying out of new combinations, authorizes people, in the name of society as it were, to form them. He is the ephor of the exchange economy.

—Joseph Schumpeter (1912)

The relationship between the state and the banking system constitutes a defining feature of a national political-economic system, with implications for many other things. The previous chapter described how U.S. authorities reversed political course in Japan and enforced a policy of credit-capital restriction in 1948–49. This chapter explains how Japanese financial authorities simultaneously preserved and consolidated the core financial circuits of Japan's capitalist economy. It contextualizes that process within the historical stream of the development of Japan's state-bank complex.

From the early 1940s into the 1980s, the Japanese system of industrial finance relied mainly on direct financing by banks. In Schumpeterian terms, this system of industrial finance itself had the aspect of a "new combination." In the historical timing of its appearance, it also fits with the cyclical framework developed by

Schumpeter in regard to the temporal "clustering" of new combinations (see 9.1). This new financial system began to take shape during the deflation and recessions of the 1920s and 1930s.[1] Total war and wartime totalitarianism after 1937 drove forward this transformation and caused the state to assign a quasi-administrative role to the banks. The changes of the occupation era tended to consolidate rather than reverse this transformation, and the system that emerged out of the capital constriction crisis of 1949–50 proved enduring. Viewed in terms of Schumpeter's cyclical schema, the system of direct bank financing thus emerged out of the crisis of the semiliberal prewar economic order and functioned as an innovatory infrastructural element supporting the long economic upswing that began in the 1950s. The banking system was also at the center of the 1989 bubble. The period of troubles since the bubble's collapse conforms also to Schumpeter's schema: what worked as a developmental factor at one stage ceased to do so at the next. More than that, it became a dysfunctional element and obstacle to the tasks of the present.

8.1 Banking as Economic Governance

Japan's modern state-society structure is now widely understood to be characterized by an extensive, diverse, and well-articulated set of institutions "in between" state and society. This picture has appeared from many vantage points in the English-language scholarship of the last quarter century. In Chalmers Johnson's account, large corporations themselves played such an intermediate role. The paternalistic bureaucratic state delegated authority to them, expected them to follow state directives, and protected and nurtured them as its own. Peak business organizations have played similar mediating and self-governance roles, as emerges in the work of Miles Fletcher, Ulrike Schaede, and Lonny Carlile. In Carol Gluck's study of the construction of the ideology of the modern imperial state, a large part was played not only by state officials but also by ideological entrepreneurs from "among the people" who competed to serve the state, to make the state's messages their own, and to make their own messages those of the state. Sheldon Garon has anatomized the in-between places of civil-society organizations such as women's groups, religious bodies, and social reform groups as they sought representation in the state and were co-opted and deputized by it. Often enough, such organizations were themselves first organized at the initiative of state authorities or of people very close to state authorities. Gregory Kasza has explored the character of mass civil organizations in international comparative perspective and delineated a "conscription society" that shares key features with Fascist Italy and the Soviet Union. Similar "parastatal" dynamics appear in numerous social domains.[2]

The place of banking must be understood within this context. Numerous analysts have noted the special role of banks in Japan. In general, however, most specialized studies of Japanese banking are not set within the frame of a wider social-historical analysis that would allow this central feature to be grasped. The same is true of other countries. Japan is more "normal" than unique in this respect. In fact, banks in Japan have been peculiarly close to the state and so tightly articulated with it that it is analytically useful to think of the two as forming a single complex. This aspect was never more salient than in the wartime and early postwar years.

The fact of a tightly linked state-bank complex was not new to postwar Japan but went back seven decades, to the origins of Japan's modern capitalism.[3] Western banking provided the model for modern banking in Japan, but historically the place of banks in the Japanese political-economic system has been substantially different from their place in the Western countries to which comparison is usually made. In fact, to describe this system using English terms in the received English sense can obscure its key features. Among these features are the debt-as-control mechanisms that link business, banking, and the state, and in particular the quasi-ownership rights frequently exercised by banks vis-à-vis their clients. But this is not only a matter of difference. Indeed, to clarify the actual relations of state-bank governance of the economy also clarifies features of the actual functioning of Anglo-American political economy, as opposed to supposed, idealized pictures of it.

The capital for Japan's industrial development was from the beginning mainly developed internally, and Japanese authorities early on recognized the developmental functionality of banks. The first modern, Western-style banks were founded, like modern, Western-style industry, as a response to state initiatives. Thus, the Bank of Japan's Yoshino Toshihiko traced "the traditional supremacy of our banking system" to the beginning of the modern period. "If we had waited for the gradual increase of voluntary savings raised from a low level of national income," Yoshino wrote in 1957, "it would have been impossible to accomplish our conversion from an agricultural state to an industrial one and furthermore from a light industry to a heavy one in a short time." The state "introduced a modern banking system" precisely "to compensate for this shortage of *voluntary* capital formation." Nakayama Ichirō and Ōkita Saburō both thought in the same way.[4]

The problem of credit inflation was also therefore built in from the beginning. Again Yoshino: "This method of finance . . . relying upon the credit creating power of the banking system to its full extent, might inevitably lead to an inflationary movement." The situation faced by the country after the 1868 Meiji revolution was repeated after World War II, when bank credit "was really the sole support" for national economic recovery. Therefore, "there was no resort but compulsory saving by means of relying upon the credit creating power of the banking system—which inevitably would involve a violent inflationary process, as was shown in the case of the primary capital accumulation of the early Meiji era."[5] Yoshino, the bank's distinguished historian and himself a future BoJ director, understood this history very well, and further reading of it bears out his judgment.

Not only were Japan's first modern banks founded with "catch-up" developmentalist goals in mind. The organization of Japan's Western-style banking system also largely *preceded* the founding of Japan's Western-style industry. In 1872, four years after the Meiji revolution, the new government established a system of "national banks," which could issue their own banknotes based on their holdings of central-government bonds. This system was modeled on the one developed in the northern United States during the Civil War, a system that was decentralized on the one hand but designed to fund the war credits of the U.S. central government (as it then became) on the other.[6] Each of these aspects had their appeal in the new Japan. The initially decentralized organization of the banks made a place for members of former regional ruling elites, who were prominent as founders of the new national banks. The capital of the former lords and high retainers consisted of the bonds—that is, state promises to pay—with which the new government pensioned them off. The elite social background of these new capitalists gave banking in Japan a high social status that it has retained, and it differentiated the new Western-style banks from the old "exchange shops" (*ryōgae*) run by members of the hereditary merchant class, toward whom the samurai were by custom supposed to feel contempt. Banking thus came to be seen as a middle way between holding state office and following a career in business. Bank of Japan governor Ichimada Hisato saw it this way. In this, he was following his mentor Inoue Junnosuke, who likewise thought that bankers occupied a place "at the head of the business world," between the elite state bureaucracy and the directors of private industry.[7]

Among the institutional features of the Japanese banking system as it developed in the twentieth century, two deserve special notice. First, there was a large group of parastatal banks that carried out policy lending under state direction. Most relevant here is the specialized industrial development bank, the Industrial Bank of Japan. Second, the private banking sector itself was highly concentrated and hierarchically organized. Concentration arose as a response to depression and financial crisis in the 1920s and 1930s. Then, during World War II, private banking too was put under state direction. After the war, the character of this control changed, and its thrust was redirected, but institutional and personal relations established during the war persisted.

8.1.1 Parastatal Banks: The Extended State

The parastatal banks were half owned by the state and were under state (i.e., Ministry of Finance) direction. Together with the state, the parastatal sector formed a kind of "extended state" that placed a large set of extra resources at the service of state objectives. Or, as Ōkita Saburō described it, the use of the parastatal banks for long-term capital funds and the use of postal savings funds by the Deposit Bureau of the Ministry of Finance meant that "the government itself was a large banking institution."[8]

The first of the parastatal banks was the Yokohama Specie Bank, established in 1880, which was designed to finance foreign trade and concentrate foreign-exchange money (specie). GHQ ordered the Yokohama Specie Bank to be privatized in 1946, because of its role in the financial governance of Japan's overseas empire. It was renamed the Bank of Tokyo. GHQ itself took charge of Japanese trade accounts during the first part of the occupation. The Yokohama Specie Bank's former function of concentrating foreign-exchange funds was taken over directly by the Ministry of Finance itself. A centralized system of foreign-exchange budgeting, joined with a link system connecting imports with exports, subsequently became a core element of the High-Speed Growth system.

The second formally parastatal bank established by the Ministry of Finance was the Bank of Japan, Japan's central bank of issue, established in 1882. The Bank of Japan was also intended to concentrate specie and collect savings from the domestic banking system as a whole, to fund the government. It was further designated to oversee and coordinate the entire private banking system, "somewhat in the same way as a head office looks upon its branch offices," in the words of finance minister Matsukata Masayoshi, who directed the bank's establishment.[9]

Japanese conditions and institutions are often seen as exceptional, and it is good to consider also their generic aspects. It is also nice when a theoretical schema finds confirmation that its originator did not know of or did not adduce to it. Here, the schema is that of "late development," as outlined by Alexander Gerschenkron, which featured a special place for banks. Gerschenkron's idea was that in the countries that industrialized after England did, the process of industrial development has become, by stages, more conscious, concerted, and temporally compressed. The second wave of European industrialization in the mid-nineteenth century was characterized by the new role of industrial-bank financing, exemplified by the activity of the Péreire brothers (and animated by their Saint-Simonian ideas). Schumpeter likewise understood the role of the

Péreire brothers and their Crédit Mobilier as a further stage in the development first announced by John Law (see 3.2.1). Gerschenkron did not discuss Belgium in this framework, but he should have, for Belgium was the second industrialized country, after England, and what Gerschenkron called a "German" bank-centered model of development might better be called a Belgian model. The National Bank of Belgium also provided the direct model for the Bank of Japan and for the central banks of several other countries.[10] The bank-centered actualities of continental European industrialization influenced Schumpeter's theory of capitalist development, and they are described by it. The third wave of national industrialization, beginning late in the nineteenth century, was characterized by a large role for specialized industrial development banks and by an expanded role of the state and of mobilizing ideologies, including Marxism.[11] Gerschenkron did not include Japan in his analysis either, but students of Japanese development have been struck by its applicability.

In Japan, a new flurry of parastatal financial institution building began around 1896. The gold standard was adopted in 1897, and between 1896 and 1902 five "special" semigovernmental banks (*tokushu ginkō*) were chartered under their own enabling laws to provide long-term industrial, colonial, and agricultural financing. These were the Hypothec Bank of Japan (Nihon Kangyō Ginkō, 1896), the Agri-Industrial Bank (Nō-kō Ginkō, 1896), the Bank of Taiwan (Taiwan Ginkō, 1897/99), the Hokkaidō Development [or Colonization] Bank (Hokkaidō Takushoku Ginkō, 1899), and the Industrial Bank of Japan (Nihon Kōgyō Ginkō, 1902). In 1911 the colonial Bank of Korea (Chōsen Ginkō) was added. The 1900 Industrial Association Act simultaneously provided a legal framework for credit associations. Thus a banking system that was both state-centered and capitalistic was mainly set in place in its early twentieth-century form by 1902. These new parastatal banks were part of a larger system of parastatal corporations charged with key developmental tasks. Prominent among the parastatal corporations were colonial development companies, such as the South Manchurian Railway Company (1906) and the Oriental Development Company (1908).[12] This parastatal system was then substantially reorganized in the late 1940s and early 1950s.

Formally, the parastatal banks were established as joint-stock banks with their own boards of directors. Their staff were not government officials. Ownership followed the same formula as that of the Yokohama Specie Bank and the Bank of Japan. The government (practically speaking, the Ministry of Finance) owned half of the stock of each of the specially chartered banks. The imperial family owned large blocks of shares. The rest of the stock was held mainly by members of the Meiji state's new aristocracy (who were themselves "made" by and closely tied to the imperial state) or by favored businessmen closely connected to top state officials. These banks were run for profit but returned those profits to the state and (before the war) to their elite, state-connected shareholders. The minister of finance appointed or approved top management, and in practice, these banks took direction from the Ministry of Finance and from the Bank of Japan.

After the war, U.S. occupation authorities ordered the special banks to be privatized or dissolved. At the same time, as we have seen, a new parastatal bank, the Reconstruction Finance Bank, was organized in 1946. In the early 1950s, a new set of special banks was established.[13] These included the Japan Development Bank, established as successor to the RFB in 1951; the Japan Export Bank, established in 1950 and renamed the Japan Export-Import Bank in 1952, in effect to replace the Yokohama Specie Bank; and the Long-Term Credit Bank of Japan (also 1952). These special banks, but particularly the Industrial Bank of Japan, which was now formally privatized, controlled a very large proportion of capital flows through the 1950s.

8.1.2 Consolidation and Mobilization of the Private Banks

The outlines of banking-system expansion are described by the growth of the volume of bank balances (see appendix table A-1). Modern (Western-style) banking started in 1873. Account balances in the banks grew rapidly, but as late as 1891 they still totaled less than a third of the amount of paper and metallic cash-currency in circulation. The volume of bank balances reached parity with the volume of currency in 1897, the year the gold standard was enacted. Thereafter, the increase of bank balances rapidly outstripped that of currency. By 1920, at the peak of the post–World War I bubble, the amount of bank balances was five times that of currency. If one compares this to national economic activity as a whole, total credit (i.e., debt) balances in the banks and postal savings system equaled only about 4 percent of annual national income in 1893. They reached a level of 100 percent of national income in 1931.[14]

By the end of the World War I boom, there were more than 2,000 banks. This was an exceptionally large number by European standards, though not by U.S. standards. The deflation and depression of the 1920s and early 1930s brought a phase of shakeout and amalgamation. Especially after the great bank panic of 1927, the Ministry of Finance strongly promoted banking concentration. The requirements of the new bank law of 1927, adopted in the wake of the panic, reduced the number of banks to fewer than 700 by 1932. Consolidation of the private banking sector simplified the challenges of coordination and control for the MoF and BoJ. State direction was intensified by the so-called quasi-war in Manchuria after 1932. According to Hugh Patrick, the Bank of Japan was relatively loosely connected to the private banks before 1932, although under Inoue Junnosuke's tenure in the 1920s, the central bank did engage in great bailouts of the private banks. After 1937, wartime mobilization laws placed the banks under direct government and BoJ control. Consolidation was pushed much further during the war.[15] By the end of 1945, the number of banks was reduced to sixty-nine. A clear hierarchy of banks was also established. At the core of the system were eight national-level "city" banks. Regional banks, merged in line with the MoF's idea of "one prefecture, one bank," had the function of absorbing funds locally and funneling them to the city banks. The savings banks were consolidated into one great national savings bank, which was later converted into a city bank. The giant Imperial Bank (Teikoku Ginkō) was split after the war, and three of the parastatal special banks became regular city banks. There were now thirteen city banks.

The banks also acquired a central role in governing the whole industrial economy during the war. Corporations' previous mixed reliance on bank credit, self-financing, bonds, and to a lesser extent stock issues was replaced with a state-directed system of industrial finance via bank lending. This created another distinctive feature of the High-Speed Growth system of industrial finance.

Ichimada Hisato reappears in this connection. The Bank of Japan's charter was due to expire in 1942. In early 1941, having risen through the Bank of Japan ranks to the post of Inspection Section chief, Ichimada was a junior member of the bank's Special Survey Committee, which had the task of reforming the bank's structure in line with the needs of a "high-degree national defense state" (*kōdo kokubō kokka*) and "planned economy." Concretely, this meant that the central bank moved directly into industrial financing.[16] Thus in 1942, at a moment when Japanese military forces were fanning out across Southeast Asia, the bank was reorganized on the basis of a new Bank of Japan law, modeled on the Nazi-era revision of the Reichsbank law. Internally, the 1942 law centralized power further in the office of the central bank's governor. The new law also gave the Ministry of Finance even more direct control over the BoJ, while simultaneously strengthening BoJ control over the national credit system. The purport of the law could not have been clearer:

> *Article 1*: The purpose of the Bank of Japan shall be to adjust currency, to regulate financing, and to develop the credit system in conformity with policies of the state so as to ensure appropriate application of the state's total economic power.
>
> *Article 2*: The Bank of Japan shall be operated exclusively with a view of accomplishing the purposes of the state.[17]

Modestly revised under the occupation, this law remained the governing charter of the central bank for fifty-five years, when it was replaced by the new Bank of Japan law of 1997. This time it was modeled more on U.S. ideas of "central bank independence."

It was also in 1942 that a Nationwide Financial Control Association (Zenkoku Kin'yū Tōseikai) was established and given power over private banks, along the same lines as the control associations established in other branches of industry and commerce. To manage it, the BoJ's Inspection Section (Kōsa-bu) was expanded into the Inspection Bureau. (Later it was redesignated the Control Bureau [Tōseikyoku].) Ichimada was promoted to bureau chief (*kōsa kyokuchō*). In this position, although formally the lowest ranked member of the executive committee, he functioned in fact as "informal secretary general," responsible for the day-to-day management of the Nationwide Financial Control Association.[18] That is, he was responsible for coordinating the provision of capital funds to industry. The BoJ itself thus shifted from its former commercial orientation to a new industrial orientation. The central bank's close postwar contact with industry grew out of this experience. By 1943, bank credit was the primary source of long-term industrial financing. Almost all large companies were officially designated "munitions companies." In the spring of 1944, state authorities designated particular financial institutions to finance each particular company. These designated financial institutions were backed by BoJ or government credit. This new combination of wartime institutions established the framework for the BoJ's postwar institution of credit control under the name "window guidance," and for the postwar "main bank" system and bank-centered *keiretsu* system. The parastatal special banks also had an enlarged wartime role. The role of the Industrial Bank of Japan especially was greatly expanded.[19]

After the war, as mentioned, U.S. occupation authorities substantially reorganized the parastatal banks, excepting the BoJ. The Imperial Bank, created by the wartime merger of the Mitsui and Dai-ichi banks, was split back into its two component pieces.[20] But this is about all that was done. Unlike other sectors of the Japanese corporate system, the private banking system was neither deconcentrated nor significantly liberalized. A pyramidal hierarchy was retained. The banks were therefore in place in the 1950s to serve as centers of the giant bank-centered *keiretsu* such as Mitsui, Mitsubishi, and Sumitomo, which reconstituted the old *zaibatsu* groups. They continued to depend on the BoJ and continued to take direction from the MoF and BoJ.

8.1.3 Who Owed Whom?

The government's debts, in theory, signified claims on future government revenues. Who held the government debt? In short, the Japanese state owed its debt mainly to its "extended" self. Formally, this looked like a Western state-debt system under which future state revenues were mortgaged to private credit-creators. In fact, the state debt was in large part an accounting fiction. As of the end of March 1948, the parastatal Bank of Japan held some 28 percent of all domestic government bonds issued. The state itself, mostly the Deposit Bureau (Yokinbu) of the Ministry of Finance, directly held some 23 percent of its own bonds. As it worked out, exactly 51 percent of the bonds were thus held by the state and central bank. This was the same standard controlling ratio as the ratio of shares that the state conventionally held in parastatal enterprises. Commercial banks held another 28 percent of government bonds. Corporations held only 0.3 percent of government bonds. Individuals held only 0.1 percent.[21] These numbers failed to account for some 21 percent of government bonds, presumably held by special (parastatal) financial institutions. Moreover, the state's private "creditors"—the commercial banks—were themselves actually client debtors of the extended state (see 12.1.2). Not only did they depend financially on the Bank of Japan, but the BoJ closely regulated their lending and, jointly with the Ministry of Finance, instructed them as to their purchases of government bonds. Practically speaking, the "creditors" of the state were thus components of the state-bank complex.

8.2 Superdirect Finance

The system of industrial finance by banks is often mischaracterized as "indirect" financing. This system, especially as practiced in Japan, is in fact better described, in line with Schumpeter's conception of capital, as *superdirect* financing.

The idea that bank finance is "indirect" embodies an entire theory. Indeed, it embodies a "cover story," for there is an unofficial bankers' party line when it comes to telling the public what banks do. As the story goes, private individuals begin the process by depositing their money with the bank; banks collect these savings, and then lend out this same money, thereby serving as "intermediaries" between savers and borrowers. Hence, when banks lend to companies, their depositors are said to be investing indirectly in those companies. This story, taught to schoolchildren and otherwise widely disseminated, is not a satisfactory account, for it elides the fact that only a small fraction of the "deposit money" that the banking system creates corresponds to cash deposits actually paid in by depositors. As Schumpeter emphasized (see 3.2.1), the alleged norm, while it may constitute one historical origin of the system, is actually a special case. The normal case is that banks create new credit funds by the act of lending something that did not exist before it was "lent"; the great bulk of bank balances originate in this way.

According to the Bank of Japan's authorizing definition, the institutions that could create deposit-money (that is, credit-money) included city banks, local banks, trust banks, long-term credit banks, and a few more specialized financial institutions.[22] All of these institutions could accept monetary deposits and, more to the point, could "leverage" these deposits, creating balances many times larger through lending. As creators of credit-money, the city banks had the main role. The Industrial Bank of Japan also played an extraordinarily large role, described further below. Of the thirteen postwar city banks, seven were former *zaibatsu* banks (Mitsubishi, Mitsui, Fuji, Sumitomo, Daiwa, Tōkai, Kōbe). Three were former parastatal banks privatized during the occupation: the Bank of Tokyo (the former Yokohama Specie Bank), the Kangyō (Hypothec) Bank, and the Hokkaido Colonial (Hokkaidō Takushoku) Bank. These former parastatal banks retained especially close connections to the Ministry of Finance. The remaining three city banks (Dai-ichi, Sanwa, Kyōwa) were more or less independent. Bank of Japan credits to banks served as the base money for the system. In a usage opposite to Anglo-American usage, some Japanese writers have used the term "indirect" to describe finance via the stock market, which also depended ultimately on money created by banks.

8.2.1 The Marginality of the Stock Market

Before the war, new fundraising in Japanese financial markets was centered on bonds, and a large proportion of corporate shares were tightly held by the *zaibatsu* families rather than being offered and traded on the public markets. New share issues became much less significant during the war. On August 10, 1945, the day after the atomic bombing of Nagasaki, Japanese authorities closed the exchanges to prevent panic selling.

The officially recognized stock exchanges remained closed until May 1949. Finance minister Tsushima Juichi attempted to reopen the Tokyo exchange on September 26, 1945, but GHQ intervened to prevent it. The Americans used the Tokyo Stock Exchange building as a gymnasium. Occupation authorities did tolerate a "black-market" exchange that operated unofficially nearby. They did not think much of it, complaining that the "extralegal" market operates in a "dirty, dark, and poorly ventilated room. It not only does not inspire confidence but looks disgraceful." Graceful or not, the unofficial exchange became very active. From the end of 1945 to early 1949—that is, for the duration of the high-inflation era—there was a historic boom in share trading, the biggest since the inflationary boom of World War I, stimulated by the confiscation and public sale of *zaibatsu* shares.[23] Trading in company shares also retained the highly speculative character it had had before the war. Most of this trading was unconnected to providing capital funds to businesses, and new public offerings of company shares did not emerge as a major method of financing industrial development.

To the extent that public offerings of shares did provide new capital, it was largely funded, as in other countries, by new bank credit, making this the more indirect method of financing.

The stock-market boom accompanied the growth of the black market in goods, and black-market proceeds were a major source of the funds wagered on stocks. The shares of former *zaibatsu* companies served as relatively liquid assets whose value kept pace with inflation. Expectations of inflation thus caused people to prefer holding shares over cash. The stock boom was further stimulated by the laundering of "old yen" accounts through the stock market: when the government froze existing bank deposits in February 1946 and limited the conversion of old yen into new yen, a loophole in the law allowed funds to be transferred to brokerage houses. As the underground stock market burgeoned, people transferred money into company shares and then sold the shares for new yen. In this narrowly contained domain, there was indeed a postwar inflationary bubble. The feverish trading in shares was part of a speculative craze that ranged from dealing in stockpiled industrial materials to petty black marketeering and *pachinko* (pinball machine) gambling. The "Nikkei-Dow Jones Average," printed daily in the newspapers to track the unofficial market, rose from 65 in the autumn of 1946 to 700 in May 1949. By January 1948, daily trading activity reached a peak of more than 6 million shares—six times the prewar average. The Securities Dealers Association (who mainly administered themselves) temporarily suspended trading to try to rein things in. By February 1948, trading volumes had fallen back to about 2 million shares per day. On January 31, 1949, shortly before Joseph Dodge came to Japan, GHQ announced that the stock exchange would be officially reopened. On the eve of the opening of the relegalized exchange on May 16, 1949, trading volume reached a final peak of 8 million shares.[24] The market then crashed, ironically as a result of the Dodge policies, and became inactive as an adjunct facility for credit generation.

8.3 The Privatization of the Positive Policy

As described in chapter 7, Dodge's cutoff of industrial finance from the Reconstruction Finance Bank caused an immediate capital shortage—reminiscent of the circumstances that had led to the RFB's founding in the first place. This shortage of capital was the "essence of a stabilization crisis" in Dodge's private reckoning. In these constrained circumstances, Japanese financial authorities developed a new, more privatized structure of state-directed industrial credit. That is, within the framework of Dodge's macro-level "negative policy," a bank-centered micro-level "positive policy" emerged. This was more than simply another case of American form (or façade) and Japanese function. In fact, this seemingly contradictory policy mix established the framework within which first recovery and then sustained high growth would unfold for the next several decades.

Ikeda Hayato was minister of finance from February 1949 to October 1952—the entire period of the Dodge Line and six months beyond it. As governor of the Bank of Japan, Ichimada Hisato had a much longer tenure, from June 1946 to December 1954. This was the longest term of any governor in the central bank's history. Ichimada was also the most "independently" powerful governor in the central bank's history—because he had powerful foreign backing. His tenure in office was, moreover, the period when capital allocation was most closely directed by the central bank.[25] Ikeda and Ichimada also came to be sharp rivals. In their public and private statements, both men presented themselves as agreeing in principle with the Dodge Line. Both attempted to work around Dodge's strict rules with the shared goal of continuing to direct funds to prioritized large enterprises. Despite their personal rivalry for control, Ikeda's thinking on this point was close to Ichimada's.

As minister of finance, Ikeda became closely identified with Dodge's deflation policy (see 7.3). He tried to give it a good name, "balanced public finance," with limited success. "I realize it is the feeling of the public that this thing called 'balanced public finance' is unaccommodating, stubborn, and oppressive," Ikeda acknowledged in his book *Balanced Public Finance* (*Kinkō zaisei*), ghostwritten by a team of MoF officials in 1952.[26] He therefore tried to explain its rationale. The credit system, he said, was built of "closely mutually interdependent" parts "like the gears of precision machinery" and "extends in a complicated fashion." Failure here would affect the whole economy, and one must be very cautious. "Especially in the postwar Japanese economy, which is described with the phrase 'shallow economy,' capital, especially liquid capital, is insufficient." At the same time, however, "it is no good to have simply a general monetary easing which would promote once again a sweet dream of inflation." Monetary adjustment was a delicate matter, "and if you loosen even a little, inflation will reappear." In order to gain a "suitable overall balance," the proper technique was "to go with tightening in general, but to pour capital into the most important areas such as basic industries, medium and small business, and trade promotion in especially necessary areas."[27] In essence, this was a continuation of the logic of priority production and targeted RFB financing, within a macro-level, anti-inflationary framework that restricted the flow of money and credit everywhere else. Like Ikeda, Bank of Japan governor Ichimada represented himself as being in general agreement with the Dodge plan, but with modifications: "I thought that in order to control inflation we had to accept that sort of thing [the Dodge plan] unconditionally. However, though the aim of controlling inflation was good, looked at in terms of timing, I was worried that if we did it as demanded, at that time, it could really become a deflation."[28] Much more than Ikeda, Ichimada was in a position to do something about it.

8.3.1 The General Headquarters of Monetary Indication

"Indeed, it may have looked like a main temple [*honzan*]," Ichimada later acknowledged, referring to the occupation-era image of the central bank as "the Vatican." And Ichimada himself exercised an autocratic power there, to the extent that he was dubbed "Rōma Hō-ō," the "Pope of Rome." Here was another kind of divided governance. General MacArthur, from his headquarters in the Dai-Ichi Insurance building, looking out over the Imperial Palace, played the role of American shogun and presided over the secular world of administrative indication and enforcement, which would be done "at gun-point" if need be. Undisturbed in the Bank of Japan's head office not far to the north, Ichimada as "King of the Dharma" governed the esoteric world of financial indication.[29] During this time, Ichimada recalled that he met personally with MacArthur about twice a month. His nominal superior, Minister Ikeda, meanwhile worked out of temporary offices across town in Shinjuku, GHQ having requisitioned the MoF head office in the government district of Kasumigaseki.

Ichimada himself seems not to have minded being called pope. He preferred it, he joked, to being called the "gargoyle of Notre Dame," which he had been called in reference to his physiognomy. The power of the central bank itself was greatly enhanced by several special factors, according to Yoshino Toshihiko. First, GHQ saw the Bank of Japan as more "impartial" than the government. Thus GHQ officials ignored the Japanese chain of command and dealt directly with Ichimada, bypassing the Ministry of Finance, which they mistrusted. Ichimada also said that ESS chief General William Marquat, being a military man, mostly listened to Ichimada's advice on financial matters (though Marquat's own letters to Dodge expressed considerable distrust of Ichimada).[30] Thus the Bank of Japan gained a strong position relative to the Ministry of Finance: if GHQ okayed the bank's policy, the MoF was compelled to go along. Ichimada later recalled this period—of foreign military occupation—as the time when Japan had a "real central bank," which could concern itself solely with "the national interest" and nothing else.

A second factor enhancing the central bank's influence was the importance of industrial financing, with which the BoJ was closely concerned, and in particular the critical role of the Reconstruction Finance Bank, whose activity was closely coordinated with the BoJ. Ichimada avoided discussing these questions in public, even long after the fact.

A third factor enhancing the central bank's power was GHQ's purging of other financial powers. First, *zaibatsu* dissolution rendered inactive the giant capital of the *zaibatsu* groups. The personnel purge also removed many of the most senior *zaibatsu* leaders from their executive positions. Before the war, the *zaibatsu* had regarded even temporary reliance on the Bank of Japan as a disgrace.[31] Heads of the great *zaibatsu*, for example Mitsui Bank head Ikeda Seihin, had seen themselves as standing at the same level as the BoJ governor. Now, the central bank's system of "overloan" support to the private banks focused especially on the former *zaibatsu* banks. It was these BoJ credits that kept the pieces of the former *zaibatsu* afloat and made them beholden to the central bank, which could now look on them, indeed, "as a head office looks upon its branch offices." A similar effect followed from GHQ's reorganization or shutting down of the parastatal banks, which had engaged in policy lending and could issue bonds. When these pivotal banks were shut down, the Bank of Japan by default assumed an even larger direct role.

A fourth factor indicated by Yoshino was the personal position of Ichimada Hisato, whose power was deeply rooted within the Bank of Japan itself (see 2.4). This position was rooted also in the wartime financing of industry. In 1944, having managed the wartime industrial financing system since its formation in 1942, Ichimada was appointed to the BoJ's board of directors. In 1945, continuing as a BoJ director, he was posted to Nagoya and then to Osaka as branch chief. This move out of Tokyo was timely, for GHQ officials would almost surely have purged Ichimada if they had understood his wartime role. In June 1946, GHQ did purge BoJ governor Araki Eikichi, together with all but three BoJ directors. Ichimada now became governor, with a new board of directors. Four of the newly appointed directors served for less than a year, further enhancing Ichimada's primacy.[32] The purge of top BoJ officials and private bankers made Ichimada at one bound the dominant figure in the postwar banking world.

The continuation of the wartime Bank of Japan law contributed to Ichimada's power. Under the prewar rules, all BoJ directors had a vote on policy. Under the 1942 revisions, decision-making power was concentrated in the governor. Thus, within the bank as well, Ichimada was "Pope of Rome." In part, this was a heritage of Tōjō-era "war dictatorship" thinking, known at the time as the "leadership principle" (*shidōsha genri*), a translation of the German *Führerprinzip*.[33] It reflected also a "one-man," or "American" executive style, as exemplified by Prime Minister Yoshida. Despite the powers accumulated by both Yoshida and Ichimada, this one-man style became impossible after 1952, when it was no longer so closely backed by American power.

Ichimada's experience in post–World War I Germany and his admiration for Reichsbank governor Hjalmar Schacht have also been mentioned. One aspect of this is seen in Ichimada's professed "stabilization first" viewpoint. In Japan, as in those days in Germany, Ichimada explained, "the first thing is to give all of our power to currency stabilization." The key to monetary stabilization in Germany was the fact that "despite the government's pressure, Governor Schacht never yielded on the matter of issuing [more] currency." Ichimada, however, could not do the same in Japan. His own policy during the Dodge Line was more significant in the opposite direction. This reflected the expansive, credit-creation aspect of Schacht's policy as it later developed.[34]

Dodge's termination of lending by the Reconstruction Finance Bank threatened the core circuits of industrial financing. Ichimada therefore modified the Dodge plan, in order to turn deflation to disinflation: "Having ourselves up to then . . . had a policy of stabilization based on expanding the economy by all means, [I thought that] if we hastily took a strong deflationary policy, there was probably a danger that it would become more than a stabilization panic [*antei kyōkō*]."[35] Again, the lessons of the 1920s were in play. What Ichimada feared, according to his deputy Yoshino, was "a panic brought about by policy." That is, he feared a stabilization depression like that produced in Germany during his sojourn there.[36] The German "stabilization crisis" of 1924 was only the first of three deflationary crises. The worst was the third, the disastrous Brüning deflation of 1930, which inaugurated a period of rule by decree that eventuated in the Nazi seizure of power in 1933. Brüning himself escaped Germany only a few steps ahead of Hitler's secret police. Japan in 1930 had undergone its own self-induced "stabilization" depression, directed by Ichimada's mentor Inoue Junnosuke. Inoue's campaign had ended in his own assassination. No one at the Bank of Japan had forgotten this experience. Ichimada's own version of balanced finance was thus to balance Dodge's restriction of credit with new credit creation:

> We judged that we might not be able to control the Japanese economy; therefore, opposing Mr. Dodge's intention, on my own responsibility, and only within the scope of the excess of withdrawals [i.e., from monetary circulation] in the government budget, we hammered out a policy of filling in [this shortfall] by putting out funding from the Bank of Japan. In calling this "disinflation," we gave it the meaning of having neither inflation nor deflation.

"It wasn't that I was completely against Mr. Dodge's Nine Principles," Ichimada later explained; "it was just that as the person who had been entrusted with the actual responsibility for Japan's economy, in this way of doing things, I differed somewhat from Mr. Dodge's intentions."[37] The BoJ, acting via the private banks, thus filled in for the RFB to bridge the funding gap for priority industries.

The Bank of Japan's policy was not hidden from view. The BoJ informed occupation authorities of what it was doing and provided a breakdown of bank lending by amount, by industry, and by capital funds versus operating funds. They explained that they were cooperating with the Economic Stabilization Board in order to fulfill the FY 1949 iron and steel production plan and in order to provide stopgap loans to other critical industries, such as electrical power generation and chemical fertilizer production. By Ichimada's own account, he independently decided that the Bank of Japan must increase its lending. Dodge implicitly acquiesced in the creation of this bank-centered arrangement. In fact, it appears that the initiative for this BoJ role came from the ESB, which delivered a plan describing this "stopgap" operation to GHQ on April 19, 1949. This was followed by the BoJ's own proposal to GHQ on April 28. The BoJ proposal paid lip service to known American financial conceptions: "Needless to say, industrial funds henceforth should be obtained in principle from accumulated funds." But unfortunately, that was now impossible. The BoJ further indicated that they expected these credits to be refinanced in the future by U.S. aid counterpart funds. Therefore, as a temporary measure pending the release of those funds, the BoJ would see to it that a credit syndicate was organized for each of the key enterprises, "with banks having close business relations with the enterprise as its nucleus."[38]

This "temporary" arrangement was the origin of the postwar "main bank" system. It was also a continuation of the wartime designated-bank system.[39] Needless to say, there was no sense in spelling out the latter point to the Americans. Bank of Japan stopgap lending was also a starting point for the postwar "overloan" system. The BoJ indicated to GHQ authorities that they would provide credits as needed to "smooth" syndicate funding. Because of "delays" in government payments, they reported, the BoJ "will make" city banks extend funds of approximately ¥10 billion to specified industries. The central bank would itself provide these funds to the banks. For example, Nippon Steel Tube Co. (Nippon Kōkan, NKK) had depended on the RFB, from which it had borrowed ¥943 million. In the case of a new ¥320 million loan to the steel company, the BoJ did not directly lend the money but rather put together a syndicate, led by the Industrial Bank of Japan and Fuji Bank and including five other banks. A new ¥340 million loan to Nittetsu (Japan Iron Manufacturing Co.) was similarly organized, as was a ¥500 million loan to the Nippon Electric Power Generation and Transmission Company. Further large loans were made to the Nippon Nitrogen Co. and to other priority recipients of past RFB lending. To support lending by the commercial banks, the BoJ also began to directly buy up commercial bills held by the banks—¥100 billion worth in 1949 (see appendix table A-2).[40]

Even years later, the entire subject of "overloan" was something that Ichimada refused to discuss. There were good reasons to remain silent, for the arrangements in question were part of a discreetly managed ongoing reality that concerned the core national circuits of economic wealth and power. When questioned on the point, Ichimada said only that the "overloan" was "unavoidable" and that "there were no particular questions" in the BoJ's relation with the city banks "because they depended on us." He did say that not only the banks but the whole of industry depended on the central bank, "and that's probably why I was called 'the Pope'."[41]

Thus the Bank of Japan, in cooperation with the ESB, put together its own industrial financing plan to fill in for the loss of RFB funds. The seven industries to be funded were, in order of priority: coal, electric power, iron and steel, chemicals, shipping, metals mining, and petroleum. The BoJ's use of other banks, including the Industrial Bank of Japan, greatly leveraged the BoJ's money-creation power: new BoJ credits to the banks served as a "deposit base" on which the banks could create credits many times greater. This arrangement also distributed the profits to the private banks.

Rigid enforcement of the former "class A-1, class A-2, class B, class C" categorization of borrowers also ended in 1949, but the Bank of Japan continued to screen loans to ensure that they went to priority projects. When speaking to the meeting of the Japan Bankers Association in June 1951, for example, Ichimada told them that the Bank of Japan would rigorously screen any loans for new equipment, except in the cases of electrical power and shipbuilding. He further indicated that although the city banks should lend only to profitable enterprises, they should never extend credit to ventures that were engaged in speculation and stockpiling.[42] The Bank of Japan clearly considered that it knew what was best for the overall national economy, with which Ichimada Hisato said he had been "entrusted." Given the strength and broad oversight of its research staff, this was not an unbacked claim. Because the city banks were in an "overloan" condition, the central bank had the leverage to command city bank compliance, and it had the administrative tools to ensure compliance in detail.

Inflation greatly pushed up market interest rates during the period 1945–49, but the Bank of Japan was slow to raise its own discount rate. In effect, the BoJ thus provided large subsidies to those banks on which it bestowed credits. Interest-rate increases to control inflation were not a part of the Dodge Line, even though they are typically part of anti-inflationary monetary stabilization programs. The BoJ did not raise its discount rate at all during 1949–50.[43]

The consequences of Ichimada's modifications of Dodge's principles were profound. The end result was that the Dodge Line meant not a reduction but rather a "privatization" of the money-supply process. The Dodge Line restrained the issuance of cash-currency (BoJ notes). But this reduction was more than offset by the simultaneous increase in commercial bank credit. Thus in 1949, the volume of cash currency was more or less frozen, but the total of bank balances increased by close to ¥300 billion, or nearly 60 percent.[44] In other words, total money actually increased. The Dodge and Ichimada policies together caused the ratio of bank balances to currency to jump, in a single year, from a level of one-to-one to a level of two-to-one.

8.3.2 The Question of Central-Bank Independence

In various ways, core Japanese financial arrangements proved to be surprisingly durable and resistant to U.S. occupation initiatives. This pattern can be seen again in the response to the single major U.S. initiative that really touched on the management of the central bank.

It is sometimes mistakenly said that the Bank of Japan enjoyed central-bank independence before the adoption of the new law of 1942. In fact, the BoJ was under definite state (i.e., MoF) control under the terms of the original Bank of Japan law. The central bank did develop a degree of practical autonomy, especially after 1919, when Inoue Junnosuke became the first career BoJ man to have risen through the ranks to become the central bank's governor. But the Anglo–U.S. idea of "central bank independence" was not an operative principle.

As the "reverse course" in policy gathered force in 1948, some U.S. officials did develop a plan for turning the Bank of Japan into an institution wholly owned by private banks, in the way the U.S. Federal Reserve banks were. This vision was held particularly by C. E. Cagle, an experienced Federal Reserve "money doctor" on loan to GHQ, and by Economic and Scientific Section finance chief Walter K. LeCount, who was a private banker by profession. In May 1948, the time of the Federal Reserve's Young mission to Japan, LeCount called for an extraordinary constitutional (or extraconstitutional) innovation, arguing within GHQ that a "Banking Board" with Cabinet rank should be established and entrusted with the "formulation and enforcement of all monetary and credit policies of the Government." The projected Board would additionally "regulate and supervise all banks and all other credit and financial institutions." It should be composed of bankers and businessmen, "inexperienced in politics," with the goal of preventing "domination or dictatorship over banks by the Government."[45]

This plan borrowed the then-regnant language of "democratization" to propose, in essence, an outright bankers' republic. The idea of a powerful U.S. Federal

Reserve–like structure that would locate all money-creation power in a practically self-governed banking sector would come close to describing future U.S.
realities, whose bubble-machine dynamics are now manifest. In Japan in 1948,
such an enactment would have stripped the Ministry of Finance of its power over
monetary and credit policy and of its regulatory power over the financial sector.
This is approximately what did happen fifty years later in the great financial reforms of 1997 to around 2003, when U.S. practice did serve as a model.[46]

The rhetoric of democratization also fit awkwardly with proposals to strengthen
the power of bankers. With the turn to the Dodge Line, the new rhetoric of "economic stabilization" became much more comfortable to probank reforms. Army
undersecretary William Draper also wanted to strengthen the Bank of Japan and
remove it from MoF authority. In fact, this was something his fellow Wall Street
bankers had hoped for since the 1920s, when it had been an item on a 1927 "wish
list" that J. P. Morgan and Company executives had communicated to their clients in the Japanese government.[47] Japanese authorities had ignored the idea then,
and they managed to avert it now.

The BoJ itself was an obstacle to this "Federal Reserve"–style vision. Within
the Bank of Japan, such ideas were felt as another American attack on the Japanese economy. As Yoshino Toshihiko put it, "under the name of democratization,
GHQ in the early occupation period was eager to weaken the Japanese economy,
starting with *zaibatsu* dissolution." The Bank of Japan reorganization looked like
more of the same. Although GHQ officials spoke of "independence," BoJ officials feared that changes would weaken their present powerful position. For their
part, GHQ officials criticized the Bank of Japan as a financial monopoly, in that
the same institution made financial policy and executed it, reigning over the city
banks; they wanted the BoJ to serve as a central bank only. Dodge, as a regional
private banker himself, shared this view. Cagle warned that "the Bank of Japan is
largely a one-man institution" and said that the BoJ under Ichimada had not
fought inflation.[48]

The reorganization of the Bank of Japan was the biggest issue that Ichimada
had to negotiate with GHQ. The result was on its face a compromise. A "Policy
Board" was established, but it was located within the BoJ, and its role was so reduced as to be of little consequence. It was called in Japanese the "Policy Committee" (Seisaku I'inkai), which sounded advisory rather than authoritative.
Shimomura Osamu, who was dispatched as the MoF representative to the Policy
Committee in 1953, called it a "sleeping board."[49] According to Ichimada, he
argued the matter with Dodge, and Dodge gave up, with the policy committee
being written into the otherwise modest revision of the Bank of Japan Law in
June 1949. If so, this is remarkable. Dodge was not a man to easily abandon a
position once enunciated. Indeed, he made it a matter of principle when dealing

with Japanese officials not to do so, even sticking to positions to which he was not especially attached merely to avoid setting a precedent of compromise. Finance Minister Ikeda got little or nothing from Dodge despite his best efforts. Nor was Dodge wont to confuse surface for substance. But where Dodge did relent was in his lenient treatment of Japanese banking. The "Policy Board" did represent a defeat for Ichimada, by forcing the governor to share power with the board, and Ichimada continued to regard it as an anomalous heritage of the occupation. At the same time, most provisions of the 1942 Bank of Japan Law remained in effect, including the provision that the central bank was under the supervision of the finance minister, who could "order the bank to undertake any necessary business," and the provision that the cabinet, on the finance minister's recommendation, could remove the bank's governor or vice-governor. The Ministry of Finance later reasserted its influence over the Bank of Japan, but the central bank retained a broad field of authoritative latitude. Concerning this entire encounter, William Tsutsui concluded that "the wartime 'chain of command' stretching from the bureaucracy to private-sector finance via the Bank of Japan was not broken—or even substantially weakened—by the American legislative initiative."[50] And this "chain of command" of capital was strengthened by changes that were environmental to the financial system.

THE TURNING POINT

If all produced means of production were ever to disappear, indeed if all goods, with the exception of the most necessary subsistence goods, disappeared for a certain time period, and only the natural possibilities and the organization of the economy remained—the disaster would not be as big as one might believe. If the leaders were somehow able to retain their authority, and, in the area destroyed, each and every one would in a thoroughly orderly way begin again with the productive work, then the traces of the catastrophe would soon be blurred and wiped out. *The stock [Vorrat] of produced goods does not mean that much. Much more important is the hierarchy*—the system of superordination and subordination—of the members of an economy, their dispositions to act, *and the economy's energy and goals.* The paradox in our assertion is not quite as outrageous as it may seem at first glance. The vindication of this assertion lies in the fact that wars and other catastrophes overall, where they do not cause the economic organization to collapse, do not leave permanent traces, that the consequences of such devastation actually disappear surprisingly fast.

—Joseph Schumpeter, *Theory of Economic Development* (1912)

It was Schumpeter, in *Business Cycles*, who first clearly conceptualized economic development as a succession of industrial revolutions, each based on a set of core technologies, organizational forms, and ideologies. His idea of coherent waves of industrial reorganization continues to provide a starting point for thinking about the succession of technological and organizational paradigms, regulation regimes, and other similar constructions. Schumpeter himself died in January 1950, but those who later developed this line of thinking mainly agree in finding the late 1940s and early 1950s to be a "Schumpeterian" turning point, with the solution of a long systemic crisis and the beginning of a long boom that lasted to 1973.[1] This was true at the level of the whole international system as well as at the level of most national political economies. This Schumpeterian turn coincided with the domestic and international settlements that followed World War II;

with both things happening together, the transformation was that much more sweeping and intense.

Japan's own postwar reformation, comprehensive though it was, was unique in neither intensity nor scope. Similarly profound transformations happened across Eurasia in these years. Unlike the aftermath of World War I, these transformations coincided with a great economic recovery—this world war was followed not by chronic deflation and depression but instead by the greatest globally synchronous boom in industrial history. This chapter considers this moment and offers some interim conclusions.

9.1 A Schumpeterian Turning Point

Schumpeter's *Business Cycles* is built around the idea of economic long waves: super–business cycles with a length of fifty to sixty years, which are a fundamental feature of the capitalist developmental process. These supercycles came to inflationary peaks around 1814, 1865, and 1920, as indicated by N. D. Kondratiev, from whom Schumpeter took the outlines of the long-wave idea.[2] Schumpeter's account of the process was an extension of the vision he developed in connection to shorter-term business cycles in his *Theory of Economic Development*. It came down mainly to two intertwined lines of explanation. The first is a schema in which phases of collective inflationary credit creation are followed by phases of deflationary "repayment" through an increased flow of production. A second line of explanation, much less a focus of this book, is more conspicuous and has gotten more attention from later analysts. This is a schematic history of successive technological-organizational complexes. In more recent discussion, these are called *paradigms* by contemporary neo-Schumpeterians like Christopher Freeman and Carlota Perez. The term *regimes* is used in much the same way by Regulation School theorists. In this view, new domestic social settlements were emplaced around the world in the late 1940s, establishing the new regulatory and technological regimes that would support economic development for the next quarter century. This phase of crisis and restructuring was followed by a classic Schumpeterian long boom from the 1950s to the early 1970s.[3] Industrially, the postwar "long boom" system was based on a set of mass-production (or "Fordist") technologies developed in the 1920s, mainly in the United States. This technological package was still relatively new but by now well established and available for much broader diffusion and application. The socialist countries, where the investment process was wholly state-directed, also took part in this movement. By the 1970s, however, the postwar heavy-industrial system and postwar regulatory regimes had developed limits of their own, manifested in the simultaneous onset of economic slowdown and high inflation. I'll return to this idea and its instrumentalization in Japan in the next chapter.

Schumpeter published *Business Cycles* in 1939, just before World War II and the great inflation that came with it. Partly for this reason, *Business Cycles* was poorly received in the United States, and Schumpeter's long-wave framework was ignored by most "mainstream" economists there (W. W. Rostow was a significant exception).[4] At the same time, "those big two volumes of Schumpeter" were widely read by economists in wartime Japan (see 2.1). As described already, Schumpeter's historical analysis was based on a retrospective "long nineteenth century" view, which extended from roughly the 1780s to the 1930s. Looking at this period of 150 years (that is, three long-wave periods), Schumpeter saw inflation as an essential feature of the twenty- to thirty-year upswing phases of each wave, and deflation as an essential feature of the twenty- to thirty-year downswings. In this, these super–business cycles were like the classic seven- to eleven-year business cycles of the nineteenth century (which Schumpeter dubbed Juglar cycles, after Clement Juglar), but they operated on a timescale some six times longer.[5]

The great inflation of the 1940s subsequently crosscut this long-wave pattern, ending the deflation of the 1920s and 1930s seemingly "ahead of schedule" compared to the duration of the prior nineteenth-century price waves. This great inflation then ended, internationally, by about 1952. The worldwide recovery and boom that continued from around 1950 to around 1973 was again "on time," according to Schumpeter's long-wave schedule. The long boom also conformed to the historical pattern in being a time of moderate (and increasing) inflation.

To preface the discussion in chapter 10, it is helpful to consider the era of High-Speed Growth within this framework. First, the two-decade period from the early 1950s to the early 1970s stands out, institutionally speaking, as a single political-economic unit. This is conspicuously so in Japan, where a new and remarkably stable institutional settlement came together very quickly after the return of national political independence in 1952. At the same time, a new, but already proven industrial-technological complex provided the basis for *predictable* rapid growth. For the world as a whole, industrial growth during this period was based on a set of technologies mostly created during 1925–50; innovations in the 1950s and 1960s were more characterized by application rather than creation de novo.[6] In Japan, this aspect was intensified by the fact of catch-up growth. This was especially visible in the large stock of "off the shelf" technologies available for purchase, licensing, or copying. These came mainly from the United States, a channel of technological transfer that had been blocked by the war. Despite the moderately inflationary trend of the 1950s and 1960s, decreasing production costs were especially evident in steel, automobiles, oil refining, synthetic fibers, petrochemicals, electric appliances, and machinery: the staple industries of the era (see 12.3). Low costs in many of these industries were additionally based on the supply of cheap oil, a condition that changed suddenly in 1973.

Let us cast even further ahead for a moment. Worldwide, the coincidence in the 1970s of high inflation with stagnation in the old heavy-industrial core regions seemed to signal a fundamental shift in systemic functioning. This shift was widely interpreted as the onset of a new long downswing, and a significant revival of long-wave theorizing followed. However, the 1980s were not a time of international deflation. At the least, this indicated a basic departure from the nineteenth-century pattern of "inflationary upswing, deflationary downswing" that was at the heart of Schumpeter's picture of development through cycles. This is getting ahead of the subject of this book, but some points of Schumpeter's conception of deflation are worth reconsidering in connection with his ideas of "autodeflation" and "harvest periods," as will be discussed in the concluding two chapters.

9.2 Social Sources of Keynesian Stabilization

Schumpeter avoided making policy recommendations. His Japanese students did find his work to have important policy implications, which would not have been in line with his own preferences. Schumpeter himself was fundamentally conservative, even aristocratic, in his social outlook and preferred a classic laissez-faire approach. He intensely disliked Roosevelt's New Deal and Keynesian stimulus ideas in general, and he often said more or less frankly that recessions were a necessary part of the developmental process, which had to run their course.[7] This had also been the verdict of classical economics. Such an aloof philosophical view did not offer answers to the immediate crises people faced. Looking at the various social prescriptions offered by laissez-faire, by socialism, and by fascism, it was thus to the ideas of J. M. Keynes that people across the capitalist world turned in establishing a new liberal democratic mainstream. Or rather, to Keynes plus the new "welfare–warfare state," as it happened in actuality.[8] In the case of demilitarized Japan, it was to the new capitalist investment state. On this point, Schumpeter's Japanese students, particularly Nakayama Ichirō, were more Keynesian than they were Schumpeterian.

Social inequality was another thing Schumpeter considered natural, and he did not much address its implications until the end of his career. By the late 1940s, however, social inequality was coming to be widely understood as a cause of the systemic economic collapses of the 1930s. This breakdown was now interpreted in Keynesian fashion, as a failure to realize economic growth based on domestic demand. This systematic restriction of mass demand had been identified earlier by Karl Marx, J. A. Hobson, and others as an aspect of industrial capitalism in general. In prewar Japan, Ishibashi Tanzan argued from a more practical and optimistic standpoint that it was not a necessary aspect of capitalism, and that domestic consumption was needlessly constrained by the deflation policies of the 1920s and 1930s. Nakayama Ichirō also emphasized that there was a "holding down of the domestic market" during the 1920s due to low wages and a corresponding excessive reliance on overseas demand.[9] In the 1930s, the Japanese government had followed a military-fascist path of increasing military and heavy-industrial demand rather than the peaceful civilian-oriented path favored by Ishibashi Tanzan. Thus, military consumption grew, and industrial production and profits recovered, but domestic mass consumption remained restricted. Industrialization-for-war thus temporarily seemed to stabilize Japan's domestic economic conditions in the midst of depression elsewhere in the world, but runaway militarism ultimately cannibalized a greater and greater share of social production and ate deeply into the national stock of physical productive capital.

Japanese critics of capitalism understood this history very well. What critics of capitalism did not expect was that capitalist revival after the war would be accompanied by a more truly populist economics—something Ishibashi Tanzan had expected all along. This was not only a matter of business revival but was based also on a social transformation. Nakayama Ichirō, in his role as chair of the Central Labor Relations Board, was in a central mediating position for facilitating that transformation from the standpoint of enhancing the incomes of industrial workers. In this role also, he was more a Keynesian than a Schumpeterian. Tōbata Seiichi thought in the same way and worked hard to make good, stable incomes a reality for farm families as well. In these ways, social leveling after World War II was enabled by a program of conscious social-harmony policies. Economic liberals like Ishibashi were much less interested in such policies, and liberal social conservatives like Schumpeter still less. Nonetheless, Noda Nobuo later interpreted the widening of domestic consumption as a case of "the opening of a new market," item 3 on Schumpeter's "new combination" list.[10]

This kind of social-economic leveling was part of an international process. There was a comprehensive program of such policies in Japan, most notably the labor reforms and the agricultural land reform. These were at the heart of the new social settlement. Especially significant in the case of the land reform (and in part an unintended result of inflation) was its aspect as a comprehensive agrarian debt-relief program (see 6.3). Agricultural landlords and tenants disappeared as separate social classes, as all became owner-farmers of comparably sized units. The agrarian class struggle also disappeared, and farmers became a core support base for conservative political hegemony as represented by the Liberal Democratic Party. Ikeda Hayato recognized that this was happening already in 1952 and therefore rejected conservative efforts to revise the land reform.[11]

Postwar inflation and shortages temporarily shifted the balance of market power to the side of those with goods to sell (conspicuously farmers). Inflation helped producers doubly by lightening their debts. Inflation simultaneously squeezed consumers and antagonized wage and salaried workers, who were the ones who paid for it. The inflation thus spurred labor militancy, while price stabilization subsequently helped to deradicalize the labor movement. The end result of unionization combined with price stabilization was to give factory workers, too, a greater share in national wealth and ultimately to bring them into the lower ranks of the new middle-class, mass-market Japan. The new system of "lifetime" employment and seniority-based pay now became generalized to male workers in large enterprises. Social distinctions between blue-collar and white-collar workers, previously strongly marked, were now effaced. Organized workers also formed a core of support for the leftist opposition that fought to preserve occupation-era reforms in the face of conservative efforts at rollback during the 1950s. The union-backed Japan Socialist Party gained a significant share of seats at the political table. This new balance of forces resulted in the institutionalization of a new social settlement.

Through the "forth and back" movements of reform and reverse course, the overall thrust of things was toward greater social inclusion and social-economic leveling. And this leveling was a "leveling up," which broadened and deepened domestic markets for the range of new consumer durable goods that began to flow forth from new and refurbished factories, supporting the capitalist "golden age" that followed.[12] Japan achieved one of the most egalitarian income distributions in the noncommunist world. In general, however, this did not happen on the model of the European welfare state, although that was a model Japanese socialists aspired to emulate. Ishibashi Tanzan also spoke of the welfare state as an ideal. In Western Europe, formal Conservative-Socialist accommodation took on a lasting institutional form. Ishibashi also made some efforts to build bridges between the Liberal Party and the Socialists, but the European type of accommodation was actualized only fleetingly in Japan by the three-way coalition of the Socialist, Democratic, and Cooperative parties in 1947–48. Nonetheless, national income-coordination policies were critically important in Japan. Nakayama Ichirō, the main facilitator in the institutionalization of this process, also expressed the ideal that his country should be aiming for a welfare state, supported by high productivity.

These, in the long run, were the domestic sources of social stabilization. This was also a matter of the stabilization of capitalism internationally. The empirical material in this book focuses on Japan, but the regime shift was global.

9.3 The Second Try at Global Postwar Stabilization: Some Interim Conclusions

A glance laterally at Japan's postwar regional and global contexts clarifies the dynamics at work at the national level. As Ōuchi Hyōe said, wartime finance was everywhere impossible without inflation. Noncombatant countries, in South America especially, enjoyed something more like an inflationary export boom. But everywhere prices went up and price controls became ubiquitous. Japan's inflation after World War II was also quite unlike the international inflation of 1919–20. That was a postwar boom, but this, as Ishibashi Tanzan said, was more like a famine or a depression. In terms of the model of economic long waves developed by Schumpeter, the inflationary wave of the 1910s came at the peak of an international economic long wave: it was superadded to a developmental, entrepreneurially driven inflation.[13] World War II on the other hand came after a period of international deflation and depression, and the great inflation that followed the war came at the end of a long downswing that had begun in the 1920s.

It was to be expected that a world war would generate a world inflation. More surprising, because the causes in every case seem nationally particular, is the fact that inflation was also brought under control more or less simultaneously in so many countries in 1949–50. In all but a few countries, inflation was under control by 1952, notwithstanding the temporarily great surge of commodity prices induced by the Korean War.[14] This was the end of the great inflation of the 1940s, and the end of the second round in the twentieth-century price revolution. Postwar monetary stabilization happened right across the now divided capitalist and socialist worlds: thus, postwar socialism was stabilized also. This in itself makes dubious any narrowly national efforts at explanation.

It is enlightening here to compare the fifteen-year period after World War I with the fifteen years that followed World War II. World War I was followed by a decade of deflationary stabilization policies. Almost every European country implemented such programs, as did Japan. These national programs aimed to stabilize the value of monetary claims—meaning debts—by constraining new money creation and constraining domestic demand. International debts arising out of the war were preserved and augmented. These financially oriented policies culminated in the worst synchronized depression in the history of industrial capitalism.[15] Fundamentally, the Great Depression was a debt crisis so immense that it brought down the international monetary system as it was then constituted. Fascism was presented as a solution to this crisis.[16] Fifteen years after the end of World War I, the year was 1933. The Hitler regime destroyed German democracy in a matter of weeks, preparing the way for much worse to come. Fascism, to many people in Japan and elsewhere in the world, then seemed to be the wave of the future. It is hard to imagine a worse moral and imaginative failure.

Fifteen years after World War II, it was 1960. Anticolonial national liberation was the trend of the times, and the world was in the middle of the greatest of synchronized booms. Aggregate debt levels around the world were low or moderate. The recent world war seemed less to overhang the present than to have opened the way for it. This time around, Keynesian stabilization seemed to have succeeded brilliantly, internationally and in Japan. Lessons had been learned, and on all sides there were great achievements to congratulate.

This understanding of things became ubiquitous in the 1950s and 1960s (when Keynes's influence grew ever more to overshadow Schumpeter's). This understanding also remains fairly conventional today. I agree with it too, as far as it goes. But there are, to say the least, some underappreciated aspects to it. By the 1970s, the limits, systemic dysfunctionalities, and pathologies of the Keynesian solution were also becoming manifest.[17]

"Postwar adjustment" in its financial aspect is largely a question of adjusting debt claims arising out of the war. Unlike debt claims arising out of industrial investment, these claims to future revenue streams correspond to no increased flows of real wealth. "Postwar adjustment" is often a euphemism for popular austerity. As a general rule, this adjustment proceeds either by an inflation policy or by a deflation policy, and typically by each in succession. The shift from an inflation policy to a deflation policy is very often accompanied by changes in political leadership. These political struggles determine who will gain from the war and who will pay for it, and who will gain and who will pay in the postwar reconstruction process. Like debt-destruction crises in general, this is a divisive and crisis-ridden process.

Inflationary "adjustment" has historically tended to happen first. It has also usually happened in an ad hoc way, neither fully thought out nor stated openly as a policy. In this regard, Ishibashi Tanzan's acceptance of inflation was unusually conscious and unusually open. At heart, Ishibashi was an engaged public economist and publicist rather than a politician, and his attention was focused by the failures of the international deflation policy after World War I. Ishibashi also exemplified the new tide of Keynesian thought, which removed the former moral stigma associated with deliberate inflation.

Postwar inflation reduced the actual value of debts denominated in national currency. It diminished or destroyed the purchasing power of monetary savings and reduced the purchasing power of monetary incomes. An inflation policy also serves, at least for a time, to sustain the inflated structures of wartime credit. This can enable industrial reconversion from war to civilian production, the hiring of returned soldiers, and so on. In Japan after World War II, as in Germany after World War I, postwar inflation issued also from industrial financing: subsidies to designated industrial producers, mainly in a few vital sectors such as coal and steel. The greater part of this funding was conducted through the banking system. Easy inflationary financing also develops powerful constituencies and can become a habit that is hard to break, as Joseph Dodge clearly understood.

Deflationary policies, contrariwise, have tended historically to be consciously concerted, pulled together as an act of political will in order to reverse a prevailing inflationary trend. Deflation preserves and enhances the purchasing power of existing monetary claims—of existing debts. Morally, the restoration of "sound money" is also traditionally orthodox: it is only since World War II that it has become politically taboo to openly announce a program of austerity and liquidation, and that such policies have become ones to be implemented by stealth.

Stabilization policies after World War II also constituted the second round in a process that began after World War I. Social learning effects were very strong. For many Japanese intellectuals, in many connections, the experience of Germany served as a mirror. Nowhere after World War II was there anything like the international deflation campaign that followed World War I. On the contrary, there was a program, also coordinated internationally by U.S. authorities, of active expansionary financial policies.

Marshall Plan aid to Western Europe has been well described as international Keynesianism, or as international Cold War Keynesianism. It also involved a high degree of economic planning—in fact, this kind of financing was itself a form of planning. Japanese politicians asked for Marshall aid, too, but they didn't get it. The "providential assistance" Japan received in 1950 as a result of the Korean War was an unintended and unplanned consequence of U.S. policy rather than a consciously planned Keynesian stimulus. The results were similar, however. This is another case of the historical phenomenon of different "causes" bringing out common "effects." A high degree of planning was already present on the Japanese side: this was also a case of preparation meeting opportunity. The deeper causes for the economic successes that followed lay in the preparation itself.

9.4 Dollar Capital as Divine Providence

On June 25, 1950, war broke out in Korea. The perverse result was an international economic recovery. This is also when full economic stabilization came to Japan, where massive U.S. military procurements effectively ended Dodge's stabilization depression. After four and a half years of postwar economic difficulties, a robust recovery began. The Korean War was followed by a brief postwar recession, but in retrospect, this appears as a pause, an in-gathering of forces for the great leap that followed. The long worldwide boom that began then continued into the early 1970s. For Japan, the pump-priming effect of Korean War spending by the United States was thus the functional equivalent of U.S. Marshall Plan aid to Western Europe. Compared to the effects of the European Recovery Plan, however, war procurements were a case of relying on external demand—of producing for U.S. military consumption—and even this recovery of production seemed to come initially at the expense, relatively speaking, of domestic consumption.

The Korean War windfall lifted the realization crisis provoked by the Dodge Line, bringing an influx of foreign-exchange money in advance of Joseph Dodge's expectations and in a much bigger and more sudden way. In this way, Japan's international financial circuit began to function again, after an interval of more than eight years. This new access to foreign-exchange funds did not change the essential nature of Japan's circuit of domestic capital provision. In the new global political order, Japan was incorporated into the U.S.-centered system. In the core financial respect of capital provision, however, Japan was quite independent.

In its geographical theatre of operations, the war in Korea was terribly concentrated, as vast productive forces mobilized by the new Eurasian and Atlantic blocs were brought to bear for a work of destruction in a zone of less than 100,000 square miles. The destruction was thus contained, while the production, wasteful as much of it was, occupied many hands in many countries. Not only in the national history of Japan, but in histories of Germany and other countries, one can read that the war in Korea set off a boom that ended a period of postwar depression. The economic effects were greater in Japan than in any country but Korea itself. Coming at a time of dollar scarcity and international depression, the surge of dollar receipts had heightened effects. In several branches of industry, recovery was already quietly under way in the first half of 1950, but in general the Dodge Line depression had not lifted when the war began.

The first economic effects of the war seemed to be negative, as the Tokyo stock market, reacting to early reports from Korea, crashed on July 6, 1950, falling in one day to half of its former paper value. The sudden expansion of military production in the United States also caused an international increase of the prices of commodities of all kinds. Because of Japan's position as America's main forward supply base, the price rise "was more marked in Japan than in other countries," according to Ōkita Saburō at the Economic Stabilization Board. The surge in international raw-material prices fed directly into Japanese producer prices, as did the doubling of shipping costs. After the U.S.-China phase of the war began in December 1950, the United States restricted Japanese trade with continental China, cutting off imports of Chinese iron ore, coking coal, salt, and other basic goods, which now had to be sought from more distant sources. On the domestic side, the prior removal of price controls under the Dodge Line weakened the "price stabilizing function of the government," in the view of the ESB's Ōkita. War and import constraints now became a reason for the Japanese government to reimpose controls that had been lifted under the Dodge Line. Dollar rationing was strengthened and systematized. At the same time, the Bank of Japan's "usance" system initiated in the fall of 1950 increased the supply of credit.[18]

Within this framework, a war boom unfolded—"divine providence" was Prime Minister Yoshida's description of it. Nevertheless, Japanese industrial companies initially supplied a large part of U.S. military procurements out of unsold inventory accumulated during the Dodge Line depression, so company profits increased, but production (and employment) increased much less. After September 1950, industrial production also increased strongly. It was now that the industrial recovery really got under way. In October, industrial production finally surpassed the 1932–36 level. (This was still only half of wartime peak production levels reached in 1944.) At the same time, the national population, re-concentrated in the Japanese archipelago after the repatriation of Japanese from overseas, was more than 20 percent greater than it had been in the mid-1930s.[19]

At the time, Ōkita emphasized the distorting effects of the boom. The shift of resources into military production caused some fallback in the production of consumer goods in the second half of 1950. Production in the food, beverages, and tobacco category actually fell, against the trend of increase in other categories. This suggests that part of the profitable increase in war production came, as it had during World War II, at the expense of domestic consumption. In Ōkita's judgment, the war thus caused a "leveling off" in the recovery of living standards. Average family consumption levels remained about 75 percent of the levels of the mid-1930s—still below the depression-era lows of the early 1930s but an improvement over 1949. Average industrial wages were now increasing at a rate slightly ahead of the increase in the cost of living. Workers in large enterprises tended to pull ahead, while those in smaller enterprises tended to fall behind.[20] The recovery was thus most conspicuous in business profits, in branches of business most directly connected to war production.

In connection with Schumpeter's schema of successive industrial paradigms, it is also significant that the special procurement boom was primarily a rehabilitation of the *old* industrial structure. It was led by established industries like coal and textiles, which would soon go into terminal decline. Some wartime armaments factories were even temporarily reopened. In contrast, High-Speed Growth after 1955 was based on a transformed industrial structure—on "innovation," as Ōkita's number-two man, Gotō Yonosuke, would famously describe it, taking the idea from Schumpeter (see 10.2).[21]

Japan's balance of international payments briefly swung into surplus in the second half of 1950, for the first time in many years. The recovery of textile production was extraordinary. By the end of 1950, Japan was again the world's number-one exporter of cotton cloth. As before the war, these exports went primarily to Asian countries, whose own export earnings were buoyed by high commodity prices. The government's store of foreign-exchange currency, although still at "poverty" levels, more than doubled, to the $500 million level. Imports remained highly constrained. Price levels rose sharply, especially for producer goods.[22] Against this overall movement, the relative stabilization of food prices adversely affected farmers, who on the whole had gained greatly in the inflation years. By the same token, it stabilized the livelihoods of consumers.

Limits to the boom began to appear in 1951. By early 1951, bottlenecks were apparent in the supply of electric power and raw materials. Ishibashi Tanzan perceived a credit bottleneck as well. Even in the midst of the Korean War inflation, Ishibashi continued to think the situation was essentially deflationary. His Tōyō Keizai group of publications held to his "liberal inflationist" line, opposing both economic controls and monetary stringency. The argument ran as follows. During the first four months of the Korean War boom, the Bank of Japan increased its note issue by 11 percent. But at the same time, industrial output increased by 20 percent, while prices increased by 30 percent. With higher prices for industrial inputs, the relative limitation of the BoJ's note issue thus objectively intensified the existing tight-money situation. Meanwhile, under Dodge's orders, the government continued to run surplus budgets and to retire debt ("government funds withdrawal," as Ishibashi, Ikeda, Ichimada, and the ESB were all agreed in calling it). Indeed, the budget surplus (i.e., withdrawal of government funding flows) was greater in early 1950 than in 1949. As in 1949, the monetary gap was filled by increased BoJ loans. The overall situation, in Ishibashi's view, was thus one of an "acute shortage of money."[23]

Ishibashi's concerns were those of the wider business community. They were echoed by the Keizai Dōyūkai (now being called in English the Business Managers

Association of Japan). In an open letter to Finance Minister Ikeda and Bank of Japan governor Ichimada, published in the *Nihon Keizai Shinbun* on New Year's Day, 1951, the Keizai Dōyūkai declared that present financial and monetary policies were an unsuitable extension of the outdated "stabilization" policy.[24] Despite the remarkable economic recovery, there was thus a widespread sense that the scope, scale, and speed of the recovery was being unnecessarily constrained. Later experience tended to confirm this view.

9.5 "Dangerous Delusions"

Japan's "Minister of Deflation," Joseph Dodge, paid his final official visit to Tokyo in late October 1951. The signing of the San Francisco Treaty in September meant that Japan would regain formal national sovereignty in April 1952. The Korean War procurements boom continued. Knowing Dodge's straight-spoken manner, Finance Minister Ikeda feared he would make a public statement that would make the soon-to-be independent government appear weak. To forestall Dodge before he could deliver a sermon to reporters, Ikeda sent his deputy Miyazawa Kiichi ("Keech," as he signed his bouncy letters to Dodge) to meet Dodge aboard his ship in Tokyo Bay. At Miyazawa's request, Dodge reluctantly refrained from reading the statement he had prepared. But Dodge was still concerned to control the budget for the coming year, and he ended up speaking his mind anyway.[25]

With the return of independence, Japan "needed to tighten its loincloth," as Miyazawa nicely expressed Dodge's meaning. At a time when other Americans were congratulating the Japanese people on their coming independence and fine progress under American tutelage, Dodge in his own farewell address in November 1951 did not waste words on happy talk. "No one could fail to note the visible signs of material progress made by Japan in the past year," he began. "But at the same time," he continued, "any study of the underlying circumstances will provide just cause for concern about the firmness of the foundation upon which this higher structure has been built." He then offered a characteristically blunt warning: "At present, Japan is suffering from a plague of false legends, which include some dangerous delusions."

In his dogged and orderly way, Dodge listed fifteen specific delusions. These included:

> That Japan is a "special case" not affected by economic events that are affecting most other nations. . . .
> That granting progressively larger amounts of commercial bank credit for capital purposes can be substituted for the normal processes of capital accumulation. . . .

That increased production without a parallel increase in exports represents
   sound progress. . . .

That any future trade with Communist China will have the same advantages
   as it had before the war.

That the Korea wind-fall will be followed by another equally good or even
   better fair wind.

That the inflation is a temporary phenomenon instead of a continuing
   pressure in an economy short of domestic supplies of raw materials, and
   that inflation easily can be offset by increased production. . . .

That a nation [that] must export to live can afford to price itself out of its
   export markets with a domestic inflation. . . .

That every difficulty caused by excessive debt, speculative purchasing and
   similar acts of bad management . . . should be borne by the Government
   or the consumers.

"The progress and present favorable status of Japan," Dodge concluded, "has
been the result of a series of extremely fortunate external circumstances, which
cannot be expected to be repeated and continued indefinitely."[26]

Ten years on, Dodge's prescriptions seemed to have aged poorly. Even the
London *Economist*, which espoused a right-wing Keynesian standpoint, held up
Japan as a model from which Britain had much to learn. For Norman Macrae,
the *Economist*'s correspondent, Dodge's farewell lecture was a classic case of
Westerners having gotten it wrong:

> In the decade since [1951,] Japan, continuing and following almost pre-
> cisely the policies that Mr Dodge had castigated and opposed, has seen
> its real national product increase at an average pace of over 9 per cent a
> year, its industrial production and rate of manufacturing exports more
> than quadruple, its urban population make the great breakthrough into
> the first modern consumer-oriented economy in Asia.[27]

This analysis, subsequently published in the book *Consider Japan*, was the *Economist*'s famous announcement of the "Japanese miracle" to the world, and to Japan itself. It also forms a neat counterpoint to the *Economist*'s tuneless neoliberal
refrain on Japan in the 1990s—which in its own way was a return to the financially oriented economics of Joseph Dodge. But in 1962, Japan and the world
were manifestly in a "capitalist construction" phase, and it was Dodge's ideas
that were out of step with the policy tone of the times. The preference for inflationary financing that Dodge castigated—the aggressive logic of "expand production first"—also sounds like a resumé of the antidepression policies first developed in the early 1930s by Finance Minister Takahashi Korekiyo, and then
carried further by Ishibashi Tanzan. Dodge's own policies, judged successful by

Dodge himself and by many others at the time, more resembled the failed Bank of England–style deflation policy of Inoue Junnosuke in 1929–31.

From his side, Ishibashi Tanzan viewed Dodge's parting comments as a specific attack on his own policies. After June 1949, GHQ authorities had put Ishibashi under surveillance, suspecting him of promoting opposition to the Dodge Line. His purge, like that of Hatoyama Ichirō, lasted until nearly the end of the occupation, despite that fact that most purgees, many accused of extremely serious offenses, were depurged before that time.[28] But GHQ had greatly eased its censorship, and Ishibashi responded to Dodge's criticism directly. The continuation of the tight-money policy, Ishibashi said, hampered Dodge's professed aim of export expansion: "Japanese business and industrial enterprises today are suffering from an acute money shortage. . . . Hence, many of them are unable to accept and execute attractive orders from abroad." Japan did not need foreign credit-capital, Ishibashi said. What mattered was labor and physical capital:

> *The only question is how to raise the necessary funds in Japan.* Thus, Japan today stands in the same situation [as it did when] funds were raised for boosting the coal output shortly after the war's termination.[29]

HIGH-SPEED GROWTH

The Schumpeterian Boom

> The "postwar" is already over. We are now facing a new situation. Growth through recovery is over. Future growth will be sustained by modernization. . . . The present urgent necessity is to begin a new nation building, riding the world wave of technological innovation.
>
> —Economic Planning Agency [Gotō Yonosuke],
> Economic White Paper (July 1956)

> *Why is it that industrial and commercial change is not continuously distributed in time, but proceeds by leaps . . . ?*
>
> It is simply because as soon as any step in a new direction has been successfully made, it at once and thereby becomes easy to follow. . . . The first success draws other people in its wake and finally crowds of them, which is what the boom consists in.
>
> —Joseph Schumpeter, "The Explanation of the Business Cycle" (1927)

Even inside Japan, the novelty of High-Speed Growth was theoretically underregarded. It still is underregarded by most Western analysts. In fact, it was the beginning of a new epoch in world industrial history. In the prior history of world industrialization, rates of increase in national production had never reached the level of double-digit annual percentage increases for more than a few years, and then only in the extraordinary circumstances of recovery from a war or comparable catastrophe. Knowledgeable people therefore expected economic growth to slow down as the nation exited the postwar recovery phase. Instead, beginning around 1955, growth accelerated, to a level that fluctuated around 10 percent per year. It held to that level until 1973.[1]

High-Speed Growth is usually credited to a long list of factors. Surveying the explanations on offer, one could name dozens of pro-growth processes, including technological, industrial, demographic, political, and social-psychological ones.[2] The variety of the positive-feedback cycles now working for growth was extraordinary. So, too, was their mutually reinforcing character: the way they combined to form an integrated system. Many of these factors could be grouped under the head of "innovation" in the broad sense. This was the conclusion of the 1975 *Shōwa-Era Economic History*, written under the direction of Arisawa Hiromi: the "motive force" of rapid growth in the decade of the Shōwa thirties (1955–65) was *inobēshon* (innovation). Arisawa highlighted here Gotō Yonosuke's language in the 1956 White Paper. Arisawa explained further that "it was Schumpeter who emphasized that innovation is the basic motive force of economic development and conjunctural cycles." Schumpeter's wide understanding of innovation, Arisawa concluded, "fit perfectly" Japan's High-Speed Growth. When asked later if there was a single "Merkmal" for High-Speed Growth, Shimomura Osamu specified the same word: *inobēshon*.[3] On the financial side of this process, the institutions of bank-centered industrial finance, high investment, high savings rates, and moderate inflation worked as a system to generate new capital for the work of "new combination."

This chapter considers High-Speed Growth as an exemplary Schumpeterian long boom and outlines its business-cyclic character. Business cycles were driven by industrial investment, which proceeded so fast that it repeatedly bumped up against external monetary constraints. The outer, containing circuit of monetary circulation was the sphere of U.S. dollar circulation. From Japan's standpoint, this was a sphere of "hard," non-creatable money. It was in their management of the inner, impelling circuit of domestic credit-money creation, discussed further in chapter 11, that Japanese authorities were free to create "New Economic Space," to borrow another of Schumpeter's terms. These inner and outer monetary spheres were organically connected, and this connection was manifested in a business-cyclic process, but in this inner sphere, the constraints were substantially self-determined.

10.1 The Restoration of the Business Cycle

Japan's High-Speed Growth came in surges, assuming a cyclic or wavelike character. With the restoration of a stable political-economic framework, the reappearance of regular business cycles was to be expected. The notable feature of business cycles in the era of High-Speed Growth is their character as *growth* cycles and more particularly as *investment* cycles.[4] Nakayama Ichirō's student Shinohara Miyohei, cited earlier, was a prominent econometrician and policy adviser. He also became the most influential interpreter in Japan of Schumpeter's long-cycle theory. As Shinohara explained it, the periodic overshooting that happened at the peak of each of these short growth cycles enabled faster growth. His thinking here was in line with Schumpeter's. It was also in line with early views of Hayek, whom Shinohara also credited as a source of his ideas:

Economic fluctuations must probably be regarded as necessary accom-
paniment of the accelerated development experienced by countries of
the Western world in the last 150 years. Such fluctuations, in turn could
be entirely eliminated only if the tempo of this development was substantially lessened.[5]

Whether faster growth was *better* growth is another question. In a hyper-
competitive world, when the choice seemed to be to seize the moment or else fall
behind, it is also a question that appeared more philosophical than practical.

Compared to the past history of Western industrial development, there was
also a critical difference in Japan in the 1950s: this cyclical overshooting was *not*
followed by mass liquidations of businesses, as it would have been under a
strictly liberal and laissez-faire policy order. In fact, government agencies and
business leaders consciously coordinated their efforts to prevent this from happening. This idea—that the new economic construction of the boom phase of
the cycle was "too valuable an asset to be left lightheartedly to the natural course of
shrinkage"—guided policy at least as early as the 1920s. By the 1950s it was fully
worked out and institutionalized in practice.[6]

One can date the restoration of normal business cycles from the trough of the
Dodge Line recession in early 1950—this was Shinohara's judgment.[7] The Economic Planning Agency (EPA) dated the turning points of growth cycles after
that time as shown in table 10-1. Also indicated are the points in each cycle when
the Bank of Japan began to tighten credit due to concern over the shrinkage of
national foreign-exchange balances.

None of the "Japanese-style recessions" of this period were recessions at all according to the standard U.S. economists' definition of the term. In fact, these
"recession" rates of growth would qualify as booms in other times and countries.
As Ōkita Saburō explained in 1974: "negative growth, a real recession, has not
been experienced since the end of World War II."[8] Nonetheless, even these relative
slowdowns could be threatening to overleveraged companies, as so many companies were.

It was not the mild recessions but the booms that characterized the era. Journalists and EPA writers gave proper names to their booms, characterizing them
as unprecedented since the age of the enterprising gods who first created and
populated the Japanese islands. The superlatives became increasingly inflated:
the "Jinmu" boom of 1955–57, the greatest boom since the age of the legendary
first emperor, was followed by the "Iwato" boom of 1958–61, the greatest boom
since the sun goddess emerged from her hiding place. These were followed by
the "Olympic" boom of 1962–64 and the "Izanagi" boom of 1965–70, named for

TABLE 10-1.   Growth cycles, 1950–1962

TROUGH	BOOM	PEAK GROWTH RATE*	DATE BoJ TIGHTENS	PEAK	RECESSION	TROUGH GROWTH RATE†
Early 1950	Korean War boom (c. 16 months)	—		June 1951	"Truce recession" (4 months)	
Oct. 1951	"Consumption boom" (27 months)	13.0 (1951)	Nov. 1953	Jan. 1954	"1954 recession" (10 months)	5.4 (1954)
Nov. 1954	"Quantity boom"** (31 months)	9.0 (1955)	Mar. 1957	June 1957	"Pot-bottom recession" (12 months)	5.6 (1958)
June 1958	"Iwato boom" (42 months)	14.6 (1961)	July 1961	Dec. 1961	"1962 recession" (10 months, to Oct. 1962)	6.9 (1962)

Sources: Shinohara 1969: 73, 74, 92, referring to EPA dating; annual growth rates in real GNP by EPA reckoning given in Andō 1979.

*Annual growth rate (%) for peak year of boom.
†Annual growth rate (%) for trough year of recession.
**Also called the "Jinmu boom."

the male procreator of the islands of Japan. These nicknames entered common discussion and fostered a wider public consciousness of business cyclicity. Such an awareness well predates the 1950s, but it then became much more highly developed. In this, Japanese conceptions fit well with Schumpeter's own conjunctural vision. The first volume of Schumpeter's *Business Cycles* was not translated into Japanese until 1958. But, as Nakayama Ichirō reported in the preface to that book, Schumpeter's three-cycle schema was already well known before this. Economists had discussed it since the wartime (see 2.1). Mass-market books on business cycles also began to take Schumpeter's schema of multiple waves and their interference patterns as a starting point and have continued to do so since then.[9] This widespread awareness of waves, cycles, and revolutionary structural transformation also exemplifies the historical relativism seen everywhere in Japanese economic discourse: a dynamic, developmental understanding combined with a consciousness of stages, phases, and transitions in economic structure. With this came the natural understanding that different paradigms in economic theory and policy inevitably went with each stage or phase.[10]

10.1.1 Business Cycles and Policy Swings

Following the return of independence in 1952, Japanese macroeconomic policy resumed the aspect of being driven by peacetime domestic considerations for the first time in twenty years. As regular business cycles reappeared, so did the regular alternation of the "positive" and "negative" macroeconomic policies (see 6.1.1). In this context, "positive policy" meant, roughly, more inflationary capital creation, and "negative policy" meant less. The "positive" growth policy was now an impelling force, while "negative" policies of fiscal and monetary constraint aimed to modulate its excessive application. This had more or less been the case through Japan's modern history as a whole. However, the last time Japanese political economy had been characterized by a regular peacetime alternation of policies, in the 1920s, the tone of monetary policy had been on balance deflationary and "negative," with the "positive policy" relatively constrained.[11] In the 1920s, these opposed policy positions had been championed by two rival conservative parties, contributing to the bitter political divides of the era. These divides were now brought *intra muros* within the united Liberal Democratic Party. The question accordingly became less a matter of ideologized party positions and more a matter of policy technique. This, too, was part of the general "technocratization" of the postwar system.

Growth cycles interacted with swings in policy. The national policy space itself shifted, altering the nature of the policy swings that constituted it.[12] In the environment of a fast-growing world economy, aggressive growth policies worked to prolong the booms and dampen the reactions, and after 1960 the ongoing growth boom created a new consensus around the positive policy. In this "positive–negative" dimensionality, fiscal and monetary policies from the war's end to the Ikeda cabinet's Income Doubling Plan can be schematized as follows.

1945–48   Positive policy (inflationary reconstruction under the Ishibashi line and ESB line)

1949–50   Negative policy (Dodge Line and stabilization panic)

1951–53   Positive policy (Korean War financial expansion but within ongoing Dodge Line restraints)

1954–55   Negative policy (Ichimada line; "second retrenchment" following the Korean War boom)

1956–57   Positive policy (Ishibashi–Ikeda line)

1957–59   Negative policy, but only relative to the foregoing and succeeding periods (second Ichimada line)

1960–64   Positive policy (Ikeda cabinet's Income Doubling Plan)

In the business-cyclic renormalization after 1949, these policies became re-aligned with Japan's balance-of-payments cycle and with phases of recession and boom.

Rival policy positions did continue to be closely identified with individual political leaders. From when he first took office as finance minister in April 1946, Ishibashi Tanzan conspicuously represented a polar "positive" position within this policy field. "Positive policy *is* Japan's path to life," Ishibashi reaffirmed in 1952.[13] Joseph Dodge in 1949 took it on himself to serve as a "negative" pole in this policy field. And although Dodge was only a sojourner in Japanese policy space, the impression he made persisted long after he was gone. In particular, Dodge succeeded in reestablishing the balanced-budget principles that would persist as orthodoxy inside the Ministry of Finance, where officials took pride in the fact that they did not issue any deficit bonds before 1965. Even after bonds were issued in response to the temporary economic slowdown of that year, the MoF largely held the state budget in balance until the 1970s.[14] Dodge himself was awarded a Japanese imperial medal in 1962. The Dodge-Ikeda line was thus institutionalized in the budgetary domain.

Nonetheless, when the occupation ended, Ishibashi Tanzan reemerged as a champion of the positive policy. "If I were to become minister of finance," Ishibashi explained in print a week after the return of national sovereignty, the first order of business would be a "production-first" policy. That was what Japan needed in 1946, and that was what Japan needed now. "Production first" meant improving people's lives and preparing the basis for realizing a "welfare state."[15] This same Keynesian-style ideal would be the basis for Nakayama Ichirō's original call for "wage doubling" in 1959. The former executor of Dodge's policy, Ikeda Hayato, also joined Ishibashi's cause, adopted Nakayama's slogan, and carried the pro-growth program to the pinnacle of its success. Ikeda's transit from the negative to the positive policy was thus one of the most consequential policy conversions of a pivotal decade. It took some time for Ikeda to make this change, and his own learning process reveals the character of the national transition.

On the political surface of events, the formal return of national sovereignty on April 28, 1952, did not seem to change very much. More than 100,000 U.S. troops remained in Japan. Prime Minister Yoshida remained in office. There was no sudden shift of policy, nor was the heritage of the Dodge Line wholly gone. Even under the Yoshida cabinet, however, numerous occupation-era measures were quickly and quietly reversed. One of the first American impositions to be dropped was Joseph Dodge's insistence on what the Japanese government called an "overbalanced budget" (meaning balance not only in the general account but also in the special accounts, which the Japanese government considered to be investment accounts that would naturally show "deficits"). This principle of overall balance was already gone in the 1952 budget.[16] In January 1952, even before the reversion of sovereignty, Japanese authorities also resurrected the Reconstruction Finance Bank as the Japan Development Bank (JDB). Those RFB loans still outstanding were transferred to the new bank. The JDB resumed lending to the priority industries the RFB had supported: coal, steel, electric power, and shipbuilding.

In October 1952, Yoshida formed his fourth cabinet. Ikeda was minister of trade and industry. He was concurrently director-general of the Economic Council, the short-lived successor to the Economic Stabilization Board and predecessor to the Economic Planning Agency.[17] It can be thought that Yoshida delegated Ikeda to gut the agency. Within weeks, however, Ikeda himself was forced from office, an early victim of a mounting political attack on Yoshida. During an interpellation in the Diet, Minister Ikeda stubbornly held to his earlier "misstatement" about the suicide of small businessmen, compounding the fault by his condescending manner. Opposition party members seized on the chance to renew the furor and moved to censure Ikeda. The anti-Yoshida faction within the Liberal Party, led by Hatoyama Ichirō, allowed the no-confidence motion against Ikeda to pass on November 28, 1952, forcing Ikeda's resignation and making him, too, a belated political victim of the "so-called stabilization panic."

10.1.2 The Second Dodge Line

The outer context of Japanese policy also shifted at this point, as the Dodge Line came to America itself. This can be called the second Dodge Line. Following the November 1952 presidential election, the Eisenhower administration took office in January 1953. It was the first Republican Party executive administration since that of Herbert Hoover in 1929–33. Joseph Dodge was Eisenhower's first director of the Bureau of the Budget, from January 1953 to April 1954. Dodge was the second official Eisenhower appointed to his administration. Eisenhower simultaneously raised the position of budget director to cabinet status and made Dodge a member of the new National Security Council.

Dodge directly set to work cutting the large Truman budget. Eisenhower called it a "subtraction process," to counter the Democratic Party's "additive process" of the past two decades. In Japanese terms, it would be called a "negative policy." Dodge directed the same sort of criticism at the U.S. government that he had at the Japanese, telling his fellow businessmen back home in Detroit that the federal government "resembled a family that had consistently lived well beyond its means." He mandated spending cuts of 10 percent by each federal agency. To his credit, he attempted to cut the military budget in the face of the newly institutionalized military-industrial complex, as Eisenhower later named it.[18]

Dodge also presided over another recession. The Korean War ended in July 1953, and a phase of postwar deflation and recession followed. Reduced U.S. demand for goods and services fed back into international trade circuits. In addition, U.S. military procurements in Japan fell off, and Japan's balance of payments worsened.

In this context, the Yoshida administration also conducted what was called a "second stabilization program." In October 1953, responding to the deteriorating balance of payments, BoJ governor Ichimada Hisato initiated an unpopular policy of monetary tightening. The boom peaked in Japan at the end of 1953, and the monetary contraction that followed was more severe than that occasioned by the original Dodge Line.[19] There was briefly outright deflation in mid-1954, as wholesale prices fell by about 9 percent from March to August. In September, the Bank of Japan also began a new system of directly regulating city bank borrowing. The recession affected small and medium-sized businesses especially, although the economy was by this time much more robust than it had been in 1949. In 1954–55, the government also adopted a policy of budgetary retrenchment.

Criticism of Yoshida's government continued to grow. In late 1954, Hatoyama Ichirō formed the rival Japan Democratic Party, joined by dissidents from the Liberal Party. Ishibashi Tanzan headed the new party's Policy Committee. Hatoyama and Ishibashi were united in thinking that Yoshida had played an underhanded role in their respective political purges by GHQ. The combined opposition finally forced Yoshida from office in December 1954, when Hatoyama formed a new cabinet, with the support of both wings of the divided Socialist Party.[20] The Yoshida era, with its strong political continuities with the occupation, thus ended at the end of the 1954 recession. The new political era that opened in 1955 featured the return of Ishibashi Tanzan's "positive policy" and of growth-oriented national planning.

10.2 "The Postwar Is Over": The Schumpeterian Boom Begins

The global economic expansion supported Japanese export growth, and the "quantity boom" got under way in early 1955. The name itself was originally Yoshino Toshihiko's translation of West Germany's "Mengenkonjunktur," and it captures the dynamic of the boom. What was happening from this point was no longer so much a matter of ongoing institutional "new combination." The new institutional order was settling in place, and it was more a matter of massive quantitative growth within an established institutional infrastructure. Prewar production levels were now finally regained and surpassed. It was this that signified the "end of the postwar era," as declared in the July 1956 Economic White Paper authored by Gotō Yonosuke.[21] Journalists and popular writers embraced this statement, which is now presented in hundreds of Japanese history books as an announcement of the onset of High-Speed Growth. But Gotō's point was in fact a Schumpeterian one: the national economy could no longer grow on the basis of a reflexive bounce-back effect but must instead advance on the basis of technological innovation. The "theoretical core" of the 1956 White Paper, as Ishibashi Tanzan's *Oriental Economist* pointed out, was "the doctrine of the business cycle." Specifically, it was Schumpeter's doctrine of the business cycle.

The 1956 White Paper's presentation itself showed only a rough grasp of Schumpeter's long-cycle theory, which had not yet been translated into Japanese.[22] But that was enough for its purpose, which was to emphasize that Japan was now in the *early* phase of a great economic upswing, which was based on the emplacement of a new set of productive technologies (see 9.1). Heavy investment was therefore justified. It was necessary to seize the moment. This was the "actionable" message of the 1956 White Paper.

Gotō later explained that he had Schumpeter's idea of innovation in mind when he wrote the 1956 White Paper. "Technological renovation" (*gijutsu kakushin*) was his own translation of the loan-word "innovation" (*inobēshon*), which Schumpeter had originally called "new combination." Gotō also clarified in conversation with Nakayama Ichirō and Arisawa Hiromi that he understood innovation to go well beyond technology. In effect, Gotō also added a sixth point to Schumpeter's list of what constitutes innovation (see 3.1) by expanding the notion to include the modernization of the national economic structure as a whole. Only state authorities could conceivably act intentionally at the level of the whole national industrial structure. If innovation defined the entrepreneur, then to shift the question of innovation to this scale level was to constitute the responsible state agencies themselves as Schumpeterian entrepreneurs. We have already seen this move incipiently in Tōbata Seiichi's 1936 analysis of Japanese agriculture.[23]

Another of Schumpeter's ideas, that of the superior efficiency of big business, was also in harmony with the moment. The U.S.-imposed Anti-Monopoly Law was relaxed during the early phase of the Dodge Line. By 1953 or 1954, component companies of the old *zaibatsu* were relinking themselves into bank-centered *keiretsu* groups. This regrouping was quite rapid. Mitsubishi Trading (Mitsubishi Shōji), for example, was split into 139 companies during the anti-*zaibatsu* campaign. By 1953, the first full year of national independence, it had regrouped into four companies, which reunited as a single company in 1954. Mitsui Trading (Mitsui Bussan) was split into some 200 companies. By 1955 it regrouped into two companies and re-formed as Mitsui Bussan in 1959. These reconstituted general trading companies (GTCs; *sōgō shōsha*), closely tied to their respective group banks, were core components of the new *keiretsu*. The general trading companies also developed the practice of entrepreneurship to a new scale level and to a new level of routinization, making it their business to systematically identify new business opportunities and to organize and fund subsidiary companies to take advantage of them.[24] This was another form of collective, corporate entrepreneurship that extended the entrepreneurial process in a way that Schumpeter had not really grasped as a possibility.

Something Schumpeter did point out was that nonbank business enterprises may be in a position to create their own means of payment—meaning their own entrepreneurial capital. This is especially so for companies on which networks of suppliers or distributors depend. The general trading companies thus had considerable power to create their own credit-capital within the sphere of their own interbusiness handlings.[25] As international trading companies, the GTCs also fell within the jurisdiction of the International Trade Bureau of the Ministry of International Trade and Industry. Thus their financial operations remained outside the purview of the MoF and BoJ. In addition, MITI's International Trade Bureau managed foreign-exchange budgeting during the period 1952–66. The trading companies themselves depended almost entirely on borrowed funds for their operations.[26]

MITI itself was the state-entrepreneurial agency par excellence, in the sense Gotō envisioned. MITI was the descendant of the former Ministry of Commerce and Industry, which during the war became the Ministry of Munitions and gained an enormous range of direct administrative powers over industry. When the ministry was reorganized as MITI in May 1949, Prime Minister Yoshida, who was no friend of the control-oriented Ministry of Commerce and Industry, staffed key foreign trade positions with officials from his own Foreign Ministry. It was only after Yoshida's political overthrow at the end of 1954 that MITI re-emerged in its new form as a power in the government.[27] This was also when Ishibashi Tanzan was made minister of MITI.

10.3 Ishibashi and Ikeda: The Ascent of the Positive Policy

In economic policy, the cabinets led by Hatoyama Ichirō from December 1954 to December 1956 present a mixed picture. Ishibashi Tanzan, the champion of industrial expansion, was minister of trade and industry, pushing for an expansive investment policy. Ichimada Hisato, having been eased out of the Bank of Japan via promotion, was minister of finance, and he attempted to hold the national budget to a limit of ¥1 trillion, to moderate what he regarded as excessive stimulation. One sees in this opposition a characteristic interministry polarity: an expansion-minded MITI opposed by a limitation-minded MoF.[28]

The political flux of the early postwar era was also ending. In October 1955, after long talks, the divided left and right wings of the Socialist Party reunited. In November, the conservative parties united as the Liberal Democratic Party (LDP). The primary partisan opposition now took a clear capitalist-versus-socialist form. This also meant the shift from multiparty flexibility to two rigidly opposed parties. The procapitalist LDP formed what turned out to be a permanent majority, constituting Japan as a one-party state for most practical administrative purposes. Within the LDP, policy divisions along the axis of the positive and negative policies persisted, but the differences between these positions became less marked ideologically. A new status quo was being attained, and a number of compromises built around the new situation had by now been worked out.

In December 1956, Ishibashi Tanzan succeeded Hatoyama as prime minister. He named Ikeda Hayato minister of finance. In light of Ishibashi's espousal of a positive policy, reporters at his first press conference questioned his appointment of Ikeda, who still retained his image as an advocate of retrenchment. Ishibashi told them that public opinion was mistaken about Ikeda, and he glossed over their past differences. Ishibashi explained that when he himself had been finance minister in 1946, the first thing had been to revive production. Some inflation was inevitable. When Ikeda became finance minister in 1949, it was a time when disinflation was necessary. In fact, Ishibashi insisted that Ikeda adhere to a positive policy as a condition for joining the cabinet.[29] Influenced by his adviser Shimomura Osamu and by economic analyst Takahashi Kamekichi, Ikeda thus came around to Ishibashi's view. Ikeda had long favored tax cuts. As finance minister, he combined these with spending increases in his "¥100 billion tax cut, ¥100 billion government expenditure" program for fiscal year 1957.

Consequent on this conversion, Ikeda's role in Japan's High-Speed Growth has been evaluated very highly. When Ikeda himself became prime minister in 1960, he presided over the famous Income Doubling Plan. He died in office in 1964, the year of the great "Olympic boom." This final image of Ikeda is the one that has remained. Nakamura Takafusa, a leading student of Arisawa Hiromi and the most prominent and prolific economic historian of twentieth-century Japan, wrote that Ikeda was "the single most important figure in Japan's rapid growth." Chalmers Johnson shared this judgment. For journalist Shioguchi Kiichi, the very words High-Speed Growth conjured up the picture of Ikeda Hayato "in a double exposure with his master, Ishibashi Tanzan."[30]

Prime Minister Ishibashi suffered a stroke and had to retire in February 1957. Kishi Nobusuke replaced him as prime minister. Set against Ishibashi's grand vision, his actual ten-week tenure as prime minister was thus an anticlimax. But, parallel to what the 1956 Economic White Paper had suggested concerning Japan's economic position in general, Ishibashi's fleeting premiership was less the close of an era than the opening of one, and it created a prototype for Ikeda's successes in 1960–64.[31]

Ikeda continued for a time as finance minister in the subsequent cabinet led by Kishi Nobusuke, but the policy tide temporarily turned against him. The "quantity boom" that began in 1955 was characterized by prosperity without inflation, the beginning of a harvest period for investments made since 1952. But surging investment meant a surge in capital-goods imports. Prices again began to increase, and the balance-of-payments constraint was already pressing when Ikeda began to push his expansionary policy. These circumstances provoked a sharp debate on economic policy. Ikeda's adviser Shimomura Osamu took the lead in arguing on the side of positive policy. Gotō Yonosuke argued for restraint.[32] In the short run, Ikeda and Shimomura were proved wrong. The Suez crisis in late 1956 caused companies to stockpile raw materials and temporarily pushed up materials prices. Ikeda's expansion policy simultaneously induced companies to increase their orders for capital goods. The balance of payments worsened, and in June 1957, the government announced emergency countermeasures and initiated a deflationary policy. In July, Ikeda resigned. He was replaced as finance minister by Ichimada Hisato, who followed a retrenchment policy into 1958. The government resorted to emergency IMF dollar loans totaling $137 million in July and August 1957, and IMF advice added to the "negative policy" pressure to restrict credit and cut government spending.[33] In the longer run, the Ikeda-Shimomura line was the wave of the future.

10.4 The International Circuit: The External Capital Constraint

In its monetary aspect, the national economy consisted of an inner, yen-based circuit of national monetary circulation and an outer, dollar-based circuit of foreign exchange. In this, the Japanese economy was like all other national economies in the postwar world, except for one, the United States, which enjoyed the "exorbitant privilege" of having its own national money serve also as the world's foreign-exchange money. Americans paid for their imports with U.S. dollars created by U.S. banks. The rest of the world needed dollars in order to purchase U.S. products and services. They also needed dollars in order to settle trade among each other, for U.S. dollars were wanted universally. This arrangement offered an enormous field of money-creation opportunities—"bank seigniorage"—to U.S. banks. Internationally oriented U.S. bankers had dreamed of this possibility and had worked to create it since before the establishment of the U.S. Federal Reserve system in 1913, and now it had come to pass.[34]

In postwar Japan as in most of the postwar world—and as had not been the case in the prewar gold-standard system—there was also a strict separation between the circuit of inner, national money and that of outer foreign-exchange money (see 7.5). The interface between the two was closely controlled by the Ministry of Finance. A black market in foreign exchange developed during the occupation and persisted through the 1950s. As late as 1959, U.S. dollars sold for ¥400 per dollar in the freely traded (illegal) market, as against the official rate of ¥360 per dollar. This is to say that scarce dollar funds were still being officially rationed, and to receive them at the official exchange rate was a de facto subsidy. It has also been alleged that enormous secret dollar funds, known as the "M fund," were employed as a political slush fund by LDP fixers.[35] But in the main, the MoF closely controlled foreign exchange via a system of foreign-exchange controls and centralized foreign-exchange budgeting, computed on a quarterly basis. This was a powerful lever of control.

Japan had been chronically short of foreign-exchange money before the war also, despite the fact that the Japanese state then governed large overseas agricultural and mining areas from which the country could import raw materials and pay for them in yen. After the war the country depended more than ever on imports of raw materials and food for which it could not pay in domestic currency. Here was a wall limiting the efficacy of domestic capital creation. To pay for imported materials and machinery required the acquisition of externally valid capital funds, meaning dollar and sterling funds.

The first international "dollar gap" had appeared as a result of World War I.[36] After World War II, the problem of the dollar gap was greatly magnified, as war-damaged countries attempted to rebuild their productive capacity by importing capital goods from the only source then available, the United States. Americans had much less need for the products of other countries. In Japan, as in Britain and many other countries, the business cycle of the 1950s was accordingly marked by cyclic foreign-exchange shortfalls, conditioned by persistent deficits in the national balance of payments. In Britain, where financial interests attempted to hold up an overvalued currency, these "dollar-gap" recessions had the character of currency crises. In Japan, they were "high-growth recessions." Japan's trade balance remained in deficit until 1965. The 1954, 1957, 1962, and 1964 recessions were all preceded by a worsening of the national balance of payments, which provoked the Bank of Japan to tighten credit (see table 10-1).[37] The investment-led expansion thus repeatedly ran up against the limits of foreign-exchange reserves, which were needed to buy capital goods and raw materials. Demand for imported consumer goods, other than wheat and other raw-material foodstuffs, was comparatively insignificant.

Exports were critically important in balancing Japanese trade, but High-Speed Growth was at its core a domestic investment-led process.[38] Many otherwise well-informed analysts have missed this point and mischaracterized Japan's High-Speed Growth as an example of export-led growth. It is true that Japanese authorities consciously and systematically promoted exports, and that over the course of the 1960s, Japanese industrial growth did become increasingly driven by exports. After 1973, in a global environment of slower growth, the continuation of relatively strong Japanese economic growth became all the more export driven. Exports have also had a leading role in rapid industrial growth in other East Asian countries, since the 1980s especially. But in the late 1950s, while Japanese production levels surged ahead of their prewar levels, exports as a share of total national production remained well below their prewar levels. The New Long-Range Economic Plan issued in December 1957 (see 11.3) continued to foresee development based on the domestic market and projected a relatively restricted role for exports, which were expected to continue substantially below prewar levels.[39]

Exports to Asia did have a strategic *developmental* importance that went beyond the need to earn foreign-exchange money. This point, and the dynamic, historical sense of comparative advantage that underlay it, was well understood by Ōkita Saburō, who was a guiding spirit behind the New Long-Range Economic Plan. As Ōkita explained, Japan's current exports to the richer, more industrialized countries of North America and Europe were labor-intensive products.[40] These were the exports of the past. The strategic exports of the future were capital-intensive products. These were the products that Japan exported to poorer, less industrialized countries in Asia, Africa, and South America in the 1950s. These were also the sorts of goods Japan had formerly exported to its own empire. As their quality improved, these were the goods Japan began to export to rich-country markets in the 1960s. In the mid-1950s, about half of Japan's exports were sold into each type of market.

Ōkita's developing "Asia vision" is also evident here. In 1950, Ōkita was one of the first Japanese officials to travel abroad again after the war, dispatched by the Economic Stabilization Board on a study tour of twenty-three nations. In 1951, he became Japan's first, informal representative at the meeting of the United Nations Economic Commission for Asia and the Far East (ECAFE), which met in Lahore, Pakistan. In 1952, Japan could join ECAFE formally. Ōkita became a member of the secretariat and in 1952–53 was stationed in Bangkok as chief of ECAFE's Economic Analysis Section. Tsuru Shigeto was assigned as an economic officer to ECAFE in Bangkok in 1954–55. Ōkita became a leading figure within ECAFE, and he organized the ECAFE session in Tokyo in March–April 1955, the largest international conference held in Japan since the war. It was as important a milestone for Japanese economic diplomacy as the Bandung Conference in April 1955. The latter, which Ōkita also attended, itself signified an economic "return to Asia" for Japan. Ōkita thus launched a second career as postwar Japan's leading international development adviser and as Japanese representative to numerous international bodies, including the Club of Rome and the Trilateral Commission. This role culminated in his appointment in 1979–80 as foreign minister in the cabinet led by Ōhira Masayoshi, Ōkita's old colleague from their days in occupied Beijing.

It is further interesting to see that while members of the UN Economic Commission for Latin America (ECLA) were developing "dependency theory" to explain why the world economic system made it difficult for Latin America to develop industrially, Ōkita was quietly developing ideas of how Asia could and would develop. Like the "dependency" thinkers, Ōkita was informed to a degree by socialist ideas, but he took them in a different direction. The ECLA analyses may have been insightful and indeed true as descriptions of the world, but they were much less empowering in the willful, entrepreneurial sense of making the possible *become* true.

HIGH-SPEED GROWTH
Indication and Flow

> No matter how much Japan's economy shows all the special charac-
> teristics of a cygnet's development, if you look at it with a duck's
> eyes it must appear abnormal and unbalanced. But it seems that
> Japan was not a duckling. Finally we begin to see that when the time
> arrives, splendid snow-white wings will beat and it will be able to soar
> high into the sky.
>
> —Shimomura Osamu, *Japan's Economy Will Grow* (1963)

In 1963, flush with the spectacular overfulfillment of the Income Doubling Plan, Prime Minister Ikeda's economic adviser Shimomura Osamu declared that when he heard commentators persist in describing Japan as a "lesser-developed country," with its "dual structure" (e.g., Arisawa) and its "low wages" and "income gaps" (e.g., Nakayama), it reminded him of Hans Christian Andersen's story *The Ugly Duckling*. "These people may be mistaking themselves for ducks," he said. But Japan's new style and pace of development had its own dynamic balance and its own norms. In a longer retrospect, what was now being revealed was a new developmental norm, whose main field of action was opening in East Asia. In fact, the Japanese economy had entered what Schumpeter liked to call a "New Economic Space."

This chapter ties together several threads in this book by considering this New Economic Space from the aspects of credit creation, investment, and planning. The consultative national planning process itself can be considered a pragmatic extension of Schumpeter's model in a direction he did not imagine or think possible: toward an entrepreneurial role for the state. Here, Nakayama Ichirō and Ōkita Saburō served as chief facilitators.

11.1 The Domestic Circuit: Imagined Capital for Real Growth

First, a bracketing observation: deeper consideration leads one to ask whether the hydraulic analogies of *liquidity* and *flow* are at all apt for describing monetary processes, when most monetary claims exist only as bookkeeping entries maintained by the banking system and have no persistent physical form. The question appears most sharply in the case of banks' creation de novo of new money-capital. A different and in ways more apt description is of money-capital as *indication* (see 3.4). This idea is considered further later in this chapter. For now, I continue with the metaphor of money flow, which is ubiquitous as well as convenient. The question to be deferred is whether the "flow" metaphor, with its implications of continuity and *conservation* of some kind of substance, may not also conveniently mislead.

To begin here with the idea of flow, it is informative to consider the Bank of Japan's own analysis of the monetary flows of the economy. In a 1958 report that adapted U.S. "flow of funds" conceptions, the Bank of Japan offered a description that, while slightly cryptic, goes to the heart of the banking system's place in the processes of investment and savings. The report is phrased in the conventionally orthodox language wherein bank financing is described as "mediated" and "indirect," but in fact both the process and the central bank's understanding of it can again be described as Schumpeterian:

> The banks are playing today various roles [as] suppliers of deposit currency and equipment funds, and as saving institutions to absorb personal savings. This form of indirect financing, chiefly operating through the medium of the banks, has shown such tendencies as enterprises making investments with *funds supplied by the banks in advance*, and *incomes and savings coming up afterward* arising from such investments, and as the great part of *personal savings are absorbed by the banks*. This form of financing has contributed a great deal to the rapid economic growth, but has brought about a tendency of credit expansion dependent upon Bank of Japan credit.[1]

This, too, is a clear recognition that the banking system "authorized" industrial investment by creating credit-money in the act of investment. The report says funds are "supplied" "in advance"—this is to say, that they are newly created. Monetary savings spared out of people's incomes, reabsorbed by the banks, happened afterward as a result of these investments. The conventional and commonsensical idea that savings (S) come first and investment (I) later, as expressed for instance by Joseph Dodge, was thus the reverse of the reality.

Here is the place to recall Shinohara Miyohei's statement that Japan, more than other countries, followed a "typical Schumpeterian course of development." Shinohara posed the relevant distinction precisely as follows: "the question is whether the cause and effect relationship is $I \rightarrow S$ or $S \rightarrow I$." As for which of these offered the better description of reality, "we will follow the theories of Schumpeter and Keynes and attach a greater importance to the $I \rightarrow S$ relation." Shinohara thus agreed with the authors of the Bank of Japan report and with Nakayama Ichirō: "Movement of overall investment *precedes*, and is followed by movement of savings *as its effect*. A high savings ratio can, after all, be said to be a reflection of a high investment ratio."[2] Ōkita Saburō, as he ventured into overseas development advising, also began to draw general developmental lessons from Japan's experience. He emphasized the same point:

> In most underdeveloped countries, domestic voluntary savings are rather scarce, and *if the amount of new investment [were] to be confined strictly to the amount of savings collected by the financial institutions or by the government, not much could be done*. Throughout the course of economic development, Japan was always short of capital, and the government did not hesitate to take every possible measure to augment the supply of credit.[3]

Ōkita's voice in Asia in this respect also constitutes a significant dissemination of the heritage of Japanese practice.

Far from being uncapitalistic, this foreshortened investment process is hypercapitalistic. What "the miser strives after," wrote Marx, "by seeking to save his money from circulation, is attained by the more acute capitalist, by constantly throwing it afresh into circulation."[4] Now, following Schumpeter, we can say further: the capitalist entrepreneur does this by throwing "his money" into circulation *before it is even his*. This reversal in the former order of operations is precisely the vital point. That is, the capitalist entrepreneur throws new purchasing power into circulation at a point when it still consists of a pair of contractual promises to pay. The first of these promises is the entrepreneur's promise to repay to the bank the loan principal plus interest. Paired with this is the bank's promise to pay, to the extent of the credit extended, whomever the entrepreneur directs it to pay.

In its 1957 Economic White Paper, the Economic Planning Agency likewise highlighted the recursive, self-augmenting character of banks' creation of new balances. These newly created deposits (so-called)

> are made by loaning out funds, and these deposits are again withdrawn [i.e., when expended by corporate borrowers], but they all become deposits in other banks. *Consequently, from the viewpoint of banks as a whole, something is created from nothing.*[5]

Coming from an official source, this is an unusually clear statement.

Bank "overloaning," reliant on the central bank, was at the heart of this process. The city banks all charged the same interest rates ("coordinated" by the Ministry of Finance and Bank of Japan). They competed only via advertising and the establishment of branch offices (though the MoF controlled this as well). In 1958, the thirteen city banks accounted for 64 percent of bank balances and 59 percent of bank loans. Only 1.3 percent of city bank assets consisted of actual cash holdings (at the end of FY 1958–59); 76.5 percent consisted of outstanding loans and credits. Another 9.3 percent of city bank assets consisted of corporate stocks and bonds. Stocks and bonds alike functioned essentially as a form of credit at the time. The banks themselves purchased most bonds (more than 80 percent in 1956). They purchased or directly funded the purchase of a large share of stocks (in 1956 about 60 percent altogether, including direct purchases and loans to securities companies and investment funds).[6] The regional banks formed a lower tier in the banking hierarchy. They tended to absorb personal savings and to channel (relend) them back to the city banks to which they were connected as subordinate partners.

As the Bank of Japan summarized the results in 1958, Japan's "enormous growth in comparison with other countries" was "attributable mainly to brisk investment activities, which were backed by the so-called 'indirect financing' through bank loans." As explained earlier, this is better described as *superdirect* financing (see 8.2). On the "downstream" side, industrial corporations relied heavily on direct borrowing from the banks. This continued the pattern established during the war and contrasted with the pattern of industrial financing before the war. In 1936, 61 percent of total capital in industrial corporations was accounted as firms' own capital (paid-in capital and reserves). The rest was liabilities, mainly loans from banks. In the years 1951–55, this ratio was nearly reversed. The weight of corporations' own capital had fallen to the range of 35–40 percent, and borrowing from banks now made up the greater part.[7] In 1956 and 1957, some 50 percent of corporate funds were directly borrowed. In the United States, only 12 percent of corporate funds in 1956 and 4 percent in 1957 were directly borrowed from banks (though the entire monetary system was equally based on credit creation by banks). And, as mentioned, the ratio of funds supplied by the banks was actually even higher than the statistics for direct corporate borrowing indicate, because financial institutions directly purchased about 30 percent of corporate stocks and bonds and created credit to purchase most of the rest of the new securities on offer. "Such holdings [of stocks and bonds] are in substance considered as borrowings from the [financial] sector," according to the Bank of Japan report.[8]

The Bank of Japan allocated credit to the banks under a system of "window guidance." This was a system of direct but "informal" lending controls that replaced the formal controls of the occupation period. In legal terms, this type of regulation was a matter of informal advice, meaning that it could operate outside MoF purview. In its actual operation, however, "window guidance" was anything but informal, consisting of "daily fund guidance" and bank loan controls based on regular monthly meetings and detailed BoJ review of each bank's lending. The BoJ Business Bureau's director-general (*eigyō kyokuchō*) played the key managerial role.[9] This secretive system was neither well documented nor well understood by outsiders to it. Many analysts have considered this kind of credit rationing to be a uniquely Japanese practice. But here again, according to Schumpeter's view of central banks there was nothing unexpected: "*Rationing* [of credit] *was not an emergency measure but part of the ordinary routine of bankers' banks.*" This rationing of credit, Schumpeter explained, is done in the context of a close and watchful monitoring. It also has a strongly social and even clubbish aspect:

> If the writer may judge from the practice of the only great central bank which he thoroughly knew and from such indications as he was able to gather about the practice of two others, every member bank was closely watched, not only as to its balance sheet, but also as to its personnel, the nature of the transactions it entered into, its affiliations, and the kind and quality of its customers [as to industry, geographical location, etc.]. . . . Gossip about them and their leading men was carefully collected. Thereupon, it was decided what its "ration" was to be. This was then varied cyclically [i.e., in accord with the general business cycle], besides being currently revised on the merits of the individual case.[10]

In Japan such "ordinary routine" circumstances of credit rationing were joined with actual emergency measures during the wartime and occupation periods. Many of these emergency practices were then institutionalized. They were linked with state policies of industrial targeting that developed out of the same contingencies of war and occupation.

The sectoral distribution of this newly created credit-capital tells its own story. In 1959, 48 percent of city bank lending went to manufacturing, and 34 percent to commerce. Only 1.4 percent went to the financial sector. Only 0.7 percent went to real estate.[11] Lending to the "finance (insurance) and real estate" (FIRE) sector, which became notorious for its place in the world economic bubble that peaked in 2007, was thus highly restricted under the High-Speed Growth system. As mentioned already, interest payments and rents also had a very small place in postwar income flows (see 6.3).

11.2 Monetary "Flows," "Leakages," and "Absorption"

"Economic activities of a nation are developed through two flows, real and monetary, the former a flow of goods and services, and the latter a flow of currency, deposits, loans, etc."—this was the starting point of the social-sectoral accounting of money flows produced by the Bank of Japan in 1958. Here again is the idea of distinct physical and monetary flows, neither of which can be reduced to the other. People readily think of money as a fluid substance, and hydraulic metaphors abound in monetary discussion. But in what sense does money actually "flow"? As we have seen, monetary flows (as they are ordinarily thought of) themselves consist of two distinct spheres of circulation (see 7.4.1). The first is the sphere of cash-currency. Here, money retains, at least residually, a representational kind of materiality as metal tokens or pieces of paper. And here the metaphor of *flow* is at least partially apt, for these tokens and pieces of paper do pass from hand to hand. And in the case of paper banknotes, this physical flow is indeed circular, as banknotes originate from the central bank and when worn out are delivered back to it for destruction. The second, quantitatively much larger monetary sphere is the sphere of credit (debt) circulation. This is purely a world of presentation and representation, where money maintains its social existence in the form of entries on the balance sheets of banks. Banks accordingly function as "social accountants," in the apt description of Stiglitz and Weiss, who themselves drew on Schumpeter for this understanding.[12]

When it comes to money and credit, the metaphor of *flow* sometimes hits but sometimes misses the processes at work. The analogy of money to a fluid, like the analogy of electricity to a fluid, highlights and clarifies some of its features. But on other points (as also with electricity), the hydraulic analogy can mislead. I have not avoided the hydraulic analogy here, but for several reasons, the idea of *indication* is a better fit. This is true especially in the provision of credit-capital for investment. Or one might speak of a "flow" of indications, as in a computer program. The rest of this chapter will develop this idea of indication in connection with other themes that emerge from the foregoing pages.

The capital-creation process discussed in this book concerns the sphere of bank balances, where corporate accounts predominate and where money consists of credits (debts). By 1958, both the volume of cash currency and bank balances had grown to record levels. Bank balances totaled more than seven times the amount of cash-currency, also a new record. The question of monetary "flows" focuses attention on the interface between these two spheres. By the nature of their business, bankers seek to minimize "leakages" out of the banking system into cash. Concerning this point, the Bank of Japan noted in 1958 that increased credit creation by banks does not make the money market tight *as long as the increase in bank loans equals the increase in bank balances*—that is, as long as the newly created purchasing power remains "socially accounted for" within the banking system. The banks made every effort to make sure this was so, using their powerful position to require their client (debtor) companies to retain on deposit a substantial share of the funds that the bank created for (lent to) them. These were called "compensating balances." This is also a chief reason banks were eager to form enterprise groups—to keep payments internal to their own systems and minimize the need to settle their credits.[13] "If intra-group transactions increase, a loan to Company *A* in the group, for example, usually becomes a deposit by Company *B* in the same group," as Yoshihara Kunio explained.[14] This is so for a single bank and a single enterprise group. The same principle applies at the level of the banking system as a whole, which is not called on to pay out cash-currency as long as the newly created purchasing power remains within the banking system and is transferred, for example, from one corporate account to another.

This brings us to the question of household incomes. "What makes the money market tight," the BoJ report explained, "is indeed the drain away from the banks through an increase in cash currency in circulation, *which is usually brought about by the expansion of personal incomes.*" The payment of wages thus tends to create a "drain" into cash from the standpoint of the banking system. This points also to the pivotal role of personal bank accounts in absorbing purchasing power (cash) from households. In the self-understanding of the monetary authorities, the question was thus not expressed as one of *saving* as such—that was the viewpoint of the individual saver and the viewpoint addressed in public propaganda. It was rather a matter of "fund [i.e., cash] *absorption.*"[15] This underlines the difference between insider understandings and the exoteric picture presented to the public. Personal saving was needed after the fact of credit creation and investment, to absorb "excess" purchasing power in the hands of households.

For individual savers, of course, savings meant not "fund absorption" but rather the storing up of claims on the future—the difference of perspective is radical. This is not a matter of one view being true and the other false: it is a matter of the viewpoint of the individual versus the viewpoint of the banking system. In the 1957 Economic White Paper, the Economic Planning Agency also took note of the great increase in personal savings, which concentrated in bank deposits (¥447 billion in 1956).[16] At the same time, the financial savings of corporations shrank, as they relied on credit and put everything available into investment.

11.3 Credit Creation as Planning; Planning as Credit Creation

Neoclassical economists have tended to imagine a hard boundary between allocation of resources through markets and allocation of resources through administrative decisions, and they have made this distinction part of the framework of their analytical language. As a matter of academic disciplinary boundaries, the analysis of market determination thus belongs to economics, and the analysis of administrative determination belongs to other disciplines. This stance turns an empirical question in need of careful study into a preanalytical assumption that shuts off much of actual economic functioning from examination. In fact, the question of administrative determination is at the heart of economics, because so much of the decision-making within corporations, the fundamental social organizations of modern capitalism, has much more an administrative than a market character.[17] The allocation of capital *within* corporations, as a budgetary process, is also a distinct question that needs detailed empirical study.

The coordination of capital allocation among corporations also has an administrative aspect. Again, Japanese experience sharpens the question. At the industry and business-group levels, one sees active coordination—of pricing, market sharing, technology acquisition, and so on—in countless connections in 1950s Japan. Schumpeter's idea that capital creation itself is a kind of planning, in which banks act as authorizing agencies, is also very apt to the Japanese situation. National-level planning in the formal sense should be considered in this connection.

The early postwar economic plans were based on "techniques and experiences" of wartime materials mobilization planning, according to Shinohara Miyohei, who himself became involved in the national-level planning process. Wartime materials mobilization planning was where Arisawa Hiromi, Ōkita Saburō, and others got their start as planners, and this style of planning carried over into the early postwar period. Ōkita noted that the early postwar plans calculated investment needs only, and showed a strange lack of attention to the savings-investment balance. In fact, the latter consideration, of savings, was not even introduced until the New Long-Range Economic Plan produced in 1957.[18] This prolonged absence reflects the reality that in the first phase of the postwar investment cycle, there was not much monetary savings to balance against. As Ōkita himself said, if a newly industrializing country were to start out by relying only on savings, "not much could be done."

In December 1955, with the announcement of the "Five-Year Plan for Economic Self-Support," the shift was made from planning based on the materials-mobilization model to planning based on a national-income model. The national consultative planning process instituted then is another, underappreciated aspect of the "1955 system."[19] The drafting of the five-year plan was begun in August 1955. The plan's goals were "economic stability," "full employment," and "economic independence" (*keizai jiritsu*), meaning particularly a balancing of external payments based on normal exports rather than U.S. military procurements. The Economic Planning Agency, reorganized under that name in July 1955, now reasoned from a macro "national accounts" level, using the method developed by Gerhard Colm, who had been a German government statistician during the Weimar era, had worked in the U.S. government during the war years, and was now chief economist of the (U.S.) National Planning Association. Colm had also collaborated with Joseph Dodge and Raymond Goldsmith (Raimund Goldschmidt) on the "Colm-Dodge-Goldsmith" currency reform in western Germany. Ōkita later translated Colm's "Ten Year Prospect of the U.S. Economy."[20] The Colm method, however, was dropped after a year, and a new round of planning was begun. Despite the 1955 plan's rapid supersession, it had concrete results in the form of the affiliated investment plans of various state and public-private agencies. These are seen in the Electric Power Development Six-Year Plan of January 1956; the March 1956 Provisional Textile Promotion Law; the May 1956 MITI Long-Range Steel Supply Plan; the August 1956 Japan National Railways First Five-Year Plan; and in five-year port development and other plans.[21] It may not be necessary to say that no government agency in Cold War America would have called what they were doing a "First Five-Year Plan." On the other hand, "Four-Year," "Five-Year," and "Six-Year" plans were usual in much of the rest of the world in the 1950s and 1960s.

Japan's next "five-year" development plan was issued two years later, in December 1957. It was called the "New Long-Range Economic Plan." The membership of the committee that wrote this five-year plan illustrates several points that have already come up. In terms of formal responsibility, the plan was drawn up by the Economic Deliberation Council, a public-private advisory board of the Economic Planning Agency. As usual, much of the real work was done in the specialized committees, and in practice, EPA officials coordinated the process from the beginning. Again, EPA Planning Bureau chief Ōkita Saburō had an unobtrusive but central role. The formally executive-level Economic Deliberation Council itself was chaired by Ishikawa Ichirō, the founding chairman of Japan's most powerful peak business association, Keidanren, and was composed mainly of top industrial and banking executives, joined by government officials. The executive council included only two professional economists—none other than the Schumpeterians Nakayama Ichirō and Tōbata Seiichi. Formally beneath the Economic Deliberation Council in the planning process was the General Committee and eight specialized committees. The General Committee was where much of the real executive work was done. Here, top officials from every ministry of the government were present. The committee was chaired by Nakayama Ichirō. Nakayama thus played a key role in coordinating between the level of the executive committee full of big names and the specialized committees that conducted the actual work. A few more economists were also present on the General Committee: Tōbata Seiichi (again), Inaba Hidezō (who sat also on the Industry, Energy, and Agriculture committees), and two other Hitsotsubashi University economists involved in the Long-Term Economic Statistics (LTES) project, Ōkawa Kazushi and Yamada Yūzō. Also present was Noda Nobuo of the Japan Productivity Center (where Nakayama was also active). Arisawa Hiromi chaired the Employment Committee and cochaired the Energy Committee. Tōbata Seiichi chaired the National Life Committee, which was also the only committee that seems to have had any women members. Shinohara Miyohei was a member of the Industry Committee. The eight functional committees also included dozens of business executives, government officials, and other experts.

The makeup of the Finance and Banking Committee is particularly interesting. Several business executives sat on this committee, but remarkably, it included only a single banker from a purely private bank. Represented instead were bankers from the parastatal or former parastatal banks. The committee was chaired by the president of the Industrial Bank of Japan. The vice-president of the Bank of Japan was also a member, as was the IBJ's executive director. But outnumbering the committee's twenty-six civilian members (many of whom were themselves retired bureaucrats) were thirty-six government bureau directors and section chiefs. The largest shares of seats was held by the Ministry of Finance, which sent four bureau directors and five section chiefs to this committee.

Concerning the core financial circuit of the developmental process—the capital side of the capitalist developmental process—the Economic Planning Agency's published report was also almost completely uninformative as to details.[22] One would be hasty to take this as evidence that nothing was happening here. One does read, again and again, that postwar Japanese economic plans did not amount to much, that the EPA had no administrative power, and that being "informational" rather than mandatory, they were not "real" plans. In part, this evaluation is a matter of the explicit or implicit comparison being made to the hardest, Soviet type of mandatory planning. But if this were truly a case of talk and no action, one might wonder at the way these overworked business executives and government officials wasted their time, at such a busy time in such a busy country. The composition of the planning committee itself tells part of the story—some 150 of the country's most powerful business executives, an even greater number of executive bureaucrats, and assorted famous experts; these were the people who managed and directed the major organizational components of the Japanese economic system. Even discounting the ceremonial and extended nature of many Japanese meetings, it appears that some actual work of coordination was going on. What went into the published report was not necessarily the most significant part of the process.[23]

The Industrial Bank of Japan itself also directly financed an extraordinary share of Japanese industrial development. As Alice Amsden has outlined in a broad transnational account, this type of parastatal development-bank lending has been a vital and practically worldwide phenomenon that has been invisible or misperceived in many Western-centric views of postwar economic development.[24] Here, too, the numbers tell their own story: the IBJ created more than a third of the funding for total investment in industrial equipment in 1957. It was particularly dominant in the heavy and chemical industries and in energy. The question of which enterprises got capital from the IBJ, and how much they got, went far in determining the shape of the country's industrial structure. These decisions were articulated with the national consultative planning process. The state-owned Japan Development Bank, as successor to the Reconstruction Finance Bank, played a similar role, as did the privately-owned Long-Term Credit Bank (LTCB). In 1956, the JDB, IBJ, and LTCB together provided some 60 to 90 percent of all lending for new plant and equipment for the machinery, chemicals, textiles, mining, iron and steel, shipping, and electric power industries. These banks thus continued to function as parts of the extended state described in chapter 8. Ōkita Saburō described the state itself as "one giant financial institution."[25] The Postal Savings System was the country's largest savings institution, and the MoF's Deposit Bureau (Yokinbu) invested these funds through the Fiscal Investment and Loan Program. This giant financial institution looks much more gigantic if one includes the parastatal or near-parastatal banks.

It is notable that Ōkita described the state in this way, and gave a brief history of the Japanese banking system, in a book entitled *Economic Planning*. His explanation of the connection between banking and planning was that banking was "used by the government as a method of capital accumulation." This was part of a process Ōkita called "*inflationary accumulation*." One can also call it Schumpeterian accumulation. Looking around Asia and Africa at the newly independent formerly colonized countries that were now trying to develop industrially, Ōkita further understood the *absence* of national banking—which meant dependence on Western banks—to be a critical lack.[26]

The long-term credit banks' issue of their own bonds (debentures) and their arrangement of corporate bond issues were other forms of capital creation. The IBJ headed the Bond Arrangement Committee (Kisai Kondan Kai), which met monthly to determine the details of new industrial bond issues. These were determined by methods rather like those that govern budget politics.[27] As already described, the banks themselves bought most of these bonds. The Ministry of Finance in turn subsidized the IBJ by buying IBJ bonds. The IBJ also had close ties to the management of the securities market, and IBJ veterans retired into executive posts in the big securities companies.

The occupation-era Reconstruction Finance Bank had itself originated as a department of the IBJ in 1946. Its successor, the Japan Development Bank, continued to be staffed by IBJ managers. In addition, JDB lending was coordinated by the Funds Committee of the Council on Industrial Rationalization. Because of the JDB's position as a state investment bank, its own lending functioned as a kind of signaling or indicative planning. The private banks combined to fund projects that had received the JDB's official blessing, which they took as an implicit guarantee, thus leveraging JDB loans into much larger volumes of private bank lending.[28]

The Long-Term Credit Bank's official ten-year history in 1962 described how the practice of "cooperative financing" worked from the standpoint of the credit banks: "we supplied long-term funds to the client firms of the commercial banks, which were the main holders of our bank debentures, in order to relieve those banks' burdens, and we also take care to make the funds [lent to these client firms] return to those banks as deposits." The city banks thus extended credit (created funds for) the long-term credit banks, who typically then lent (created) twice that amount as loans to client companies, to be recorded as balances in the city banks, enabling the city banks to lend still further. To complete the circle, the Bank of Japan provided funds to the city banks in order to purchase the bonds issued by the credit-banks.[29] One can get a bit dizzy considering all of this. The MoF and BoJ coordinated the entire process.

At the political level, the national consultative planning process also happened in communication with the governing Liberal Democratic Party (whose Ikeda faction had close MoF ties and whose Kishi faction had close MITI ties). Thus, in the case of the New Long-Range Economic Plan, the LDP's Policy Deliberation Board issued its own statement in support of the plan on November 19, 1957, the day after the specialized committees submitted their reports to the General Committee. The planning confab thus served to coordinate expectations at the executive levels of government, industry, banking, and the party.

In his autobiography, Ōkita states that as EPA Planning Bureau chief, he was "responsible" for the 1957 five-year plan. To replace the discarded Colm formula, he worked with Hitotsubashi University economics professors Yamada Yūzō and Ōkawa Kazushi to develop a new method for estimating how fast the national economy could grow, consistent with stability. To do this, they targeted three balances: of savings and investment (the domestic capital circuit); of external receipts and payments (the external capital circuit); and of labor supply and demand. They came up with a target growth rate of 6.5 percent per year.[30] The five-year plan's targets were actually fulfilled in three years. A new long-range plan, the Income Doubling Plan, was then adopted.

11.4 The Investment Doubling Plan

The origin of the "Income Doubling" idea is usually credited to Nakayama Ichi-rō. Here Nakayama took another step beyond Schumpeter's vision. In 1951, Nakayama and Tōbata published their translation of Schumpeter's 1942 book *Capitalism, Socialism and Democracy.* In it, Schumpeter had guardedly projected a long-run average rate of production increase for the United States of 2 percent per year, meaning that U.S. production, and U.S. average incomes, would more than double over the fifty-year period from 1928 to 1978. By such a doubling of incomes, Schumpeter said, "all the desiderata that have so far been espoused by any social reformers . . . either would be fulfilled automatically or could be ful-filled *without significant interference with the capitalist process.*"[31] In his role as chair of the Central Labor Relations Council, Nakayama first advocated "wage doubling" in a column written for the *Yomiuri* newspaper for New Year's Day, 1959. There, Nakayama explained that he had recently visited Czechoslovakia and met with officials at the Central Planning Agency there. In discussions with them, he realized that Japan and Czechoslovakia had overcome similar postwar challenges and faced similar questions in planning their long-run futures. This mention of his meeting with planners in a socialist country itself appears to have been a bid for domestic Socialist Party and labor union support. The future ideal of the Japanese economy, Nakayama said, was the "construction of a welfare state." And "as the concrete form by which we can approach that [ideal], I want to advocate a wage-doubling economy."[32] This was the first step to a future tri-pling and quadrupling of wages. And the prerequisite for doubling wages, Na-kayama said, was to double productive capacity. Compared to Schumpeter's fifty-year prospect, Japan's income doubling was to be done five times faster. But Nakayama's goal was likewise one of automatic social reform, produced as an effect of the capitalist developmental process. Prime Minister Kishi followed up on this idea by asking the Economic Council (whose General Committee was chaired by Nakayama) to develop a plan for wage doubling. Kishi adopted the slogan himself and announced his own stimulus plans. "Professor Nakayama re-ally took care of matters in his capacities as general section chair of the Economic Council and as the real leader in planning the Income Doubling Plan," Ōkita Saburō later stated.[33] Ōkita himself played the actual day-to-day leadership role.

Politically, the Income Doubling Plan is most closely associated with Ikeda Hayato. As part of his own ongoing political reinvention, Ikeda had undergone a further conversion in 1958, dropping his former opposition to economic planning as something socialistic and instead becoming a champion of expansionist capitalist planning. In a June 1959 cabinet reshuffle, Ikeda rejoined Kishi's cabinet as minister of MITI. His appointment was reportedly due to his support from business. By now the image change was complete—Ikeda had become known in the press as the "minister of expansion" (*kakudai daijin*). In the 1959 electoral campaign, Ikeda also adapted Nakayama's popular idea as his own slogan, calling for "income doubling."[34] The national planning project was completed when Ikeda was prime minister and was announced in November 1960 as the ten-year Income Doubling Plan. The political success of this optimistic vision also represents the success of Ishibashi Tanzan's economically oriented, nonmilitary vision of Japan's future. Ikeda's adviser Shimomura Osamu echoed the Schumpeterian language of Gotō's 1956 Economic White Paper, saying that a moment of "comprehensive modernization revolution" was at hand.[35]

The Income Doubling Plan is regarded as the most consequential of postwar economic plans and as the representative policy statement of the High-Speed Growth era. As first proposed by the Economic Planning Agency, the plan set a wage-growth target of 7.2 percent per year. Shimomura Osamu, who was appointed a director of the Japan Development Bank in July 1960, thought that Japan was being held back from truly spectacular growth by insufficiently "positive" policies on the part of the Ministry of Finance and Bank of Japan. Shimomura thus wanted to go faster than Nakayama and Ōkita thought wise, and the Ikeda cabinet followed Shimomura's advice by proposing a "special express" growth-rate target of 9 percent per year. The final plan settled on the lower "subexpress" rate because, in Nakayama Ichirō's words, an excessively high growth rate such as that experienced during the 1956 "quantity" boom "would generate contradictions in the structure between the economic base and the superstructure."[36] Again, the analytical vocabulary is unusual for a neoclassical economist. The specific contradictions Nakayama foresaw fell into three categories. First, limited capacity in the core industries of transport, steel, and electric power would create bottlenecks. Second, overly fast growth would demand imports too quickly, and excessive imports would again push up against foreign-exchange limits. Third, overly fast growth would create new income differentials between industries in which productivity could be quickly raised and those in which it could not. As incomes were standardized between these branches of industry, the result would be productivity-gap inflation (owing to wage increases that exceeded productivity increases in the technologically lagging sectors).

Income doubling was based on capital investment doubling, and it promoted a great investment boom.[37] As a matter of national psychological indication, the plan served to authorize both investment and consumption. In fact, even the 9 percent rate proposed by Shimomura and Ikeda was less than the rate actually achieved. In 1960, GNP grew by more than 13 percent and in 1961 by close to 12 percent. This indeed led to a shortage of foreign-exchange money and the adoption of tightening measures in 1962. In its overall effect, Japan's system of capitalistic, indicative planning thus interacted with the basic system of capital provision to supercharge the development process and carry the pace of industrial growth *well beyond* the expectations of those who were attempting to plan it. As Shinohara Miyohei explained, the economic plans were not intended as comprehensive models but as common "guideposts" for the government, business enterprises, and financial institutions. Thus, financial institutions were guided in determining the direction of their loans to various industries.

This reinforces the idea that the iterative consultative process of actually drawing up these plans may have been its own most important result. As mentioned, Shinohara, together with his mentor Nakayama Ichirō, was one of the few academic economists who participated in the process. Almost all of these economists were from Hitotsubashi, where Nakayama Ichirō had been university president. From the standpoint of business enterprises, as Shinohara saw it,

> the economic plan depicts some *balanced* development of various industries, so that entrepreneurs in one industry can establish an outlook [such] that, if the other industries follow the courses scheduled in the plan, they will be also justified in following along the established course. Since the plan will enhance the feeling of certainty in entrepreneurial behavior, the growth will be more accelerated than if we have no economic plan as a guide-post.

This, too, sounds vague, if less vague than the planning committees' bland published reports. In effect, what was happening was that the planning process activated a set of self-reinforcing feedback circuits, as enterprises were assured of receiving a certain minimum amount of capital funds (bank credit), which would be forthcoming in accordance with the plan's targets for production growth in their industrial sector. The process was even more assured in cartelized, oligopolistic industries such as steelmaking, where the market share of firms was fixed by a MITI-brokered consultative system and firms strove to stay even with each other. But there was more to it than this, because a competitive dynamic was present that drove Japanese entrepreneurs regularly to outstrip the announced guideposts, ambitious though they were. This happened, Shinohara explained, because "once a plan is announced, each firm regards it as a *mini-*

mum figure, and jumps into cutthroat competition in investment or tries to accelerate the target investment so as to achieve it not after ten years [in the case of the 1960 Income Doubling Plan] but within only a few years."[38] The astounding result was that the 1960 plan's ten-year target for producer's durable investment was surpassed in the plan's first year.

The losers in this process were those firms that failed to borrow and invest in new productive capacity *ahead* of the rate designated in the plan: "those enterprises who faithfully followed the plan's course cannot but lose their market [share], and the market share has actually been enlarged only for aggressive entrepreneurs," Shinohara said. This conclusion ought to be underlined: in this highly leveraged, hypercapitalist environment, merely to grow even at so historically high a rate as, say, 7 percent per year would guarantee that one fell behind. This recalls Schumpeter's explanation—which Nakayama and Shinohara knew well—that the process of capitalist development "sweeps away those types whose pride it was that they never took any credit." That is, it swept away the kind of people Ikeda Hayato had hailed in 1952 as "the old-fashioned entrepreneurs, who felt the bitterness of a debt economy to the marrow of their bones." But that was Ikeda in his pre–"positive policy" iteration. Schumpeter's own conclusion: "in the end all businesses—old as well as new ones—are drawn into the circle of the credit phenomenon."[39]

CONCLUSIONS

Credere and *Debere*

> How is a Debt created? By the mutual consent of two minds. . . .
> When two persons have agreed to create a Debt—whence does it
> come? Is it extracted from the materials of the globe? No! It is a
> valuable product, created out of the Absolute Nothing, by the mere
> fiat of the Human Will.

—H. D. Macleod, *The Theory of Credit* (1889)

> In no other case is it difficult to distinguish between an object and a
> claim to it, but in the case of money, claims can serve as money
> substitutes. I cannot ride on a claim to a horse, and everybody
> realizes that the creation of such a claim does not increase the
> available quantity of horses and that it would be inadmissible
> double-counting to put a horse and a claim thereto on the same level.
> But with a claim to money, I can in certain circumstances do exactly
> the same as with the object to which the claim gives title.

—Joseph Schumpeter, "Money and the Social Product" (1917)

Schumpeterian capital—credit-capital as the counterpart of innovation—can be described as prescriptive or prefigurative capital. This description highlights both its virtuality—its socially *imagined* quality—and its aspect as the willful calling into existence of new forms and productions. Questions of credit ("belief," in its Latin root) and debt ("obligation") are also questions of social and political power. Credits created by banks and entrusted to entrepreneurs act as "orders" on the economic system—this was another of Schumpeter's basic points. He further compared this decentralized (or semicentralized) indicative process to the mandatory indicative process in a state-socialist system. Both imply hierarchy, and both imply a social distribution of claims to or command over services of labor, land, goods, and natural resources. In the case of liberal capitalism, these commands are mediated through market mechanisms, and the relations between buyers and suppliers are in theory contracted voluntarily. Entrepreneurs are disciplined by the fact that they must repay the social credit advanced to them. The aspect that Schumpeter explored less is the question of credits as debts, and the questions of control, hierarchy, and ownership implied by debt. These relations are highly variable legally, culturally, and historically. Credit creation, debt repayment, and debt destruction create powerful business-cyclic dynamics. Credit creation, when disconnected from production, also creates financial bubbles. These processes characterize modern capitalist systems in general. East Asian capitalist practice reveals the nature of some general capitalist realities in a way that is both historically distinctive and exceptionally clear.

12.1 Norms and Exceptions

By the close of the twentieth century, Japan, Taiwan, South Korea, and China had all experienced runs of two decades or more of high-speed growth, during which increases in GDP per capita ran at over 7 percent per year. The people of each of these countries thus gained a five to six times increase in GDP per capita, socially fairly widely spread, over the course of their high-growth periods.[1] The speed of China's industrial growth since the final decades of the twentieth century has broken all previous records for both speed and scale. It has also been funded in ways that seem wrong and paradoxical to many observers. In fact, a look at the academic journal literature in English on the financing of China's industrial boom will leave one with the strong impression that the whole thing is impossible. One might alternatively conclude that the orthodox neoclassical framework cannot "see" what is actually happening.[2]

In the face of high-speed growth across eastern Asia, "orthodox" economic treatments tended to maintain an established verbal façade rather than to inquire more deeply. A typical instance was given in the World Bank's famous 1993 report on "the East Asian Miracle." This report was widely considered to be unprecedentedly sympathetic to East Asian economic perspectives and to be (for the World Bank), a departure from the straight and narrow path. But on the basic point of capital creation, it could say simply: "in a closed economy, savings is the only source of investment, and the two [savings and investment], by definition, must be equal. But in an open economy, investment can be financed by borrowing from abroad as well, that is, with foreigners' savings." The possibility, or inevitability, of investment in excess of preexisting monetary savings—the fact that "saving" is forced from the wider society via credit creation—was not even mentioned.[3] Something that was widely understood by Western economists in the middle decades of the twentieth century had seemingly been "forgotten" in a world constructed by definitions and algebraic identities.

In all modern capitalist systems, new credit-money is created mainly by banks, but the direct way banks created investment capital in Japan offers an unimpeded view of the basic capitalist developmental process at work. State authorities in the Republic of Korea adopted this system in a very systematized way—if anything, more systematized than in Japan—in constructing their own high-growth system.[4] In capitalist Taiwan, the banking system remained through the 1980s mainly state owned, part of the extended state bureaucracy, closely controlled by the Ministry of Finance and the central bank.[5] China since the 1980s has achieved the greatest and longest sustained high-speed growth of all, also characterized by massive credit creation conducted through a banking system that has grown directly out of the socialist state structure. Credit creation there has also operated in an extraordinarily active way at the municipal level, where land itself, as in John Law's vision, has been the basis for a radically expansionary system of credit creation. Here, too, a kind of "land standard" has operated. "Land may be convey'd by paper," as Law explained in his 1705 *Proposal for Supplying the Nation with Money*, and land has the "qualities necessary in money, in a greater degree than silver." For Chinese municipal governments, which hold ultimate land ownership rights, "entrepreneurial bureaucrats" have made "land conveyance" (the literal term used) into a main source of revenue; on the basis of land, credit has been created as "a seemingly inexhaustible and renewable asset."[6] Bafflement concerning the financial mechanisms of Chinese high-speed growth must be reconsidered in this light. China is certainly not following a *Japanese* model. But in the broad financial sense described in this book, it seems that China does exemplify *Schumpeterian* credit-creation dynamics, in an intense and concentrated way.[7]

To view things in this way means to consider industrial capitalism not from the standpoint of idealized ideological definitions; nor from an analysis of the system's British origins; nor from the system's imagined omega point in the United States. Rather, it is to consider actually existing industrial capitalism from the standpoint of its historically newest East Asian form. Japan's High-Speed Growth system was only the opening movement in this wider regional process and is certainly not itself normative. Investigators are only beginning to chart the actualities of China's own high-speed growth system, and only beginning to understand it in its own *capitalist* terms rather than as a departure from or convergence toward some other norm. With any new technology or new social form, when one looks back to its early days, one notices cul-de-sac developments and various forms and features that later seem quirky or accidental and may fall away entirely. Doubtless this will be the case with modern industrialism also.

In connection to these questions, we can usefully reverse the direction of inquiry, and reverse the sense of norm and exception, for to consider Japanese experience also makes one more conscious of actual as opposed to idealized dynamics of Anglo-American capitalism. Schumpeter's account of capital creation by banks and other credit-creating agencies applies to the Anglo-American world as well. There are, however, significant differences concerning the time (term) structure of the financing of businesses. These differences make it appear that in the Japanese system we are dealing more with *flows* of investment, while in the Anglo-American system, on the face of things, it is more a case of *stocks* of investment, structured not as direct bank loans but as debts in the form of long-term bonds or as "ownership shares" (or "stocks"). But these forms of investment, too, are ultimately forms of credit creation. Behind the screen of stock and bond markets, the British and U.S. systems are themselves much more centered on the biggest banks, with the central bank backing them, than is commonly represented. The structural similarities between the Japanese system and the U.S. and British systems were revealed most definitely in the U.S. and British bubbles that began to collapse in 2007–8, and in the nature and conduct of the bailout of the great banks that followed. This Anglo-American bubble was of the very type of the Japanese bubble that came to its own peak at the end of 1989. Before turning to that question, it is appropriate to take stock of what Japanese experience reveals about the nature of credit, investment, and debt.

12.1.1 Balancing the Investment → Inflation Loop

Concerning investment and savings, Japanese experience illustrates a general point in a very sharp way. It is useful to recall Jerome Cohen's observation that the Japanese system paradoxically combined a "strong propensity to inflation" with a "devotion to frugality and thrift." The next questions to ask are: Inflation for whom? And whose frugality and thrift?

As we have seen, the investment of newly created credit-capital, considered from the side of the productive services that entrepreneurs hire or purchase, appears as preemption vis-à-vis competing uses of the same services. This kind of preemption—"buying before" or "buying for more"—characterizes the first, instantiating stage of the circuit of "new combination" (see 3.3). Thus, in the process of Japan's recovery after World War II, the inflationary creation of capital came first. The purchasing power that banks made available to companies was not something accumulated through prior thrift on the part of savers. The postwar moment presented this situation in an extreme way. Clear-sighted observers, including Ōkita Saburō, Yoshino Toshihiko, and Shinohara Miyohei, found Japan's modern capitalist history to be characterized by this pattern of "first investment, then saving." These economists tended to think this was a particularly Japanese phenomenon. In fact, it was something much more general. One can compare here Friedrich Hayek's early (1925) judgment about modern capitalism as a whole:

> There can be no doubt at all that the development of the capitalistic economy over the last hundred years would not have been possible without the "forced saving" effected by the extension of additional bank credit.[8]

Any newly created means of payment that corresponds to nothing yet existing has this aspect of monetary expropriation. Seen from the other side, it constitutes an additional claim against things already existing. In Schumpeter's vision, when harnessed to productive enterprise, this was a kind of *creative* expropriation. Here we obviously enter into controversial questions of the balance of social gains and losses, which will be felt differently by different people and will differ from one investment to the next.

In early postwar Japan, the question is presented all the more clearly because the savings loop did not function for a time. High inflation erased existing monetary savings, while the continuation of inflation discouraged and penalized monetary saving. The bank-account freeze of February 1946 saved the banking system but did not necessarily instill popular confidence in bank-money. Until 1949, money remained something to recirculate quickly. The Dodge policy then restabilized the value of money, and with the increase of income that followed the Korean War boom, personal thrift grew by leaps and bounds. By the 1960s, Japanese could boast of the industrialized capitalist world's highest rates of personal savings, close to 20 percent of income. While high, this level remained within the range of historical experience of several other high-saving countries. At the same time, investment surged to levels substantially higher than savings, running at more than 35 percent of GNP. This level was far higher than in any of the other industrial capitalist countries. It was more comparable to the forced investment levels in the socialist countries.[9]

As for inflation, we can compare Cohen's statement on the Japanese propensity to inflation with the very different judgment of another close observer of Japanese society, Ezra Vogel, who wrote twenty years later, at the peak of the worldwide price revolution of the 1970s, that "inflation control" was "immeasurably easier" in Japan than in the United States. Vogel attributed Japan's success to conscious and coordinated policies of balancing incomes across various social sectors. The public-private institutionalization of this "income balancing" process owed much to the active administrative work of the Schumpeterian duo Nakayama Ichirō and Tōbata Seiichi, as Nakayama took a leading role in the domain of labor incomes and Tōbata in the domain of farm incomes. In its basic intellectual grounding, the success of this process also owed something to the concern for economic dualism shared by Arisawa Hiromi, Shinohara Miyohei, and many others. Japan's social-political balance, Vogel concluded, "helps explain why the Japanese economy recovered so quickly from [post 1973] oil-shock inflation and why it has maintained an inflation rate significantly lower than America's in recent years."[10]

In fact, from the 1870s through the 1940s, the Japanese political-economic system did produce a consistent inflationary bias relative to other countries. If we understand this as a political economy of inflation, then such a political economy was already operating in Japan in the second half of the nineteenth century, some four or five decades before it was institutionalized in most Western countries.[11] Inflation was reduced to low levels in Japan in the 1950s, but moderate inflation picked up again circa 1960. High inflation returned to Japan in the early 1970s, as it did around the world.

Contrary to Cohen's statement, however, Japan since the early 1950s came to have a low propensity to wholesale price inflation compared to other countries. In fact, Japan during the long postwar boom had the *lowest* rate of wholesale price inflation among the major industrialized capitalist countries. Thus, from the first full year of independence, 1953, to the last full year of High-Speed Growth, 1972, wholesale prices rose 18 percent in Japan. Germany was famous for a national aversion to inflation, following the experience of two destructive postwar inflations, but nevertheless West Germany experienced a substantially higher rise in wholesale prices, 26 percent, over the same twenty years. In the United States, wholesale prices rose 36 percent over the period. In Britain, wholesale prices rose 77 percent during the same period, boosted by the stepwise depreciation of the national currency combined with a one-sided reliance on imports.[12]

The story is very different for consumer prices. Between 1953 and 1972, consumer prices indeed increased by the *greatest* rate in Japan compared to these other industrialized countries: 122 percent, as against 56 percent for the United States. This gulf between the "input" prices paid by businesses and the "output" prices charged to consumers in itself suggests that Japanese consumers continued to be the fount of social "forced savings," to the benefit of Japanese producers and distributors. However, amid this generalized consumer-price inflation, retail prices of *manufactured goods* tended actually to fall, even as their quality increased. The point is an important one, for it appears to be a case of Schumpeter's autodeflation mechanism (see 12.3). That is, it appears that manufacturing industry was "returning goods to the social stream." Retail price increases came mostly for agricultural goods, services, and the products of small and medium-sized enterprises. Wages also increased. A kind of social-sectoral leveling up is thus indicated.

The great inflation of the 1970s was worldwide. At the same time, however, the substantial appreciation of the yen against the dollar moderated the increase of prices Japanese companies paid for raw materials and other imported goods. This movement began in 1971. Japanese inflation thus came to look quite low in international comparison. Although High-Speed Growth ended in 1973, Japanese industry in the 1970s and 1980s continued to expand at rates substantially higher than in other industrialized countries. By the middle of the 1980s, the yen's great appreciation had so reduced the internal (yen) price of imported raw materials that it brought actual wholesale price *deflation* to Japan.[13] This was a historic turn that has been little noticed, even in the flood of recent analyses of Japan's postbubble deflation. The onset of wholesale price deflation thus happened a decade in advance of the headline consumer-price deflation that commenced in the mid-1990s. Consumer prices in the 1980s maintained their old high levels.[14] Again, this gap between the economic system's "input" and "output" prices meant an expropriation of consumers' purchasing power, or "forced savings." The windfall profits created by this gap formed an underlying aspect of the bubble economy of the late 1980s.

In addition to the yen's appreciation, systematically *dis*inflationary dynamics were at work. Two distinct disinflation loops operated, on the production side and on the monetary side. On the production side, increased industrial investment tended to increase production, triggering the "autodeflation" process discussed later in this chapter. A second modulating feedback loop operates through savings. This is the question of investment and savings discussed by Shinohara Miyohei (see 11.1). Taxation also functions in a way parallel to savings (see 6.4).

From the "naive" standpoint of the individual saver who puts money in a bank—we can call it the standpoint of *thrift*—it appears that one's personal monetary savings are invested onward by the bank, which leads finally to a future "return" of the money, plus interest. This $S \rightarrow I$ story is also the conventional "commonsense" view propagated by banks to the public. It is a hydraulic, "flow" view of money. But of course, money does not originate in the household sector. This should be repeated: new purchasing power is never *created* by the personal saver. It is therefore strange that so many banking-system public representations begin from this point. (I offer examples in the notes.)[15] From the standpoint of the capitalist process itself, it is instead Shinohara's description, $I \rightarrow S$, that captures the dynamic at work. Banks create new purchasing power *for* investment; it is created *in the act* of investing, as Schumpeter explained it. Personal savings is purchasing power withdrawn from the income flows originally generated by investment and returned to the banking system. There follows the critical question of what part of this purchasing power "returned" to the banking system is then extinguished, and what part is recirculated. Saving is neither the beginning nor the end of the process.

Investment in excess of savings is clearly an inflationary process, meaning a net injection of purchasing power into the system. And saving in excess of investment is a force for deflation, a withdrawal of purchasing power from circulation. Savings diverted into *overseas* investment (i.e., into purchases made overseas) is also, by and large, a force for deflation from the standpoint of the domestic economy.[16] Japanese investment overseas has also become very large since the mid-1980s, although its deflationary effects were temporarily masked by the bubble dynamics that developed at the end of the 1980s.

12.1.2 Hierarchy and Debt: State-Bank Capitalism versus Bank-State Capitalism

In a philosophical sense, *all* money, silver and gold money included, is social credit: it signifies claims on future production. In a modern capitalist economy, money creation also means credit creation in the ordinary sense, of banks creating book-money, which consists of a set of bookkeeping entries and the bank's promise to make payments for or to the account holder, in exchange for the borrower's promise to repay the loan principal plus interest. It is commonly said that governments create money. However, as ordinarily measured, governmental "seigniorage" profits have become trivial in modern times. Modern money in the broad sense used by economists is mainly created by private banks in the act of lending money they do not yet "have." As the Economic Planning Agency's July 1957 White Paper put it, from the viewpoint of banking system "something is created from nothing." As Stiglitz and Weiss put it, banks themselves have "seigniorage rights" under anything less than a system of 100 percent reserve requirements.[17] And these seigniorage rights collectively now dwarf those of states.

Again, this point is well known to economists, as it was in Schumpeter's time, and one can find the fact that money is created by banks explained, more or less, in introductory textbooks. There would be no need to repeat such a basic point were it not for the way this fact is so quickly and so routinely lost from view. This is true even in academic discussion. In public economic discourse, the fact that most money is "created from nothing" by banks is practically buried.[18] There are good reasons for this avoidance. It is one of the ways social power occults itself—a case of holders of extraordinary power and privilege managing to create a field of discretion around the realities of their own agency.

In any modern capitalist economy, the respective places in this money-creation process of the state, the central bank, and the commercial banks will define the power relationships at the heart of the capitalist circuit. International comparison of the main sources of new money can, accordingly, reveal fundamental features of a national political economy. Sakakibara and Noguchi have pointed out some significant national differences in this regard. In the postwar United States, they said, the main source of new high-powered money for the banking system was federal government debt. This debt is mainly purchased by means of credits created by private banks; the banks "invest" these new credits in the government, and they are accounted as public debt. The process of public money creation in the United States is thus largely one of private "bank seigniorage." In the postwar Federal Republic of Germany, Sakakibara and Noguchi said, the main source of new high-powered money was increased foreign-exchange (mainly dollar) reserves. If this description is correct, it means that the West German system during the "economic miracle" of the 1950s and 1960s worked more like the prewar gold-exchange standard: externally created U.S. dollars served as the monetary base of the system, in the place that foreign gold-standard currencies once had. In Japan, Sakakibara and Noguchi said, the main source of new high-powered money was increased lending by the Bank of Japan.[19] Thus, to the extent that these highly elastic and managed monetary systems held to any single standard, we can speak, respectively, of a U.S. government-financing standard, a West German export-financing standard, and a Japanese industrial-financing standard. New "high-powered money" in these three motors of the postwar capitalist world thus came, respectively, from the growth of government (including military) spending; from the growth of exports; and from the growth of industry. The latter two overlap but are far from identical.

This brings up another question of "norms" and "departures" from supposed norms. The question is further complicated by ideological façades that create acute gaps between understanding and reality on both sides. In the United States, in an arrangement that has its origins in the national bank system created during the Civil War, the government in effect licenses private banks to create credit-money, then borrows this money at interest, with its bonds serving as capital for the banks. This arrangement constitutes an enormous ongoing public subsidy to private financial interests. This roundabout system of public finance is said to impose a price—a "tax"—on public spending, and so it does. This is the essential character of America's bank-centered monetary system, and it is at the core of the structures of political and economic power in the United States.

In Japan, the relationship worked differently. On paper it looks similar. But in fact, during the period under discussion, most Japanese government "debt" was debt only in the formal sense that it was denominated as government bonds. But these bonds from the time of their inscription were held mainly by the quasi-governmental Bank of Japan and by government agencies—it was debt that the government largely "owed to itself" (see 8.1.3). In effect, via the instrumentality of its central bank, the government directly created money without going through the business of permitting the private banks to create credit-money to be lent to the government at interest. The implications for relative power relationships are considerable. So, too, are the implications for the real public debt loads associated with money growth.

As late as 1965, central government debt was "of negligible importance" in Japan, as Hugh Patrick reported. The total amount was small, and less than one-tenth of this government debt was held by banks or by private individuals. Nor was all of it even negotiable, that is, even "ownable" in theory. That is, it was an accounting convention, debt in name only. The government issued virtually no bonds, and short-term treasury bills were sold to the Bank of Japan. One reason for this lack of government debt was the fact that high postwar inflation virtually erased former government debts. Then under the Dodge Line there was a virtual freezing of further government bond issues, which in any case carried a low interest rate.[20] The contrast with the U.S. system was thus profound.

But it went beyond that. Not only was the Japanese government not "in debt" to the private banks—instead, the private banks were in debt to the central bank. In effect, this meant the banks were in debt to the state, which owned the central bank. The process of private bank "overloan" and dependence on the Bank of Japan continued into the 1960s. In 1959, 8.0 percent of city bank liabilities consisted of loans from the Bank of Japan. This is an average for the year, and at times the banks depended on the central bank for much more than this. During some months in the years 1949–54, for example, the eleven largest banks had debts to the Bank of Japan in excess of one-third of their own outstanding loans. The story is told less by the averages than by the highest levels, and by the fact that banks knew they could fall back on BoJ credit. Significantly, the Ministry of Finance would not allow the city banks to issue more stock to cover their chronic capital shortage.[21] (And in Japanese circumstances, such stocks would have been purchased predominantly with credits created ultimately by the private banks themselves.) That is, the government in effect *required* the city banks to remain in debt to the Bank of Japan. The MoF argued that this capital was better directed to industry, but the desire to keep the city banks directly beholden to the Bank of Japan would appear to be an obvious if unstated motivation.

This financial structure was thus unlike the Anglo-American arrangement in which private investors, chiefly major financial institutions, owned the government debt. To an arguable extent, these private interests accordingly "owned" the state. In England particularly, this statement would describe a long-enduring social-political reality that goes back to the founding of the Bank of England and the National Debt.[22] In Japan, things were more the other way around. The difference is fundamental and is all the more significant in a society in which indebtedness has such close historical associations with subordination. The Japanese state did not own the private banks, but it certainly claimed a share of the executive power we associate with ownership rights. In the same way, the "main banks" came to dispose of a significant degree of executive power with respect to their client companies. The "overloan" policy, joined with direct BoJ guidance of the extent and direction of commercial bank lending, thus turned out to be more than a set of temporary work-arounds. Despite Joseph Dodge's advocacy of industrial financing via stocks and bonds, it seems that as a commercial banker himself, Dodge acquiesced in the overloan policy, seeing commercial banks as a more appropriate funding mechanism than government banks. This combination of policies formed the basic financial circuits of the High-Speed Growth system.

In contrast to the U.S. economic system, the emphasis in this control-via-debt formula is less on formal ownership than on creating a structure of ongoing obligation and control. Banks also exercised considerable powers of surveillance over their client companies. Indeed, banks' "governance" role has been seen as the functional equivalent of that of boards of shareholders in the Anglo-American system. Intercorporate credit also had a very great role, especially in the relations between large corporations and the small and medium enterprises that served as their suppliers and distributors.[23]

The idea of "capitalism without capitalists," expressed by Arisawa Hiromi and many others since the 1940s, can be considered in this context.[24] In describing the postwar system in this way, these analysts are focusing on the peak levels of the economic structure, the large corporations. Small and medium enterprises continued to fit a more classic capitalist mode. Small and medium enterprises also served as supports for the large corporations, which subordinated and to a degree exploited most of them. In regard to the ownership of large corporations, cross-shareholding among corporations and banks meant that corporations and banks, organized as enterprise groups, collectively owned themselves. They were immune from Anglo-American-style financial takeovers funded by the new creation of debt capital. The percentage of shares held by individuals increased as a result of *zaibatsu* dissolution but then declined again as corporations regrouped and reconcentrated their own shares over the course of the 1950s. This highly leveraged system was backed by implicit government guarantees, which enabled extremely high levels of investment and rapid industrial expansion. The postwar financial system thus assumed a highly stable, cartelized aspect, tightly regulated by the MoF, who ran a "convoy system" under which banks were not permitted to fail. That is, they were not permitted to fail until it became practically unavoidable, in the great wave of Schumpeterian restructuring that happened in the late 1990s.[25]

12.2 Stocks of Debt and Debt-Destruction Crises

The creation of credit capital has a powerfully reflexive, self-referential aspect. "Demand for credit makes possible . . . a corresponding supply," Schumpeter wrote, "and every supply makes possible a corresponding demand, so that supply and demand in this case do not confront each other as independent forces."[26] In the "virtual reality" of the credit-creation circuit, this kind of self-reinforcing feedback process can produce big effects very quickly. The potential bubble dynamics are obvious. Modern telecommunications and computerization only magnify the possibilities. Here, Frederick Soddy's term *virtual wealth* is freshly apt in light of computer-age usage, for the world of monetary claims now exists as an electronic presentation of economic activity that gains a shadow life of its own.

This consideration reconnects us to some big questions. The accumulation of financial wealth means the accumulation of social credits. Except for the small fraction of financial wealth that consists of actual cash currency, the accumulation of credits identically means the accumulation of indebtedness on the part of other parties. This recalls the basic points made by Soddy, Hixson, and others. That is, financial saving is the saving or storing up of debt. The social buildup of interest-bearing monetary claims and their periodic destruction is a core capitalist process.[27] Here is where the "verbal" world of monetary representation diverges from the physical world of matter and energy. Money belongs to a world of indication and mathematical possibility where weight, friction, entropy do not apply. Or at least they do not apply until that world is brought "down to earth," back into closer connection with the social-economic structure of material-energetic flows that it represents (at least notionally) and that it definitely commands and directs. This "bringing down to earth" can be brought about by means of good institutional practice or by uncontrolled periodic crises.

Schumpeter himself tended to ignore the *systemicity* of debt crises in the capitalist process. He imagined, without investigating it empirically, that the problem of debt buildup could resolve itself simply through increased production and automatic deflation. In fact, debt-destruction crises appear to be inherent in the credit-creation process he described. The historical record makes clear both the scale and the regularity of debt crises—which were conspicuous especially in the process of late nineteenth-century deflation that Schumpeter considered normative for his model. A full account must therefore encompass these crises as well. In short, debt claims, which may be created "by an agreement of two minds," tend to self-augment and proliferate over time relative to a slower growing base of "services" of land, resources, goods, and labor. When new monetary claims are invested into new production, they can increase this underlying supply of services, as emphasized by Schumpeter and indeed by John Law. (Land, as such, does not increase, but development projects may increase the amount of usable land, and the intensity of land use may increase greatly.) We have seen this in Japan. But the facility of creating new monetary claims is also incomparably greater than the facility of creating productive services, whose growth frequently runs up against definite material and social limits. In an argument that deserves to be better known, William Hixson, drawing on the insights of Irving Fisher, has argued in detail that the excessive growth of debt is foundational to depressions— that by the very process of money creation under bank-centered capitalism, debt grows inexorably along with the money supply, until a great crisis takes place in which great amounts of debt are liquidated.[28] Those moments when economic functioning seems to leave behind material constraints are called *bubbles*. Far from being accidental and epiphenomal (as Schumpeter sometimes suggested), they are of the essence of the capitalist process. Before locating Japan's bubble economy in this history, one more feature of Schumpeter's explanation needs further thought. This is the cyclically occurring process of "automatic deflation," which also appears fundamental to the development of the late 1980s bubble.

12.3 Autodeflation

For Schumpeter, the primary developmental and ultimately disinflationary force was the increase of production that followed from new industrial investment. In the sequence of development, the creation of new credit for investment would first increase the monetary numerator, but over the long run, the resulting expansion of production would correct, even overcorrect, the balance of purchasing power to goods by enlarging the goods denominator. In postwar Japan, massive investment led to massive increases in industrial production. And, as mentioned, retail price increases were greatest in sectors other than manufactured goods, suggesting the generation of relative deflationary pressure in the manufacturing sector.

In the 1890s, when Schumpeter was forming his own intellectual view of the world, the idea that capitalist development was ultimately deflationary would have appeared sensible and even commonsensical. The newly industrializing economies of that era were manifestly undergoing an unprecedented technical and organizational revolution, generating an astounding outpouring of production. Prices simultaneously fell, in a series of wavelike conjunctural movements, to lower and lower levels. These facts were well described in statistics, which made it clear to "scientific men" that price levels in the mid-1890s were on the whole lower than at any time since the eighteenth century.[29] Such an age seems hard to imagine now.

The idea that industrial capitalism was intrinsically deflationary retained its plausibility in 1912, when Schumpeter published his *Theory of Economic Development*. One could argue the point even more forcefully in 1926, when Schumpeter revised his book, or in 1934, when he collaborated in the English translation of it, for in the aftermath of the great World War I inflation, the world was again in the throes of a great deflation. And this renewed deflation—what Schumpeter called in 1927, "*the secular downward trend of prices during the period of Capitalism*"—progressed precisely in the midst of another wave of industrial revolution, in the form of electrification and mass production.[30] But then the deflation ended. As the price revolution of the twentieth century rolled onward, the idea that modern capitalism was automatically deflationary seemed nonsensical, and it was largely forgotten. It is therefore interesting to see Nakayama Ichirō writing at the very height of the inflationary High-Speed Growth boom—and describing an autodeflationary process that was entirely Schumpeterian:

> From [1949] until the present [1973] the productivity of manufacturing industries has increased three times. During the course of this three-fold expansion, quality improved and new products appeared continuously *while prices fell as fast as products grew.*[31]

That is, the price of manufactured products fell even in the midst of an overall inflationary national and world trend. Other factors were operating here besides Schumpeter's autodeflation dynamic. Above all was the fact that the prices of imported materials were stable or actually falling. But the productivity revolution was surely the key to it.

The advantage of low-cost raw materials disappeared suddenly in the early 1970s, when prices for oil and other commodities skyrocketed, propelling the worldwide inflation forward. But in fact, autodeflation dynamics reasserted themselves afterward. Indeed, they became even more comprehensive in their effects. By the late 1980s, Japan had the world's highest price levels, at least as measured in foreign currency. People noticed the "Japan as number one" syndrome in prices but took less notice of the fact that Japanese wholesale prices had been *falling* on the whole since 1982.[32] (And 1982 was also the year the historic run-up in world stock markets began.) In the 1990s came the deflation of prices in general.

12.4 Mirrors and Miracles

It is in the nature of credit-money that it can somehow be "in" (i.e., be represented in) two places at once, without really being "anywhere" at all. One may not be able ride on a claim to a horse, but one may be able to create new claims on the basis of that claim. Here even Adam Smith had permitted himself an uncharacteristic moment of surreality, offering ("if I may be allowed so violent a metaphor") that "the judicious operations of banking" could provide "a sort of waggon-way through the air." It is this that carries the question of money-capital into the domains of socially constituted will and imagination. It is what economist Hans Christophe Binswanger, returning to Goethe for inspiration, described as "the modern economy's alchemical core."[33]

Contrast this with the neoclassical economic view. When Keynes's theory was cast in what became its orthodox postwar form, "money became an object, like peanuts, corn, and tobacco, for which there was a demand and supply," as Stiglitz and Weiss have explained.[34] This misequation was motivated by a desire to establish a set of clear mathematical symmetries, descriptively inapt though it may have been. That people in the second half of the twentieth century could imagine that money was essentially like a physical commodity also shows the persistence of primitive, substance ideas of money, which derive from a long-gone age of exclusively metallic currency. As for that presumed historical ground—metallic money itself—several acute analysts have pointed out that money of whatever sort has always represented a kind of social debt.[35]

We have also seen credit-capital working as a system of active indication and prefiguration. Its modus operandi is "buying before" and "buying for more," or competitive preemption and inflation. *Investment* and *inflation* begin the process; it is therefore appropriate to conclude by considering the output side, meaning the subjects of harvest and deflation. In this connection, Schumpeter developed a sophisticated justification for the modern system of capital creation and provision. This point rarely gets raised in public discussion. Economists routinely, often quasi-ritualistically, blame political authorities for inflation. They rarely implicate banks, even though any trained economist knows that it is banks that create the overwhelming bulk of purchasing power. But even to start discussing this subject opens a Pandora's box of questions. Schumpeter, rather than engaging in an intellectual cover-up, attempted to offer a rational, procapitalist justification for thinking that new purchasing power created by banks will not ultimately be inflationary, *if it is directed to the expansion of production.* His idea that the funding of new production was only temporarily inflationary is a credible description of the main direction of capital investment during the era of High-Speed Growth. This was also a time when Japanese governmental and central bank authorities actively restricted the use of capital for nonproductive purposes.

But what of capital created by banks for speculation in land or commodities? And what of capital created for the even more reflexive, recursive business of purely financial speculation, capital scarcely or not at all mediated by investment into the world of material commodities? This brings us to the bubble economy.

As mentioned at the outset, the credit-inflationary funding process at the heart of modern capitalism happens on a level distinct from that of value creation and exploitation operating within the process of production itself. This operation is in its nature a form of wealth transfer and expropriation. At the level of the whole society, it may be compensated or more than compensated by the productive works it has enabled. When it does not fund productive investment that returns value to the social stream, it becomes purely a form of wealth transfer and expropriation, a taking without a giving.

Many economists, especially American ones, came in the 1980s and 1990s programmatically to eschew the word *speculation* and to deny that it has an economic meaning. Indeed, many economists justified financial speculation as healthful arbitrage and risk management, thus throwing a convenient ideological veil over it. This collective denial happened precisely in the era when speculative financial operations grew internationally to dwarf in their monetary scale the actual transactions of commerce and industry to which they must ultimately refer; at a global (dollar-system) level, the notional scale of the "two flows" radically diverged. In the same way that money creation in general works as an "inflation tax" imposed on those outside of the new-money loop, this kind of financial churning, too, is an enormous tax on the rest of economic activity. The entire process remains underanalyzed, little quantified, and poorly understood, even at a time when it manifestly moves national economies. This question concerns the U.S.-centered credit bubble that culminated in 2008, and it is more than a little interesting to see the process beginning to unfold first, eighteen years earlier, in Japan.

In fact, the Japanese High-Speed Growth system eventuated in two significant bubbles.[36] The first was minor in comparison to the second and now gets little notice. In 1972, the government's "positive" spending policy culminated in prime minister Tanaka Kakuei's "Plan to Remodel the Japanese Archipelago." This massive infrastructure development plan generated a bubble based on land speculation, which happened just on the eve of the 1973 oil shock and "stagflation" crisis and thereby intensified its effects. But Japan's economic recovery from the crises of the early 1970s was relatively quick in international comparison, and industrial expansion in Japan continued to be the highest among the industrialized countries amid the general world slowdown of the 1970s.

The second bubble was that of 1988–89. Annual GDP growth slowed to an average level around 4 or 5 percent per year in the 1970s and 1980s. At the same time, the government eased its regulation of the financial sector. Japanese banks globalized their operations, and credit creation expanded into new frontiers. Successful big manufacturing corporations, the big banks' best "blue-chip" clients, also became self-financing on the strength of year after year of large profits. They no longer relied on the banks for investment funds. This can also be described as a partial return to the situation that existed before the war. Bank lending officers, under pressure to maintain and increase loan levels, began pushing loans toward nonmanufacturing clients that were less financially sound.[37] As the credit bubble fed on itself, any business that owned land seemed worthy of receiving big new credits, unconnected to any realistic appraisal of its future revenue flows. New purchasing power that was created (lent) on the security of land boosted the value of land, in turn making a given property worthy of still more bank credit. Indeed, the credit system was often described as a "land standard." More credit did not create more land (except in the case of costly projects to remove mountaintops and claim new land from the sea). But if one looked only at the land valuation column, one might have thought that it had, for land values were "growing" by leaps and bounds.

The physical epicenter of the land bubble—the place where prices soared the highest—was none other than the credit-creation district of Tokyo itself. At work here was the idea that Tokyo's financial sector had now become the credit-creation center of the world, succeeding Wall Street in this role. This understanding was not wholly baseless, but it led to the false assessment that Tokyo real estate would only go up in price, and that any price paid now was better than a price paid later. As mentioned, the overseas diversion of investment, meaning a relative withdrawal of purchasing power from the national economy and creation of purchasing power overseas, was also for Japan another underlying deflationary force temporarily masked by the bubble. Much more could be said about the bubble, but for the purposes of this book, the main point is that Japan's core capital-creation circuits were at the center of it.

Japan's great bubble was followed in the 1990s by the first general and sustained deflation, anywhere in the world, since the 1920s and early 1930s. This was also a phase of Schumpeterian reorganization, in the sense for which Schumpeter became most famous in the neoliberal age: so-called creative destruction. Indeed, Schumpeter's justification for "destruction" became in the 1990s an excuse for financial looting. Schumpeter had stressed the evolutionary functionality of the destructive side of this dual process. That is a rather abstract view. Attending to the actualities of the process, one cannot fail to see also its contingent and political character. Thus, right through the crises of systemic restructuring in Japan in the late 1990s and early 2000s, what ended up being conserved and protected politically was the bankrupt core of the banking system, even as other formerly protected interests were sacrificed.

In some ways, the same thing had happened in the previous great crisis of systemic restructuring, in the late 1940s. In that case, one can easily imagine that the big banks might have been broken up during the early phase of the occupation, along the lines of the bank breakup that U.S. authorities actually did push through in the western zones of Germany. In the 1990s, however, the preservation of the core big banks was only to be expected, given the configuration of political-economic power. All the same, it is striking that the very part of the economic system that generated the bubble should be that part of the system that came through the crisis with its power apparently most concentrated and enhanced, as a result of mergers of the great banks and their swallowing up of smaller banks, backed up by record-shattering bailouts directed to the new megabanks by the Bank of Japan. Simultaneously, the autonomous authority of the Bank of Japan was greatly extended, in line with the idea of Anglo-U.S.-style "central bank independence."[38] The central bank's ability to subsidize the private banks was also massively enlarged and extended.

Since the great American bubble began to collapse in 2007 and 2008, much the same thing has happened in the United States. The same can be said of Britain and of the ongoing debt crisis in Europe. These deep commonalities point to the systemic character of the crisis and to the systemic character of the political response. If one were to judge from the standpoint of competitive market functioning, this seems more a case of radical dysfunctionality than of evolutionary dynamism. Evidently, competitive market functioning is not the quality that this system is working to conserve, notwithstanding some of the stories that get told to children.

The twenty-first century has been prospectively cast by more than one writer as Schumpeter's century.[39] It does seem that we will be hearing more from Schumpeter rather than less. But precursive, preemptive Schumpeterian *finance*, on the scale of the credit creation that funded the first great age of industrial capitalism, seems to have outlived its usefulness in much of the already industrialized world. More than that, it appears radically incompatible with the emerging circumstances of countries that are experiencing no population growth and need now to embark on a course of qualitative development rather than rapid, extensive industrial growth. Massively leveraged finance, flowing in ever greater volume, cannot continue to correspond to an ever greater torrent of production. Ever more production itself becomes pathological past a certain point of sufficiency. In these changed environmental circumstances, the type of banking system that funded the first great age of capitalism now functions more and more as a bubble machine, casually throwing up immense debts that act as a dead weight on everything else. In this dimension, the second age of industrial capitalism will need to be a post-Schumpeterian age.

In considering our twenty-first-century world, Japanese experience may have a more universal significance than has hitherto been recognized. Japan has been, at the least, a highly sensitive indicator of these global movements. More than that, it appears to have been at the leading edge of them, a fact that is not widely grasped, much less understood. Japan's modern price revolution itself began in the 1860s, a generation in advance of the onset of the worldwide price revolution of the twentieth century. This early onset of modern inflation can be put down to a difference of monetary standards and to a catching-up to international price levels, but it also had to do with the creation of a characteristic and precociously modern system of bank-funded industrial development. This points to the highly compressed character of Japanese development as a whole. Again, the exaggerated character of Japan's World War I boom, and the fact that the post–World War I crash began first in Japan, might be taken as indications of the same precocity. Japan's forerunner position in the implementation of "Keynesian"-style reflation and recovery from the Great Depression in 1932 appears even more systematically related to the innovation of "rationalized" capitalist forms. This book has focused on some of the ways that High-Speed Growth after 1955 constituted a historic supercompression of capitalist development. Now it seems also that Japan is the country that completed the modern inflationary process first. This is happening simultaneously with Japan's highly compressed transit from the "first" to the "second" demographic transition—meaning prospective population decline, which is already incipiently under way. There are profound structural reasons for thinking that underlying forces now tend in the direction of deflation rather than inflation.

We have here a convergence of factors acting on multiple time scales, from that of macro-level price revolutions on the scale of centuries to the meso-level where Schumpeter's long-cycle analysis was centered. In this connection, Schumpeter once wrote of an earlier period of falling prices:

> In a socialist society, such periods might be hailed as *periods of harvest*. In capitalist society, they do not cease to be that. But this aspect is entirely lost in the fears, sufferings, and resentments generated by the dislocation of existing industrial structures that is the first consequence of technological or commercial progress.[40]

Again we face the problem of the distribution of this harvest, and the distribution of fears, sufferings, and resentments. As I have suggested, it now begins to appear that the present harvest, and the present dislocation, are something more than that which comes as the fulfillment of one of the long cycles of fifty-some years delineated by Schumpeter. It does seem to be that: for Japan, the great cycle from the late 1940s to the turn of the twenty-first century was a great one indeed, and very clearly marked. Shinohara Miyohei, more than any other analyst, has delineated the unfolding of this process.[41] But increasingly, the present great slowdown and continued deflation appears to be significant also as a turning point on a substantially longer timescale, as the culmination of Japan's modern era of inflationary industrial-capitalist development. That is a question for another book.

It is also a question much in the spirit of Schumpeter's own approach. Schumpeter inherited and remained attached to the static equilibrium structure of late nineteenth-century neoclassical economics. At the heart of his intellectual approach, however, was a much more organic vision of economic life—we could just say life—as a dynamic developmental process. This was discerned by Schumpeter's junior colleague Wassily Leontief, who in his obituary of Schumpeter noted the affinity between Henri Bergson's idea of "creative evolution" (1907) and Schumpeter's theory of economic development, which Schumpeter articulated mainly in 1907–9. Leontief recalled in this connection Schumpeter's "peculiar concern with the science, with the process of knowledge itself." United with this was Schumpeter's realization "that in the fields of intellectual endeavor no harvest is final, all fruit is perishable and only as good as the new seed it might contain."[42] In regard to human understanding itself, this too is a "flow" and a "revenual" vision of things.

Table A-1 gives basic statistics for total currency in circulation and for total bank balances. The most evident trend was for bank balances to increase as a share of total money, reflecting a seemingly universal modern tendency. It is also evident that deflationary programs have historically focused on reducing cash-currency rather than bank balances.

The total volume of bank balances first came to equal the volume of cash-currency in 1897, which was also the year Japan adopted the gold standard. Bank balances then increased very rapidly in both absolute and relative terms for the next two decades. This trend reversed during the wartime and early postwar years, when the relative increase in cash-currency brought the volume of currency temporarily back to parity with bank balances in 1947. The historical tendency for bank money to increase then resumed.

In 1949, the year of the Dodge Line, the Bank of Japan began to discount bills in large volume and to buy bills outright. This makes it appear that the BoJ "loans" category declined as a result of the Dodge Line, but in fact there was a major increase in BoJ credit creation. The central bank's outright purchase of bills was extremely large. These were the amounts purchased, in billions of yen:

1949	1950	1951	1952	1953	1954	1955
100	63	39.6	38.3	11.5	1.2	1.2

This Dodge-era program was discontinued after 1955. Later BoJ statistics combine loans, discounts, and bills bought and list them all together as "Bank of Japan lendings," as I have also done in table A-2.

Second to manufacturing, commerce was the other great destination of bank lending. At a time when both volumes increased very rapidly, the share of total bank lending that went to manufacturing was remarkably stable, fluctuating in a range between 47 and 51 percent during the years 1952–65. During the first three years of the Income Doubling Plan, 1961–63, the percentage varied even less, remaining between 50.1 and 50.7 percent. This, too, suggests active management of the investment process.

TABLE A-1. Basic indicators of money and credit, 1868–1965 (in millions of yen to 1916; in billions of yen from 1917)

YEAR	CURRENCY (A)	% CHANGE	BANK BALANCES (B)	% CHANGE	RATIO OF BANK MONEY TO CURRENCY (B/A)
1868	24				
1869	50	108.0			
1870	56	12.0			
1871	62	10.7			
1872	72	16.1			
1873	97	34.7	2.9		0.03
1874	114	17.5	3.5	20.7	0.03
1875	113	(−0.9)	1.5	(−57.1)	0.01
1876	124	9.7	2.5	66.7	0.02
1877	140	12.9	4.5	80.0	0.03
1878	189	35.0	8.1	80.0	0.04
1879	189	0.0	16.2	100.0	0.09
1880	183	(−3.2)	17.5	8.0	0.10
1881	178	(−2.7)	24.5	40.0	0.14
1882	170	(−4.5)	23.4	(−4.5)	0.14
1883	159	(−6.5)	37.3	59.4	0.24
1884	153	(−3.8)	39.9	7.0	0.26
1885	153	0.0	43.9	10.0	0.29
1886	168	9.8	49.8	13.4	0.30
1887	171	1.8	46.2	(−7.2)	0.27
1888	172	0.6	65.6	42.0	0.38
1889	178	3.5	68.5	4.4	0.39
1890	201	12.9	62.7	(−8.5)	0.31
1891	209	4.0	66.2	5.6	0.32
1892	212	1.4	85.2	28.7	0.40
1893	231	9.0	112	31.5	0.49
1894	230	(−0.4)	134	19.6	0.58
1895	260	13.0	184	37.3	0.71
1896	275	5.8	235	27.7	0.86
1897	296	7.6	305	29.8	1.0
1898	279	(−5.7)	371	21.6	1.3
1899	340	21.9	536	44.5	1.6
1900	317	(−6.8)	576	7.5	1.8
1901	303	(−4.4)	579	0.5	1.9
1902	323	6.6	692	19.5	2.1
1903	325	0.6	759	9.7	2.3
1904	384	18.2	811	6.9	2.1
1905	423	10.2	974	20.1	2.3

TABLE A-1. *(continued)*

YEAR	CURRENCY (A)	% CHANGE	BANK BALANCES (B)	% CHANGE	RATIO OF BANK MONEY TO CURRENCY (B/A)
1906	469	10.9	1,395	43.2	3.0
1907	509	8.5	1,325	(−5.0)	2.6
1908	499	(−2.0)	1,304	(−1.6)	2.6
1909	521	4.4	1,506	15.5	2.9
1910	586	12.5	1,649	9.5	2.8
1911	634	8.2	1,776	7.7	2.8
1912	649	2.4	1,941	9.3	3.0
1913	628	(−3.2)	2,110	8.7	3.4
1914	561	(−10.7)	2,112	0.1	3.8
1915	623	11.1	2,569	21.6	4.1
1916	827	32.7	3,464	34.8	4.2
1917	1.1	35.1	5.1	48.6	4.6
1918	1.6	45.5	7.2	38.5	4.6
1919	2.1	31.3	8.7	20.8	4.2
1920	1.8	(−14.3)	8.8	1.1	4.9
1921	2.0	11.1	9.5	8.0	4.9
1922	1.9	(−5.0)	9.6	1.1	5.1
1923	2.2	15.8	9.7	1.0	4.4
1924	2.2	0.0	10.2	5.2	4.7
1925	2.1	(−4.5)	10.8	5.9	5.1
1926	2.1	0.0	11.3	4.6	5.5
1927	2.2	4.8	11.3	0.0	5.1
1928	2.3	4.5	11.7	3.5	5.1
1929	2.2	(−4.3)	12	2.6	5.5
1930	1.9	(−13.6)	11.6	(−3.3)	6.0
1931	1.8	(−5.3)	11.1	(−4.3)	6.1
1932	2.0	11.1	11.5	3.6	5.8
1933	2.1	5.0	12.1	5.2	5.7
1934	2.3	9.5	12.8	5.8	5.6
1935	2.5	8.7	13.6	6.2	5.5
1936	2.6	4.0	14.7	8.1	5.7
1937	3.2	23.1	16.4	11.6	5.2
1938	3.8	18.8	20.7	26.2	5.5
1939	4.9	28.9	27.6	33.3	5.6
1940	6.3	28.6	34.3	24.3	5.4
1941	7.9	25.4	41.5	21.0	5.3
1942	9.3	17.7	50.0	20.5	5.4
1943	13.2	41.9	56.3	12.6	4.3

(continued)

TABLE A-1. *(continued)*

YEAR	CURRENCY (A)	% CHANGE	BANK BALANCES (B)	% CHANGE	RATIO OF BANK MONEY TO CURRENCY (B/A)
1944	22.8	72.7	77.9	38.4	3.4
1945	56.7	148.7	120	54.0	2.1
1946	95.9	69.1	145	20.8	1.5
1947	221	130.4	234	61.4	1.1
1948	357	61.5	505	115.8	1.4
1949	358	0.3	792	56.8	2.2
1950	425	18.7	1,049	32.4	2.5
1951	510	20.0	1,506	43.6	3.0
1952	581	13.9	2,224	47.7	3.8
1953	643	10.7	2,708	21.8	4.2
1954	637	(−0.9)	3,037	12.1	4.8
1955	695	9.1	3,724	22.6	5.4
1956	812	16.8	4,764	27.9	5.9
1957	869	7.0	5,505	15.6	6.3
1958	931	7.1	6,484	17.8	7.0
1959	1,083	16.3	7,414	14.3	6.9
1960	1,297	19.8	8,872	19.7	6.8
1961	1,549	19.4	10,332	16.5	6.7
1962	1,821	17.6	12,119	17.3	6.7
1963	2,146	17.8	15,648	29.1	7.3
1964	2,419	12.7	17,846	14.0	7.4
1965	2,698	11.5	20,653	15.7	7.7

Sources: Nihon Ginkō Tōkeikyoku 1962: 58, 67–72; Nihon Ginkō Tōkeikyoku 1966.

TABLE A-2. Credit creation and industrial investment, 1940–1965 (in billions of yen)

YEAR	TOTAL BoJ LENDING	TOTAL BANK LENDING	BANK LENDING TO MFG.	MFG. LENDING / TOTAL LENDING	PERSONAL SAVING	SAVING AS % OF INCOME
1940	0.8	21.7			7.5	28.1
1941	0.9	24.3			10.1	32.7
1942	1.8	26.7			11.4	32.4
1943	3.6	32.4			14.1	35.2
1944	9.9	51.2			20.1	43.1
1945	49.1	97.6			—	—
1946	58.0	146.4			8	2.4
1947	85.5	168.2			(−40)	(−4.6)
1948	135.4	381.3			(−8)	(−0.5)
1949	188.6	679.0			(−43)	(−1.9)
1950	331.9	984	535	0.54	410	14.6
1951	400.7	1,506	831	0.55	718	19.2
1952	356.0	2,111	1,060	0.50	442	10.3
1953	402.5	2,655	1,261	0.47	394	7.8
1954	266.3	2,894	1,415	0.49	549	9.6
1955	45.8	3,176	1,493	0.47	853	13.4
1956	142.9	4,021	1,895	0.47	952	13.7
1957	551.9	4,981	2,465	0.49	1,219	15.6
1958	379.3	5,767	2,844	0.49	1,248	15.0
1959	337.8	6,751	3,285	0.49	1,547	16.7
1960	500.1	8,117	4,035	0.50	1,864	17.4
1961	1,284	9,698	4,856	0.50	2,402	19.2
1962	1,285	11,405	5,778	0.51	2,691	18.6
1963	1,156	14,451	7,266	0.50	3,026	18.0
1964	1,110	16,713	8,221	0.49	3,156	16.4
1965	1,628	19,076	9,210	0.48	3,884	17.7

Sources: Bank lending: outstanding loans and discounts by industry (banking accounts of all banks) are Bank of Japan data given in HSJ 3: 184–185 and Nihon Ginkō Tōkeikyoku 1966: 192–193. The numbers for BoJ total lending given in HSJ, vol. 3, used here for the period after 1950, differ slightly from those in Nihon Ginkō Tōkeikyoku 1966. Personal savings and personal saving ratio (as percent of personal disposable income) are EPA figures, in HSJ 3: 356–357.

TABLE A-3. Prices and wages, 1936–1965

YEAR	WHOLESALE PRICE INDEX*	ANNUAL % CHANGE	CONSUMER PRICE INDEX†	ANNUAL % CHANGE	MFG. WAGES**	ANNUAL % CHANGE
1936	1.04		1.04			
1937	1.26	21.2	1.14	9.6		
1938	1.33	5.6	1.30	14.0		
1939	1.47	10.5	1.46	12.3		
1940	1.64	11.6	1.70	16.4		
1941	1.76	7.3	1.72	1.2		
1942	1.91	8.5	1.77	2.9		
1943	2.05	7.3	1.87	5.6		
1944	2.32	13.2	2.10	12.3		
1945	3.50	50.9	3.08	46.7		
1946	16.3	366	18.9	514		
1947	48.2	196	51	170		
1948	128	166	150	194		
1949	209	63.3	243	62.0		
1950	247	18.2	238	(−2.1)		
1951	343	38.9	310	30.3		
1952	349	1.7	301	(−2.9)	5.5	
1953	352	0.9	311	3.3	6.2	12.7
1954	349	(−0.9)	321	3.2	6.5	4.8
1955	343	(−1.7)	308	(−4.0)	6.8	4.6
1956	358	4.4	307	(−0.3)	7.4	8.8
1957	369	3.1	314	2.3	7.7	4.1
1958	345	(−6.5)	310	(−1.3)	7.9	2.6
1959	348	0.9	309	(−0.3)	8.5	7.6
1960	352	1.1	313	1.3	9.2	8.2
1961	356	1.1	323	3.2	10.2	10.9
1962	350	(−1.7)	333	3.1	11.2	9.8
1963	356	1.7	349	4.8	12.3	9.8
1964	357	0.3	356	2.0	13.6	10.6
1965	359	0.6	374	5.1	14.8	8.8

Source: Bank of Japan price data given in HSJ 4: 330–333, 348–349. Ministry of Labor wage data given in HSJ 4: 307.

Calendar year averages of current prices; 1934–36 = 1. Current wages; 1980 = 100.
*Bank of Japan wholesale price index.
†BoJ consumer price index for Tokyo.
**Ministry of Labor index of manufacturing wages for establishments of thirty or more workers.

TABLE A-4. Indicators of manufacturing production, 1936–1965

YEAR	TOTAL MFG.	% INCREASE (DECREASE)	IRON AND STEEL	MACHINERY	TEXTILES	CONSUMER DURABLES
1936	31.5		21.9	11.4	74.9	9.6
1937	37.2	18.1	25.3	15.3	85.3	9.6
1938	38.2	2.7	29.0	16.8	70.4	9.6
1939	42.1	10.2	31.1	20.6	70.4	9.7
1940	44.3	5.2	32.4	25.0	63.7	10.8
1941	45.8	3.4	33.4	28.8	51.5	7.9
1942	44.5	(−2.8)	35.3	29.9	40.7	6.5
1943	45	1.1	39.5	32.8	26.7	4.8
1944	46.2	2.7	36.9	38.6	14.2	2.1
1945	19.6	(−57.6)	13.1	16.4	5.5	0.7
1946	7.4	(−62.2)	4.3	5.0	9.1	2.3
1947	9.2	24.3	5.7	6.0	12.2	3.7
1948	12.3	33.7	9.5	9.2	13.9	5.2
1949	16.3	32.5	16.3	11.5	18.5	6.4
1950	20.4	25.2	22.9	11.9	26.4	6.2
1951	28.8	41.2	30.9	19.2	37.4	8.3
1952	31.1	8.0	31.4	19.7	42.5	10.3
1953	38.5	23.8	37.4	25	51.2	13.3
1954	42.2	9.6	39.2	28.2	55.6	15.2
1955	45.7	8.3	43.8	28.5	62.0	18.9
1956	56.4	23.4	53.3	41.4	73.7	27.0
1957	66.9	18.6	60.8	57.6	81.3	38.7
1958	65.7	(−1.8)	57.2	56.5	72.6	48.5
1959	79.6	21.2	76.3	72.6	84.8	75.2
1960	100.0	25.6	100.0	100.0	100.0	100.0
1961	119.9	19.9	126.1	129	107.9	125.8
1962	130.1	8.5	125.5	145	113.5	143.9
1963	143.7	10.5	140.4	159.5	122.5	160.1
1964	169.1	17.7	172.8	194	136.9	175.7
1965	177.2	4.8	177.7	198.8	147.1	157.2

Sources: MITI data, given in Nihon Ginkō Tōkeikyoku 1966: 92–93.

Weighted index of value-added for each product category. Index: 1960 = 100.

Notes

ABBREVIATIONS OF COMPILATIONS, ARCHIVES, JOURNALS, AND REFERENCE WORKS

ESJ   Economic Planning Agency (Keizai Kikakuchō). *Economic Survey of Japan* [Economic White Paper], various years.

HSJ   Sōmuchō Tōkeikyoku (Statistics Bureau, Management and Coordination Agency), ed. 1988. *Nihon chōki tōkei sōran*. [Historical statistics of Japan]. 5 volumes. Tokyo: Nihon Tōkei Kyōkai (Japan Statistical Association).

ITZ   *Ishibashi Tanzan zenshū* [Collected works of Ishibashi Tanzan]. 15 vols. Tokyo: Tōyō Keizai Shinpōsha, 1970–72.

JMDP   Joseph M. Dodge Papers, Burton Historical Collection, Detroit Public Library. Abbreviated by box and file number; for example, "Japan-1949-1" is box "Japan-1949," file 1.

LTES   *Chōki keizai tōkei, suikei to bunseki* [Estimates of long-term economic statistics of Japan since 1868]. Ed. Oʜᴋᴀᴡᴀ Kazushi, Sʜɪɴᴏʜᴀʀᴀ Miyohei, and Uᴍᴇᴍᴜʀᴀ Mataji. 14 vols. Tokyo: Tōyō Keizai Shinpōsha, 1965–88.

NGHS   *Nihon Ginkō hyakunenshi* [One-hundred-year history of the Bank of Japan]. 6 vols. Tokyo: Nihon Ginkō Hyakunenshi Iinkai, 1982–86.

NKS-SZ   *Nihon kin'yūshi shiryō, Shōwa zoku hen* [Materials on Japanese financial history, Shōwa era continued]. Ed. Nihon Ginkō Kin'yū Kenkyūjo. 29 vols. Tokyo: Ōkurashō Insatsukyoku, 1978–96.

OE   *The Oriental Economist* [English-language publication of *Tōyō keizai shinpō*]. Tokyo.

SCAP   Supreme Commander for the Allied Powers (U.S. occupation administration). See note on U.S. occupation archives below.

SZS-SK   *Shōwa zaisei shi: Shūsen kara kōwa made* [History of public finance in the Shōwa period: From the end of the war to the peace treaty]. Ed. Ōkurashō Shōwa Zaiseishishitsu [Ministry of Finance, Shōwa Financial History Editorial Office]. 20 vols. Tokyo: Tōyō Keizai Shinpōsha, 1976–82.

TKS   *Tōyō keizai shinpō* [The oriental economist]. [Japanese-language ed.] Tokyo.

U.S. OCCUPATION ARCHIVES

U.S. occupation (SCAP) records held in the National Archives are in Record Group 331. They are abbreviated by SCAP section, box number, and folder number. For example, SCAP/GS 2275E-8 would be SCAP, Government Section, box 2275E, folder 8. CIE = Civil Information and Education Section; ESS = Economic and Scientific Section; GS = Government Section. Microfilmed copies of the SCAP records are also held in the Kensei Shiryōshitsu in the National Diet Library, Tokyo.

INTRODUCTION

Epigraph: Goethe, *Faust*, pt. 2, act 1, lines 4929–4930 (translation by Philip Wayne 1959: 33).

1. Crafts and Venables (2003) analyze Asian industrialization as Phase III of the global industrialization process.

2. Machlup 1943; chapter 3 in this book.

3. Ōkita 1957: 36.

4. Young Schopenhauer, through his mother's mediation, became part of Goethe's circle at Weimar, though Goethe rejected Schopenhauer's solipsism. A line also connects Schopenhauer (and Faust) to the stormy ruminations of Friedrich Nietzsche, and onward to Joseph Schumpeter's heroic visions of the entrepreneur and the cycle of "creative destruction" (Brown 1997; Reinert and Reinert 2006).

1. THE REVOLUTION IN PRICES

Epigraphs: Schumpeter 1954b [1918]: 119; Ōuchi in Ichimada and Ōuchi 1949: 9–10; "Budget Analysis by Jerome B. Cohen," July 15, 1949, Japan-1949-1, JMDP. Cohen repeated this point in Cohen 1949: 85 and 1958: 84.

1. Binswanger 1994. Binswanger, a senior professor of finance, has brought Goethe back into discussion in the aftermath of the 2007 bubble, e.g., in conversation with his Ph.D. student Josef Ackermann, chief of Deutsche Bank; see Josef Ackermann and Hans Christoph Binswanger, "Es fehlt das Geld. Nun gut, so schaff es denn!," June 30, 2009, *Frankfurter Allgemeine Zeitung*, FAZ.net. Notably, Binswanger's work was translated into Japanese before it was translated into English. Berman 1982 includes a classic essay on "Faust the developer."

2. "Zu wissen sei es jedem, der's begehrt: / Der Zettel hier ist tausend Kronen wert. / Ihm liegt gesichert, als gewisses Pfand, / Unzahl vergrabnen Guts im Kaiserland." *Faust*, pt. 2, act 1, ll. 6057–6060, my translation.

3. Binswanger 1994, and Taylor's notes to his translation, Goethe 1876: 310–313. Law's story has been well told so many times that it is hard to know where to begin. Larry Neal has offered a series of modern economic-historical analyses. Philip Mirowski (1981, 1985) has traced the origin of major business cycles (which Schumpeter called Juglar cycles) to the 1720 bubble in England.

4. Cantillon 1931; Schumpeter 1954c: 222; Murphy 1986. Schumpeter said that Cantillon made "the first systematic attempt to work over the whole field of economics" and that he was, "so far as I know, the first to use the term entrepreneur" (Schumpeter 1954a: 29–30; 1954c: 555).

5. Metzler 2006b. My book *Lever of Empire* looked at the outside of the national capital-creation process by focusing on Japan's relation to its international "capital environment," particularly to British and American banks in the years before and after World War I. This book focuses on the "inside" of the capital circuit, domestic capital creation.

6. The *Great War → Great Depression* connection has been least visible to U.S. scholars, who often fail to grasp deflation and depression as international processes that began in 1920. I discuss this aspect of the depression in Metzler 2006b, especially chaps. 6 and 8 and pp. 260–263.

7. Schumpeter 1918: 119, emphasis added.

8. Bresciani-Turroni 1937: 103–105, 196–212, 415–422; quotation from p. 365.

9. Metzler 2006b, chap. 5; Lewis 1990.

10. Metzler 2004; for some Asia-wide aspects of this inflation–deflation wave, see Metzler forthcoming.

11. Schumpeter 1943: 115; chapter 7 in this book.

12. Fisk 1924; Moulton and Pasvolsky 1926, 1932.

13. Smethurst 2007; Metzler 2006b. Takahashi himself was not a militarist, nor was he a Keynesian in any literal sense, for his economic ideas were developed in advance of Keynes's own writing on the subject.

14. Nihon Ginkō Tōkeikyoku 1962; the numbers are given in appendix A in this book. An English translation of the Bank of Japan law is given in Shinjo 1962: 179–197; Japanese text in *NGHS* 6 (Shiryōhen).

15. Patrick 1965b; Metzler 2006b.

16. Ōuchi 1947: 118–119.

17. Nakamura 1989b: 26, 31–32.

18. Ōuchi 1947: 117–120. Details of Japanese monetary missions are given in Schiltz 2012, and a summary discussion of the origins of the yen bloc is given in Metzler 2006b. Full histories in Japanese are provided by Shimazaki 1989 and Tadai 1997.

19. Ōuchi 1947: 120.

20. Metzler 2006b, chap. 13; Tsushima 1966; Hashimoto 1989: 69–71.

21. Havens 1978: 36, 94; Griffiths 2002.

22. Griffiths 2002: 825, 828.

23. Havens 1978: 94–95, 124–125; Griffiths 2002.

24. Garon 2000; Havens 1978.

25. Nihon Ginkō Tōkeikyoku 1966: 76–77.

2. DRAMATIS PERSONAE

Epigraph: Schumpeter 1934: 85.

1. Yagi 2004; Hein 2004; Gao 1994. Barshay (1988: 64–97) discusses some related questions.

2. Yasui Takuma was Ōuchi's junior colleague in the Economics Faculty of the University of Tokyo, where he was the first neoclassical mathematical economist. He also served as an academic mentor to Shimomura Osamu.

3. Ōuchi 1959: 266–267.

4. Nei 2001: 116, 125–126, 153–154, 171.

5. Arisawa 1948: 233–235; Maier 1988: 140–141; "Sozialisierungskommission," http://de.wikipedia.org/wiki/Sozialisierungskommission (accessed August 12, 2012). Arisawa 1948 features an extended discussion of the German Sozialization Commission (125–150).

6. Ōuchi 1959: 125–127, 151–153. Lederer subsequently went to Tokyo Imperial University as a visiting professor. Ōuchi hosted him in Tokyo a second time after Lederer left Germany to escape Nazi persecution. Some likenesses of Lederer's and Schumpeter's economic thought are discussed by Michaelides et al. 2010. Arisawa Hiromi translated Lederer's work; Ōuchi also said that people used Lederer's work in an effort to integrate Marxism and neoclassical economics (Hein 1994: 756).

7. März 1991: 147–63; see Sargent 1982: 48–56 on Austria's inflation and its end. Schumpeter's biographical details are drawn from McCraw 2007, Swedberg 1991, Stolper 1994, Haberler 1950, and Smithies 1950. McCraw's biography is especially engaging and Haberler's tribute especially brilliant.

8. Ōuchi 1974–75, 12: 199. Widdig (2001) describes the culture of inflation in Germany and Austria after World War I.

9. Schumpeter 1925.

10. I describe the theory and practice of 1920s "stabilization" depressions in Metzler 2006b: 159–74.

11. McCraw 2007: 97–111, 543–545.

12. Shionoya 1990b: 9–10.

13. Ōuchi 1959. Laura Hein's 2004 study offers a fascinating group portrait of Ōuchi and his circle, which included Arisawa.

14. Hein 2004: 22, 28–30, 44; Ōuchi 1959: 129.

15. Ōuchi, "Infurēshon jidai no Doitsu" (September 25, 1947), in Ōuchi 1974–75: 195–201.

16. Arisawa is the central figure in Bai Gao's important study (1994, 1997).

17. Arisawa 1948: 1–2; Gao 1994: 118–119.

18. Arisawa 1934.

19. Hein 2004: 64–76.

20. Here see especially Gao 1994, 1997.

21. Ichimada's name is subject to several readings. Many biographical dictionaries render his given name as Naoto, and his family name is occasionally rendered as Ichimanda. He signed his name in roman letters as Hisato Ichimada (examples may be found in the Bank of Japan archives and in JMDP).

22. Ichimada 1950: 62–66, 99, 106; Yoshino 1975: 284–285; Yoshino 1976: 263. For Inoue Junnosuke's life and death, see Metzler 2006b.

23. Ichimada 1950: 114–117; Yoshino 1976: 264–265; Gerald Feldman, personal communication.

24. James 1985, 1986; McNeil 1986; Katalin Ferber, personal communication.

25. Nishizawa 2001; Morris-Suzuki 1991: 68–69, 92–94; Pyle 1974; Bassino 1998: 85–87.

26. Tōbata 1984: 3. Tōbata began his memoir *My Teachers, My Friends, My Scholarship* (*Waga shi • waga tomo • waga gakumon*, 1984) with a long appreciation of Schumpeter.

27. Nei 2001: 113–117.

28. Nakayama 1972–73, 1: i–iii; Nakayama 1933: 4, 115–126. The first volume of Nakayama's collected works also included a series of essays on Schumpeter's life and work (pp. 305–385).

29. Nakayama 1972. Scott O'Bryan (2009) examines the influence of Keynesianism in Japan.

30. Tōbata 1936; Yagi 2004; on the latter point, Francks 1984 and related considerations in Morris-Suzuki 1994: 88–104.

31. Schumpeter 1937; Tōbata 1984: 13–14.

32. Ōuchi 1959: 214, 267.

33. Arase 1995; "1968 Ramon Magsaysay Award for Public Service," www.rmaf.org.ph/Awardees/Biography/BiographyTobataSei.htm. (Ōkita Saburō received the same award.) Akamatsu Kaname's idea of the "flying-geese pattern" of development also developed in this context (Ikeo 2008).

34. Arisawa discussed the Akimaru Institute (Akimaru Kikan) in a 1956 magazine article, and Arisawa and Nakayama discussed it further in Nakayama 1972–73 (Bekkan): 61–62.

35. Tsuru 2000.

3. WHAT IS CAPITAL?

Epigraphs: Schumpeter 1934: 116; Shinohara 1964b: 32 (emphasis in originals). In the quotations from Schumpeter that follow, I supplement emphasis in the original with my own.

1. This discussion sets aside for separate consideration more metaphorical constructions of capital such as Pierre Bourdieu's idea of "cultural capital" (which, like money-capital, is subject to its own inflation and bubble dynamics!). The literature on money itself is vast. An outstanding general statement and introduction to some of the most penetrating thinking on the subject is given by Geoffrey Ingham (2005a).

2. Schumpeter 1934: 116, 120, 122; Schumpeter 1939: 129 for a later statement. Biondi 2008 translates a fuller statement in Schumpeter's 1926 book that was not included in the 1934 English translation.

3. The fullest exploration of this theme is the excellent essay by Jean-Pascal Bassino (1998); Bai Gao (1997) has made further important indications in this connection.

4. Smithies 1950: 632; Bassino 1998: 80.

5. Chakravarty 1980; a recent introduction to Schumpeter's system is given by Andersen 2011.

6. "Jedes neue Kapital betritt in erster Instanz die Bühne, d.h. den Markt, Warenmarkt, Arbeitsmarkt oder Geldmarkt, immer noch als Geld, Geld, das sich durch bestimmte Prozesses in Kapital verwandeln soll." Marx 1967: 146, translation modified, emphasis added.

7. Schumpeter 1934: 45–46.

8. Practically, it might be very difficult to distinguish investment in "reproduction" from investment in "innovation," especially when they happen within the same firm. Nonetheless, this analytical distinction focuses attention on the basic process of innovation. Schumpeter's ideal construction of the "circular flow" of the economy is less interesting. Much of it now reads as a forced effort to retain the received mathematicized model of equilibrium (to which Schumpeter was strongly attached) as a metaphysical ground for his theory of development—as the basis from which to perceive change. In essence, however, he was proposing an evolutionary model that broke the old equilibrium framework. März (1991) points out another aspect: that Schumpeter's circular-flow model offers an abstract picture of the dynamics of Austria's old agrarian economy in the absence of capitalist entrepreneurship.

9. Schumpeter 1934: 74–75, 66.

10. Schumpeter 1934: 95, 96–97.

11. Schumpeter 1934: 98–99, citing Frank A. Fetter, *Principles of Economics*; Schumpeter 1954c: 1116.

12. Schumpeter 1954c: 321–322.

13. Schumpeter 1934: 99.

14. Schumpeter 1939: 118; 1934: 98.

15. Schumpeter 1934: 102–104, 106–107.

16. Schumpeter 1934: 107, 108.

17. Schumpeter 1934: 108–109, 109n.

18. Schumpeter 1934: 109n; Machlup 1943: 27–28. Hayek traced the idea of inflationary or "forced" accumulation back to British economists writing at the beginning of the nineteenth century (Hayek 1932; 1935: 18–31; Schumpeter 1954c: 724). He cited J. S. Mill (1844), who explained that bankers convert future revenue streams into capital: "and thus, strange as it may appear, the depreciation of the currency [i.e., inflation], when effected in this way, operates to a certain extent as a forced accumulation." This idea is at the center of Hayek's analysis in *Prices and Production*.

19. Machlup 1943: 27. The Japanese word *setsuyaku* 節約 suggests *economizing* but without the sense of *accumulation* carried by other standard words for *saving* such as *chochiku* 貯蓄 or *chikuseki* 蓄積. Thanks to Laura Hein for the "forced investment" suggestion. In 1955, Shinohara Miyohei attended Machlup's seminar, and the two became close (Amsden and Suzumura 2001: 347).

20. Schumpeter 1934: 109.

21. Schumpeter 1934: 110; also 1927: 302–303.

22. Schumpeter 1934: 123, 125, 126.

23. Schumpeter 1939: 111.

24. Schumpeter 1939: 111–112. Tsuru Shigeto focused on this passage in a 1941 essay written at Harvard for Schumpeter's seminar (in Tsuru 1993a: 43–44; also in Tsuru 1976).

25. Schumpeter (1939: 641–642) also qualified the idea that banks' provision of credit "orders" corresponded to the directives of a planning board in a socialist state. As a rule,

he emphasized, the initiative and actual project planning comes from the side of the entrepreneur. Banks' role in planning is one of reacting, judging, deciding, and monitoring. When banks go too far beyond that—when bankers begin to actively urge projects on their clients—there is danger. That is, a bubble is usually under way, and a crash in the works.

26. As recorded by Tsuru Shigeto. Schumpeter's fullest discussion of Marx is given in *Capitalism, Socialism and Democracy.*

27. Marx 1967: 154, 163. Marx presented a lengthy construction of the creation of value through production in volume 2 of *Capital.*

28. Marx 1967: 189.

29. Marx 1967: 94.

30. Schumpeter 1934: 119.

4. FLOWS AND STORES

Epigraphs: Soddy 1922; Nakayama Ichirō, in Arisawa, Tōbata, Nakayama, Wakimura, and Ōkita 1960: 262–263.

1. Quoted in Arena and Festré 2005: 384.

2. Smil 2008: 12–13; Soddy 1922.

3. Barnhart 1987.

4. Beaudreau 1999; Mirowski 1989 for some connected concerns. Schumpeter himself recognized that there was much more to say about electricity, and he placed electrification at the heart of the "new industrial revolution" of the early twentieth century (1939: 397–398).

5. Grandy 1996: 27–30, 39–41; Sclove 1989. For Soddy's ideas, see also Daly 1980 and Martinez-Alier 1987: 127–148.

6. Soddy 1926: 9.

7. Ōkita 1983: 9; Ono 2004; Baba 1933; Baba 1936. The Systems Analysis Society was later renamed the Academic Association for Organizational Science.

8. Iwasaki 1998; economic "planification" (*keikakuka*) is treated in Nakamura 1989d, especially in the chapter by Hara Akira, and by Okazaki (1998, 1999b). Janis Mimura (2011) treats the larger subject of planning in connection to Japanese "techno-fascism."

9. Berndt 1985. The Ottawa government also surely disliked Scott's vision of an Anschluss of Canada to the "Technate of North America."

10. Smil 2008: 341–346 (who seems also to have in mind the conceptual tangles in which Marx tied himself with a one-factor "embodied labor" theory of value); Berndt 1985; for energy as a factor of production, Stern and Kander (2012); thanks to Kaoru Sugihara for ideas in this connection.

11. A recent popular introduction to systems thinking is Meadows 2008. The Wikipedia "Systems Science" portal offers a good entryway to the subject: http://en.wikipedia .org/wiki/Portal:Systems_science.

12. Soddy 1926: 108.

13. Rosovsky 1961; *LTES* 3, 1966; Ohkawa and Rosovsky 1973; Ohkawa and Shinohara 1979; see Mosk 2004 for an introduction to Japanese economic growth in general. Thanks also to Ōshima Mario for his thoughts on this subject.

14. Soddy 1926.

15. Soddy 1926: 70; Daly 1980: 474. Daly emphasized the "limits to growth" aspect of Soddy's work. But also characteristic of Soddy, and shared by the Technocrats, was a view of practically unlimited future technological possibilities.

16. Daly 1980: 475–476. On this point, see also Hixson 1991, whose analysis productively combines the ideas of American populism, Milton Friedman, and Karl Marx.

17. Schumpeter 1939: 146–147, 909; Fisher 1933.

18. Soddy cited in Daly 1980.

19. Soddy in Daly 1980, my emphasis.

20. Leontief 1950; Shionoya 1997: 186. Shionoya (1997: 100–104) sees also the influence of Ernst Mach and Henri Poincaré.

21. Nakayama in Arisawa, Tōbata, Nakayama, Wakimura, and Ōkita 1960: 262–263; Ōkita 1957: 37; Ōkita 1962: 239–240.

22. See also Morris-Suzuki 1991: 145–149. Ōkita's own biographer, in a laudatory account (Ono 2004), acknowledged the insipidity of Ōkita's prose. Ōkita's most inspired literary performance may have been the 1946 report of the Special Survey Committee itself, in which he was assisted by the talented writer Gotō Yonosuke.

23. On the South Manchurian Railway Company, see Matsusaka 2001; also Ito 1988 and Young 1998. Emer O'Dwyer is writing an up-close history of Japanese Dairen.

24. Ono 2004: 13–15.

25. For wartime technocracy in Japan, see Mimura 2011; Pauer 1999; Kerde 1999.

26. Ōkita 1983; Ono 2004. On NTT, see Anchordoguy 2001; on Matsumae, see Yang (2010), who discusses the Technicians' Movement: 154–158.

27. Ono 2004: 153–159; O'Bryan 2009: esp. 154–157.

28. Fletcher 1982; Fletcher (185) calls Ōkita the most famous alumnus of this academy.

29. Omori 1992.

30. Peattie 1975.

5. JAPANESE CAPITALISM UNDER OCCUPATION

Epigraphs: Schumpeter 1934: 220; Ōkita Saburō, in conversation with Arisawa Hiromi, "Keizai saiken to keisha seisan," in Andō 1966: 293.

1. Tsutsui 1998: 122; Dower 1999: 530.

2. Moore 1983.

3. "Anchor chain": compare Redish 1993.

4. Ōuchi 1959: 329, quoted in Ōkita 1961: 14 and in Ōkita 1983: 32.

5. Ohno n.d.; Ōkita 1983: 32; Ōkita 1961: 13. The postsurrender numbness and psychological depression is evoked by Dower 1999: 87–105.

6. Mercado 2002: 174–180.

7. Takahashi 1963: 260–262. Takahashi Kamekichi may have been the most active writer on the subject of "controlled economy." His role deserves more attention.

8. These other members were Taira Teizō, Rōyama Masamichi, Kameyama Naoto, Tatsumi Yoshitomo, Ōno Kazuo, and Sugihara Arata.

9. Dower 1988 [1979]: 265–272.

10. Ōkita, "Sengo fukkō," in Arisawa 1989: 3–7; Ōkita in Andō 1966, 2: 276–277. The Japanese and English versions of the report have been republished by Tokyo University Press. Further discussion of this group can be found in Ōkita 1961: 13–25; Nakamura introduction to Ōkita et al. 1992; Ōkita 1983; and O'Bryan 2009: 21–36.

11. Schumpeter 1934: 85.

12. Arisawa 1989: 6. "Kōza" and "Rōnō" were not party labels, but to say "Communist" and "Socialist" captures much of the intellectual-political divide between the two; see Hoston 1986 and Ōshima 1991.

13. Minoguchi et al. 2000: 210–212. Other participants in the lunchtime meetings included Arisawa Hiromi, Tōbata Seiichi, Uchida Shun'ichi, Hori Yoshiaki, Shirasu Jirō, and Wada Hirō. The significance of the Japan Productivity Center is explored by Tsutsui 1998: 135–149; Gordon 1998: 47–49; and O'Bryan 2009: 139–142, 163–170.

14. Quoted in Minoguchi et al. 2000: 213.

15. Ōkita 1983: 33.

16. O'Bryan 2009: 43–46.

17. Ōuchi quoted in Hein 2004: 94.

18. Saga 1991: 229–237.

19. Kaplan and Dubro 2003: 31–55; Whiting 1999: 7–38; Aldous 1997: 216–217.

20. Griffiths 2002: 836.

21. *NGHS* 5: 8–13; Andō 1966: 293.

22. Ōuchi quoted in Hein 2004: 92; Yoshino 1996: 174–177.

23. Yoshino 1996; *NGHS* 5: 20–21; SCAP orders of September 2 and 4, 1945, in *NKS-SZ* 25: 35–37; and for more on Tsushima, Metzler 2006b. Internal (secret) U.S. occupation directives stated, "The Japanese authorities will remain responsible for the management and direction of the domestic fiscal, monetary, and credit policies subject to the approval and review of the Supreme Commander"; "United States Initial Post-Defeat Policy Relating to Japan," August 22, 1945, in *SZS-SK* 20: 63–67.

24. Nolte 1987: 295–296; Johnson 1982: 178; Nakamura 1981: 32.

25. Kimura 1948: 113, 116–117; *NGHS* 5: 23–24; Nakamura 1981: 22; Nihon Ginkō Tōkeikyoku 1962, summarized in appendix A here.

26. Dower 1999: 45–54; Nakamura 1994: 124–125; Miwa 1989: 181.

27. Nakamura 1994: 125.

28. Kōsai 1989c: 494.

29. [Economic Stabilization Board] 1947: 372–379; Cumings 1981: 204.

30. Hein 1990: 30–31.

31. Hein 1990: 75, 36.

32. Hein 1990: 32–36 (quotation from 131); Samuels 1987: 74–75, 89–91; see also the chapter entitled "Are Coal Miners Human Beings?" in Ishimoto 1984 [1935].

33. Moore 1983: 33–47, 59–61; Hein 1990: 65–67, 87–97.

34. Hein 1990: 73; [Economic Stabilization Board] 1947: 381–382.

35. See Tsutsui 2003 for the environmental effects of the war.

36. [Economic Stabilization Board] 1947: 366–371, 378–379; Nakamura 1989b: 42. On the "bamboo-shoot" existence, see Dower 1999: 89–97 and Griffiths 2002.

37. Arisawa 1948: 18, 20–30; Nihon Ginkō Tōkeikyoku 1966: 46–47, 335–337.

38. State-War-Navy Coordinating Committee (SWNCC) Report 150/3, in SZS-SK 20: 63–67.

39. Noda Nobuo on this point cited Schumpeter's idea that the breaking up of a monopoly position could be a factor for new combinations (Nihon Seisansei Honbu 1960: 14). Tsuru (1993a) offered a wider, Schumpeter-inspired conception of "creative defeat."

40. Ishibashi, "Yondai zaibatsu no kaitai," November 24, 1945, in ITZ 13: 67–70; Ishibashi 1951a: 196.

41. Ishibashi 1951c: 603.

42. Central Committee of the Communist Party of Japan 1973: 102–103.

43. T. Cohen 1987: 154–170.

44. T. Cohen 1987. The crucial exception was petroleum, where U.S. oil industry executives did have a central role in shaping GHQ policy (Hein 1990: 77).

45. Hein and Metzler 2013; Ishibashi 1951a.

46. Kuroda 1993: 35–36.

47. *NGHS* 5: 30, 34–36; Teranishi 1993: 67, 71; Schumpeter 1954 [1918].

6. INFLATION AS CAPITAL

Epigraphs: Cohen 1958: 83; Noguchi 1986: 37. Compare the conclusion of Hugh Patrick: "Despite high saving propensities, there has been a tendency toward inflation in Japan . . . inflationary tendencies are an indication of the high investment demand" (or, one could say simply, of high investment) that is "greater even than the supply of savings" (1962: 22).

1. Morozumi 1956: 55; Shiotani 1956: 34.

2. Schumpeter in 1939 criticized the term *forced savings* as a description of his idea of developmental credit inflation, because he disliked the implication that households in general ended up paying the cost of this new investment. He claimed that "it is primarily the purchasing power of other *firms* that is reduced in order to make room for the requirements of entrepreneurs, and the reduction of the 'real' purchasing power of some *households* is a secondary phenomenon which, moreover, is compensated in part by the increase in the real purchasing power of others" (Schumpeter 1939: 112n). Here he was obviously thinking of the separate markets for producers' goods and consumer goods. But these markets are not unconnected. In any case, the term *forced savings* seemed apt to other people, and its use persisted.

3. Yoshino 1957: 587; Nihon Ginkō Chōsakyoku 1946.

4. Kimura 1946: 189. Ishibashi's role has often been dismissed by Americans, since the time when American officials officially "dismissed" him during the occupation itself. Ishibashi is the subject of an excellent biography in English by Sharon Nolte (1987), who concentrated on his education and his prewar journalistic career as a Taishō-era liberal. I discuss Ishibashi's prewar economic thought in Metzler 2004 and 2006b. Indicative of the ongoing Ishibashi boom in Japan is the fact that more than thirty Japanese-language books have been published on him since 1990 (according to a quick search of the online catalog of the National Diet Library).

5. Ishibashi, "Yondai zaibatsu no kaitai," November 24, 1947, in *ITZ* 13: 67–70; Ishibashi 1951b: 196–197. As author of such books as *The Theory and Actuality of Inflation* (*Infureshon no riron to jissai*, 1932), Ishibashi was recognized as an authority on inflation. Ishibashi was also a counselor to the Cabinet Planning Board from July 1937 to November 1943 and was for two years a member of the Central Price Committee. Details can be found in Ishibashi Tanzan Kankei Monjo [Ishibashi Papers], Kensei Shiryōshitsu [Modern Japanese Political History Materials Room], National Diet Library.

6. Bronfenbrenner 1950: 286; Schumpeter 1939: 114. On Bronfenbrenner, see Ikeo 2011.

7. Ishibashi 1951b: 200, 203; Metzler 2006b: 257.

8. Ishibashi 1951c; Nolte 1987: 322–323. On Takahashi as "Japan's Keynes," see Smethurst 2007 and Metzler 2006b; for Japanese Keynesianism after World War II, O'Bryan 2009.

9. Ishibashi, "Infure hassei sezu (1)—defure koso mushiro hitsuzen," September 22, 1945, in *ITZ* 13: 93–98; Ishibashi 1946: 117. Ishibashi made the same argument when he was running for the Diet in March 1946 ("Shūgiin giin rikkōho ni saishite," March 16, 1946, in *ITZ* 13: 183).

10. Ishibashi 1951b: 199.

11. Yoshino 1996: 174.

12. Hein 2004: 88–89; Hein and Metzler 2013.

13. Nolte 1987: 289–290.

14. Gao 1994: 139, 134–135.

15. *NGHS* 5: 57.

16. Ishibashi 1951c: 634; Nihon Ginkō Tōkeikyoku 1966: 76–77.

17. "Mr. Ishibashi's Obstructionism on Extraordinary Tax Legislation" (n.d., written some time after October 1946), SCAP/ESS 7497-6. Kimura (1948: 112) presented a widely held contemporary view: the reason the government paid these wartime claims was because it was not the people's government; it was serving the munitions companies. Ishibashi's account is given in Ishibashi 1951b: 205–207; see also Nolte 1987: 298.

18. Quoted in Nolte 1987: 312.

19. Ishibashi's purge is documented in SCAP/GS 2275E-8 and 9. Accounts are given by Nolte 1987: 297–98, 305–320 and Masuda 1988: 147–175. Ishibashi's defense is documented in *ITZ* 13: 223–332.

20. Johnson 1982: 178–179.

21. Ishibashi to Lower House, "Shōwa 21-nendo Shūgiin zaisei enzetsu," July 25, 1946, in *ITZ* 13: 186–202; also Ishida 1985: 204–223 and *NGHS* 5: 57–59. Literally, Ishibashi said, the present situation was like "a famine or panic [*kyōkō*]." As in nineteenth-century English usage, *panic* was practically synonymous with depression (thus the great depression of 1929 was called in Japan the "Shōwa panic").

22. [Economic Stabilization Board] 1947: 372–379.

23. Later, while under purge, Ishibashi wrote his own summary history of the German inflation and deflation. He laid the main blame for that inflation on reparations and the Ruhr occupation—meaning he laid the main blame on the Western allies ("Sengo Nihon no infurēshon," in *ITZ* 13: 387–404). He feared the same thing would happen to Japan (Ishibashi 1951b: 210).

24. Ishibashi to Lower House, July 25, 1946, in *ITZ* 13: 192–194.

25. Smethurst 2007; Metzler 2006b; Cha 2003.

26. Ishibashi to Lower House, July 25, 1946, in *ITZ* 13: 194–200.

27. Metzler 2006a.

28. E.g., Ishibashi 1951b: 213–214. Ishibashi, despite his long-standing sympathy with the plight of tenant farmers, thought that small-scale farming was economically inefficient and favored a shift to large-scale farming. Nolte (1987) describes Ishibashi's advocacy for tenants in the 1920s.

29. Miwa 1993: 140; Okazaki 1999a: 123.

30. Schumpeter 1954; März 1991: 85–86. Schumpeter was drawing here on the fiscal sociology of Rudolf Goldschied.

31. MoF Banking Bureau, memo of December 1, 1949, p. 1, in SCAP/ESS 7513-7; Nolte 1987: 299. The RFB was sometimes also called the Reconversion Finance Bank in English; its Japanese name was Fukkō Kin'yū Kinkō, or Fukkin.

32. Arisawa and Ōkita in Andō 1966, 2: 283–287; Ōkita 1983: 38–39.

33. Economic Investigation Agency 1950: foreword (n.p.); Okazaki 1998: 248–250; Ōkita 1983: 39; Ono 2004.

34. Nolte 1987: 300; Johnson 1982: 181–183; Hein 1990: 118–128.

35. MoF Banking Bureau memo of December 1, 1949, pp. 7, 12, 24–25, in SCAP/ESS 7513-7; Yoshino 1976: 267. The 1946–47 fiscal year lasted only nine months, from August 1, 1946, to March 31, 1947.

36. Ichimada in November 1947, quoted in Asai 1993: 209; Calder 1993: 85–87; Okazaki 1999a: 124.

37. Nihon Ginkō Tōkeikyoku 1966.

38. Hein 1990; MoF Banking Bureau, "Reconversion Finance Bank," December 1, 1949, pp. 33–34, SCAP/ESS 7513-7.

39. [Economic Stabilization Board] 1947: 372–379.

40. Ishibashi to Lower House, "Shōwa 22-nendo Shūgiin zaisei enzetsu," March 3, 1947, in *ITZ* 13: 207, 212; Ishida 1985: 232–33.

41. A collection of Ishibashi's prewar anti-imperialist essays, including his well-known argument for a "little Japanism" (in the mold of Gladstone's "little Englandism") are collected in Ishibashi 1995b. In February 1944, Ishibashi's second son was killed at the battle of Kwajalein. Some ambiguities of the wartime position of Ishibashi and his *Tōyō keizai shinpō* are described by Shorb 1997. Ishibashi's pro-China peaceful policy in the 1950s is discussed further by Ishida 1985: 199–201.

42. Memorandum, May 1, 1947, SCAP/GS 2275E-8 and 9.

43. *OE*, January 1957, 1–2; also Ishibashi 1951b: 210.

44. These statements can be found in SCAP/GS 2275E-8 and 9.

45. Ikeda 1952: 3–4; Shimomura Osamu in Ekonomisuto Henshūbu 1999: 14. Ikeda's 1952 book was actually written by a team of his MoF subordinates.

46. Johnson 1982: 176; also Johnson 1978: 75–79; Ōuchi 1959: 155. On America's wartime controlled economy, see Higgs 1992.

47. Adams 1964: 252.

48. That is, central-bank monetary regulation by the supposedly orthodox methods of altering interest rates, altering banks' reserve requirements, and buying and selling government bonds from and to the banks.

49. This moral question is a central concern in Hein 2004 and in Barshay 2004.

50. Ono 2004: 78–79; Arisawa and Ōkita in Andō 1966, 2: 287; Ōkita 1983: 40; Ishibashi 1951b: 221.

51. Economic Investigation Agency 1950: foreword (n.p.).

52. Kohno 1997: 49–67 provides an insightful analysis.

53. Carlile 1989: 257.

54. Ōtake 1987. The Keizai Dōyūkai is now called the Japan Association of Corporate Executives; see the association's website, www.doyukai.or.jp/. For the "renovation bureaucrats," see Mimura 2011. The transformation from "class society" to "system society" is described by Yamanouchi 1998. Here, too, systems thinking and approaches were gaining force, if not necessarily under that name.

55. Carlile 1989: 216–217. Lonny Carlile's unpublished dissertation is invaluable on this subject.

56. Matsumoto 1991; Carlile 1989: 215; Tsutsui 1998: 123–129; Hirschmeier and Yui 1975: 252.

57. Ōkita et al. 1992: 128–129.

58. Fletcher 1982: 127, 184; and for a full discussion, Gao 1994 and Gao 1997. For corporatism in the Japanese context, see Pempel and Tsunekawa 1979 and Garon 1987: 242–248.

59. ESS Finance Division, "Reconversion Finance Bank," March 2, 1948, SCAP/ESS 7515-1; Economic Investigation Agency 1950 (quotations from foreword [n.p.]); Johnson 1978: 78–79.

60. Ōkita 1961: 52–53; Arisawa and Ōkita in Andō 1966, 2: 292; Ōkita (May 1948) in Ōkita 1949: 227–229. For more on the economic white papers, see O'Bryan 2009.

61. Economic Investigation Agency 1950: foreword (n.p.); Dower 1999: 100.

62. Nihon Ginkō Tōkeikyoku 1966: 46–47.

63. Tylecote 1991: 248–251.

64. Hayek 1935: 8–9, 11; Schumpeter 1954: 222–223. The reference is to Cantillon's discussion of "the augmentation and diminution of the effective quantity of money in a state." Hella Hayek, the wife of Friedrich Hayek, translated Cantillon's book into German in 1931.

65. Dore 1985 [1959]: 212–213.

66. Nihon Ginkō Tōkeikyoku 1966: 46–47.

67. Hein 1990: 7, 98–105.

68. Nolte 1987: 300.

69. Maier 1987: 189, 196, 221.

70. This section draws on Hein and Metzler 2012, where more detail is given.

71. Taxation is thus basic to the constitution of money for a reason additional to those argued by G. F. Knapp in his influential "chartalist" analysis.

72. Brownlee et al. 2013 for the Shoup mission and its effects.

73. Bronfenbrenner 1950.

74. Ikeda 1952: 92–93.

75. Ikeda 1952: 93–94, 251; Bronfenbrenner 1950: 284.

76. Bronfenbrenner 1951: 983.

77. Ikeda 1952: 93–94, 251; Military Intelligence Section, General Staff, "Anti-tax Activities of Japan Communist Party," February 2, 1948, SCAP/Military Intelligence Section 7497-6.

78. Nakamura Takafusa has emphasized this point; also Nanto 1976; Kuroda 1993: 32–34.

79. R. E. Philips, memorandum of March 2, 1948, p. 8, SCAP/ESS 7515-1.

80. Hein 1990: 128, 132–135; details can be found in "Showa Denko," SCAP 7456-3 and "Working Papers (RFB)," SCAP 7515-1.

81. The Liberal Party was actually renamed the Democratic Liberal Party at that point. For the sake of simplicity, I refer to it as the Liberal Party throughout.

82. Arisawa 1948: 1–3, my emphasis; Yagi 2004.

7. INTERLUDE (DEFLATION)

Epigraphs: Schumpeter 1943: 115; Dodge, "Inflation Notes" (summer 1949), Japan-1949-6, JMDP.

1. Okazaki Tetsuji has produced a series of detailed reports on wartime economic planning; it is enlightening to compare the analysis of the "classic" socialist system by Kornai (1992), on which Okazaki drew. Other seminal work includes that of Hara Akira and Nakamura Takafusa, and in English, Erich Pauer (1999). I owe many basic ideas on this subject to discussions with Katalin Ferber. It is not the point of this discussion, but this combination of authoritarian control with capitalism also acquired a proper name: *fascism*. Of course, there are varieties of fascism also.

2. Miwa 1989: 130–132.

3. Dodge's mission falls within a history of U.S. "money doctoring." These monetary and fiscal experts' missions, often delegated with authoritative political powers, were first conducted in colonial and semicolonial settings after the turn of the twentieth century. The term was first applied to the monetary adviser Dr. Edwin Kemmerer, who in the 1920s led a series of international missions to put countries on dollar-based standards managed by internationally controlled central banks. Interest in the subject burgeoned because of U.S. and IMF interventions in "third world" and postsocialist settings in the 1980s and 1990s, most famously in the "shock therapy" treatments administered by Jeffrey Sachs. Some starting points to the growing literature on "money doctors" are Drake 1989, 1993; Rosenberg 1999; and Flandreau 2003. For World War II–era and early postwar international monetary experts missions, see Helleiner 2003a, especially 187–189, and Helleiner 2003b. For Japan's own prewar monetary missions to its own colonial and semicolonial periphery, see Schiltz 2012.

4. Schumpeter 1939: 117–118, 640–641.

5. Dodge, "Inflation Notes" (summer 1949), Japan-1949-6, JMDP.

6. Woodford 1974: 181–184, 200–204, 207; Joseph M. Dodge, biographical file, JMDP. There is still no biography of Dodge.

7. Dodge, "Appointment Correspondence [1948–49]," Japan-1949-1, JMDP.

8. Dodge, "Inflation Notes" (summer 1949), Japan-1949-6, JMDP, where Dodge refers to Bresciani-Turroni 1937, Dupriez 1947, Foa 1949, and Dieterlen and Rist 1948.

9. Dodge was here quoting Bresciani-Turroni 1937: 363.

10. Compare Bresciani-Turroni 1937: 363.

11. Schumpeter 1934: 232, here quoting Emil Lederer; Ichimada (July 1949), in Ichimada 1950: 228–229.

12. The protectionist national economics of Friedrich List responded even more directly to the deflationary postwar conjuncture that commenced in the late 1810s (Metzler 2006a).

13. For the reasons discussed here, the invention of "eurodollar" lending in the 1970s—the creation of U.S. dollar credits by overseas banks—was an extraordinary departure in the history of money creation that deserves deep analysis.

14. Ōkita et al. 1992: 13.

15. Metzler 2006b.

16. Schonberger 1989; Davis and Roberts 1996.

17. Oral History Interview with General William H. Draper, Jr., January 11, 1972, Truman Presidential Library. For both Draper and Dodge, see Schonberger 1989: 161–235.

18. Chernow 1990: 374–377.

19. Chernow 1990: 463–475.

20. Vatter 1985; Higgs 1992; C. Gordon 1994. America's own wartime economic planning and its postwar heritage needs much fuller analysis. This moment, when the modern military-industrial complex came together, often seems to be a collective blind spot.

21. T. Cohen 1987: 405–407; Schaller 1985; Schonberger 1989; summary biographical details of U.S. occupation officials are given in SZS-SK 3: 52–67. Theodore Cohen was chief of the Labor Division in GHQ's Economic and Scientific Section; his own political standpoint was that of an anticommunist New Dealer.

22. Dodge to Detroit Bank board, December 13, 1948, "Appointment Correspondence [1948–49]," Japan-1949-1, JMDP.

23. Concerning the significance of the Cold War for American policy-making toward Japan, readers can turn to several excellent studies, including those of Schaller (1985), Schonberger (1989), Dower (1993), and Sugita and Thorsten (1999). For the U.S. side of the international monetary context, see Kirshner 2007: 122–153.

24. Hogan 2000 provides a close study.

25. Bronfenbrenner 1950: 285.

26. Dodge, quoting MacArthur, who was himself quoting Churchill (Dodge speech, stamped Dept. of State, July 7, 1949, "Econ. Stabiliz. Pgm.," Japan-1949-4, JMDP).

27. Cohen 1987: 415–416; Forrestal 1951: 328–329; Borden 1984: 77–81.

28. Tsutsui 1988: 55–58; Calder 1993: 42.

29. Ralph A. Young et al., "Report of the Special Mission on Yen Foreign Exchange Policy," June 12, 1948, Sproul Papers, Federal Reserve Bank of New York archives; Yoshino 1996: 130–149; NGHS 5: 202–205; T. Cohen 1987: 412, 417, 419, 420.

30. T. Cohen 1987: 405, 410; Schonberger 1989; Davis and Roberts 1996.

31. "Information Objectives and Themes on the Nine-Point Economic Stabilization Program," February 20, 1952, SCAP/CIE 5216-8.

32. Ōkita (1961: 45–47) said the Dodge Line meant "the revival of the price mechanism," but he also called it an old-fashioned response driven by Cold War imperatives. Writing shortly after the end of the Cold War, against the background of worldwide neoliberal reforms, neoclassical economists Teranishi and Kosai (1993: 1, 14) also presented the Dodge Line as part of Japan's "transition to a market economy" after a time of heavy state control. As such, they thought Japan's experience under U.S. occupation could be a model for "the former socialist countries currently making an attempt to move towards a market economy" and for "developing countries as they work to draw up policies for the structural adjustment and stabilization of their economies." This view, that financially

oriented "shock therapy" could be a developmental model, contrasts greatly with Japanese postwar development advising as it actually happened, led by Ōkita Saburō.

33. Metzler 2004.

34. Tsuji 1956: 10.

35. Miyazawa 1956; see Shimomura Osamu, "Seichō seisaku no seika," in Ekonomisuto Henshūbu 1999: 15–16, for Ikeda's memoir; Metzler 2008 for a summary of "positive–negative" policy alternation in the 1990s.

36. Dodge, paraphrased by Miyazawa 1956: 14–15. The minister of finance was then Ōya Shinzō. Ikeda formally took office as minister later in the month.

37. Miyazawa 1956: 14–17; Masumi 1985: 187.

38. Dodge, memo of March 1, 1949, meeting, Japan-1949-1, "Budget–Ikeda Interviews," JMDP; Hein 2004: 97.

39. Orville J. McDiarmid, "Counterpart Fund and Credit Policy," April 7, 1949 (JMDP, reprinted in *NKS-SZ* 25: 277–281); Borden 1984.

40. MoF memorandum of December 1, 1949, SCAP/ESS 7513-7; Masumi 1985: 187.

41. Dodge, "Budget—Ikeda Interviews," Japan-1949-1, JMDP. The quotations are from Dodge's memos of meetings with Ikeda on March 1, March 25, and March 28, 1949. Ikeda (1952) called the talks "tax-cut negotiations," but in 1949 Dodge would not negotiate. For more on the tax question, see Brownlee et al. 2012.

42. Dodge, memos of March 24, 1949, and April 21, 1949, meetings with Ikeda, "Budget—Ikeda Interviews," Japan-1949-1, JMDP.

43. Ikeda 1952: 213, 95, 251–253; see Hein and Metzler 2012 and other essays in Brownlee et al. 2012.

44. Quoted in Schonberger 1980: 74.

45. International Financial Committee, Japan Federation of Economic Organizations, "Views on the Currency Reform" (n.d. [other documents in the file are from January–February 1949]), "Currency," Japan-1949-3, JMDP. On the postwar Keidanren, see Allinson 1987 and Fletcher 2012.

46. Ralph A. Young et al., "Report of the Special Mission on Yen Foreign Exchange Policy," June 12, 1948, Sproul Papers, Federal Reserve Bank of New York archives; Yoshino 1996.

47. Dodge, memos of March 9, March 24, and March 25, 1949, meetings with Ikeda, "Budget—Ikeda Interviews," Japan-1949-1, JMDP.

48. Dodge, "Inflation Notes" (summer 1949), Japan-1949-6, JMDP; compare Bresciani-Turroni 1937: 104, 105. On the role of industrial finance in the German inflation, see Bresciani-Turroni 1937: 103–105, 196–212; also Feldman 1993: 272–305, 840–846.

49. Ichimada and Ōuchi 1949: 27–30, 151–153. Ōuchi further saw the Dodge Line as a first step toward the restoration of the gold standard, which he thought was the only true basis for a monetary system ("Kinhon'isei fukki e no shuppatsu," June 1949, in Ōuchi 1974–75, 6: 455–470).

50. Dodge, "Inflation Notes" (summer 1949), Japan-1949-6, JMDP.

51. Dodge, "Inflation Notes" (summer 1949), Japan-1949-6, JMDP, my emphasis.

52. Dodge, "Inflation Notes" (summer 1949), Japan-1949-6, JMDP.

53. Ikeda 1952: 15. This heritage of wartime controls and inflationary finance corresponds to Janos Kornai's analysis of "soft budget constraints" under socialism (Kornai 1992; thanks to Katalin Ferber for ideas on this point).

54. Ikeda 1952: 16. The possible apprehension of "irony" seems to be Ikeda's allusion to the pre-1945 conception of "dangerous thought."

55. Ikeda quoted in Shioguchi 1975: 67–68 (*Asahi* newspaper, March 3, 1950, front page).

56. Dodge, memo of March 24, 1949 meeting with Ikeda, "Budget—Ikeda Interviews" (summer 1949), Japan-1949-1, JMDP.

57. Anchordoguy 2001. Ōkita's family lived in Kajii's house for some time after the war.

58. Ministry of Labor statistics, in MITI report to Dodge, November 2, 1950, Japan-1950-6, JMDP; Price 1997: 76; Partner 1999: 64, 66.

59. Dodge to MacArthur, July 13, 1949, "Appointment," Japan-1949-1, JMDP.

60. Dodge to Marquat, September 16 and September 29, 1949, both in "Correspondence—Marquat," Japan-1949-2, JMDP.

61. Price 1997: 83; Cumings 1981.

62. Ishibashi, "Obā-rōn kokufuku saku," January 19, 1952, in ITZ 14: 82–83; Kuroda 1993: 32–33; Bank of Japan index, given in OE, February 3, 1951. We see also by these black-market price indices how carefully official agencies tracked the illegal markets. This in itself raises big questions of legality and regulation.

63. Patrick (1962: 77) notes another relevant point, that in the mid-1950s, increases in cash currency lagged behind increases in loans and bank balances by about six to nine months.

64. Metzler 2006b; Bytheway forthcoming.

65. Sakakibara and Noguchi 1977: 101, 112.

66. Ōkita 1962: 229, 242; Bytheway 2010; Bytheway, forthcoming; Mason 1992.

67. Tsuru (1963) in Tsuru 1976: 242–244.

68. Yoshino 1996: 173–180; Ōuchi published the results as a book in 1947.

69. Asai 1993: 218. That is, Japan's prewar "gold standard" was in fact a gold-exchange standard; see Metzler 2006b.

70. Borden (1984: 18–38) discusses the postwar dollar gap in reference to Japan. At this writing, the "hard" euro is also forcing "peripheral" European countries into bankruptcy and now seems at the point of breaking.

71. Triffin 1960: 59; further context in James 1996.

72. Nakakita 1993: 335–336; Fukao et al. 1993.

73. Asai 1993: 218–221; Murphy 1997; Angel 1991.

74. GHQ, SCAP, Office of the Financial Advisor, "Dodge Press Statement," March 7, 1949, SCAP 7455-8.

75. Iguchi 2003: 222–229, 231–233; Schonberger 1989: 196–197.

76. GHQ, SCAP, Office of the Financial Advisor, "Dodge Press Statement," March 7, 1949, SCAP 7455-8.

77. Friedman and Schwartz 1963: 596.

78. "Two-Billion Dollar Failure in Japan," Fortune, April 1949: 67; MacArthur to Dodge, July 7, 1949, "Appointment Correspondence (1948–1949)," Japan-1949-1, JMDP.

79. Dodge, memo of October 25, 1950, meeting with Ikeda; Dodge to Ikeda, June 30, 1950, both in Japan-1950-7, JMDP. Concerning Dodge and export promotion to Asia, see Borden 1984: 124–131, and for Kennan's "crescent" vision, Cumings 1993 and Borden 1984.

80. Kunz 1991: the British government's decision was then announced to the world on September 21, 1931.

81. Asai 1993: 222–224; Ichimada 1950: 245–247.

8. THE STATE-BANK COMPLEX

Epigraphs: Sakakibara and Noguchi 1977: 99, 109; Schumpeter 1934: 74; ephor: one of five ancient Spartan magistrates having power over the king.

1. This "semiliberal" economic order is described by Teranishi (2004) as the "Meiji-Taishō order."

2. Johnson 1982; also Johnson 1978; Fletcher 1989; Schaede 2000; Carlile 1989; Gluck 1985; Garon 1997; Kasza 1995. Many more studies could be added to this list.

3. Ōkita 1962: 235. Many Japanese economic historians since the 1980s have recast the Meiji era (1868–1912) as an age of "small government" and laissez-faire. It may seem so compared to the extremely state-directed system that followed in the 1930s and 1940s. In its own temporal context, however, the Meiji system stands out as the most concerted, developmentalist economic system in the late nineteenth-century world.

4. Tamaki 1995; Bytheway 2008; Yoshino 1957: 574–575, emphasis added; Nakayama in Arisawa et al. 1960: 261–262; Ōkita 1962: 239–240.

5. Yoshino 1957: 577–578.

6. Miyajima and Weber 2001.

7. Yamamura 1967; Yoshino 1976: 285; Metzler 2006b: 11.

8. Ōkita 1957: 35; Ōkita 1962: 235; Ferber 2002 for details and important further considerations.

9. Matsukata, memorandum, March 1, 1882, reprinted in Matsukata 1899: 43–67.

10. Cameron 1967b; Schiltz 2005. It was the St.-Simonians who first came up with a total, and global vision "to entrust the banking system with the responsibility of allocating the means of production" (Eckalbar 1979: 84).

11. Gerschenkron 1962. Rondo Cameron's 1967 volume remains invaluable on this subject. Debate over Gerschenkron's formulation has often gotten lost in the details and policy implications of the argument; his broader historical insights continue to find new confirmation.

12. Tamaki 1995: 98–103; Bytheway forthcoming; Matsusaka 2001; Johnson 1978.

13. Tamaki 1994; Packer 1994: 145–153.

14. Data from Nihon Ginkō Tōkeikyoku 1962, 1966, given in appendix A here; Ōkita 1957: 34.

15. Okazaki and Sawada 2007; Patrick 1960: 51; on bailouts, Metzler 2006b and further details in NGHS 3; Baxter 2007.

16. NGHS 4: 466–467, 486–487.

17. Sakakibara and Noguchi 1977; NGHS 4: 478–479, 488–489.

18. Okazaki 1999b: 165; NGHS 4: 331–332.

19. Nakamura 1981: 16–18; Okazaki and Okuno-Fujiwara 1999b; Teranishi 1999; Ueda 1999.

20. On Mitsui Bank, Ogura 2002 (pp. 45–56, 59–60 for the merged Imperial [Teikoku] Bank).

21. MoF, Financial Bureau, Treasury Section, memo, January 1949, "Treasury Section," SCAP/ESS 7455-7. MoF figures show a total of only 28.6 percent of FY 1947–48 state debt of all forms held by the "private sector," meaning almost exclusively the private banks.

22. Patrick 1960: 60, 62.

23. Arisawa et al. 1978: 190; quotation: ESS to Marquat (draft), January 28, 1949, "Stock Exchange," SCAP/ESS 7464-10; Alletzhauser 1990: 133; Okazaki 1999a for historical contextualization.

24. F. A. March, ESS Research and Statistics Div.), memo, February 2, 1948; J. J. Simonelli to Morrow, January 25, 1949; Nippon Times, June 23, 1949, clipping, all in "Stock Exchange," SCAP/ESS 7464-10.

25. Calder 1993: 15.

26. Ikeda 1952: 3–4. The construction of Ikeda's 1952 book was described by Shimomura Osamu, who was part of the effort (Shimomura in Ekonomisuto Henshūbu 1999).

27. Ikeda 1952: 16–17. Given Ikeda's actual policies and comments at the time, one could doubt his sincerity in listing "medium and small business" as a sector to which priority capital should be directed—this seems to be a statement for political consumption.

28. Quoted in Yoshino 1976.

29. Ichimada, "Sengo no kin'yū seisaku" [Postwar financial policy], in Andō 1966: 307. The term "Hō-ō, the conventional translation for "Pope," can be translated literally as "King of the Law" or "Dharma King."

30. Ichimada in Andō 1966: 299, 307; Yoshino 1975: 277–280; Ichimada 1969: 209; Marquat to Dodge, JMDP.

31. Yoshino 1975: 279; Baxter 2007: 176.

32. Ichimada in Andō 1966: 294; *NGHS* 5 (Shiryōhen): 447.

33. Yoshino 1975: 280; *NGHS* 4: 331.

34. Ichimada 1950: 114–117; Yoshino 1976: 264; thanks to Simon Bytheway for the latter point.

35. Yoshino 1976: 270.

36. Yoshino 1976: 271.

37. Ichimada, excerpted in Yoshino 1976: 271; Ichimada 1950: 222–229; Ichimada in Andō 1966: 298–301.

38. Economic Stabilization Board, "Stop-Gap Loans," April 19, 1949; Y. Yano (BoJ) to R. E. Phillips (Finance Div., ESS), April 28, 1949, "BOJ Misc. Statements and Reports," SCAP/ESS 7455-8.

39. Okazaki 1995; Teranishi 1994, 1999. Bhatt (1995: 77) calls the main-bank system an innovation in the Schumpeterian sense and compares it to the Indian "lead bank" system. More detail and some wider considerations are given in Aoki et al. 1994; Ueda 1994; and Aoki 1994.

40. Y. Yano to R. E. Phillips, April 28, 1949, "BoJ Misc. Statements and Reports," SCAP/ESS 7455-8; Y. Fukichi (BoJ) to ESS Finance Division, June 17, 1949, and June 23, 1949, "B. of Japan Stop-gap Loans," SCAP/ESS 7455-5; Ichimada 1950: 226–227.

41. Ichimada, "Sengo no kin'yū seisaku," in Andō 1966: 307.

42. *OE*, June 23, 1951: 481.

43. Yoshino 1976: 269; *NGHS* 5 (Shiryōhen): 376–379. Wartime rates were fixed at 3.29 percent, then a historically low level. Altogether, Ichimada's Bank of Japan raised its discount rate four times. This happened on October 14, 1946 (to 3.65 percent); on April 26, 1948 (to 4.38 percent); on July 5, 1948 (to 5.11 percent); and then during the Korean War boom, on October 1, 1951 (to 5.84 percent). Looking back, Ichimada said he did not raise rates often enough.

44. Teranishi 1993: 66, 77; Nihon Ginkō Tōkeikyoku 1962 and appendix A here.

45. Tsutsui 1988: 73–77; my explanation draws mainly on Tsutsui's account. There is further detailed discussion in Asai 1993: 193–202 and *NGHS* 5: 282–323.

46. Amyx 2004; Grimes 2001; and the summary in Metzler 2008.

47. Metzler 2002.

48. Yoshino 1975: 273; Tsutsui 1988: 84–85.

49. Shimomura in Ekonomisuto Henshūbu 1999: 16, 17, 18.

50. Patrick 1960: 57; Tsutsui 1988: 86.

9. THE TURNING POINT

Epigraph: Schumpeter 2003: 101–102; Backhaus's translation slightly modified, emphasis added. This is from the original seventh chapter of Schumpeter's book, which he left out of later editions.

1. Hanusch and Pyka 2007; Freeman and Louçã 2001 offer one of the best examples of this kind of Schumpeterian analysis.

2. Kondratiev 1926. Great wars evidently caused these price peaks, as Kondratiev observed. Schumpeter attempted to exclude these wars from analysis, considering them accidental political events, in order to focus on "pure" economic dynamics. Kondratiev himself, thanks to Vincent Barnett (1998), is finally getting some of the scholarly attention he deserves.

3. Kleinknecht 1989. My own sense is that Schumpeter's long-wave idea is correct in many of its basic insights but radically incomplete, with much remaining to be worked out. A comprehensive statement of the state of this exploration is given by Freeman and Louçã (2001). Yamada 1993 and Jessop 2001 give comprehensive introductions to regulation theory, which has had its main centers in France. The U.S.-centered "social structures of accumulation" approach is similar; see Kotz et al. 1994, and McDonough et al. 2010.

4. E.g., Rostow 1978; Auguello 1990: 81, 83–84.

5. *Conjuncture* is still not a standard term in English. The word usually translates into English as "business cycle" but has a significantly wider sense, meaning also the general economic situation or tendency. One might describe it as the total "wave situation" at a point in time. *Konjunkturzyklen*—"conjunctural cycles"—is the title of the German translation of Schumpeter's *Business Cycles* (which he originally wrote in English). *Business Cycles* appeared in Japanese as *Shunpētā keikijunkanron* (景気循環論), in five volumes between 1958 and 1964. The team translation effort was supported by Nakayama Ichirō, Tōbata Seiichi, and Tsuru Shigeto, and it received funding from the Mitsui Bank. A German translation of *Business Cycles* was not published until 1961.

6. Shibagaki 1988: 44; Murakami 1987: 44. Transistorization, as a new but very quickly applied technology, forms an important exception to this statement.

7. Nei 2001: 125–126, 153–154, 171.

8. Reifer 2000.

9. Metzler 2004; Nakayama 1963: 11.

10. Nihon Seisansei Honbu 1960: 56.

11. Dore 1985 [1959]: 422.

12. In a somewhat Keynesian reading of the long-wave process, Tylecote (1986, 1991) makes the question of social inequality central, singling out the importance of the postwar Japanese reforms in this connection.

13. Schumpeter (1939) called this a "secondary" wave. Whether the U.S. wartime revival of industry ought to be called a boom or not is an open question: see Higgs 1992 for some valuable considerations.

14. See also A. J. Brown 1955.

15. This is the main subject of my book *Lever of Empire* (2006).

16. In Italy, where Fascism with a capital *F* originated, the first phase of Mussolini's policy followed the lines of classical liberalism as dictated by the prevailing orthodox consensus. Fascist economic policy as now thought of really began only at the end of the 1920s.

17. Stabilization policies in Western Europe after the two world wars have been studied intensively. Influential work includes that of Charles Maier (1987, 1988) and Barry Eichengreen (1992); Kindleberger's classic study of the Great Depression can also be read in this light.

18. Ōkita 1951; Nihon Ginkō Chōsakyoku 1953: 5; ESS Finance Division, "Foreign Exchange," "Classified Material, 1951," SCAP/ESS 7498-9; *NGHS* 5: 386–389; Ichimada to Marquat, "Future Financial and Banking Policies" (memo), April 4, 1951, SCAP/ESS 7498-9.

19. Dower 1988 [1979]: 316, 424; Ōkita 1951.

20. Ōkita 1951.

21. Shibagaki 1988: 43.

22. *OE*, February 10, 1951, 125–126; Ōkita 1951; Kōsai 1989a: 289–290. $500 million was equivalent to the amount spent on imports in the first quarter of 1951.

23. *OE*, January 13, 1951: 21–23.

24. *OE*, January 20, 1951: 50.

25. Miyazawa 1956: 133–135.

26. Dodge 1951: 581–583.

27. Economist 1962: 11–12. In Britain, the finance-driven effort to hold up the value of the pound involved the repeated application of deflationary austerity policies, reflected in the "stop-go" policy cycles of the 1950s. This was an implied focus of Norman Macrae's criticism.

28. Nolte 1987: 315–316, 318–320.

29. *ITZ* 14: 61–75; *OE* October 6, 1951: 778; Ishibashi 1951c: 648, emphasis added; Ishibashi 1951b: 239. Dodge's criticism appeared in the *Yomiuri* newspaper of September 18, 1951. In the *Yomiuri* of September 24, Ishibashi responded by openly expressing "our doubts about the so-called Dodge Line" (*ITZ* 15: 35–39).

10. HIGH-SPEED GROWTH: THE SCHUMPETERIAN BOOM

Epigraphs: Keizai Kikakuchō 1956: 42–43; Schumpeter 1927: 297–298, emphasis in original.

1. Average growth rates in 1946–55 topped 9 percent per year. Growth rates in 1955–70 averaged 11 percent (Kōsai 1989a: 284). For the new attention GNP statistics—"the measures that rule," in Scott O'Bryan's words—see O'Bryan 2009.

2. For introductions to High-Speed Growth, the reader may turn to multiple English-language studies by Nakamura Takafusa and to the standard works by Kōsai (1986), Odaka (1989b), and Johnson (1982).

3. Arisawa, Andō et al. 1976, 2: preface and 194; Shimomura Osamu in Ekonomisuto Henshūbu 1999: 22.

4. Odaka 1989b: 163–166.

5. Hayek (1925), quoted in Festré 2002: 464; compare Shinohara 1970a: 362–363; Amsden and Suzumura 2001: 347.

6. Yasuba and Inoki 1989a: 47; the quotation is from Fukai Eigo of the Bank of Japan, writing to Morgan and Company's Thomas W. Lamont in 1927 (in Metzler 2002: 288). The institution of "recession cartels" is one conspicuous example (Kōsai 1989b: 245–246).

7. Shinohara 1994: 177; also Nakamura 1989a: 59–60.

8. Ōkita 1974: 714. Even the Dodge Line recession had some of the character of a growth recession, as explored in new work by Temple Jorden.

9. Nakayama, preface to *Shunpētā keikijunkanron* [Business cycles] 1 (1958): 4. In Schumpeter's three-cycle schema, "Kitchin" cycles were short-term inventory cycles that averaged about three years in duration; "Juglar" cycles were major business cycles with an average duration of about nine years; "Kondratiev" cycles were economic long waves fifty-plus years in duration. The first of these varied greatly from country to country. Schumpeter centered his attention on major business cycles and long waves, both of which were international processes. To Schumpeter's three-cycle mix, Shinohara and others later added "Kuznets" growth waves of approximately eighteen to twenty years in duration. These, too, varied greatly from country to country, sometimes even running in reverse phase between countries. Kuznets waves were strongly marked in production indices.

Kondratiev long waves were weakly or not at all marked in production indices and were most strongly marked in value indices (prices and, more than that, interest rates and international debt-default cycles; see the work of Christian Suter [1989, 1990, 1992] for the latter, underappreciated point). In the 1950s and 1960s, "up" phases in both Kuznets and Kondratiev waves seem to have coincided.

10. Metzler 2006b.

11. Metzler 2006a. This conclusion differs from the emphasis of Hara Akira's fundamental 1981 work, which was a starting point for my own analysis.

12. See Metzler 2010 for policy space and policy dimensionalities. There the timescale is different, with a focus on temporally macro-level (typically, generation-long) policy regimes. Here, it is a temporally meso-level consideration, involving policy swings on the scale of months and years.

13. Ishibashi's words: "sekkyoku seisaku koso Nihon no ikiru michi," in "Nihon no jinkō to nōgyō" [Japan's population and agriculture], January 1952, in ITZ 15: 80–81. Ishibashi contrasted this with a "negative [or passive: shōkyoku] pessimistic Malthusian theory."

14. Kōsai 1989b: 220–221; Campbell 1977: 235–271; Wright 2002.

15. Ishibashi, "Moshi Ōkura daijin ni nattaraba" [If I were to become minister of finance], May 5, 1952, in ITZ 15: 118.

16. NGHS 5: 424; NKS-SZ 12: 189–216.

17. The Economic Council (Keizai Bangichō) was alternatively called in English the Economic Counsel Agency or Economic Deliberation Agency.

18. Morgan 1990: 13; Sloan 1991: 29–30, 50–51, 71–72, 75; quotation in Morgan 1990: 50.

19. Yoshino 1957: 573, 592–593.

20. Fukui 1970: 47–48; Kohno 1997: 69.

21. NGHS 5: 472–474; Hashimoto 1989: 58; O'Bryan 2009: 148–149. The White Paper's author, Gotō Yonosuke, later said that his own meaning was that growth would slow down with the end of the recovery phase; therefore, Schumpeterian-style "modernization" (i.e. "innovation") was needed (Gotō in Arisawa et al. 1957: 24). The economic white papers are themselves high-quality works of economic reportage and analysis, with an open-ended and empirical flavor that still feels fresh. They were also presented in English translation. Gordon 1993a, Gluck 1993, and Hein 1993 offer wider thoughts on the "postwar" and its end.

22. Keizai Kikakuchō 1956: 34–35. This point became practically incoherent in the English translation. A similar rough statement of Schumpeter's technological-cyclic schema was earlier given by Akamatsu Kaname (Ikeo 2008: 90–97).

23. Gotō in Arisawa et al. 1957: 24–25; Yu 1997 for related considerations. Gotō equated his use of the word modernization (kindaika) to Schumpeter's innovation, which he also translated as shin-kijiku (literally, "new axis"). Arisawa discussed the same point in Arisawa, Andō, et al. 1976; see also Gao 1997: 64, 207–209. Noda Nobuo at the Japan Productivity Center expressed a similar Schumpeterian point of view (Nihon Seisansei Honbu 1960: 12–19), as did Shinohara Miyohei (1960: 37). Bai Gao (1997: 210) adds the significant point that the "innovation paradigm changed the time span" considered relevant to planning.

24. Masumi 1985: 244; Gerlach 1992; Yoshihara 1982.

25. Schumpeter 1939: 113. Some of the multiple varieties of credit creation by and involving the general trading companies are listed in Yoshihara 1982: 174–175, 180–182, 198–199, 215–218.

26. Calder 1993: 141, 148–149; ESJ 1957–58: 242–243.

27. Johnson 1982: 229; Johnson's book remains the classic account.

28. Nakamura 1981a: 80; Shioguchi 1975: 149–159; Johnson 1982.

29. Ishida 1985: 156–157; Shioguchi 1975: 166; Ishibashi on Ikeda, in *ITZ* 14: 512–513. Ishibashi's old friend Takahashi Kamekichi, who headed his own economic research institute, gave Ikeda a series of economic briefings that helped to bring him around to a more expansive vision.

30. Nakamura 1981: 80; Johnson 1982: 202; Shioguchi 1975: 5.

31. Ishida 1985: 157.

32. *OE*, September 1956, 434–436; Shimomura in Ekonomisuto Henshūbu 1999: 16, 20–21. Shimomura was a leading MoF intellectual and an avowed Keynesian. While working as an MoF official, he completed a Ph.D. in economics; his dissertation (Shimomura 1952: 3–18) included an effort to formulate Keynes's theory in terms of the new systems-theoretic ideas of automatic servomechanisms and feedback loops, explaining conjunctural fluctuations as oscillations driven by "responsive investment" (*kannō tōshi*).

33. Calder 1988: 90; James 1996: 116.

34. "Bank seigniorage": Stiglitz and Weiss 1988, citing Schumpeter; see chapter 12 here. In advocating for a U.S. central bank, bankers had posed this matter of bank seigniorage as a national question. For instance, Paul Warburg in July 1914: "a foreign purchaser will rather buy merchandise to be paid for in sterling than in dollars and for the shipping of goods purchased abroad, be it South America or Asia, the American merchant has to provide European bank acceptances, because the acceptance of the American banker, no matter how good his credit, has no market. We pay an annual tribute of millions to Europe for the financing of our trade" (Warburg 1914: 167). Broz 1997, especially 142–159, provides the larger context.

35. Ryuzo Sato in Backhouse and Middleton 2000, 1: 242; Johnson et al. 1995.

36. Falkus 1971; Metzler 2006a for the case of Japan.

37. BoJ 1958: 8; Nakamura 1981: 53; Shinohara 1969: 74, 92. For Japan, the 1953–54 and 1956–57 foreign-exchange shortfalls also had the character of sterling gaps (Narvekar 1961).

38. Shinohara 1970a; Odaka 1989b.

39. Ōkita 1956: 6–13; Hollerman 1960: 220; Shinohara 1970a: 355. Exports as a proportion of GNP increased from 7.0 percent in 1953 to 11.4 percent in 1965.

40. Ōkita cited by Hollerman 1960: 225; Ōkita 1962: 258.

11. HIGH-SPEED GROWTH: INDICATION AND FLOW

Epigraph: Shimomura 1963: 1–2.

1. BoJ 1958: 20, emphasis added. Yoshino (1960: 119–134) discusses BoJ money-flow analysis in detail.

2. Shinohara 1970b: 356–357, emphasis added; also Shinohara 1960: 32–33 and chapter 4 here. A recent reconsideration of the $I \rightarrow S$ "Schumpeter-Keynes" process is given by Dullien 2009.

3. Ōkita 1957: 36, emphasis added. Arisawa (1960: 5, 23) made a similar point.

4. Marx 1967: 153.

5. *ESJ*, 1956–57, 199, emphasis added.

6. Patrick 1960: 61, 64–66, 71; *ESJ*, 1956–57, 197–198; Suzuki 1980: 51–53.

7. Yoshino 1957: 586.

8. Patrick 1960: 99; Bank of Japan 1958: 16, 18.

9. Patrick 1962: 141–157; Suzuki 1980: 166–179; Calder 1993: 88–91.

10. Schumpeter 1939: 651. The central bank Schumpeter thoroughly knew was surely the Austrian central bank; the two others were likely the German and U.S. central banks.

11. Patrick 1960: 68. The volume and direction of banks' lending was also actively self-regulated by the Federation of Bankers' Associations via its Funds Adjustment Committee, in line with MoF and BoJ guidance (Patrick 1962: 163–165; Okazaki 1995: 99–101).

12. Stiglitz and Weiss 1988.

13. "Compensating balances" typically averaged about 25 percent of the credit extended, according to Suzuki (1980: 29, 46–51; 1986: 7–8, 31). Patrick (1962: 135–136) reported that they sometimes went much higher. More than 90 percent of large U.S. banks in the mid-1950s also required compensating balances that ranged up to 20 percent of the credit extended. On banks and industry groups, see Yoshihara 1982.

14. Yoshihara 1982: 182. Direct bank transfers are used in Japan rather than checks. To minimize their external payments, Japanese banks encourage their customers to keep their payments within the bank by charging fees for transfers to accounts in other banks while making it free to transfer funds to other accounts within the same bank. People therefore routinely open accounts in each of the various banks to which they need to make regular payments.

15. BoJ 1958: 13, 18, emphasis added. Compare Patrick (1962: 76–77): in this view from the standpoint of the banking system, "drain" means currency (Bank of Japan notes) outside of the banks—in effect, cash currency *is* a "drain." In this case, the operation of the central-planning system, with its radically simplified capital system, also sheds light on the actual functioning of capitalist systems. Compare Richard Portes's description of the Soviet system: "The CPE [centrally planned economy] has a single, combined central and commercial bank with many branches. The monobank facilitates central control over enterprises and monitoring of households' financial behavior. It also enforces a separation of the *types of money* used by these two sectors: transactions between enterprises are conducted entirely with deposit money—entries on the monobank's books—while those between enterprises and households, and within the household sector, are conducted in cash." Moreover, "wages determine the supply of money to the household sector. This relation is the key to the monetary economics of the CPEs. . . . At the center of monetary control is the balance of money incomes and expenditures of the population" (Portes 1983: 151, 157, emphasis added).

16. *ESJ*, 1956–57, 198.

17. An awareness of the *administrative* character of the corporation was far stronger among analysts sixty or seventy years ago, when the modern corporate form was much newer, than it has since become. An unbiased observer will notice that an ideology of "market determination" and of "internal markets" has since then been built up to "explain" (or explain away) the functioning of massive corporate internal administrative hierarchies that, at their largest, rival small states in their size and complexity.

18. Ōkita 1962: 206.

19. Shinohara 1964a: 210; Ikeo 2000a; Okazaki 2005; Hashimoto 1989: 75–78.

20. The title in English of Colm's 1960 book was *Long-Range Projections for Economic Growth: The American Economy in 1970.*

21. Okazaki 2005.

22. Economic Planning Agency 1957.

23. Work by Okazaki Tetsuji particularly has begun to develop a detailed view of the interaction of state-level "strategic" concerns and business-level commercial concerns, not as a simple "either-or" question but as a realistic "both-and" picture; see also Komine 1993.

Casting further ahead in time, it is also interesting to note the existence of the Japan Association for Planning Administration, founded in 1977. The first president was Nakayama Ichirō, the second was Arisawa Hiromi, and the third Ōkita Saburō.

24. Amsden 2001: 125–160; also Bhatt 1995. Calder (1993) offers a careful study of the IBJ's early postwar role that downplays its strategic aspect; Okazaki (1997a: 90–91) has discovered evidence that suggests a more strategic picture. Packer's detailed 1994 study tends to confirm this view.

25. Packer 1994: 162; Ōkita 1962: 235.

26. Ōkita 1962: 236–241.

27. Calder 1993: 164–166.

28. Yoshino 1957: 580–582; Packer 1994: 161–165; Okazaki 1995: 101–102; Okazaki 1997a. Calder (1993: 161) called the JDB a de facto subsidiary operation of the IBJ.

29. Quoted in Okazaki 1995: 102; Packer 1994: 155–156.

30. Ōkita 1983: 76–77.

31. Schumpeter 1950: 69; p. 123 of Nakayama and Tōbata's 1951 translation.

32. Nakayama cited in Shioguchi 1975: 188–189.

33. Shinohara (1973) cited in Minoguchi et al. 2000: 213–214.

34. Arnold 1984: 202, 204; Yanaga 1968: 143; Morris-Suzuki 1991: 138–141; Shioguchi 1975: 185, 189; Uchino 1983: 113–114.

35. Kōsai 1989b: 210; Tsutsui 1992: 132; Ishida 1985: 157, 200–201; Shimomura 1963: 2.

36. Shimomura in Ekonomisuto Henshūbu 1999 : 24; Nakayama (1981) cited in Minoguchi et al. 2000: 214; Ōkita 1961: 115–118.

37. Shinohara 1964b; Kōsai 1989b: 210.

38. Shinohara 1964a: 213–214.

39. Shinohara 1964a: 214; Ikeda, quoted in chapter 6 in this book; Schumpeter 1934: 103.

12. CONCLUSIONS

Epigraphs: Macleod 1889: 54; Schumpeter 1956: 167. Concerning Macleod, Schumpeter (1954: 1115) wrote, "The first—though not wholly successful—attempt at working out a systematic theory that fits the facts of bank credit adequately . . . was made by Macleod." Schumpeter judged Macleod to be "an economist of many merits" who failed "to put his many good ideas in a professionally acceptable form."

1. Maddison 2006. Synthetic discussion of Asian high-speed growth is still limited. In one brief comparison, Boltho and Weber (2009) identify the "East Asian" path with Japan, Taiwan, and South Korea, whose experiences of high-speed growth they find similar enough to label "JTK." They conclude that China did follow the "East Asian" path, with significant differences and innovations.

2. See also Dullien 2009. Contributing to the perceptual confusion is the fact that corruption in the Chinese system is currently so raw and visible on the surface of things, while in the British and American systems it is better covered by polished façades.

3. World Bank 1993: 40–41. Later in the report, the authors used "forced savings" in a way oblivious to the historical (and highly relevant) sense of the term, using it to refer to mandatory pension schemes and to limitations on consumer borrowing. For more on the politics of the "East Asian Miracle" report, see Shiratori 1998.

4. Woo (1991) gives a compelling account of the origins of South Korea's bank-centered high-growth system. See also Amsden 1992, which should be read together with the account of development banks in Amsden 2001.

5. Wade 1990: 263–265.

6. McGee et al. 2007: 19–26; John Law, *Money and Trade Considered: With a Proposal for Supplying the Nation with Money* (1705).

7. For China, Liang (2012a: 4, 2012b: 19), citing Herr, argues that credit creation by banks promoted a "Schumpeterian-Keynesian credit-investment-income-creation process" and that credit creation is not constrained by the lack of prior savings. Naughton 1995 and Yang 1996 discuss the initial phase of China's capitalist high-speed growth; introductions to the credit financing of development are given by Naughton 1995, esp. 253–259 and 263, and by Lardy 1998, esp. 76–92. Right through China's long run of high-speed growth,

much of the English-language writing would lead one to think the system of industrial finance was simply bad and getting worse; these judgments suggest another gap between understanding and reality. Compare Wade (1990: 159–172) on Taiwan's bank-centered financial system, which funded an extraordinary run of high-speed growth while leaving neoclassical economists "unimpressed." R. Bin Wong (1997) considers the larger question of supposed Western norms and supposed Asian exceptions in an encompassing way. Nor should we confine the discussion to East Asia. The description of the "overdraft economy" (économie d'endettement) in postwar France by Loriaux (1991) is also highly productive of comparative perspective. The postwar French story is often told from a financially "orthodox" viewpoint, as if it, too, were a story of failure, but had the country ever done better for its people?

8. Hayek quoted in Festré 2002: 464. More discussion of the point, and a different valence, can be found in Hayek 1939: 183–197.

9. See Shinohara 1970a: 40–78; Ōkita 1957: 32; Kornai 1992; and see Garon 2012 for the social and political sides of mass saving.

10. Vogel 1979: 124.

11. Kang 1960; chapter 1 in this volume; Maier, "Politics of Inflation," in Maier 1987. Between 1873 and 1896, a difference of monetary standards was also operative: in the Western countries, the newly internationalized gold standard produced a deflationary bias, while in Japan a silver standard produced a moderately inflationary bias.

12. United Nations Monthly Bulletin of Statistics reproduced in Miyazaki et al. 1981: 142; Abe K. 1969: 21–22.

13. Hasegawa 1986 offers an early account.

14. Ito 1992 summarizes contemporary explanations for Japan's stickily high price structure at the time (much of which now reads as history).

15. A representative simplified statement comes from a description produced by the U.S. Federal Reserve and offered as a resource for educators: "Where do banks get the money to lend? They get it from people who open accounts. Banks act as go-betweens for people who save and people who want to borrow. . . . Your savings are combined with the savings of others to form a big pool of money, and the bank uses that money to make loans." And again: "When you and other customers deposit money in a bank, the bank 'puts most of it to work.' Part of the money is set aside and held in reserve, but much of the rest is loaned to people who need to borrow money." Federal Reserve Boston, "Banking Basics," rev. January 2007, www.federalreserveeducation.org/resources/, accessed March 21, 2011. Even expert scholars repeat this kind of story, in more sophisticated language. The reality is indeed hard to explain to children, but this kind of self-representation easily misleads. While the individual bank lends out "most" of its deposits, these loans create new balances in other banks, which become the deposit basis for new lending by those banks, and so on—banks collectively do not lend "most" of what individuals save from their incomes, but rather many times more. The explanation must be rephrased: Where do banks, collectively, get the money they lend? Mostly by creating it, by announcing to one another the existence of a monetary balance in an account. This activity is pure representation, which proceeds in a mirroring fashion. Tangible, physicalistic expressions such "depositing" and "holding" are here metaphorical—historical remains of a past age.

16. The case of the United States from the 1980s into the early 2000s is a kind of mirror image, as massive but relatively noninflationary credit creation was enabled by overseas absorption or "saving" of U.S. dollars.

17. ESJ, 1956–57, 199; chapter 7 here; Stiglitz and Weiss 1988: 8.

18. In the U.S. system, a "Schumpeterian" financial process—the creation of money by banks—also underlies corporate finance by means of stocks and bonds: ultimately,

both the Japanese "bank-centered" model of industrial finance and the American "stocks and bonds" model are bank centered. The difference is one of the temporal (term) structures and formal ownership structures of this financing.

19. Sakakibara and Noguchi 1977: 114; for the gold-exchange standard, Metzler 2006b.

20. Patrick 1965–66: 327; Suzuki 1980: 29–31; Suzuki 1986: 19–20. In 1964, Japanese government debt (formally speaking) was equivalent to 4.7 percent of GNP. United States government debt was then equivalent to 50 percent of GNP, and UK government debt to more than 90 percent of GNP.

21. Ehrlich 1957: 469; Patrick 1960: 75, 76. Interbank short-term lending developed rapidly at the same time, also closely monitored and supported by the central bank (Ezekiel 1961).

22. A close reading of Cain and Hopkins (2001) brings out this point forcefully. Early British public controversies over the question of government bonds ("stocks," as they were often called) are very revealing in this context.

23. Okazaki 1999a; Aoki and Patrick 1994; Hoshi and Kashyap 2001; Ibata-Arens 2005.

24. Sakakibara 1993 and Uchino 1983 offer similar points of view.

25. Gao 2001; Amyx 2004; Metzler 2008.

26. Schumpeter 1956: 207; Festré 2002: 456; Arena and Festré 2005.

27. Cycles of debt buildup and destruction began many centuries before the development of modern capitalism. This point alone raises immense questions concerning the relationship of money economy/market economy to capitalist development, for modern capitalism did indeed arise out of and develop through this cyclic process.

28. Hixson 1991.

29. E.g., Sauerbeck 1894. I explore the late nineteenth-century deflation as a global process in a forthcoming book. Landes (2003: 234) offered a production-side explanation of the nineteenth-century deflation similar to Schumpeter's interpretation. Supply-side explanations were standard among gold-standard advocates at the time; monetary-side explanations were common among bimetallists and other critics of the gold standard.

30. Quotation from Schumpeter 1927: 303, emphasis in original.

31. Nakayama quoted in Minoguchi et al. 2000: 215, emphasis added.

32. Metzler 2012: 135–136.

33. Smith 1937: 305; Binswanger 1994: 33.

34. Stiglitz and Weiss 1988: 2–3. Compare Schumpeter (1939: 544): money may be linked to a commodity, "but it never is a commodity" (see also Schumpeter 1956: 167). Further, "since certain claims to 'money' serve, within wide limits, the same purposes as legal tender itself, . . . the very concept of quantity of money becomes doubtful. It is, in fact, impossible to speak of the quantity of 'money' in the sense in which we speak of the quantity of a commodity" (Schumpeter 1939: 546).

35. E.g., Graziani 1990.

36. See also Gao 2001: 154–157.

37. Noguchi 1994; Gao 2001: 183–189.

38. See Metzler 2008 for a review.

39. For a very early statement, Drucker 1983. In place of the defunct "Fordist accord" established in the late 1940s, some writers have even identified a prospective "neo-Schumpeterian accord," although it is not clear where the "accord" might lie (Petit 2001).

40. Schumpeter 1954: 760, my italics.

41. E.g., Shinohara 1987, 1994, 1999, 2006.

42. Leontief 1950: 104. Was there a source of inspiration in Goethe, whom Schumpeter greatly admired? Goethe envisioned biological development as "metamorphosis," a

rhythmic, holistic process that was realized through alternating stages of expansion and contraction. Metamorphosis was also a process of "new combination," which can tear "parts of a body" "out of [their] earlier combination" to create something new (Adler 1990, quoting Goethe). The "constituents" appear "to wait for a new, or under certain circumstances, a re-combination."

References

ABE Kazunari. 1969. *Nihon keizai bukka jōsho no kikō* [Structure of price increase in the Japanese economy]. Tokyo: Nihon Hyōronsha.

ABE Yasuji. 1955. *Ichimada Hisato den* [Biography of Ichimada Hisato]. Nihon Zaikai Jinbutsu-den Zenshū, vol. 7. Tokyo: Tōyō Shokan.

T. F. M. ADAMS. 1964. *Financial History of Modern Japan*. Tokyo: Research.

T. F. M. ADAMS and Iwao HOSHII. 1972. *A Financial History of the New Japan*. Tokyo: Kodansha.

Jeremy ADLER. 1990. "Goethe and Chemical Theory in *Elective Affinities*." In Andrew Cunningham and Nicholas Jardine, eds., *Romanticism and the Sciences*. New York: Cambridge University Press, 263–279.

Christopher ALDOUS. 1997. *The Police in Occupation Japan: Control, Corruption and Resistance to Reform*. London: Routledge.

Albert J. ALLETZHAUSER. 1990. *The House of Nomura: The Inside Story of the Legendary Japanese Financial Dynasty*. New York: HarperCollins.

Gary D. ALLINSON. 1987. "Japan's Keidanren and Its New Leadership." *Pacific Affairs* 60:3 (Autumn), 385–407.

———. 1993. "The Structure and Transformation of Conservative Rule." In GORDON 1993b, 123–144.

Alice H. AMSDEN. 1992. *Asia's Next Giant: South Korea and Late Industrialization*. Oxford: Oxford University Press.

———. 2001. *The Rise of "The Rest": Challenges to the West from Late-Industrializing Countries*. Oxford: Oxford University Press.

Alice H. AMSDEN and Kotaro SUZUMURA. 2001. "An Interview with Miyohei Shinohara: Nonconformism in Japanese Economic Thought." *Journal of the Japanese and International Economies* 15:3, 341–360.

Jennifer A. AMYX. 2004. *Japan's Financial Crisis: Institutional Rigidity and Reluctant Change*. Princeton, N.J.: Princeton University Press.

Marie ANCHORDOGUY. 2001. "Nippon Telegraph and Telephone Company (NTT) and the Building of a Telecommunications Industry in Japan." *Business History Review* 75:3 (Autumn), 507–541.

Esbeth Sloth ANDERSEN. 2011. *Joseph A. Schumpeter: A Theory of Social and Economic Evolution*. Houndmills, England: Palgrave Macmillan.

ANDŌ Yoshio, ed. 1966. *Shōwa keizaishi e no shōgen* [Testimony on Shōwa economic history]. Vol. 2. Tokyo: Mainichi Shinbunsha.

———, ed. 1979. *Kindai Nihon keizaishi yōran* [Handbook of modern Japanese economic history]. Tokyo: Tōkyō Daigaku Shuppankai.

Robert C. ANGEL. 1991. *Explaining Economic Policy Failure: Japan in the 1969–1971 International Monetary Crisis*. New York: Columbia University Press.

Masahiko AOKI. 1994. "Monitoring Characteristics of the Main Bank System: An Analytical and Developmental View." In Aoki and Patrick 1994, 109–141.

Masahiko AOKI, Hyung-Ki KIM, and Masahiro FUJIWARA-OKUNO, eds. 1997. *The Role of Government in East Asian Economic Development: Comparative Institutional Analysis*. Oxford: Clarendon Press.

Masahiko Aoki and Hugh Patrick, eds. 1994. *The Japanese Main Bank System: Its Relevance for Developing and Transforming Economies.* Oxford: Oxford University Press.

Masahiko Aoki, Hugh Patrick, and Paul Sheard. 1994. "The Japanese Main Bank System: An Introductory Overview." In Aoki and Patrick 1994, 1–50.

David Arase. 1995. *Buying Power: The Political Economy of Japan's Foreign Aid.* Boulder, Colo.: Lynne Reinner.

Richard Arena and Agnès Festré. 2005 [1996]. "Banks, Credit, and the Financial System in Schumpeter: An Interpretation." Reprinted in Ingham 2005b, 375–385.

Arisawa Hiromi. 1934. *Sangyō dōin keikaku* [Industrial mobilization planning]. Rev. ed. Nihon Tōsei Keizai Zenshū, vol. 6. Tokyo: Kaizōsha.

———. 1948. *Infurēshon to shakaika* [Inflation and socialization]. Tokyo: Nihon Hyōronsha.

———. 1949. *Keizai seisaku nōto* [Notes on economic policy]. Tokyo: Gakufū Shoin.

———. 1960. "Nihon no shihonshugi" [Japan's capitalism]. In Arisawa, Tōbata, and Nakamura 1960, 3–28.

———. 1989. *Sengo keizai o kataru, Shōwa shi e no shōgen* [Speaking of the postwar economy, testimony on Shōwa-era history]. Tokyo: Tokyo Daigaku Shuppankai.

Arisawa Hiromi, Abe Yasuji, et al. 1978. *Shōken hyakunenshi* [One-hundred-year history of securities]. Tokyo: Nihon Keizai Shinbun Sha.

Arisawa Hiromi, Andō Yoshio, et al. 1976. *Shōwa keizaishi* [Economic history of the Shōwa period]. Tokyo: Nihon Keizai Shinbun Sha.

Arisawa Hiromi, Nakayama Ichirō, and Gotō Yonosuke. 1957. *32-nenban Nihon no keizai—Keizai hakusho no kaisetsu to hihan.* [1957-edition economy of Japan—interpretation and criticism of the Economic White Paper]. Tokyo: Shiseidō.

Arisawa Hiromi, Tōbata Seiichi, and Nakayama Ichirō, eds. 1960. *Keizai shutaisei kōza* [Lectures on economic selfhood]. 7 vols. Tokyo: Chūō Kōronsha.

Arisawa Hiromi, Tōbata Seiichi, Nakayama Ichirō, Wakimura Yoshitarō, and Ōkita Saburō. 1960. "Keizai shutai kara mita Nihon shihonshugi" [Roundtable discussion: Japanese capitalism seen from the standpoint of economic selfhood]. In Arisawa, Tōbata, and Nakayama 1960, 245–315.

Aritake Shūji. 1967–68. *Shōwa Ōkurashō gaishi* [Unofficial history of the Ministry of Finance in the Shōwa era]. Ed. Tsushima Juichi. 3 vols. Tokyo: Shōwa Ōkurashō Gaishi Kankōkai.

Walter Arnold. 1984. "The Politics of Economic Planning in Postwar Japan: A Study in Political Economy." Ph.D. diss., University of California, Berkeley.

Asai Yoshio. 1993. "Sengo senryōki (1945–1952 nen)" [The postwar occupation era (1945–1952)]. In Nihon Ginkō Kin'yū Kenkyūjo 1993: 188–227.

Massimo M. Augello. 1990. *Joseph Alois Schumpeter: A Reference Guide.* Berlin: Springer-Verlag.

Baba Keiji. 1933. *Gijutsu to keizai* [Technology and economy]. Tokyo: Nihon Hyōronsha.

———. 1936. *Gijutsu to shakai* [Technology and society]. Tokyo: Nihon Hyōronsha.

Jürgen Backhaus, ed. 2003. *Joseph Alois Schumpeter: Entrepreneurship, Style and Vision.* Dordrecht: Kluwer.

Roger E. Backhouse and Roger Middleton, eds. 2000. *Exemplary Economists.* 2 vols. Cheltenham, England: Edward Elgar.

Bank of Japan, Economic Research Department. 1958. *Monetary Development, 1954–1957, and Essential Features of the Financial Structure of Japan: A Study on Moneyflow in Japan.* [Tokyo]: Bank of Japan, December 1958.

Vincent BARNETT. 1998. *Kondratiev and the Dynamics of Economic Development: Long Cycles and Industrial Growth in Historical Context.* Basingstoke, England: Macmillan.

Michael A. BARNHART. 1987. *Japan Prepares for Total War: The Search for Economic Security, 1919–1941.* Ithaca, N.Y.: Cornell University Press.

Andrew E. BARSHAY. 1988. *State and Intellectual in Imperial Japan: The Public Man in Crisis.* Berkeley: University of California Press.

———. 1996. "Toward a History of the Social Sciences in Japan." *Positions* 4:2 (Fall), 217–251.

———. 2004. *The Social Sciences in Modern Japan: The Marxian and Modernist Traditions.* Berkeley: University of California Press.

Jean-Pascal BASSINO. 1998. "The Diffusion and Appropriation of Schumpeter's Economic Thought in Japan." *History of Economic Ideas* 6:1, 79–106.

James C. BAXTER. 2007. "Japanese Private Sector Banks, 1931–1945: A Business Perspective." *Japan Review* 19: 161–214.

Bernard C. BEAUDREAU. 1999. *Energy and the Rise and Fall of Political Economy.* Westport, Conn.: Greenwood Press.

Markus C. BECKER and Thorbjørn KNUDSEN. 2002. "Schumpeter 1911: Farsighted Visions on Economic Development." *American Journal of Economics and Sociology* 61:2 (April), 387–403.

Marshall BERMAN. 1982. *All That Is Solid Melts into Air: The Experience of Modernity.* New York: Penguin.

Ernst R. BERNDT. 1985. "From Technocracy to Net Energy Analysis: Engineers, Economists and Recurring Energy Theories of Value." In Anthony D. Scott, ed., *Progress in Natural Resource Economics.* Oxford: Clarendon Press, 337–367.

V. V. BHATT. 1995. *Financial Systems, Innovations and Development.* New Delhi: Sage.

Hans Christoph BINSWANGER. 1994 [1985]. *Money and Magic: A Critique of the Modern Economy in the Light of Goethe's Faust.* Trans. J. E. Harrison. Chicago: University of Chicago Press.

Yuri BIONDI. 2008. "Schumpeter's Economic Theory and the Dynamic Accounting View of the Firm: Neglected Pages from the *Theory of Economic Development.*" *Economy and Society* 37:4 (November), 525–547.

Andrea BOLTHO and Maria WEBER. 2009. "Did China Follow the East Asian Development Model?" *European Journal of Comparative Economics* 6:2, 267–286.

William S. BORDEN. 1984. *The Pacific Alliance: United States Foreign Economic Policy and Japanese Trade Recovery, 1947–1955.* Madison: University of Wisconsin Press.

Costantino BRESCIANI-TURRONI. 1937. *The Economics of Inflation: A Study of Currency Depreciation in Post-war Germany 1914–1923.* London: Allen and Unwin.

Martin BRONFENBRENNER. 1950. "Four Positions on Japanese Finance." *Journal of Political Economy* 58:4 (August), 281–288.

———. 1951. "Review of Report on Japanese Taxation by the Shoup Mission, Second Report on Japanese Taxation by the Shoup Mission by Carl S. Shoup." *American Economic Review* 41:5 (December), 983–985.

———. 1965a. "Economic Miracles and Japan's Incomes-Doubling Plan." In Lockwood 1965, 523–553.

———. 1965b. "Formalizing the Shimomura Growth Model." *Economic Development and Cultural Change* 14:1 (October), 85–90.

———. 1968. "The American Occupation of Japan: Economic Retrospect." In G. Goodman, ed., *The American Occupation of Japan: A Retrospective View,* International Studies, East Asian Series Research Publication no. 2. Lawrence: Center for East Asian Studies, University of Kansas, 11–25.

A. J. Brown. 1955. *The Great Inflation, 1939–1951*. Oxford: Oxford University Press.

William Robert Brown Jr. 1997. "Schopenhauer and Faust II." Founders Prize Essay. *Postscript* (Journal of the Philological Association of the Carolinas) 14, 15–27; www2.unca.edu/postscript/postscript14/ps14.2.pdf. Accessed October 14, 2012.

W. Elliot Brownlee, Eisaku Ide, and Yasunori Fukagai, eds. 2013. *The Shoup Mission and the Reform of Public Finance in Japan, 1945–1952: A Transnational History*. New York: Cambridge University Press.

J. Lawrence Broz. 1997. *The International Origins of the Federal Reserve System*. Ithaca, N.Y.: Cornell University Press.

Roger Buckley. 1982. *Occupation Diplomacy: Britain, the United States, and Japan, 1945–1952*. Cambridge: Cambridge University Press.

Simon Bytheway. 2008. "Money, Banks and the State: The Role of the State in Japanese Finance, 1868–1945." Paper presented at Twelfth Conference of the European Association of Japanese Studies, Lecce, September 20–23.

———. 2010. "Liberalization, Internationalization, and Globalization: Charting the Course of Foreign Investment in the Finance and Commerce of Japan, 1945–2009." *Japan Forum* 22:3–4, 433–465.

———. Forthcoming. *Investing in Japan's Future: From Black Ships to Globalization*.

P. J. Cain and A. G. Hopkins. 2001. *British Imperialism, 1688–2000*. 2nd ed. London: Longman.

Kent E. Calder. 1988. *Crisis and Compensation: Public Policy and Political Stability in Japan*. Princeton, N.J.: Princeton University Press.

———. 1993. *Strategic Capitalism: Private Business and Public Purpose in Japanese Industrial Finance*. Princeton, N.J.: Princeton University Press.

Rondo E. Cameron, ed. 1967a. *Banking in the Early Stages of Industrialization: A Study in Comparative Economic History*. Oxford: Oxford University Press.

———. 1967b. "Belgium, 1800–1875." In Cameron 1967a: 129–150.

John C. Campbell. 1977. *Contemporary Japanese Budget Politics*. Berkeley: University of California Press.

Richard Cantillon. 1931 [1755]. *Essai sur la nature du commerce en général*. Ed. Henry Higgs. London: Macmillan.

Lonny E. Carlile. 1989. "Zaikai and the Politics of Production in Japan, 1940–1962." Ph.D. diss., University of California, Berkeley.

Central Committee of the Communist Party of Japan. 1973. *The Fifty Years of the Communist Party of Japan*. Tokyo: Communist Party of Japan.

Myung Soo Cha. 2003. "Did Takahashi Korekiyo Rescue Japan from the Great Depression?" *Journal of Economic History* 63:1 (March), 127–144.

Sukhamoy Chakravarty. 1980. *Alternative Approaches to a Theory of Economic Growth: Marx, Marshall and Schumpeter*. R. C. Dutt Lectures on Political Economy, Centre for Studies in Social Sciences, Calcutta. New Delhi: Orient Longman.

Ron Chernow. 1990. *The House of Morgan: An American Banking Dynasty and the Rise of Modern Finance*. New York: Simon and Schuster.

Jerome B. Cohen. 1949. *Japan's Economy in War and Reconstruction*. Minneapolis: University of Minnesota Press.

———. 1958. *Japan's Postwar Economy*. Bloomington: Indiana University Press.

Theodore Cohen. 1987. *Remaking Japan: The American Occupation as New Deal*. Ed. Herbert Passin. New York: Free Press.

Nicholas Crafts and Anthony J. Venables. 2003. "Globalization in History: A Geographical Perspective." In Michael D. Bordo, Alan M. Taylor, and Jeffrey G. Williamson, eds., *Globalization in Historical Perspective*. Chicago: University of Chicago Press and National Bureau of Economic Research, 323–364.

Bruce CUMINGS. 1981. *The Origins of the Korean War*. Vol. 1, *Liberation and the Emergence of Separate Regimes, 1945–1947*. Princeton, N.J.: Princeton University Press. Reprint, Seoul: Yuksabipyungsa, 2002.

———. 1993. "Japan in the World System." In Gordon 1993b, 34–63.

Herman E. DALY. 1980. "The Economic Thought of Frederick Soddy." *History of Political Economy* 12:4, 469–488.

James W. DEAN. 1981. "The Dissolution of the Keynesian Consensus." In Daniel Bell and Irving Kristol, eds., *The Crisis in Economic Theory*. New York: Basic Books, 19–34.

Glenn DAVIS and John G. ROBERTS. 1996. *An Occupation without Troops: Wall Street's Half-Century Domination of Japanese Politics*. Tokyo: Yenbooks.

Jeffry M. DIEFENDORF, Axel FROHN, and Hermann-Josef RUPIERER. 1993. *American Policy and the Reconstruction of West Germany, 1945–1955*. Washington, D.C.: German Historical Institute and Cambridge University Press.

Pierre DIETERLEN and Charles RIST. 1948. *The Monetary Problem of France*. New York: Carnegie Endowment for International Peace.

Joseph M. DODGE. 1951. "Statement Issued by Ambassador Joseph M. Dodge on the Occasion of His Departure from Japan, November 29, 1951." *Contemporary Japan* 20:10–12 (October–December), 581–583.

Ronald P. DORE. 1956. "Japanese Election Candidates in 1955." *Pacific Affairs* 29:2 (June), 174–181.

———. 1985 [1959]. *Land Reform in Japan*. London: Oxford University Press. Reprint: New York: Schocken.

Rudiger DORNBUSCH, Wilhelm NÖLLING, and Richard LAYARD, eds. 1993. *Postwar Economic Reconstruction and Lessons for the East Today*. Cambridge, Mass.: MIT Press.

John W. DOWER. 1988 [1979]. *Empire and Aftermath: Yoshida Shigeru and the Japanese Experience, 1878–1954*. Harvard East Asian Monographs no. 84. Cambridge, Mass.: Harvard University Press.

———. 1993. "Occupied Japan and the Cold War in Asia." Reprinted in Dower, *Japan in War and Peace: Selected Essays*. New York: New Press, 155–207.

———. 1999. *Embracing Defeat: Japan in the Wake of World War II*. New York: Norton.

Paul W. DRAKE. 1989. *The Money Doctor in the Andes: The Kemmerer Missions, 1923–1933*. Chapel Hill, N.C.: Duke University Press.

———, ed. 1993. *Money Doctors, Foreign Debts, and Economic Reforms in Latin America from the 1890s to the Present*. Wilmington, Del.: Scholarly Resources.

William H. DRAPER Jr. 1972. Oral history interview, January 11, 1972. Truman Presidential Library and Museum. Available at http://www.trumanlibrary.org/oralhist/draperw.htm.

Peter F. DRUCKER. 1983. "Modern Prophets: Schumpeter and Keynes?" Available at www.druckersociety.at/.

Sebastian DULLIEN. 2009. "Central Banking, Financial Institutions and Credit Creation in Developing Countries." United Nations Conference on Trade and Development (UNCTAD) Discussion Papers, no. 193 (January).

Leon H. DUPRIEZ. 1947. *Monetary Reconstruction in Belgium*. New York: Carnegie Endowment for International Peace.

Peter DUUS, ed. 1989. *The Cambridge History of Japan*. Vol. 6, *The Twentieth Century*. Cambridge: Cambridge University Press.

Peter DUUS and Daniel OKIMOTO. 1979. "Fascism in Japan: Notes on the Failure of a Concept." *Journal of Asian Studies* 39:1 (November), 65–76.

John C. Eckalbar. 1979. "The Saint-Simonians in Industry and Economic Development." *American Journal of Economics and Sociology* 38:1 (January), 83–96.

Economic Investigation Agency [Government of Japan]. Liaison Section. 1950. *Major Activities of the Economic Investigation Agency, 1948–1950.* Tokyo, August 22. Copy in SCAP/ESS 7465-1.

Economic Planning Agency, Government of Japan. 1957. *New Long-Range Economic Plan of Japan.* Tokyo: Tokyo Education Research Institute.

[Economic Stabilization Board, Government of Japan.] 1947. "Official 'White Paper' Issued by the Japanese Government, July 4, 1947." *Contemporary Japan* 16:7–9, 362–402.

Economist. 1962. *Consider Japan.* London: Duckworth.

E. E. Ehrlich. 1957. "Note on Postwar Credit Policies in Japan." *Review of Economics and Statistics* 39:4 (November), 469–471.

Barry Eichengreen. 1992. *Golden Fetters: The Gold Standard and the Great Depression, 1919–1939.* New York: Oxford University Press.

Ekonomisuto Henshūbu, ed. 1999. *Kōdo seichōki e no shōgen (jō)* [Testimony on the era of high-speed growth (1)]. Tokyo: Nihon Keizai Hyōronsha.

Basil Entwistle. 1985. *Japan's Decisive Decade: How a Determined Minority Changed the Nation's Course in the 1950s.* London: Grosvenor Books.

Hannan Ezekiel. 1961. "The Call Money Market in Japan." *Staff Papers—International Monetary Fund* 13:1 (March), 26–51.

M. E. Falkus. 1971. "United States Economic Policy and the 'Dollar Gap' of the 1920's." *Economic History Review* 24:4 (November), 599–623.

Gerald D. Feldman. 1993. *The Great Disorder: Politics, Economics, and Society in the German Inflation, 1914–1924.* New York: Oxford University Press.

Katalin Ferber. 2002. "Run the State like a Business: The Origin of the Deposit Fund in Meiji Japan." *Japanese Studies* 22:2 (September), 131–151.

Agnès Festré. 2002. "Money, Banking and Dynamics: Two Wicksellian Routes from Mises to Hayek and Schumpeter." *American Journal of Economics and Sociology* 61:2 (April), 439–480.

David Hackett Fischer. 1996. *The Great Wave: Price Revolutions and the Rhythm of History.* New York: Oxford University Press.

Irving Fisher. 1933. "The Debt-Deflation Theory of Depressions." *Econometrica* 1:4, 337–357.

Harvey E. Fisk. 1924. *The Inter-Ally Debts: An Analysis of War and Post-war Public Finance, 1914–1923.* New York: Bankers Trust Company.

Marc Flandreau, ed. 2003. *Money Doctors: The Experience of International Financial Advising, 1850–2000.* London: Routledge.

David Flath. 2005. *The Japanese Economy.* 2nd ed. New York: Oxford University Press.

William Miles Fletcher III. 1982. *The Search for a New Order: Intellectuals and Fascism in Prewar Japan.* Chapel Hill: University of North Carolina Press.

———. 1989. *The Japanese Business Community and National Trade Policy, 1920–1942.* Chapel Hill: University of North Carolina Press.

———. 2011. "The Challenge of Recovery and of Globalization: The Japan Spinners Association and the Japanese Cotton Textile Industry, 1945–1952." Unpublished manuscript.

———. 2012. "Dreams of Economic Transformation and the Reality of Economic Crisis: Keidanren in the Era of the 'Bubble' and the 'Lost Decade' from the Mid-1980s to the Mid-1990s." *Asia Pacific Business Review* 18:2, 149–165.

Bruno Foa. 1949. *Monetary Reconstruction in Italy.* New York: Carnegie Endowment for International Peace.

James FORRESTAL. 1951. *The Forrestal Diaries*. New York: Viking Press.

Penelope FRANCKS. 1984. *Technology and Agricultural Development in Pre-War Japan*. New Haven: Yale University Press.

Chris FREEMAN and Francisco LOUÇÃ. 2001. *As Time Goes By: From the Industrial Revolutions to the Information Revolution*. Oxford: Oxford University Press.

Milton FRIEDMAN and Anna Jacobson SCHWARTZ. 1963. *A Monetary History of the United States, 1867–1960*. Princeton, N.J.: Princeton University Press.

FUJINO Shōzaburō. 1965. *Nihon no keiki junkan—junkanteki hatten katei no rironteki • tōkeiteki • rekishiteki bunseki* [Business cycles in Japan—theoretical, statistical, and historical analysis of the cyclical development process]. Tokyo: Keisō Shobō.

———. 1966. "Business Cycles in Japan, 1868–1962." *Hitotsubashi Journal of Economics* 7:1 (June), 56–79.

Masahiro FUJITA. 1954. "Two Deflations in the Showa Era." *Kobe Economic and Business Review* 2, 53–76.

Mitsuhiro FUKAO, Masao OUMI, and Kimihiro ETOH. 1993. "Japan's Experience in the Immediate Postwar Period: Moving toward a Single Exchange Rate and Dena-tionalization of Trade." In Teranishi and Kosai 1993, 105–125.

Haruhiro FUKUI. 1970. *Party in Power: The Japanese Liberal-Democrats and Policy-Making*. Berkeley: University of California Press.

———. 1972. "Economic Planning in Postwar Japan: A Case Study in Policy Making." *Asian Survey*, 12:4 (April), 327–348.

Haruhiro FUKUI, Peter H. MERKL, Hubertus MÜLLER-GROELING, and Akio WATANABE, eds. 1993. *The Politics of Economic Change in Postwar Japan and West Germany*. Vol. 1, *Macroeconomic Conditions and Policy Responses*. New York: St. Martin's Press; London: Macmillan.

Bai GAO. 1994. "Arisawa Hiromi and His Theory for a Managed Economy." *Journal of Japanese Studies* 20:1 (Winter), 115–153.

———. 1997. *Economic Ideology and Japanese Industrial Policy: Developmentalism from 1931 to 1965*. Cambridge: Cambridge University Press.

———. 2001. *Japan's Economic Dilemma: The Institutional Origins of Prosperity and Stagnation*. Cambridge: Cambridge University Press.

Sheldon GARON. 1987. *The State and Labor in Modern Japan*. Berkeley: University of California Press.

———. 1997. *Molding Japanese Minds: The State in Everyday Life*. Princeton, N.J.: Princeton University Press.

———. 2000. "Luxury Is the Enemy: Mobilizing Savings and Popularizing Thrift in Wartime Japan." *Journal of Japanese Studies* 26:1 (Winter), 41–78.

———. 2012. *Beyond Our Means: Why America Spends While the World Saves*. Princeton, N.J.: Princeton University Press.

Michael L. GERLACH. 1992. *Alliance Capitalism: The Social Organization of Japanese Business*. Berkeley: University of California Press.

Alexander GERSCHENKRON. 1962. *Economic Backwardness in Historical Perspective: A Book of Essays*. Cambridge, Mass.: Harvard University Press.

Carol GLUCK. 1983. "Entangling Illusions—Japanese and American Views of the Occupa-tion." In Warren I. Cohen, ed., *New Frontiers in American–East Asian Relations: Essays Presented to Dorothy Borg*. New York: Columbia University Press, 169–236.

———. 1985. *Japan's Modern Myths: Ideology in the Late Meiji Period*. Princeton, N.J.: Princeton University Press.

———. 1993. "The Past in the Present." In GORDON 1993b, 64–95.

Johann Wolfgang von GOETHE. 1876 [1832]. *Faust. A Tragedy by Johann Wolfgang von Goethe. The Second Part*. Trans. Bayard Taylor. Leipzig: F. A. Brockhaus.

————. 1959 [1832]. *Faust, Part Two*. Trans. Philip Wayne. Penguin Books.

Andrew GORDON. 1988. *The Evolution of Labor Relations in Japan: Heavy Industry, 1853–1955*. Cambridge, Mass.: Harvard University Press.

————. 1998. *The Wages of Affluence: Labor and Management in Postwar Japan*. Cambridge, Mass.: Harvard University Press.

————. 1993a. "Conclusion." In Gordon 1993b: 449–464.

————, ed. 1993b. *Postwar Japan as History*. Berkeley: University of California Press.

Colin GORDON. 1994. *New Deals: Business, Labor, and Politics in America, 1920–1935*. Cambridge: Cambridge University Press.

Peter GOUREVITCH. 1986. *Politics in Hard Times: Comparative Responses to International Economic Crises*. Ithaca, N.Y.: Cornell University Press.

David A. GRANDY. 1996. *Leo Szilard: Science as a Mode of Being*. Lanham, Md.: University Press of America.

A. GRAZIANI. 1990. "The Theory of the Monetary Circuit." *Economies et Sociétés, Monnaie et Production*, no. 7, 7–36. Reprinted in Ingham 2005b, 386–414.

Owen GRIFFITHS. 2002. "Need, Greed, and Protest in Japan's Black Market, 1938–1949." *Journal of Social History* 35:4 (Summer), 825–858.

WILLIAM W. GRIMES. 2001. *Unmaking the Japanese Miracle: Macroeconomic Politics, 1985–2000*. Ithaca, N.Y.: Cornell University Press.

Gottfried HABERLER. 1950. "Joseph Alois Schumpeter, 1883–1950." *Quarterly Journal of Economics* 64:3 (August), 333–372.

Eleanor M. HADLEY. 1970. *Antitrust in Japan*. Princeton, N.J.: Princeton University Press.

————. 2003. *Memoir of a Trustbuster: A Lifelong Adventure with Japan*. Honolulu: University of Hawaii Press.

Horst HANUSCH and Andreas PYKA, eds. 2007. *Elgar Companion to Neo-Schumpeterian Economics*. Cheltenham, England: Edward Elgar.

HARA Akira. 1981. "1920 nendai no zaisei shishutsu to sekkyoku, shōkyoku ryō seisaku rosen" [Public expenditure in the 1920s and the positive and negative policy lines]. In Nakamura 1981b, 77–109.

————. 1989. "Senji tōsei" [Wartime controls]. In Nakamura 1989c, 69–105.

Seymour E. HARRIS, ed. 1943. *Postwar Economic Problems*. New York: McGraw-Hill.

————, ed. 1951. *Schumpeter, Social Scientist*. Cambridge, Mass.: Harvard University Press.

HASEGAWA Keitarō. 1986. *Nihon wa kō kawaru: Defure jidai no kaimaku to keiei senryaku* [Japan will change like this: The opening of the age of deflation and management strategy]. Tokyo: Tokuma Shoten.

HASHIMOTO Jurō. 1989. "1955-nen" [The year 1955]. In Yasuba and Inoki 1989b, 58–95.

William J. HAUSMAN and John L. NEUFELD. 1988. "US Foreign Direct Investment in Electric Power Utilities in the 1920s." In Mira Wilkins and Harm Schröter, eds., *The Free-Standing Company in the World Economy, 1830–1996* (London: Oxford University Press), 361–390.

Thomas R. H. HAVENS. 1978. *Valley of Darkness: The Japanese People and World War Two*. New York: Norton.

HAYASHI Fusao. 1968. *Zuihitsu Ikeda Hayato: Haisen to fukkō no gendaishi* [Essays, Ikeda Hayato: Contemporary history of defeat and revival]. Tokyo: Sankei Shinbunsha.

Friedrich A. HAYEK. 1932. "A Note on the Development of the Doctrine of 'Forced Saving.'" *Quarterly Journal of Economics* 47:1 (November), 123–133.

————. 1935. *Prices and Production*. 2nd ed. London: Routledge and Kegan Paul.

————. 1939. *Profits, Interest and Investment, and Other Essays on the Theory of Industrial Relations*. London: Routledge and Kegan Paul.

Laura E. HEIN. 1990. *Fueling Growth: The Energy Revolution and Economic Policy in Postwar Japan*. Cambridge, Mass.: Harvard University Press.

———. 1993. "Growth versus Success: Japan's Economic Policy in Historical Perspective." In GORDON 1993b, 99–122.

———. 1994. "In Search of Peace and Democracy: Japanese Economic Debate in Political Context." *Journal of Asian Studies* 53:3 (August), 752–778.

———. 2004. *Reasonable Men, Powerful Words: Political Culture and Expertise in Twentieth-Century Japan*. Washington, D.C.: Woodrow Wilson Center and Berkeley: University of California Press.

Laura E. HEIN and Mark METZLER. 2013. "Raising Taxes for Democracy: The Japanese Policy Environment of the Shoup Mission." In Brownlee, Ide, and Fukagai 2013.

Eric HELLEINER. 1994. *States and the Reemergence of Global Finance: From Bretton Woods to the 1990s*. Ithaca, N.Y.: Cornell University Press.

———. 2003a. *The Making of National Money: Territorial Currencies in Historical Perspective*. Ithaca, N.Y.: Cornell University Press.

———. 2003b. "The Southern Side of Embedded Liberalism: America's Unorthodox Money Doctoring during the Early Post 1945 Years." In Marc Flandreau, ed., *Money Doctoring: The Experience of International Financial Advising 1850–2000*. London: Routledge, 249–274.

Robert HIGGS. 1992. "Wartime Prosperity? A Reassessment of the U.S. Economy in the 1940s." *Journal of Economic History* 52:1 (June), 41–60.

Johannes HIRSCHMEIER and Tsunehiko YUI. 1975. *The Development of Japanese Business, 1600–1973*. Cambridge, Mass.: Harvard University Press.

William F. HIXSON. 1991. *A Matter of Interest: Reexamining Money, Debt, and Real Economic Growth*. New York: Praeger.

Michael J. HOGAN. 2000. *A Cross of Iron: Harry S. Truman and the Origins of the National Security State, 1945–1954*. Cambridge: Cambridge University Press.

Leon HOLLERMAN. 1960. "Industrial Structure and Economic Planning in Japan." *Pacific Affairs* 33:3 (September), 219–226.

Sidney HOMER and Richard SILLA. 1991. *A History of Interest Rates*. 3rd ed. New Brunswick, N.J.: Rutgers University Press.

Takeo HOSHI and Anil K. KASHYAP. 2001. *Corporate Financing and Governance in Japan: The Road to the Future*. Cambridge, Mass.: MIT Press.

Germaine A. HOSTON. 1986. *Marxism and the Crisis of Development in Prewar Japan*. Princeton, N.J.: Princeton University Press.

ICHIMADA Hisato. 1950. *Ningen to keizai* [People and economy]. Tokyo: Kawade Shobō.

———. 1969. "Senryōka no Nichigin sōsai—Hō-ō to iwareta hachi-nen kan [Bank of Japan governor under the Occupation—being called the Pope for eight years]. In Tōkyō 12 Channeru Hōdōbu, ed., *Shōgen, watakushi no Shōwa shi*. Vol. 6, *Konran kara seichō e* [Testimony: My Shōwa history (6), From confusion to growth] (Tokyo: Gakugei Shorin).

ICHIMADA Hisato and ŌUCHI Hyōe. 1949. *Nihon keizai no zento—Taidan, Ichimada Hisato, Ōuchi Hyōe* [The road ahead for the Japanese economy—A conversation between Ichimada Hisato and Ōuchi Hyōe]. ARISAWA Hiromi, moderator. Tokyo: Rōdō Bunka Sha.

Haruo IGUCHI. 2003. *Unfinished Business: Ayukawa Yoshisuke and U.S.-Japan Relations, 1937–1953*. Cambridge, Mass.: Harvard University Press.

IKEDA Hayato. 1952. *Kinkō zaisei* [Balanced finance]. Tokyo: Jitsugyō no Nihon Sha.

Aiko IKEO. 2000a. "Economists and Economic Policies." In Ikeo 2000b, 143–183.

———, ed. 2000b. *Japanese Economics and Economists since 1945*. London: Routledge.

————. 2008. *Akamatsu Kaname: Waga taikei o norikoete yuke* [Akamatsu Kaname: Go beyond my system]. Tokyo: Nihon Keizai Hyōronsha.

————. 2011. "The American Economist Martin Bronfenbrenner (1914–1997) and the Reconstruction of the Japanese Economy (1947–1952)." CHOPE Working Paper 2011-11. Chapel Hill, N.C.: Center for the History of Political Economy, Duke University.

Geoffrey INGHAM. 2005a. "Introduction." In Ingham 2005b, xi–xxiv.

————, ed. 2005b. *Concepts of Money: Interdisciplinary Perspectives from Economics, Sociology and Political Science.* Cheltenham, England: Edward Elgar.

Akira IRIYE. 1974. *The Cold War in Asia: A Historical Introduction.* Englewood Cliffs, N.J.: Prentice-Hall.

————. 1977. "Continuities in U.S.-Japan Relations, 1941–49." In Nagai and Iriye 1977, 378–407.

ISHIBASHI Tanzan. 1932. *Infureshon no riron to jissai* [Theory and actuality of inflation]. Tokyo: Tōyō Keizai Shinpōsha.

————. 1946. "Danger of Retrenchment Policy." *Contemporary Japan* 15:1–4 (January–April), 117–120. Reprint of a December 1945 article.

————. 1951a. "On Mr. Dodge's Criticism." *Oriental Economist* 18 (October 6, 1951), 778–779.

————. 1951b. *Tanzan kaisō* [Tanzan's reminiscences]. Tokyo: Asahi Shinbunsha, October 1951. Reprinted in *ITZ* 15: 192–241.

————. 1951c. "Ways for Japan's Economic Survival." *Oriental Economist* 18. 3 pts. August 4, 1951; August 8, 1951; August 16, 1951: 601–603, 633–635, 648–650.

————. 1954. "The World and the Japanese Economy in 1954." *Oriental Economist* 21.

————. 1970–72. *Ishibashi Tanzan zenshū* [Collected works of Ishibashi Tanzan]. Ed. Ishibashi Tanzan Zenshū Hensan Iinkai. 15 vols. Tokyo: Tōyō Keizai Shinpōsha.

————. 1981. "Zōshō jidai o furikaette" [Looking back at my time as minister of finance]. *Jiyū shisō* 18 and 19 (February and May), 24–45 and 35–57.

————. 1994 [1964]. *Tanzan zadan* [A conversation with Ishibashi Tanzan]. Tokyo: Iwanami Shoten. Republication of "Tanzan kaiko." *Keizai hyōron,* January–February 1964.

————. 1995a. *Dai Nihonshugi to no tōsō* [The struggle with Great Japanism]. Ed. Kamo Takehiko. Vol. 3 of *Ishibashi Tanzan Chosakushū.* Tokyo: Tōyō Keizai Shinpōsha.

————. 1995b. *Ekonomisuto no menboku* [The honor of an economist]. Ed. Nakamura Takafusa. Vol. 2 of *Ishibashi Tanzan Chosakushū.* Tokyo: Tōyō Keizai Shinpōsha.

————. 2001. *Ishibashi Tanzan nikki* [Diary of Ishibashi Tanzan]. 2 vols. Ed. Ishibashi Tan'ichi and Itō Takashi. Tokyo: Misuzu Shobō.

ISHIDA Hirohide. 1985. *Ishibashi seiken • 71-nichi* [The Ishibashi administration, 71 days]. Tokyo: Gyōsei Mondai Kenkyūsho.

Takaichiro ISHII. 1970. "'Overloan' of Commercial Banks in Japan." In Yao 1970a.

ISHIMOTO Shidzue [KATŌ Shizue]. 1984 [1935]. *Facing Two Ways: The Story of My Life.* Stanford: Stanford University Press.

ITŌ Masaya. 1966. *Ikeda Hayato sono sei to shi* [Ikeda Hayato, his life and death]. Tokyo: Shiseidō.

Takatoshi ITO. 1992. *The Japanese Economy.* Cambridge, Mass.: MIT Press.

ITŌ Takeo. 1988. *Life along the South Manchurian Railway: The Memoirs of Itō Takeo.* Trans. Joshua A. Fogel. Armonk, N.Y.: M. E. Sharpe.

IWAHASHI Masaru. 1996. "Bukka to keiki hendō" [Prices and economic fluctuations]. In Nishikawa et al. 1996, 55–75.

IWASAKI Minoru. 1998. "Desire for a Poietic Metasubject: Miki Kiyoshi's Technology Theory." In Yamanouchi et al. 1998, 159–180.

Harold JAMES. 1985. *The Reichsbank and Public Finance in Germany, 1924–1933: A Study of the Politics of Economics during the Great Depression.* Frankfurt am Main: Fritz Knapp Verlag.

———. 1986. *The German Slump, Politics and Economics, 1924–1936.* Oxford: Clarendon Press.

———. 1996. *International Monetary Cooperation since Bretton Woods.* Washington, D.C.: International Monetary Fund and New York: Oxford University Press.

Bob JESSOP, ed. 2001. *Regulation Theory and the Crisis of Capitalism.* 5 vols. Cheltenham, England: Edward Elgar.

Chalmers JOHNSON. 1978. *Japan's Public Policy Companies.* AEI-Hoover Policy Studies no. 24, Washington, D.C.: American Enterprise Institute and Stanford, Calif.: Hoover Institution.

———. 1982. *MITI and the Japanese Miracle: The Growth of Industrial Policy, 1925–1975.* Stanford, Calif.: Stanford University Press, 1982.

Chalmers JOHNSON, Norbert A. SCHLEI, and Michael SCHALLER. 1995. "Special Report: The CIA and Japanese Politics." JPRI Working Paper no. 11. Japan Policy Research Institute, University of San Francisco Center for the Pacific Rim, www .jpri.org/publications/workingpapers/. Accessed October 14, 2012.

KAIZUKA Keimei and ONO Eisuke, eds. 1986. *Nihon no kin'yū shisutemu* [Japan's financial system]. Tokyo: Tōkyō Daigaku Shuppankai.

Moon Hyung KANG. 1960. "The Monetary Aspect of the Economic Development in Japan with Special Reference to Monetary Policies: 1868–1935." Ph.D. diss., University of Nebraska.

David E. KAPLAN and Alec DUBRO. 2003. *Yakuza: Japan's Criminal Underworld.* 2nd ed. Berkeley: University of California Press.

Gregory KASZA. 1995. *The Conscription Society: Administered Mass Organizations.* New Haven, Conn.: Yale University Press.

KATAOKA Tetsuya, ed. 1992. *Creating Single-Party Democracy: Japan's Postwar Political System.* Stanford, Calif.: Hoover Institution Press.

KATŌ Toshihiko. 1958. "Development of the Monetary System." In Shibusawa Keizō, ed., *Japanese Society in the Meiji Era,* trans. Aora Culbertson and Michico Kimura (Tokyo: Oubunsha), 181–235.

Kazuo KAWAI. 1960. *Japan's American Interlude.* Chicago: University of Chicago Press.

KEIZAI KIKAKUCHŌ [Economic Planning Agency]. 1956. *Shōwa 31-do Nenji keizai hōkoku* [Shōwa 31 annual economic white paper]. Tokyo.

Ostrud KERDE. 1999. "The Ideological Background of the Japanese War Economy." In Pauer 1999: 23–38.

KIMURA Kihachirō. 1946. "Tanzan Ishibashi: The Man and His Policy." *Contemporary Japan* 15:5–8 (May–August), 189–201.

———. 1948. *Infurēshon no kenkyū: Nihon infurēshon no rironteki bunseki* [Research on inflation: Theoretical analysis of Japan's inflation]. Tokyo: Ginza Shuppansha.

Charles KINDLEBERGER. 1985. *Keynesianism vs. Monetarism, and Other Essays in Financial History.* London: Allen and Unwin.

———. 1986. *The World in Depression, 1929–1939.* Berkeley: University of California Press.

Jonathan KIRSHNER. 2007. *Appeasing Bankers: Financial Caution on the Road to War.* Princeton, N.J.: Princeton University Press.

Alfred KLEINKNECHT. 1989. "Post-1945 Growth as a Schumpeter Boom." *Review* (Fernand Braudel Center) 12:4, 437–456.

Masaru KOHNO. 1997. *Japan's Postwar Party Politics.* Princeton, N.J.: Princeton University Press.

Takao Komine. 1993. "The Role of Economic Planning in Japan." In Teranishi and Kosai 1993, 305–330.

Nikolai D. Kondratiev. 1926. "Die Langen Wellen der Konjunktur." *Archiv für Sozialwissenschaft und Sozialpolitik* 56:3, 573–609. Partially translated by W. F. Stolper as "The Long Waves in Economic Life," *Review of Economics and Statistics* 17:6 (Nov. 1935), 105–115.

János Kornai. 1992. *The Socialist System: The Political Economy of Communism.* Princeton, N.J.: Princeton University Press.

Kōsai Yutaka. 1986. *The Era of High-Speed Growth: Notes on the Postwar Japanese Economy.* Trans. Jacqueline Kaminski. Tokyo: University Of Tokyo.

———. 1989a. "Kōdo seichō e no shuppatsu" [Setting out for high-speed growth]. In Nakamura 1989c, 283–321.

———. 1989b. "Kōdo seichōki no keizai seisaku" [Economic policy in the era of high-speed growth]. In Yasuba and Inoki 1989b, 209–272.

———. 1989c. "The Postwar Japanese Economy, 1945–1973." In Duus 1989, 494–537.

J. Victor Koschmann. 1996. *Revolution and Subjectivity in Postwar Japan.* Chicago: University of Chicago Press.

David M. Kotz. 1978. *Bank Control of Large Corporations in the United States.* Berkeley: University of California Press.

David M. Kotz, Terrence McDonough, and Michael Reich, eds. 1994. *Social Structures of Accumulation: The Political Economy of Growth and Crisis.* Cambridge: Cambridge University Press.

Diane B. Kunz. 1991. "American Bankers and Britain's Fall from Gold." In H. James, H. Lindgren, and A. Teichova, eds., *The Role of Banks in the Interwar Economy* (Cambridge: Cambridge University Press), 35–48.

Masahiro Kuroda. 1993. "Price and Goods Control in the Japanese Postwar Inflationary Period." In Teranishi and Kosai 1993, 31–60.

Walter LaFeber. 1997. *The Clash: U.S.-Japanese Relations throughout History.* New York: Norton.

David Landes. 2003. *The Unbound Prometheus: Technological Change and Industrial Development in Western Europe from 1750 to the Present.* 2nd ed. Cambridge: Cambridge University Press.

Nicholas R. Lardy. 1998. *China's Unfinished Economic Revolution.* Washington, D.C.: Brookings Institution Press.

Gerhard Lehmbruch. 1950. "The Institutional Embedding of Market Economies: The German 'Model' and Its Impact on Japan." In Streeck and Yamamura 2001, 39–93.

Wassily Leontief. 1950. "Joseph A. Schumpeter (1883–1950)." *Econometrica* 18:2 (April), 103–110.

William E. Leuchtenburg. 1963. *Franklin D. Roosevelt and the New Deal, 1932–1940.* New York: Harper and Row, 1963.

Michael Lewis. 1990. *Rioters and Citizens: Mass Protest in Imperial Japan.* Berkeley: University of California Press.

Yan Liang. 2012a. "China's Short-Term and Long-Term Development after the 2007 Global Financial Crisis: Some Critical Reflections." *The Chinese Economy* 45:1 (January–February), 3–7.

———. 2012b. "Development Finance: China's Banking System in Light of the Global Financial Crisis." *The Chinese Economy* 45:1 (January–February), 8–27.

William W. Lockwood, ed. 1965. *The State and Economic Enterprise in Japan.* Princeton, N.J.: Princeton University Press.

Michael Loriaux. 1991. *France after Hegemony: International Change and Financial Reform.* Ithaca, N.Y.: Cornell University Press.

Douglas MacArthur. 1949. "General MacArthur Replies." *Fortune* 39:4 (April), 74–75, 188–204.

Fritz Machlup. 1943. "Forced or Induced Saving: An Exploration into Its Synonyms and Homonyms." *Review of Economics and Statistics* 25:1 (February), 26–39.

Henry Dunning Macleod. 1889. *The Theory of Credit*. London: Longmans, Green.

Angus Maddison. 2006. *The World Economy*. [Paris]: OECD, Development Centre of the Organisation for Economic Co-operation and Development.

Charles S. Maier. 1987. *In Search of Stability: Explorations in Historical Political Economy*. Cambridge: Cambridge University Press.

———. 1988. *Recasting Bourgeois Europe: Stabilization in France, Germany, and Italy in the Decade after World War I*. Princeton, N.J.: Princeton University Press.

Arthur W. Marget. 1951. "The Monetary Aspects of the Schumpeterian System." *Review of Economics and Statistics* 33:2 (May), 112–121.

Juan Martinez-Alier, with Klaus Schlüpmann. 1987. *Ecological Economics: Energy, Environment and Society*. Oxford: Blackwell.

Karl Marx. 1967 [1886]. *Capital: A Critique of Political Economy*. Vol. 1, *The Process of Capitalist Production*. Ed. Frederick Engels. New York: International Publishers.

Eduard März. 1991. *Joseph Schumpeter: Scholar, Teacher and Politician*. New Haven, Conn.: Yale University Press.

Mark Mason. 1992. *American Multinationals and Japan: The Political Economy of Japanese Capital Controls, 1899–1980*. Cambridge, Mass.: Harvard University Press.

Masuda Hiroshi. 1988. *Ishibashi Tanzan: Senryō seisaku e no teikō* [Ishibashi Tanzan: Opposition to occupation policy]. Tokyo: Sōshisha.

Masumi Junnosuke. 1985. *Postwar Politics in Japan, 1945–1955*. Trans. Lonny E. Carlile. Japan research monograph 6. Berkeley: Institute of East Asian Studies, University of California-Berkeley, Center for Japanese Studies.

Matsukata Masayoshi. 1899. *Report on the Adoption of the Gold Standard in Japan*. Tokyo: Government Press.

Koji Matsumoto. 1991 [1983]. *The Rise of the Japanese Corporate System: The Inside View of a MITI Official*. Trans. Thomas I. Elliot. London: Kegan Paul International.

Yoshihisa Tak Matsusaka. 2001. *The Making of Japanese Manchuria, 1904–1932*. Cambridge, Mass.: Harvard University Press.

Thomas K. McCraw. 2007. *Prophet of Innovation: Joseph Schumpeter and Creative Destruction*. Cambridge, Mass.: Harvard University Press.

Shannon McCune. 1989. *Intelligence on the Economic Collapse of Japan in 1945*. Lanham, Md.: University Press of America.

Orville J. McDiarmid. 1980. "The Dodge and Young Missions." In Redford 1980, 59–71.

Terrence McDonough. 1994. "The Construction of Social Structures of Accumulation in U.S. History." In Kotz et al. 1994, 101–132.

Terrence McDonough, Michael Reich, and David M. Kotz, eds. 2010. *Contemporary Capitalism and Its Crises: Social Structure of Accumulation Theory for the 21st Century*. Cambridge: Cambridge University Press.

Terry McGee, George C. S. Lin, Mark Wang, Andrew Marton, and Jiaping Wu. 2007. *China's Urban Space: Development under Market Socialism*. London: Routledge.

William C. McNeil. 1986. *American Money and the Weimar Republic: Economics and Politics on the Eve of the Great Depression*. New York: Columbia University Press.

Donella H. Meadows. 2008. *Thinking in Systems—A Primer*. London: Earthscan.

Stephen C. MERCADO. 2002. *The Shadow Warriors of Nakano: A History of the Imperial Japanese Army's Elite Intelligence School.* Washington, D.C.: Brassey's.

Marcello MESSORI. 2002. "Credit and Money in Schumpeter's Theory." Working paper, University of Rome II. Available at http://ssrn.com/abstract=320883. Accessed October 14, 2012.

Mark METZLER. 2002. "American Pressure for Financial Internationalization in Japan on the Eve of the Great Depression." *Journal of Japanese Studies* 28:2 (Summer), 277–300.

———. 2004. "Woman's Place in Japan's Great Depression: Reflections on the Moral Economy of Deflation." *Journal of Japanese Studies* 30:2 (Summer), 315–352.

———. 2006a. "The Cosmopolitanism of National Economics: Friedrich List in a Japanese Mirror." In A. G. Hopkins, ed., *Global History: Interactions between the Universal and the Local* (London: Palgrave-Macmillan), 98–130.

———. 2006b. *Lever of Empire: The International Gold Standard and the Crisis of Liberalism in Prewar Japan.* Berkeley: University of California Press.

———. 2007. "The Occupation." In William Tsutsui, ed., *Blackwell Companion to Japanese History* (London: Blackwell), 265–280.

———. 2008. "Toward a Financial History of Japan's Long Stagnation, 1991–2003." *Journal of Asian Studies* 67:2 (May), 653–674.

———. 2010. "Policy Space, Polarities, and Regimes." In Bettina Gramlich-Oka and Gregory Smits, eds., *Economic Thought in Early Modern Japan* (Leiden: Brill), 217–250.

———. 2012. "Introduction: Japan at an Inflection Point." *Asia Pacific Business Review* 18:2 (April), 135–147.

———. Forthcoming. "Thinking Laterally, Thinking Conjuncturally (Crisis as Analytical Opportunity)." In Tani Barlow, ed., *What Is Transnationalism?*

Panayotis G. MICHAELIDES, John G. MILIOS, Angelos VOULDIS, and Spyros LAPATSIO-RAS. 2010. "Heterodox Influences on Schumpeter." *International Journal of Social Economics* 37:3, 197–213.

Janis MIMURA. 2011. *Planning for Empire: Reform Bureaucrats and the Japanese Wartime State.* Ithaca, N.Y.: Cornell University Press.

Takeo MINOGUCHI, Tamotsu NISHIZAWA, and Aiko IKEO. 2000. "From Reconstruction to Rapid Growth." In Aiko Ikeo, ed., *Japanese Economics and Economists since 1945* (London: Routledge), 210–253.

Hyman P. MINSKY. 1990. "Schumpeter: Finance and Evolution." In Arnold Heertje and Mark Perlman, eds., *Evolving Technology and Market Structure: Studies in Schumpeterian Economics* (Ann Arbor: University of Michigan Press), 51–74.

Philip MIROWSKI. 1981. "The Rise (and Retreat) of a Market: English Joint Stock Shares in the Eighteenth Century." *Journal of Economic History* 41:3 (September), 559–577.

———. 1985. *The Birth of the Business Cycle,* New York: Garland.

———. 1989. *More Heat Than Light: Economics as Social Physics, Physics as Nature's Economics.* Cambridge: Cambridge University Press.

———. 2002. *Machine Dreams: Economics Becomes a Cyborg Science.* Cambridge: Cambridge University Press.

MIWA Ryōichi. 1989. "Sengo minshuka to keizai saiken" [Postwar democratization and economic reconstruction]. In Nakamura 1989c, 107–164.

MIWA Yoshiro. 1993. "Economic Effects of the Anti-monopoly and Other Deconcentration Policies in Postwar Japan." In Teranishi and Kosai 1993, 129–152.

Shigeki MIYAJIMA and Warren E. WEBER. 2001. "A Comparison of National Banks in Japan and the United States between 1872 and 1885." *Monetary and Economic Studies* (Bank of Japan), February, 31–48.

MIYAZAKI Masayasu and ITŌ Osamu. 1989. "Senji, sengo no sangyō to kigyō" [Wartime and postwar industry and enterprise]. In Nakamura 1989c, 165–235.

MIYAZAKI Seiichi, OKUMURA Shigetsugu, and MORITA Kirirō, eds. 1981. *Kindai kokusai keizai yōran* [Handbook of the modern international economy]. Tokyo: Tōkyō Daigaku Shuppankai.

MIYAZAWA Kiichi. 1956. *Tōkyō-Washinton no mitsudan* [The Tokyo-Washington secret talks]. Tokyo: Jitsugyō no Nihonsha. Reprint, Tokyo: Bingokai, 1975.

Joe MOORE. 1983. *Japanese Workers and the Struggle for Power, 1945–1947.* Madison: University of Wisconsin Press.

Iwan W. MORGAN. 1990. *Eisenhower versus "The Spenders": The Eisenhower Administration, the Democrats, and the Budget, 1953–60.* London: Pinter.

MARIANA Hideaway (EKONOMISUTO HENSHŪBU), ed. 1977. *Sengo sangyōshi e no shōgen* [Testimony on postwar industrial history]. 2 vols. Tokyo: Mainichi Shinbunsha.

MORIKAWA Hidemasa. 1956. "Trade and Industry Reviewed." *Contemporary Japan* 24:1–3, 55–67.

Tessa MORRIS-SUZUKI. 1991. *A History of Japanese Economic Thought.* London: Routledge.

———. 1994. *The Technological Transformation of Japan, from the Seventeenth to the Twenty-First Century.* Cambridge: Cambridge University Press.

Carl MOSK. 2004. "Japan, Industrialization and Economic Growth." In Robert Whaples, ed., EH.Net Encyclopedia. http://eh.net/encyclopedia/article/mosk.japan.final. Accessed October 18, 2012.

Harold G. MOULTON and Leo PASVOLSKY. 1926. *World War Debt Settlements.* New York: Macmillan.

———. 1932. *War Debts and World Prosperity.* Washington, D.C.: Brookings Institution.

Yasusuke MURAKAMI. 1987. "The Japanese Model of Political Economy." In K. Yamamura and Y. Yasuba, eds., *The Political Economy of Japan.* Vol. 1, *The Domestic Transformation* (Stanford, Calif.: Stanford University Press), 33–90.

Antoin E. MURPHY. 1986. *Richard Cantillon: Entrepreneur and Economist.* Oxford: Clarendon Press.

R. Taggart MURPHY. 1997. *The Weight of the Yen.* New York: Norton.

Yōnosuke NAGAI and Akira IRIYE, eds. 1977. *The Origins of the Cold War in Asia.* New York: Columbia University Press and Tokyo: University of Tokyo Press.

Toru NAKAKITA. 1993. "Trade and Capital Liberalization Policies in Postwar Japan." In Teranishi and Kosai 1993, 331–365.

NAKAMURA Takafusa. 1979a. "SCAP to Nihon" [SCAP and Japan]. In NAKAMURA 1979b, 3–24.

———, ed. 1979b. *Senryōki Nihon no keizai to seiji* [Economy and politics of Occupation-era Japan]. Tokyo: Tōkyō Daigaku Shuppankai.

———. 1981a. *The Postwar Japanese Economy: Its Development and Structure.* Trans. Jacqueline Kaminsky. Tokyo: University of Tokyo Press. Originally published as *Nihon keizai: Sono seichō to kōzō,* 1980.

———, ed. 1981b. *Senkan-ki no Nihon keizai bunseki* [Analysis of the Japanese economy in the interwar period]. Tokyo: Yamakawa Shuppansha.

———. 1983. *Economic Growth in Prewar Japan.* Trans. Robert A. Feldman. (New Haven, Conn.: Yale University Press).

———. 1985. *Meiji Taishō-ki no keizai* [The economy of the Meiji and Taishō periods]. Tokyo: Tokyo Daigaku Shuppankai.

————. 1989a. "Depression, Recovery, and War, 1920–1945." In Duus 1989, 451–493.

————. 1989b. "Gaisetsu, 1937–54 nen" [Outline, 1937–54]. In Nakamura 1989c: 1–68.

————, ed. 1989c. *"Keikakuka" to "minshuka"* ["Planification" and "democratization"]. Nihon Keizaishi 7. Tokyo: Iwanami Shoten.

————. 1989d. "Keiki hendō to keizai seisaku" [Business cycles and economic policy]. In Nakamura and Odaka 1989b 273–322.

————. 1993. *Shōwa shi* [History of the Shōwa era]. Vol. 1. Tokyo: Tōyō Keizai Shinpōsha.

————. 1994. *Lectures on Modern Japanese Economic History, 1926–1994.* Tokyo: LTCB International Library Foundation.

————. 1995. "Kaisetsu" [Commentary]. In Ishibashi 1995b, 337–358.

NAKAMURA Takafusa and ODAKA Kōnosuke. 1989a. "Gaisetsu, 1914–1937" [General statement, 1914–1937]. In Nakamura and Odaka 1989b, 1–80.

————, eds. 1989b. *Nijū kōzō* [Dual structure]. Nihon Keizaishi 6. Tokyo: Iwanami Shoten.

NAKAYAMA Ichirō. 1963. *The Industrialization of Japan.* Tokyo: Centre for East Asian Cultural Studies.

————. 1972. Interview. In *Geppō dai-3 go,* April 24, 1972 (Kōdansha). Insert to Nakayama 1972–73, Vol. 1.

————. 1972–73. *Nakayama Ichirō zenshū* [Complete works of Nakayama Ichirō]. 19 vols. Tokyo: Kōdansha.

Dick K. NANTO. 1976. "The United States' Role in the Postwar Economic Recovery of Japan." Ph.D. diss., Harvard University.

————. 1980. "The Dodge Line: A Reevaluation." In Redford 1980, 44–59.

P. R. NARVEKAR. 1961. "The Cycle in Japan's Balance of Payments, 1955–58." *Staff Papers—International Monetary Fund* 8:3 (December), 380–411.

Barry NAUGHTON. 1995. *Growing Out of the Plan: Chinese Economic Reform, 1978–1993.* Cambridge: Cambridge University Press.

NEI Masahiro. 2001. *Shunpētā—Kigyōsha seishin • shinketsugo • sōzōteki hakai to wa nani ka—* [Schumpeter—What are entrepreneurial spirit, new combinations, and creative destruction?]. Tokyo: Kōdansha.

Otto NEWMAN. 1981. *The Challenge of Corporatism.* London: Macmillan.

NIHON GINKŌ CHŌSAKYOKU (Bank of Japan, Survey Office). 1946. *Doitsu infurēshon to zaisei kin'yū seisaku* [The German inflation and fiscal and monetary policy]. Tokyo: Jitsugyō no Nihon Sha.

————. 1953. *Kin yushutsu saikinshi yori shūsen made no wagakuni keizai tōsei no idō* [The movements of economic control in Japan from the reimposition of the gold ban to the defeat], Chōnai no. 1, August 2. (Internal report; materials held at the Bank of Japan.)

NIHON GINKŌ HYAKUNENSHI HENSAN IINKAI, ed. 1982–86. *Nihon Ginkō hyakunenshi* [One-hundred-year history of the Bank of Japan]. 7 vols. Tokyo: Nihon Ginkō Hyakunenshi Hensan Iinkai.

NIHON GINKŌ KIN'YŪ KENKYŪJO (Bank of Japan, Institute of Monetary and Economic Research). 1993. *Nihon Ginkō seido • seisaku ron shi* [History of studies of the Bank of Japan system and policy]. Itaku kenkyū hokoku 5. Tokyo: Nihon Ginkō.

NIHON GINKŌ TŌKEIKYOKU (Statistics Office, Bank of Japan). 1962. *Nihon keizai tōkei—Meiji ikō* [Historical statistics of the Japanese economy]. [Tokyo]: Nihon Ginkō.

————. 1966. *Meiji ikō hompō shuyō keizai tōkei* [Hundred-year statistics of the Japanese economy]. [Tokyo]: Nihon Ginkō.

NIHON KŌGYŌ GINKŌ RINJI SHIRYŌSHITSU. 1957. *Nihon Kōgyō Ginkō gojūnenshi* [Fifty-year history of the Industrial Bank of Japan]. Tokyo: Nihon Kōgyō Ginkō Rinji Shiryōshitsu.

NIHON KŌGYŌ KURABU GOJŪNENSHI HENSAN IINKAI. 1967. *Zaikai kaisōroku* [Memoirs of the business world]. 2 vols. Tokyo: Nihon Kōgyō Kurabu.

NIHON SEISANSEI HONBU SEISANSEI KENKYŪJO [NODA Nobuo, director]. 1960. *Gijutsu kakushin to Nihon keizai* [Technological innovation and the Japanese economy]. Tokyo: Nihon Seisansei Honbu.

NISHIKAWA Shunsaku, ODAKA Kōnosuke, and SAITŌ Osamu, eds. 1996. *Nihon keizai no 200 nen* [200 years of the Japanese economy]. Tokyo: Nihon Hyōronsha.

Tamotsu NISHIZAWA. 2001. "Lujo Brentano, Alfred Marshall, and Fukuda Tokuzo: The Reception and Transformation of the German Historical School in Japan." In Yuichi Shionoya, ed., *The German Historical School: The Historical and Ethical Approach to Economics* (London: Routledge), 155–172.

———. 2002. "Ichiro Nakayama and the Stabilization of Industrial Relations in Postwar Japan." *Hitotsubashi Journal of Economics* 43:1 (June), 1–18.

NOGUCHI Yukio. 1986. "The Development and Present State of Public Finance." In Tokue Shibata, ed., *Public Finance in Japan* (Tokyo: University of Tokyo Press), 36–49.

———. 1994. "The 'Bubble' and Economic Policies in the 1980s." *Journal of Japanese Studies* 20:2, 291–329.

———. 1995. *1940-nen taisei: Saraba "senji keizai"* [The 1940 system: Still "wartime economy"]. Tokyo: Tōyō Keizai Shinpōsha.

Sharon H. NOLTE. 1987. *Liberalism in Modern Japan: Ishibashi Tanzan and His Teachers, 1905–1960.* Berkeley: University of California Press.

Scott O'BRYAN. 2002. "Economic Knowledge and the Science of National Income in Twentieth-Century Japan." *Japan Studies Review* 6: 1–19.

———. 2009. *The Growth Idea: Purpose and Prosperity in Postwar Japan.* Honolulu: University of Hawaii Press.

OCHIAI Emiko. 1996. *The Japanese Family System in Transition: A Sociological Analysis of Family Change in Postwar Japan.* Tokyo: LTCB International Library Foundation.

ODAKA Kōnosuke. 1989a. "Nijū kōzō" [Dual structure]. In Nakamura and Odaka 1989b, 134–184.

———. 1989b. "Seichō no kiseki (2)" [The miracle of growth, 2]. In Yasuba and Inoki 1989b, 153–208.

Shinji OGURA. 2002. *Banking, the State and Industrial Promotion in Developing Japan, 1900–73.* Houndmills, England: Palgrave.

ŌHIRA Masayoshi. 1979. *Brush Strokes: Moments from My Life.* Tokyo: Foreign Press Center.

Kazushi OHKAWA and Henry ROSOVSKY. 1973. *Japanese Economic Growth: Trend Acceleration in the Twentieth Century.* Stanford, Calif.: Stanford University Press.

Kazushi OHKAWA and Miyohei SHINOHARA, eds. 1979. *Patterns of Japanese Economic Development, A Quantitative Appraisal,* New Haven, Conn.: Yale University Press.

OHNO Kenichi. N.d. "Postwar Recovery, 1945–49." National Graduate Institute for Policy Studies. www.grips.ac.jp/teacher/oono/hp/lecture_J/lec10.htm. Accessed September 30, 2010.

OKAZAKI Tetsuji. 1995. "The Evolution of the Financial System in Post-war Japan." *Business History* 37:2, 89–106.

———. 1997a. "The Government-Firm Relationship in Postwar Japanese Economic Recovery: Resolving the Coordination Failure by Coordination in Industrial Rationalization." In Aoki et al. 1997, 74–100.

————. 1997b. "The Wartime Institutional Reforms and Transformation of the Economic System." Trans. Andrew DeWit. In Junji Banno, ed., *The Political Economy of Japanese Society* (Oxford: Oxford University Press, 1997), 277–302.

————. 1998. "The Japanese Wartime Economy and the Development of Government-Business Relations: An Overview." In Yamanouchi et al. 1998, 239–259.

————. 1999a. "Corporate Governance." In Okazaki and Okuno-Fujiwara 1999a, 97–144.

————. 1999b. "Wartime Financial Reforms." In Pauer 1999, 144–170.

————. 2005. "Chōki keizai keikaku to sangyō kaihatsu" [Long-term economic plans and industrial development]. Working paper, CIRJE-J-137. Center for International Research on the Japanese Economy. Tokyo: Faculty of Economics, University of Tokyo.

Tetsuji Okazaki and Masahiro Okuno-Fujiwara, eds. 1999a. *The Japanese Economic System and Its Historical Origins*. New York: Oxford University Press.

————. 1999b. "Japan's Present-Day Economic System and Its Historical Origins." In Okazaki and Okuno-Fujiwara 1999a, 1–37.

Tetsuji Okazaki and Michiru Sawada. 2007. "Effects of a Bank Consolidation Promotion Policy: Evaluating the 1927 Bank Law in Japan." *Financial History Review* 14:1, 29–61.

Ōkita Saburō. 1949. *Gijutsu • shigen • keizai* [Technology, resources, economy]. Tokyo: Shirabasha.

————. 1951. "Japan's Economy and the Korean War." *Far Eastern Survey* 20:14 (July 25), 141–144.

————. 1956. "The Rehabilitation of Japan's Economy and Asia." Public Information and Cultural Affairs Bureau, Ministry of Foreign Affairs, Japan.

————. 1957. "Savings and Economic Growth in Japan." *Economic Development and Cultural Change* 6:1 (October), 32–41.

————. 1961. *Nihon no keizai seisaku* [Economic policy of Japan]. Tokyo: Yūki Shobō.

————. 1962. *Keizai keikaku* [Economic planning]. Tokyo: Shiseidō.

————. 1974. "Natural Resource Dependency and Japanese Foreign Policy." *Foreign Affairs* 52:4 (July), 714–724.

————. 1983 [1981]. *Japan's Challenging Years: Reflections on My Lifetime*. Trans. Graeme Bruce. Canberra: Australia-Japan Research Centre, Australian National University. Originally published as *Tōhon seisō—watskushi no rirekisho*, 1981.

Ōkita Saburō et al. [Special Survey Committee, Ministry of Foreign Affairs]. 1992 [1946]. *Postwar Reconstruction of the Japanese Economy*. Tokyo: University of Tokyo Press.

Ōkurashō Zaisei Kin'yū Kenkyūsho Zaiseishishitsu, ed. 1998. *Ōkurashō shi—Meiji-Taishō-Shōwa* [History of the Ministry of Finance—Meiji, Taishō, and Shōwa eras]. 3 vols. Tokyo: Ōkura Zaimu Kyōkai.

Ōkurashō Zaiseishishitsu, ed. 1976–84. *Shōwa zaiseishi—shūsen kara kōwa made* [History of Shōwa-era public finance—from the end of the war to the peace]. 20 vols. Tokyo: Tōyō Keizai Shinpōsha.

Tokuko Omori. 1992. "Introduction 2." In Okita et al. 1992, xv–xxix.

Ono Yoshikuni. 2004. *Waga kokorozashi wa senri ni ari—hyōden Ōkita Saburō* [My aspiration is a thousand half-leagues distant—a biography of Ōkita Saburō]. Tokyo: Nihon Keizai Shinbunsha.

Ōshima Mario. 1991. "A Distant View of the Debate on Japanese Capitalism." *Osaka City University Economic Review* 26:2, 23–34.

Ōtake Hideo. 1987. "The *Zaikai* under the Occupation: The Formation and Transformation of Managerial Councils." In Ward and Sakamoto 1987, 366–391.

Ōuchi Hyōe. 1927. "Kin yushutsu kinshi shiron" [Historiography of the gold export embargo]. *Keizaigaku ronshū* (Tōkyō Teikoku Daigaku) 5:4, 103–142.

———. 1947. "The World Monetary System and Japan's Economic Future." *Contemporary Japan* 16:4–6 (April–June), 117–133.

———. 1948. *Financial and Monetary Situation in Postwar Japan*. Pacific Studies Series, Nihon Taiheiyo Mondai Chosakai (Japan Institute of Pacific Studies). Tokyo: International Publishing.

———. 1959. *Keizaigaku gojūnen* [Fifty years of economics]. 2 vols. Tokyo: Tōkyō Daigaku Shuppankai.

———. 1974–75. *Ōuchi Hyōe chosakushū* [Selected works of Ōuchi Hyōe]. 12 vols. Tokyo: Iwanami Shoten.

Overseas Consultants, Inc. 1948. *Report on Industrial Reparations Survey of Japan to the United States of America, February 1948*. New York: Overseas Consultants.

Frank Packer. 1994. "The Role of Long-Term Credit Banks within the Main Bank System." In Aoki and Patrick 1994, 142–187.

Simon Partner. 1999. *Assembled in Japan: Electrical Goods and the Making of the Japanese Consumer*. Berkeley: University of California Press.

———. 2004. *Toshié: A Story of Village Life in Twentieth-Century Japan*. Berkeley: University of California Press.

Hugh T. Patrick. 1959. "Monetary Policy in Japan's Economic Growth, 1945–1959." *Far Eastern Survey* 28:5 (May), 65–71.

———. 1960. "The Bank of Japan: A Case Study in the Effectiveness of Central Bank Techniques of Monetary Control." Ph.D. diss., University of Michigan.

———. 1962. *Monetary Policy and Central Banking in Contemporary Japan*. University of Bombay, Series in Monetary and International Economics, no. 5. Bombay: Bombay University Press.

———. 1965a. "Cyclical Instability and Fiscal-Monetary Policy in Postwar Japan." In Lockwood 1965, 555–618.

———. 1965b. "External Equilibrium and Internal Convertibility: Financial Policy in Meiji Japan." *Journal of Economic History* 25:2 (June), 187–213.

———. 1965–66. "Japan's Interest Rates and the 'Grey' Financial Market." *Pacific Affairs* 38, 3–4 (Fall–Winter), 326–344.

———. 1971. "The Economic Muddle of the 1920s." In James W. Morley, ed., *Dilemmas of Growth in Prewar Japan* (Princeton, N.J.: Princeton University Press), 211–266.

Erich Pauer, ed. 1999. *Japan's War Economy*. London: Routledge.

Mark R. Peattie. 1975. *Ishiwara Kanji and Japan's Confrontation with the West*. Princeton, N.J.: Princeton University Press.

T. J. Pempel. 1987. "The Tar Baby Target: 'Reform' of the Japanese Bureaucracy." In Ward and Sakamoto (1987), 157–187.

———. 1998. *Regime Shift: Comparative Dynamics of the Japanese Political Economy*. Ithaca, N.Y.: Cornell University Press.

T. J. Pempel and Keiichi Tsunekawa. 1979. "Corporatism without Labor? The Japanese Anomaly." In Philippe C. Schmitter and Gerhard Lehmbruch, eds., *Trends toward Corporatist Intermediation* (Beverly Hills: Sage), 231–270.

Carlota Perez. 1985. "Microelectronics, Long Waves and World Structural Change: New Perspectives for Developing Countries." *World Development* 13:3, 441–463.

———. 2002. *Technological Revolutions and Financial Capital: The Dynamics of Bubbles and Golden Ages*. Cheltenham, England: Edward Elgar.

Pascal Petit. 2001. "Distribution and Growth: Can the New Left Deal with the Neo-Schumpeterian 'Accord'? Some Comments on the French Experience." In Philip

Arastis and Malcolm Sawyer, eds., *The Economics of the Third Way: Experiences from Around the World* (Cheltenham, England: Edward Elgar), 120–139.

Susan J. Pharr. 1987. "The Politics of Women's Rights." In Ward and Sakamoto (1987), 221–252.

Walter N. Polakov. 1933. *The Power Age: Its Quest and Challenge.* New York: Covici Friede.

Karl Polanyi. 1957 [1944]. *The Great Transformation: The Political and Economic Origins of Our Time.* Boston: Beacon Press.

Richard Portes. 1983. "Central Planning and Monetarism: Fellow Travelers?" In Padma Desai, ed., *Marxism, Central Planning, and Soviet Economy: Economic Essays in Honor of Alexander Erlich* (Cambridge, Mass.: MIT Press), 149–165.

John Price. *Japan Works: Power and Paradox in Postwar Industrial Relations.* Ithaca, N.Y.: Cornell University Press, 1997.

Kenneth Pyle. 1974. "Advantages of Followership: German Economics and Japanese Bureaucrats, 1890–1925." *Journal of Japanese Studies* 1:1, 127–164.

Lawrence H. Redford, ed. 1980. *The Occupation of Japan: Economic Policy and Reform.* Symposium Proceedings, April 13–15, 1978. Norfolk, Va.: MacArthur Memorial.

Angela Redish. 1993. "Anchors Aweigh: The Transition from Commodity Money to Fiat Money in Western Economies." *Canadian Journal of Economics* 26:4 (November), 777–795.

Thomas Ehrlich Reifer. 2000. "Violence, Profits and Power: Globalization, the Welfare-Warfare State and the Rise and Demise of the New Deal World Order." Ph.D. diss., State University of New York, Binghamton.

Hugo Reinert and Erik Reinert. 2006. "Creative Destruction in Economics: Nietzsche, Sombart, Schumpeter." Available on the author's website, www.othercanon.org/papers/index.html. Accessed October 18, 2012.

Emily S. Rosenberg. 1999. *Financial Missionaries to the World: The Politics and Culture of Dollar Diplomacy, 1900–1930.* Cambridge, Mass.: Harvard University Press.

Henry Rosovsky. 1961. *Capital Formation in Japan.* Glencoe, Ill.: Free Press.

W. W. Rostow. 1978. *The World Economy, History and Prospect.* Austin: University of Texas Press.

Shōichi Royama. 1975. "The Financial Mechanism of Japan: Survey and Synthesis of Major Issues." *Japanese Economic Studies* 3:3 (Spring), 3–31.

Jay Rubin. 1985. "From Wholesomeness to Decadence: The Censorship of Literature under the Allied Occupation." *Journal of Japanese Studies* 11:1 (Winter), 71–103.

Saga Junichi. 1991. *The Gambler's Tale,* trans. John Bester. Tokyo: Kodansha.

Sakakibara Eisuke. 1993. *Beyond Capitalism: The Japanese Model of Market Economics.* Lanham, Md.: University Press of America. Originally published as *Shihonshugi o koeta Nihon: Nihon-gata shijō keizai no seiritsu to tenkai* (1990).

Sakakibara Eisuke and Noguchi Yukio. 1977. "Dissecting the Finance Ministry–Bank of Japan Dynasty: End of the Wartime System for Total Economic Mobilization." *Japan Echo* 4:4 (Winter), 98–123. (Partial translation of "Ōkurashō–Nichigin ōchō no bunseki," *Chūō Kōron,* August 1977.)

Richard J. Samuels. 1987. *The Business of the Japanese State: Energy Markets in Comparative and Historical Perspective.* Ithaca, N.Y.: Cornell University Press.

———. 2003. *Machiavelli's Children: Leaders and Their Legacies in Italy and Japan.* Ithaca, N.Y.: Cornell University Press.

Thomas J. Sargent. 1982. "The Ends of Four Big Inflations." In Robert E. Hall, ed., *Inflation: Causes and Effects* (Chicago: University of Chicago Press), 41–97.

Seizaburō Satō, Ken'ichi Kōyama, and Shunpei Kumon. 1990. *Postwar Politician: The Life of Former Prime Minister Masayoshi Ōhira*. Trans. William R. Carter. Tokyo: Kodansha.

Augustus Sauerbeck. 1894. "Prices of Commodities in 1893." *Journal of the Royal Statistical Society* 57:1 (March), 172–183.

Gary Saxonhouse. 1982. "Cyclical and Macrostructural Issues in U.S.–Japan Economic Relations." In Daniel Okimoto, ed., *Japan's Economy, Coping with Change in the International Environment* (Boulder, Colo.: Westview Press), 123–148.

Ulrike Schaede. 2000. *Self-Regulation, Trade Associations, and the Antimonopoly Law in Japan*. Oxford: Oxford University Press.

Michael Schaller. 1985. *The American Occupation of Japan: The Origins of the Cold War in Asia*. New York: Oxford University Press.

———. 1997. *Altered States: The U.S. and Japan since the Occupation*. New York: Oxford University Press.

Michael Schiltz. 2005. "The Bank of Japan and the National Bank of Belgium." In W. F. Vande Walle, ed., *Japan and Belgium: Four Centuries of Exchange* (Brussels: Commissioners-General of the Belgian Government at the Universal Exposition of Aichi 2005), 121–133.

———. 2012. *The Money Doctors from Japan*. Cambridge, Mass.: Harvard University Press.

Howard R. Schonberger. 1980. "The Dodge Mission and American Diplomacy, 1949–1950." In Redford 1980, 74–78.

———. 1989. *Aftermath of War: Americans and the Remaking of Japan, 1945–1952*. Kent, Ohio: Kent State University Press.

Joseph A. Schumpeter. 1925. "The Currency Situation in Austria." In Commission of Gold and Silver Inquiry, United States Senate, *European Currency and Finance*, Serial 9, Vol. 1. Washington, D.C.: Government Printing Office, 225–231.

———. 1927. "The Explanation of the Business Cycle." *Economica*, no. 21 (December), 286–311.

———. 1934 [1926]. *The Theory of Economic Development: An Inquiry into Profits, Capital, Credit, Interest, and the Business Cycle*. Trans. Redvers Opie. Cambridge, Mass.: Harvard University Press. Originally published as *Theorie der wirtschaftlichen Entwicklung: Eine Untersuchung über Unternehmergewinn, Kapital, Kredit, Zins und den Konjunkturzyklus*, 2nd ed., 1926.

———. 1937. "Preface to the Japanese Edition." In Joseph A. Schumpeter, *Keizai hatten no riron* [Theory of Economic Development], trans. Nakayama Ichirō and Tōbata Seiichi (Tokyo: Iwanami Shoten), originally published as Schumpeter 1926/1934.

———. 1939. *Business Cycles: A Theoretical, Historical, and Statistical Analysis of the Capitalist Process*. 2 vols. New York: McGraw-Hill. Translated by Kin'yū Keizai Kenkyūjo as *Shunpētā Keikijunkan ron—shihonshugi katei no rironteki • rekishiteki • tōkeiteki bunseki*. 5 vols. Tokyo: Yuhikaku, 1958–64.

———. 1943. "Capitalism in the Postwar World." In Harris 1943, 113–126.

———. 1950 [1942]. *Capitalism, Socialism and Democracy*. New York: Harper.

———. 1954a [1912]. *Economic Doctrine and Method: An Historical Sketch*. Trans. Redvers Opie. New York: Oxford University Press. Originally published as *Epochen der Dogmen- und Methodengeschichte*.

———. 1954b [1918]. "The Crisis of the Tax State." Trans. Wolfgang Stolper and Richard Musgrave. *International Economic Papers*, no. 6, 5–38.

———. 1954c. *History of Economic Analysis*. Ed. Elizabeth Boody Schumpeter. New York: Oxford University Press.

———. 1956 [1918]. "Money and the Social Product." Trans. A. W. Marget. *International Economic Papers*, no. 6 (London: Macmillan), 148–211.

———. 2003 [1912]. "Theorie der wirtschaftlichen Entwicklung" and "The Theory of Economic Development." (Chap. 7 of the 1912 ed., not included in Schumpeter's 1926 ed.) Trans. Ursula Backhaus. In J. Backhaus 2003, 5–116.

Richard E. Sclove. 1989. "From Alchemy to Atomic War: Frederick Soddy's 'Technology Assessment' of Atomic Energy, 1900–1915." *Science, Technology, and Human Values* 14:2 (Spring), 163–194.

Shibagaki Kazuo. 1988. "Studies in Japanese Capitalism: A Survey with Emphasis on the Contributions of the Marx-Uno School." *Annals of the Institute of Social Science* 30: 29–56.

Tokue Shibata, ed. 1986. *Public Finance in Japan*. Tokyo: University of Tokyo Press.

Shimazaki Kyūya. 1989. *En no shinryakushi: En kawase hon'i seido no keisei katei* [The yen's invasion history: The formation of the yen-exchange standard system]. 4 vols. Tokyo: Nihon Keizai Hyōronsha.

Shimomura Osamu. 1952. *Keizai hendō no jōsū bunseki* [Multiplier analysis of economic change]. Tokyo: Tōyō Keizai Shinpōsha.

———. 1963. *Nihon keizai wa seichō suru* [The Japanese economy will grow]. Tokyo: Kōbundō.

Hiroshi Shinjo. 1962. *History of the Yen—100 Years of Japanese Money-Economy*. Kobe: Research Institute for Economics and Business Administration, Kobe University.

Shinobu Seizaburō. 1965–67. *Sengo Nihon seijishi, 1945–1952* [Postwar Japanese political history]. 4 vols. Tokyo: Keisō Shobo.

Shinohara Miyohei. 1960. "Shihon keisei" [Capital formation]. In Arisawa, Tōbata, and Nakayama 1960, 29–75.

———. 1962. *Growth and Cycles in the Japanese Economy*. Tokyo: Kinokuniya Bookstore.

———. 1964a. "Evaluation of Economic Plans in the Japanese Economy." *Weltwirtschaftliches Archiv* 92:1, 208–219.

———. 1964b. "Factors in Japan's Economic Growth." *Hitotsubashi Journal of Economics* 4:1–2 (February), 21–36.

———. 1969. "Postwar Business Cycles in Japan." In Martin Bronfenbrenner, ed., *Is the Business Cycle Obsolete?* New York: Wiley-Interscience, 73–95.

———. 1970a. *Structural Changes in Japan's Economic Development*. Economic Research Series no. 11, Institute of Economic Research, Hitotsubashi University. Tokyo: Kinokuniya Bookstore.

———. 1970b. "Causes and Patterns in the Postwar Growth." *The Developing Economies* 8:2, 349–368.

———. 1982. *Industrial Growth, Trade, and Dynamic Patterns in the Japanese Economy*. Tokyo: University of Tokyo Press.

———. 1987. *Nihon keizai no seichō to junkan* [Growth and cycles of the Japanese economy]. Tokyo: Chikuma Shobō.

———. 1991. *Seikai keizai no chōki dainamikusu, chōki hadō to taikoku kōbō* [Long-term dynamics of the world economy: Long waves and the rise and fall of the great powers]. Tokyo: TBS-Britannica.

———. 1994. *Sengo 50-nen no keiki junkan, Nihon keizai no dainamizumu o saguru* [Fifty years of postwar economic cycles: Exploring the dynamism of the Japanese economy]. Tokyo: Nihon Keizai Shinbun Sha.

———. 1999. *Chōki fukyō no nazo o saguru* [Investigating the riddle of long-term recession]. Tokyo: Keisō Shobō.

———. 2006. *Seichō to junkan de yomitoku Nihon to Ajia* [Understanding Japan and Asia through growth and cycles]. Tokyo: Nihon Keizai Shinbun Sha.

SHIOGUCHI Kiichi. 1975. *Kikigaki: Ikeda Hayato* [Reminiscences: Ikeda Hayato]. Tokyo: Asahi Shinbunsha.

Yuichi SHIONOYA. 1990a. "The Origin of the Schumpeterian Research Program: A Chapter Omitted from Schumpeter's *Theory of Economic Development.*" *Journal of Institutional and Theoretical Economics / Zeitschrift für die gesamte Staatswissenschaft* 146:2 (June), 314–327.

———. 1990b. *Shunpētā no "Anna no nikki"* [Schumpeter's "Anna's diary"]. Tokyo: Hitotsubashi Daigaku Shakaikagaku Koten Shiryō Sentā.

———. 1997. *Schumpeter and the Idea of Social Science: A Metatheoretical Study.* Cambridge: Cambridge University Press.

SHIOTANI Tadao. 1956. "Postwar Progress in Public Finance." *Contemporary Japa,* 24:1–3, 33–46.

Masaki SHIRATORI. 1998. "Afterword to the Japanese Translation of the World Bank Report *The East Asian Miracle.*" In Kenichi Ohno and Izumi Ohno, eds., *Japanese Views on Economic Development: Diverse Paths to the Market* (London: Routledge), 77–83.

Patrick SHORB. 1997. "*Tōyō Keizai Shinpō,* Censorship, War." Paper presented at the Asian Studies on the Pacific Coast Conference, June 26–29, Monterey, Calif.

John W. SLOAN. 1991. *Eisenhower and the Management of Prosperity.* Lawrence: University Press of Kansas.

Richard J. SMETHURST. 2001. "Takahashi Korekiyo's Fiscal Policy and the Rise of Militarism in Japan during the Great Depression." In *Kindai Nihon kenkyū,* vol. 18 (Keiō Gikjuku Fukuzawa Kenkyū Sentaa), 260–288.

———. 2007. *From Foot Soldier to Finance Minister: Takahashi Korekiyo, Japan's Keynes.* Cambridge, Mass.: Harvard University Press.

Vaclav SMIL. 2008. *Energy in Nature and Society: General Energetics of Complex Systems.* Cambridge, Mass.: MIT Press.

Adam SMITH. 1937 [1789]. *An Inquiry into the Nature and Causes of the Wealth of Nations.* Ed. Edwin Cannan. New York: Modern Library.

Arthur SMITHIES. 1950. "Joseph Alois Schumpeter, 1883–1950." *American Economic Review* 40:4 (September), 628–648.

John W. SNYDER. 1969. Oral History Interview. April 16, 1969. Truman Presidential Library and Museum.

Frederick SODDY. 1922 [1921]. "Cartesian Economics: The Bearing of Physical Science upon State Stewardship." Lectures at Birkbeck College and London School of Economics, November 1921. London.

———. 1926. *Wealth, Virtual Wealth and Debt: The Solution of the Economic Paradox.* New York: Dutton.

Kurt STEINER. 1987. "The Occupation and the Reform of the Japanese Civil Code." In Ward and Sakamoto 1987, 188–220.

David I. STERN and Astrid KANDER. 2012. "The Role of Energy in the Industrial Revolution and Modern Economic Growth." *Energy Journal* 33:3, 125–152.

Joseph E. STIGLITZ and Andrew WEISS. 1988. "Banks as Social Accountants and Screening Devices for the Allocation of Credit." NBER working paper no. 2710. Cambridge, Mass.: National Bureau of Economic Research.

Wolfgang F. STOLPER. 1994. *Joseph Alois Schumpeter: The Public Life of a Private Man.* Princeton, N.J.: Princeton University Press.

Wolfgang STREECK and Kozo YAMAMURA, eds. 2001. *The Origins of Nonliberal Capitalism: Germany and Japan.* Ithaca, N.Y.: Cornell University Press.

SUGIHARA Kaoru. 1992. "Japan, the Middle East and the World Economy: A Note on the Oil Triangle." *Japan Forum* 4–1 (April), 21–31.

Yoneyuki Sugita and Marie Thorsten. 1999. *Beyond the Line: Joseph Dodge and the Geometry of Power in US–Japan Relations, 1949–1952*. Okayama: Daigaku Kyōiku Shuppan.

Supreme Commander for the Allied Powers. General Headquarters. Statistics and Reports Section (Historical Monographs). 1952a. *History of the Non-military Activities of the Occupation of Japan: No. 37, Government Finance, 1945–March 1951*. Tokyo: Supreme Commander for the Allied Powers. (National Archives—microfilm.)

———. 1952b. *History of the Non-military Activities of the Occupation of Japan: No. 39, Money and Banking, 1945–June 1951*. Tokyo: Supreme Commander for the Allied Powers. (National Archives—microfilm.)

———. 1952c. *History of the Non-military Activities of the Occupation of Japan: No. 40, Financial Reorganization of Corporate Enterprises*. Tokyo: Supreme Commander for the Allied Powers. (National Archives—microfilm.)

Christian Suter. 1989. "Long Waves in the International Financial System: Debt-Default Cycles of Sovereign Borrowers." *Review* (Fernand Braudel Center) 12:1, 1–49.

———. 1990. *Schuldenzyklen in der Dritten Welt: Kreditaufnahme, Zahlungskrisen und Schuldenregelungen peripherer Länder im Weltsystem von 1820 bis 1986*. Frankfurt am Main: Anton Hain.

———. 1992. *Debt Cycles in the World Economy: Foreign Loans, Financial Crises, and Debt Settlements, 1820–1990*. Boulder, Colo.: Westview Press, 1992.

Yoshio Suzuki. 1980. *Money and Banking in Japan: The Theoretical Setting and Its Application*. Trans. John G. Greenwood. New Haven, Conn.: Yale University Press.

———. 1986. *Money, Finance, and Macroeconomic Performance in Japan*. Trans. Robert Alan Feldman. New Haven, Conn.: Yale University Press.

Richard Swedberg. 1991. *Schumpeter: A Biography*. Princeton, N.J.: Princeton University Press.

Tadai Yoshi. 1997. *Tairiku ni watatta en no kōbō* [The yen's rise and fall on the continent]. 2 vols. Tokyo: Tōyō Keizai Shinpōsha.

Takahashi Kamekichi. 1963. *Keizai hyōron gojūnen: Watashi no jinsei to sono haikei* [Fifty years of economic commentary: My life and its background]. Tokyo: Tōshi Keizai Sha.

Takahashi Makoto. 1967. "The Development of War-Time Economic Controls." *Developing Economies* 5:4, 648–665.

Takeda Takao, Hayashi Takehisa, and Imai Katsuhito, eds. 1977. *Nihon zaisei yōran* [Outline of Japan's public finance]. Tokyo: Tōkyō Daigaku Shuppankai.

Takemae Eiji. 2002. *Inside GHQ: The Allied Occupation of Japan and Its Legacy*. New York: Continuum. Reprinted as *The Allied Occupation of Japan*.

Norio Tamaki. 1994. "The American 'Democratization' of Japanese Banking, 1945–1959." In Olive Checkland, Shizuya Nishimura, and Norio Tamaki, eds., *Pacific Banking, 1859–1959: East Meets West* (New York: St. Martin's Press), 185–198.

———. 1995. *Japanese Banking: A History, 1859–1959*. New York: Cambridge University Press.

Teranishi Jūrō. 1993. "Inflation Stabilization with Growth: The Japanese Experience, 1945–50." In Teranishi and Kosai 1993, 61–85.

———. 1994. "Loan Syndication in War-time Japan and the Origins of the Main Bank System." In Aoki and Patrick 1994, 51–88.

———. 1999. "The Main Bank System." In Okazaki and Okuno-Fujiwara 1999a, 63–96.

———. 2003. *Nihon no keizai shisutemu* [Japan's economic system]. Tokyo: Iwanami Shoten.

TERANISHI Jūrō and Yutaka KOSAI, eds. 1993. *The Japanese Experience of Economic Reforms*. New York: St. Martin's Press.

TŌBATA Seiichi. 1936. *Nihon nōgyō no tenkai katei* [The process of development of Japanese agriculture]. Tokyo: Iwanami Shoten.

———. 1984. *Waga shi • waga tomo • waga gakumon* [My teachers, my friends, my scholarship]. Tokyo: Kashiwa Shobō.

Thaddeus J. TRENN. 1979. "The Central Role of Energy in Soddy's Holistic and Critical Approach to Nuclear Science, Economics, and Social Responsibility." *British Journal for the History of Science* 12:3 (November), 261–276.

Robert TRIFFIN. 1960. *Gold and the Dollar Crisis*. New Haven, Conn.: Yale University Press.

TSUJI Kiyoaki. 1956. "The Cabinet, Administrative Organization, and the Bureaucracy." *Annals of the American Academy of Political and Social Science* 308 (November), 10–17.

TSURU Shigeto. 1941. "Economic Fluctuations in Japan, 1868–1893." *Review of Economic Statistics* 23:1, 176–189.

———. 1949. *Sengo Nihon no infurēshon* [Postwar Japan's inflation]. Tokyo: Iwanami Shoten.

———. 1955. "Business Cycles in Post-war Japan." In Erik Lundberg, ed., *The Business Cycle in the Post-War World* (London: Macmillan), 178–200.

———. 1976. *Towards a New Political Economy*. Vol. 13 of *Tsuru Shigeto chosakushū* [Selected works of Tsuru Shigeto]. Tokyo: Kodansha.

———. 1993a. *Institutional Economics Revisited* (Raffaele Mattioli Lectures). Cambridge: Cambridge University Press.

———. 1993b. *Japan's Capitalism: Creative Defeat and Beyond*. Cambridge: Cambridge University Press.

———. 2000. "Shigeto Tsuru." In Backhouse and Middleton 2000, 2: 1–28.

TSUSHIMA Juichi [TSUSHIMA Hōtō]. 1966. *Gaisai shori no tabi* [A journey to deal with foreign bonds]. Hōtō Zuisō, 16. Tokyo: Hōtō Kankōkai.

TSŪSHŌ SANGYŌSHŌ [Ministry of International Trade and Industry]. 1960. *Shōkōshō sanjūgonen shōshi* [Brief thirty-five-year history of the Ministry of Commerce and Industry]. Tokyo: Tsūshō Sangyōshō.

TSUTSUI Kiyotada. 1986. *Ishibashi Tanzan—jiyūshugi seijika no kiseki* [Ishibashi Tanzan—the path of a liberal politician]. Tokyo: Chūō Kōronsha.

———. 1992. "Toward the Liberal Democratic Party Merger: Conservative Politics and Policies." In Kataoka 1992, 119–132.

William M. TSUTSUI. 1988. *Banking Policy in Japan: American Efforts at Reform during the Occupation*. London: Routledge, 1988.

———. 1998. *Manufacturing Ideology: Scientific Management in Twentieth-Century Japan*. Princeton, N.J.: Princeton University Press.

———. 2003. "Landscapes in the Dark Valley: Toward an Environmental History of Wartime Japan." *Environmental History* 8:2 (April), www.historycooperative.org /journals/eh/8.2/tsutsui.html.

"Two-Billion-Dollar Failure in Japan." 1949. *Fortune* 39:4 (April), 67–73, 204–208.

Andrew TYLECOTE. 1991. *The Long Wave in the World Economy: The Current Crisis in Historical Perspective*. London: Routledge.

———. 1986. "On Inequality and the Rate of Profit in the Long Wave." *Economic and Industrial Democracy* 7: 29–44.

Tatsurō UCHINO. 1983 [1978]. *Japan's Postwar Economy: An Insider's View of Its History and Its Future*. Trans. Mark A. HARBISON. Tokyo: Kodansha International, 1983. Originally published as *Sengo Nihon keizaishi*, 1978.

284   **REFERENCES**

Kazuo UEDA. 1994. "Institutional and Regulatory Frameworks for the Main Bank System." In Aoki and Patrick 1994, 89–108.

———. 1999. "The Financial System and Its Regulations." In Okazaki and Okuno-Fujiwara 1999a, 38–62.

Herman VAN DER WEE. 1986 [1984]. *Prosperity and Upheaval: The World Economy, 1945–1980.* Trans. Robin HOGG and Max R. HALL. Berkeley: University of California Press. Originally published as *De gebroken welvaartscirkel,* 1984.

J. J. VAN DUIJN. 1983. *The Long Wave in Economic Life.* London: Allen and Unwin.

Harold G. VATTER. 1985. *The U.S. Economy in World War II.* New York: Columbia University Press.

Ezra F. VOGEL. 1979. *Japan as Number One: Lessons for America.* Cambridge, Mass.: Harvard University Press.

Robert WADE. 1990. *Governing the Market: Economic Theory and the Role of Government in East Asian Industrialization.* Princeton, N.J.: Princeton University Press.

Immanuel WALLERSTEIN. 1979. "Kondratieff Up or Kondratieff Down?" *Review* (Fernand Braudel Center) 2:4, 663–673.

———. 1984. "Long Waves as Capitalist Process." *Review* (Fernand Braudel Center) 7:4 (Spring), 559–575.

Paul M. WARBURG. 1914. "Circulating Credits and Bank Acceptances." In "Essays on Banking Reform in the United States." Special issue, *Proceedings of the Academy of Political Science in the City of New York* 4:4 (July), 159–172.

Robert E. WARD and SAKAMOTO Yoshikazu, ed. 1987. *Democratizing Japan: The Allied Occupation.* Honolulu: University of Hawaii Press.

Robert E. WARD and Frank J. SCHULMAN, eds. 1974. *The Allied Occupation of Japan, 1945–1952: An Annotated Bibliography of Western-Language Materials.* Chicago: American Library Association.

Richard A. WERNER. 2002. "A Reconsideration of the Rationale for Bank-Centered Economic Systems and the Effectiveness of Directed Credit Policies in the Light of Japanese Evidence." *The Japanese Economy* 30:3 (May–June), 3–45.

Robert WHITING. 1999. *Tokyo Underworld: The Fast Times and Hard Life of an American Gangster in Japan.* New York: Vintage Books.

Bernd WIDDIG. 2001. *Culture and Inflation in Weimar Germany.* Berkeley: University of California Press.

Justin WILLIAMS. 1988. "American Democratization Policy for Occupied Japan: Correcting the Revisionist Version." *Pacific Historical Review* 57:2, 179–202. Replies by John Dower and Howard Schonberger 202–218.

Jung-En WOO [Meredith WOO-CUMINGS]. 1991. *Race to the Swift: State and Finance in Korean Industrialization.* New York: Columbia University Press.

Meredith WOO-CUMINGS, ed. 1999. *The Developmental State.* Ithaca, N.Y.: Cornell University Press.

William P. WOODARD. 1972. *The Allied Occupation of Japan 1945–1952 and Japanese Religions.* Leiden: Brill.

Arthur M. WOODFORD. 1974. *Detroit and Its Banks: The Story of Detroit Bank and Trust.* Detroit: Wayne State University Press.

R. Bin WONG. 1997. *China Transformed: Historical Change and the Limits of European Experience.* Ithaca, N.Y.: Cornell University Press.

WORLD BANK. 1993. *The East Asian Miracle: Economic Growth and Public Policy.* New York: Oxford University Press.

Maurice WRIGHT. 2002. *Japan's Fiscal Crisis: The Ministry of Finance and the Politics of Public Spending, 1975–2000.* Oxford: Oxford University Press.

YAGI Kiichiro. 2004. "Japanese Theory of Modernization/Industrialization: Between Liberalism and Developmentalism." In Werner Pascha, ed., *Systemic Change in the Japanese and German Economies: Convergence and Differentiation as a Dual Path* (London: Routledge), 32–50.

YAMADA Toshio. 1993. *Regyurashon riron* [Regulation theory]. Tokyo: Kōdansha Gendai Shinsho.

YAMAMOTO Mitsuru. 1977. "The Cold War and U.S.-Japan Economic Cooperation." In Nagai and Iriye 1977, 408–425.

Kozo YAMAMURA. 1967. "The Role of the Samurai in the Development of Modern Banking in Japan." *Journal of Economic History* 27:2 (June), 198–220.

Yasushi YAMANOUCHI. 1998. "Total War and Social Integration: A Methodological Introduction." In Yamanouchi et al., 1998, 1–40.

Yasushi YAMANOUCHI, J. Victor KOSCHMANN, and Ryūichi NARITA. 1998. *Total War and "Modernization."* Ithaca, N.Y.: Cornell University East Asia Program.

Kakujiro YAMASAKI and Gotaro OGAWA. 1929. *The Effect of the World War upon the Commerce and Industry of Japan.* New Haven, Conn.: Yale University Press.

Chitoshi YANAGA. 1968. *Big Business in Japanese Politics.* Yale Studies in Political Science no. 22. New Haven, Conn.: Yale University Press.

Daqing YANG. 2010. *Technology of Empire: Telecommunications and Japanese Expansion in Asia, 1883–1945.* Cambridge, Mass.: Harvard University Press.

Haiqun YANG. 1996. *Banking and Financial Control in Reforming Planned Economies.* Houndmills, England: Macmillan.

Jiro YAO, ed. 1970a. *Monetary Factors in Japanese Economic Growth.* Kobe: Research Institute for Economics and Business Administration, Kobe University.

———. 1970b. "Supply of Funds and Currency for Economic Growth—Characteristics of the Japanese Financial Structure." In Yao 1970a, 27–59.

YASUBA Yasukichi. 1989. "Rekikshi no naka no kōdo seichō" [High-speed growth in history]. In YASUBA and INOKI 1989b, 271–309.

YASUBA Yasukichi and INOKI Takenori. 1989a. "Gaisetsu, 1955–1980" [Outline, 1955–1980]. In Yasuba and Inoki 1989b: 1–55.

———, eds. 1989b. *Kōdo seichō* [High-speed growth]. Nihon Keizaishi 8. Tokyo: Iwanami Shoten.

YOSHIHARA Kunio. 1982. *Sogo Shosha: The Vanguard of the Japanese Economy.* Tokyo: Oxford University Press.

YOSHINO Toshihiko. 1957. "Economic Recovery and Banking System." *Contemporary Japan* 24:10–12 (April), 570–595.

———. 1960. "Kin'yū no kōzō to ryūtsū" [Financial structure and circulation]. In Arisawa, Tōbata, and Nakayama 1960, 117–165.

———. 1975–79. *Nihon Ginkō shi* [History of the Bank of Japan]. Tokyo: Shunjūsha.

———. 1976. *Rekidai Nihon Ginkō sōsai ron: Nihon kin'yū seisaku shi no kenkyū* [On the successive presidents of the Bank of Japan: Research in the history of Japanese finance]. Tokyo: Mainichi Shinbunsha.

———. 1996. *En to doru* [Yen and dollar]. Tokyo: Nihon Hōsō Shuppan Kyōkai.

Louise YOUNG. 1998. *Japan's Total Empire: Manchuria and the Culture of Wartime Imperialism.* Berkeley: University of California Press.

Tony F. YU. 1997. "Entrepreneurial State: The Role of Government in the Economic Development of the Asian Newly Industrialising Countries." *Development Policy Review* 15, 47–64.

Index

Note: Page numbers followed by a *t* indicate tables.

www.ingramcontent.com/pod-product-compliance
Ingram Content Group UK Ltd.
Pitfield, Milton Keynes, MK11 3LW, UK
UKHW020902120225
454973UK00004B/15/J